D1486433

JOHN DIXON

THE MAN WHO COULD HAVE BUILT THE FORTH BRIDGE

Ian Pearce

First published in the UK in 2018 by
Tyne Bridge Publishing, City Library,
Newcastle upon Tyne, United Kingdom
www.tynebridgepublishing.org.uk

Layout | David Hepworth

ISBN-13: 9780951048887

Cover image: By permission of the National Railway Museum
(NRM Pictorial Collection/Science and Society Picture Library)
NRM Reference 1978-9160

Foreword

As great grandchildren of John Dixon we inherited artefacts appertaining to Cleopatra's Needle, the Pyramids in Egypt, Bedlington Iron Works and the Falklands Islands and this sparked an interest in our forefather.

We are immensely grateful to Ian Pearce for his diligence in researching and completing this book which documents John Dixon's worldwide work in civil engineering such as the Shanghai Railway in China, the Gibraltar water supply and even Floating Swimming Bath in the River Thames!

John Dixon belonged to an exceptional and very talented family dynasty from the north east of England and this makes us both extremely proud to be his great grandchildren.

Beth Porteous
Jean Martin

Contents

General introduction to the Dixon family and the four volumes covering their history

Researching the Dixon family

I have held a fascination for the Dixons of Raby and Cockfield for many years, and have resolved to try to give an account of the illustrious Dixons over many generations since the time of Ralph and Susanna Dixon at Staindrop in the early seventeenth century. Jeremiah Dixon, co-surveyor of the celebrated Mason-Dixon Line in America, is the only family member relatively well known today. The others are largely forgotten, a situation I now wish to put right after fifteen years of part-time research. My particular interest has been the three brothers, John, Raylton and Waynman Dixon, all successful nineteenth century engineers. John Dixon managed an international contracting business, Raylton was a major builder of iron ships on the River Tees, while Waynman worked with both of his elder brothers. Apart from their engineering achievements, I have learned much about their different personalities. John Dixon was quietly competent, devoted all his energies to his work and never hesitated to resort to the courts if he felt unfairly treated. Raylton was almost brashly extrovert, with an extremely busy social, civic and political life outside the ship building. Waynman could be said to combine the more appealing characteristics of his brothers, a practical engineer but with wider cultural interests, and an affable, almost gentle nature. Waynman spent thirty years of retirement living in Great Ayton, the North Yorkshire village where I run a local history group, and it was through this local connection that my interest in the Dixon family began.

One difficulty has been how to arrange tentative publications, since there is too much material to include in a single volume and I did not want to lose the opportunity of relating the lives and works of the Dixons in the detail they deserve. After much thought I have settled on the following division into four volumes: the early Dixons, John Dixon, Raylton Dixon and Waynman Dixon. For no particular reason, the first volume to be published is that on John Dixon.

John Dixon's portrait, dated 1885, in the records of the Institution of Civil Engineers; he had been an associate member since 1869. Photograph by Maull and Fox of Piccadilly. Henry Maull (1830-1914) was the son of a fishmonger who started working as an artist but turned to photography. From 1854 his studio was at 187A Piccadilly, where he was in partnership with his brother-in-law John Fox (1832-1907).

Summary of the four volumes

Early Dixons

Inventiveness and technological aptitude ran through generations of the Dixon family. In the 18th century their coal mining interests on Cockfield Fell and further afield provided a comfortable living, but this was carelessly lost at the start of the 19th century. This resulted in the father of John, Raylton and Waynman working in a Newcastle bank, and the three brothers were born in Newcastle. Several of their relatives were involved with the early development of the railways. Jeremiah Dixon of the Mason-Dixon survey is included, but probably briefly as a great deal has already been published about him, making the most from the few sources available and some of it quite fanciful.

John Dixon, international contractor

This volume covers the life and works of John Dixon (1835-1891). John was the eldest of the three Dixon brothers and managed an international civil engineering contracting business from offices in London. It was a contract for a bridge in Cairo that ultimately led to John and Waynman Dixon bringing the Egyptian obelisk known as Cleopatra's Needle from Alexandria to London. Press speculation of a knighthood for Cleopatra's Needle came to nothing, and John and Waynman never received proper recognition for their labours and expense with the obelisk. Many of John Dixon's contracts were for structures of wrought iron girders supported on cast iron columns, the traditional seaside pier construction as typified by his pier at Llandudno. John Dixon married Mary England and they had eleven children, nine of whom survived into adulthood. He died at the early age of fifty-six.

Raylton Dixon, the most popular man in Middlesbrough

This volume will cover the life and works of Sir Raylton Dixon (1838-1901). For many years the Cleveland Dockyard, owned by Raylton Dixon, was the largest builder of iron ships on the River Tees. Raylton led a busy social life and was soon a leading figure in Middlesbrough's civic life, being a town councillor, holding many public offices and once being voted the most popular man in the town. He was mayor of Middlesbrough at the opening of the Town Hall, and soon after received his knighthood. A staunch Conservative in a town dominated by Liberals, he unsuccessfully stood for Parliament. His later life was somewhat overshadowed by a bitter dispute with fellow Middlesbrough councillors on the Tees Conservancy Commission. Raylton Dixon married Bessie Walker, the sister-in-law of one of his close friends, and they had eight children. Raylton died of stomach cancer just three weeks after his sixty-third birthday.

Waynman Dixon, Egypt and Cleopatra's Needle

This volume will cover the life and works of Waynman Dixon (1844-1930). In many ways Waynman lived in the shadows of his two older brothers. He was content to take a supporting role in John Dixon's business for eleven years, culminating in the transportation of Cleopatra's Needle to England in 1877. At the time of the feared loss of the obelisk in the Bay of Biscay, Waynman left John and joined Raylton at the Cleveland Dockyard, where he remained until his retirement. Waynman had none of the combative tendencies of his brothers, and seems to have been more relaxed and genial person. His concern for the well-being of others was evidenced by his active support of the St John Ambulance and the North Ormesby Hospital over many years. He developed a great knowledge of Egypt and Egyptian antiquities during seven years residence

Top) Raylton Dixon, Mayor of Middlesbrough, the pinnacle of his career. In addition to the mayoral chain, Raylton wears the insignia of a Knight of the Order of St John of Jerusalem. By courtesy of Teesside Archives, Middlesbrough. Reference CB/M/C/10/33.

Above) Waynman Dixon. Reproduced by courtesy of Ann Colville, great grand-daughter of Augusta Ann Richardson, one of John Dixon's sisters.

in the country, and achieved modest fame through his discovery of the so-called 'ventilation passages' in the Great Pyramid. Although coming close to marrying an illegitimate black lady seventeen years his senior, he remained single until well into his fifties. He then married Anne Elfleda Lawrance from Australia and they had two daughters. In contrast to his brothers, Waynman lived to enjoy a long retirement until his death at the age of eighty-five.

Some themes

Technological change

The second half of the 19th century was one of unprecedented technological and economic change. Steam engines, already well-established in factories, were beginning to displace horses on the land and sails at sea. Provision, or rather over-provision, of railways in Britain was almost complete. In Europe spectacular tunnels were cut under the Alps and graceful bridges crossed the widest rivers.

It was a period of great invention. Electricity had been discovered, and electric lights were appearing in place of gas lighting, which itself had seemed revolutionary not many years before. The first steps were being taken towards electrical dynamos and motors, although this technology would not replace steam until the following century. Refrigeration became a practicable proposition, enabling imports of bananas from the West Indies and lamb from New Zealand. Sub-sea telegraph cables revolutionised international communications, and the telephone and phonograph had arrived. Photography was replacing engraving as the means of reproducing images. The bicycle, pneumatic tyre and automobile were about to revolutionise personal transport.

There were seemingly limitless supplies of coal, timber, bricks, and iron for use as castings or wrought iron. After a long inception period, steel was replacing iron, its greater strength and consistency making possible the Eiffel Tower and the Forth Railway Bridge. Manual processes were being mechanised, an example being the hydraulic riveting machine. Advanced machine tools turned out components with precision and repeatability. Specialist agents used railways and shipping to deliver of manufactured goods around Britain and across the world.

Potable water supplies were introduced in major cities, and in towns and cities sewers and sewage treatment works gradually replaced earth closets and ash pans. These developments had a dramatic effect on public health, although atmospheric and river pollution would remain problems for almost another century.

Perhaps less appreciated by historians, the rapid adoption of new techniques and inventions was greatly facilitated by innovations in business and finance. The great wealth brought about through the industrial revolution not only financed British industry but also the development of predominantly rural economies in Europe, Asia, Africa and South America. Limited liability legislation encouraged new businesses. At the same time there was a surplus of capital seeking investments, and any half-promising new venture could secure funding. With markets growing faster than manufacturing output, there was less competition between individuals, companies and countries. International exhibitions publicised the latest in technology. However, sharp swings in trade cycles brought alternating periods of prosperity and great distress. The new Union Workhouses could not cope with the worst depressions, in Middlesbrough starving and barefoot children walked to the coast at Redcar in search of shellfish washed up on the shore. Even at the other end of the social scale, leaders of industry might see their companies fail and their personal fortunes vanish in a matter of days.

Amidst all this progress there was danger. Virtually every week saw a boiler explosion, usually with fatalities. It was only when steel replaced wrought iron in boiler construction, and boiler testing regulations were introduced, that boiler explosions became a rarity. Coal mining accidents were less frequent but generally with a much greater loss of life. Railway accidents were common, as were shipping losses. Navies around the world were rapidly re-equipping with iron-clad vessels armed with ever greater fire power, and the machine gun had been invented.

The period saw a coming together of theoretical and practical engineering. Developments in the understanding of thermodynamics and fluid mechanics led to the triple-expansion marine steam engine and efficient hull design. A new generation of men emerged who combined practical and theoretical engineering abilities. Engineering institutions regulated the new professions and disseminated technical knowledge.

It was in this environment that John, Raylton and Waynman started their professional engineering careers. They could hardly have chosen a better time, with an unprecedented demand for men of their abilities both at home and around the world. Victorians worshiped invention, enterprise and hard work, virtues in which the three brothers excelled.

Engineering and business networks

Although I primarily describe John, Raylton and Waynman through their engineering works, there are several other themes which emerged during the research. As I became more familiar with the three brothers it became apparent that the British civil engineers of the second half of the nineteenth century formed a virtual extended family, and were mostly well-acquainted with each other, greatly facilitated by the Institution of Civil Engineers. As well as knowing their fellow engineers, men such as John Dixon built up relationships with suppliers of wrought iron structures, iron castings and other materials. These relationships were often with the owners of the various businesses; this was just before most businesses became limited liability companies and lost that total commitment of an individual owner with his own business. Raylton Dixon developed close ties with his suppliers of iron bars and plates, all based around industrial Middlesbrough, and also with many of men who purchased his ships. Throughout the text there are brief details of many of the men who became involved with the Dixons during their working careers, and how they were inter-connected through previous engineering projects and sometimes through inter-marriage of families.

Jeremiah and Mary Dixon, parents of John Dixon, by M Wane of Douglas, Isle of Man. Marshall Wane (1834-1903) had a photographic studio in Regent Street, Douglas, from 1861 to 1876. It appears that John took his parents over to Douglas to see the iron pier, his first large contract, and arranged for their portrait to be taken. Reproduced by courtesy of Ann Colville, great grand-daughter of Augusta Ann Richardson, one of John Dixon's sisters.

Family life

It was expected that Victorian men would marry and have children, but finding marriage partners could be difficult. In the social circles of the Dixons, which today would be seen as upper middle class, the lives of young men and young women were generally segregated. This is well evidenced in the case of Raylton Dixon's early days in Middlesbrough through the pages of the diaries of J R Stubbs. Nearly all his leisure time was spent with young men and virtually his only contact with girls was in the homes of older, married friends. Not that there was much leisure time for young engineers at the start of their careers when, at least for the Dixons, work probably took precedence over much else. For Quakers there was the additional problem of finding a partner within the Society of Friends, but who was not too closely related through previous marriages. Although brought up in the Newcastle Quaker environment, by the time of marriage the three brothers had left the Society and so were not faced with this restriction. All of this has led me to examine how John, Raylton and Waynman met the women they would marry, and some of the women they would not marry, such as Raylton's probable liaisons with London's ladies of the night and Waynman's near marriage to the black Selima Harris.

If finding their own marriage partner had not been easy, the perceived problem of ensuring their children found suitable partners emerged some years later. If marriages were not strictly arranged by the parents, it is clear that the parents exercised much influence, particularly for daughters. Accordingly marriage partners, their background and how they met their future spouses is another theme in the text.

So as not to intrude on the personal lives of the descendants of John, Raylton and Waynman I have included some details of their children but not proceeded beyond this time.

What about the workers?

It is easy to forget the many managers, foreman and workers vital to nineteenth century industrial undertakings, such as John Dixon's engineering contracting business and the Cleveland Dockyard. Much has been written on the so-called working classes, often by left-leaning historians, mainly lamenting working conditions and exploitation by all-powerful business owners. Such historians can conveniently forget that industrial work was more attractive than the alternatives of agricultural work or unemployment. While conditions were obviously very bad in coal mines and some factories, such as textile mills, the situation in engineering was rather different. The owners of engineering works were generally directly involved in the day-to-day work, and increasing union organisation resulted in shop-floor power, which could be detrimental to the business. I have chronicled the industrial relations and safety record of the Cleveland Dockyard in some detail to illustrate this.

Positioned between the owners and the shop floor were managers and foreman. Their roles were vital in engaging and organising the large labour forces involved (at its height the Cleveland Dockyard employed up to 3,000 men) yet it is difficult to find much about them. Even more critical were the resident engineers employed by John Dixon, particularly on contracts abroad. The task of assembling a local workforce to build a railway in rural China must have been daunting indeed, although not as challenging the situation faced by mining engineers in Peru (quoted here with apologies to today's sensibilities):

> 'The difficulty and expense of introducing anything new or uncommon into this region is extremely great, chiefly owing to the wonderful stupidity and ignorance of the native Indians, who are capable of doing only the meanest labour; they are, in fact, little better than beasts of burden.'

Cleopatra's Needle

John and Waynman Dixon devised and carried out the transportation of the obelisk known as 'Cleopatra's Needle' from Alexandria to London. A considerable number of publications have appeared on London's obelisk and on Egyptian obelisks in general, and there will no doubt be more as the 150th anniversary of the erection of the obelisk on the Thames Embankment in 1878 draws nigh. However biographies of John and Waynman Dixon must include this important undertaking, even given the risk of repeating information which has already been published.

References

There is no generally accepted method of referencing non-academic publications. I believe that giving references is essential to justify the text and to facilitate further research by others. I also believe that the academic Harvard system or using footnotes are distractions when reading the text. My solution has been to list all references at the end of each chapter, with a brief summary of what is relevant in each reference. I hope that readers will find this acceptable.

Acknowledgements

Specific acknowledgements are given at end of each chapter, but in addition I happily acknowledge the assistance, support and encouragement given to me by current members of the Dixon family.

The opportunities provided by the world wide web, pioneered by Sir Timothy John Berners-Lee, are invaluable to present day historical researchers. I have made much use of www.findmypast.co.uk for access to census and other records, and to old newspapers. The on-line facilities provided by Lancashire Libraries have been used to access British Library old newspapers and *The Times* archives.

Andrew Tweedie's dedication in setting up *Grace's Guide to British Industrial History* at www.gracesguide.co.uk has been greatly appreciated

Carol Morgan at the archives and library of the Institution of Civil Engineers, Adrian Clement and Sarah Rogers at the library of the Institution of Mechanical Engineers and Jennifer Hillyard at the library of the North East Institute of Mining and Mechanical Engineers have freely given their time.

David Hepworth of Tyne Bridge Publishing, part of Newcastle Libraries for his excellent support and guidance.

Finally my wife, Sue, who has put up with having the Dixon brothers as virtual lodgers in our house for many years and who has painstakingly proof-read the entire text.

Corrections and additions to the work

It is impossible to write a fully comprehensive and entirely accurate biography. I am well aware that aspects of the Dixons' lives and works, which at the time I thought correct, required later changes as additional information became available. Hence there are bound to be instances in the text which will need changing as new information comes to light, and I will always be grateful to receive details of such information.

In carrying out the research I have always tried to focus on primary sources and to check references quoted by others. There is a surprising and worrying quantity of misleading or inaccurate material in the public domain, especially on the internet.

References

Diaries of John Richard Stubbs 1853-1907
Catalogued and transcribed by Alice Barrigan
http://northyorkshirehistory.blogspot.co.uk/p/contents.html
Originals held by North Yorkshire County Record Office, Northallerton
Contain information about Raylton Dixon's early social life.

Victorian Engineering
L T C Rolt
Allen Lane, The Penguin Press, Harmondsworth, Middlesex, 1970
An authoritative yet readable history of Victorian engineering.

The Cerro de Pasco Mining District Peru
Engineering, London, 5 December 1879, pages 425-6
Description of the silver mines and the difficulties faced by engineers.

Introduction to John Dixon

1 John Dixon the engineer

Although John's engineering career might be considered as the most successful of the three brothers, John, Raylton and Waynman Dixon, it is the most difficult to research. In contrast to the unusual names of his brothers, he has a name common to countless others, rendering even the modern power of internet searches extremely difficult. Also, whereas his two brothers spent much of their working lives in one place, Middlesbrough, John Dixon worked in Europe, America, Africa and Asia. This means that the now readily-searchable nineteenth century British newspapers are of limited use in investigating his many foreign projects.

The starting point for many biographies are obituaries, which can give useful summaries of a life from birth to death and which have been written while the individual can still be remembered. This is true of John Dixon, particularly his obituary written for the Institution of Civil Engineers. It lists some of his important works, but gives little or no detail. Years of research have enabled me to piece together most of his engineering works, but there are bound to be unintentional omissions. John Dixon's younger days were spent in Newcastle upon Tyne, where he attended Dr Bruce's highly-regarded school followed by a technical apprenticeship at Robert Stephenson's works. At this time the north east of England was in the forefront of technological progress, and many of John Dixon's friends and acquaintances in Newcastle would go on to become successful engineers, forming a professional circle which would prove of great importance to John in his subsequent career. As well as this engineering network, John was brought up within the close-knit Society of Friends in Durham and Northumberland. Although he turned his back on his Quaker roots, connections into the powerful Quaker financial and business networks were important in his earlier career.

This career began in the north east iron industry but, after an unsuccessful attempt with friend to run their own iron works, John Dixon moved to London in 1866. Here he soon established himself as an international civil engineering contractor, although never achieving the fame of the great contractors such as Thomas Brassey or Sir William Arrol. Where John Dixon's name does appear in publications it is usually in his pivotal role bringing Cleopatra's Needle to London, with his brother Waynman, and erecting it on the Thames Embankment. He might have achieved even wider fame had his contract for the Forth Railway Bridge been accepted.

With the proviso that some of his contracts are undoubtedly lost, a chronological list of his work is as follows:

1856-61 Manager of the Bishopwearmoth iron works, Sunderland
1862-65 Partner in the Bedlington Iron Works with Jaspar Capper Mounsey
1866 Move to London where he became a civil engineering contractor
1867 Construction of a wharf near the Tower of London
1867 Construction of the Southport pier extension
1868 Construction of landing stages on the Thames Embankment
1869 Construction of the promenade pier at Douglas, Isle of Man
1869 Report on proposed low-water landing at Ramsey, Isle of Man
1870 Construction and operation of the Lake Windermere steam-powered ferry
1870 Design for pier at Ventor, Isle of Wight (not accepted)
1870 Civil engineering work and the discovery of fresh water sources, Gibraltar
1870s Involvement in water supply and sanitation at Rio de Janeiro, Brazil
1871 Construction of 'Pont des Anglais' bridge over the Nile at Cairo
1872-73 Design of viaducts on the Whitby to Loftus Railway, Yorkshire
1873 Construction of Eau Brink Cut bridge, King's Lynn
1874 Construction of docks and harbour extensions at Port Talbot, Wales
1874-76 Construction of the 'Muelle del Tinto' ore-loading terminal, Huelva, Spain
1875 Construction of Custom House piers at Lisbon, Portugal
1875-76 Construction of the first railway in China from Shanghai to Woosung
1876-77 Construction of a short section of the Guimarães Railway, Portugal
1876-77 Construction of the promenade pier at Llandudno, Wales
1877-78 Cleopatra's Needle, transportation from Egypt to London and erection on the Thames Embankment
1879-80 Construction of London tramways
1880 Design for a bridge over the River Douro at Porto, Portugual (not accepted)
1882-83 Rebuilding the Solway Viaduct
1882-87 Construction of water supply and sanitation scheme at Campos, Brazil
1882 Tender for the Forth Railway Bridge (not accepted)
1883-84 Construction of a loading pier at Belém on the River Pará, Brazil
1884-87 Rebuilding of the Hammersmith Suspension Bridge
1885 Tender for the Hawkesbury Bridge, Australia (not accepted)
1886-87 Construction of a breakwater at Grand Canary
1888 Shanklin Pier, Isle of Wight
1890 Plans for Waterford Free Bridge

There are some other projects about which little is currently known, such as a pier in Mexico and some bridges at Waterford in Ireland. It is hoped that this publication may bring other works of John Dixon to light.

In addition to his engineering contracts, John Dixon had several rather dubious business interests in mining companies, the Pen'Allt Mine in Wales, the Rio Malagón Mine in Portugal and the aptly-named Crooke's Mining and Smelting Company in Colorado.

2 John Dixon the man

Lives of engineers often give little attention to the underlying personalities of their subjects, their marriage partners, home life and families. Information on these aspects is more difficult to find, but some of John Dixon's life outside work will be described, although John Dixon's hectic working life must have left little time for much else.

3 The real John Dixon

At this point it should be pointed out that some publications confuse John Dixon with John Dickson (1819-1892) a notoriously unreliable railway contractor who was bankrupt three times over. John Dickson was the engineer for the construction of the Whitby, Redcar and Middlesbrough Union Railway from 1871 to 1873, when he was dismissed. John Dixon designed the five viaducts on the line, so confusion in this instance is perhaps understandable. (See chapter 13).

John Dixon has also been confused with his uncle John Dixon (1796-1865) who worked with George and Robert Stephenson on many British railways.

4 Engineering contractors in the nineteenth century

The mighty civil engineering works of the nineteenth century were achieved using a system of working developed through the construction of the railways, and well established by the time John Dixon opened his London office.

Rapid expansion of the railway network in the period following the opening of the Stockton and Darlington Railway in 1825 and the Liverpool and Manchester Railway in 1930 was only possible because of the effective organisation of the labour required to implement such projects. By the close of the railway boom, around the time that John Dixon was setting up his own business, this had matured into established engineering practice.

The first stage in any project was to set up a company with directors, sometimes chosen for their public standing rather than their knowledge of the particular business, and then to raise sufficient capital for the work. This was usually by means of issuing shares, encouraged by an often over-optimistic prospectus. With increasing prosperity and rise of the middle classes, shares issues were usually eagerly taken up, and English capital funded work around the world. The directors would then appoint a consulting engineer to carry out the overall design of the work, produce drawings and specifications. In the case of the Liverpool and Manchester Railway the engineer, George Stephenson, also recruited and directed the labour force, but these two roles were soon separated with the rise of the engineering contractor. Men such as Thomas Brassey (1805-1870) and Samuel Morton Peto (1809-1889) would be engaged by the engineer to provide the labour force, supervise their work and take care of their pay. The larger contractors, with several projects running at any time, would appoint an on site agent. The agent then took on gangers, leaders of teams of navvies. Sometimes an individual ganger would take on a specific package of work, acting as a sub-contractor. By the mid-nineteenth century, as the pace of railway building at home slowed, contractors increasingly turned to work abroad.

This was the time that John Dixon set up his engineering contracting business in London. John may well have been encouraged by his father-in-law, George England, who would have a wide experience of such matters as a supplier of engineering construction equipment and locomotives. Whereas Brassey and Peto, although superb managers of armies of workers, had no formal engineering education, John Dixon was technically competent in his own right and could act as both engineer and contractor. Furthermore, he had experience of running his own business at the Bedlington Iron Works. With an engaging personality, he had all the qualities for success. There is no doubt that he was successful, but history has tended to forget the engineering contractors while heaping praise on the consulting engineers, such as Robert Stephenson and Isambard Kingdom Brunel. Without the contractors their grand designs would never have been realised.

5 Tenders for engineering works

Organisations wishing to engage a contractor for civil engineering work would issue a call for tenders. These would sometimes appear in local newspapers, but the engineering and building press published national lists. A contractor who was interested in bidding would request drawings and specifications, and assemble the tender. Larger projects would involve a professional consulting engineer, who may well suggest suitable contractors to approach. There is no doubt that consulting engineers would have their own group of trusted contractors.

In 1867 the Board of Guardians of the Alverstoke, near Gosport in Hampshire, required a bridge to give access to the workhouse across Alver Creek. They did not advertise locally, but went to the national trade press and received nineteen tenders ranging from £425 to £920 including John Dixon's tender for £567. The number and wide range of tenders shows the problems faced by the contractor submitting the tender. With a low chance of success, the contractor could only afford to spend a minimum time on the tender, and certainly not spend time visiting the site. With the client's drawings and specifications, the tender would be put together using tables of costs based on dimensions or weight. The contractor could also be up against 'wild card' tenders. One of the tenders for the Alverstoke bridge was from a company which had not been sent plans or specifications, and is assumed to have just picked up talk of the bridge and submitted a speculative tender. The Board of Guardians accepted the lowest tender, which happened to be from the most distant company, in Manchester.

References

The Contractors
Hugh Ferguson and Mike Chrimes
Institution of Civil Engineers
Thomas Telford Limited, London, 2014
History of civil engineering contracting work, but no mention of John Dixon.

Alverstoke Board of Guardians
Hampshire Telegraph and Sussex Chronicle, and General Advertiser for Hants, Sussex, Surrey, Dorset and Wilts, Portsmouth, 10 August 1867, page 6
Discussion of tenders received for an iron bridge to the workhouse.

'The Opening of the Stockton and Darlington Railway 1825' by Terence Tenison Cuneo, 1919. Perhaps more than any other event, the opening of the Stockton and Darlington Railway heralded the industrial age of the 19th century. Terence Cuneo (1907-1996) was a prolific painter of railway and industrial scenes. His mother, father and two brothers were also artists. From the mid-1950s Cuneo's works included a small mouse, often difficult to identify but a famous trademark. Reproduced by courtesy of the National Railway Museum (NRM Pictorial Collection / Science and Society Picture Library) NRM reference 10282799

1 Early life, education and first employment

Most, but not all, generations of the Dixons of Cockfield in County Durham inherited a talent for engineering and business. One Dixon who demonstrated these talents in full was John, born in 1835 at Newcastle upon Tyne, who went on to be an international civil engineering contractor. John Dixon's education could not have been more appropriate, starting with the inspirational teaching of Dr John Collingwood Bruce at the Percy Street Academy and culminating at the foremost engineering works in the north of England, Robert Stephenson's works at Forth Banks. John Dixon began his working life at the Bishopwearmouth Iron Works with his close friend Jasper Capper Mounsey. Both men had ambitions to manage their own business and bought the Bedlington Iron Works in 1861 when John was twenty-six. Tragically Mrs Mounsey was killed in a terrible accident while touring the works in its opening week, and later the venture proved unprofitable. John Dixon left the north east in 1865 and moved to London with Jasper Capper Mounsey. It was there that he set up his civil engineering contracting business which occupied him for the rest of his life.

Dixon family talents

While it is not intended to chronicle the detailed family history of the Dixons of Raby and Cockfield here, it is important to mention some of John Dixon's ancestors. Scientific and engineering talent appeared in previous generations, and in John Dixon, although it had by-passed his father. There was also a strong line of business sense, but this had lapsed in his grandfather's generation, when the brothers George Dixon (1760-1842) and John Dixon (1762-1816) managed to lose the family coal mining wealth through incompetence. It reappeared in John and his brother Raylton, both of whom set up large and successful enterprises, John as an international civil engineering contractor and Raylton as a builder of iron ships in Middlesbrough.

The early Dixon fortunes were founded in the coal seams under Cockfield Fell. George Dixon (1701-1775) was the first documented coal owner. One of his sons, Jeremiah Dixon (1733-1779), the part-surveyor of the Mason-Dixon Line in America, is today the most often recognised family member. Jeremiah's mathematical skills were tempered by an occasional recklessness. His equally gifted brother George Dixon (1731-1785) soberly applied himself to improvements in the Dixon coal mining interests on Cockfield Fell. With an enquiring mind, he was first to light a house with coal gas and to produce coal tar, yet is virtually forgotten, such is the fickle nature of history. George's two sons, George and John mentioned above, continued the Dixon mining operations, but were the unsuccessful defendants in an action brought about when they mined under land belonging to two of their neighbours, continuing to deny any wrong-doing, even when they were caught red-handed.

With the loss of the coal mining business, the next generation turned to engineering, propitiously at the very start of the railways. John Dixon had three uncles involved in the early railways. John Dixon (1796-1865) worked with George Stephenson on the survey for the Stockton and Darlington Railway and then on the Liverpool and Manchester Railway. Edward Dixon (1809-1877) started alongside his brother on the Liverpool and Manchester Railway and later worked with Robert Stephenson. James Dixon (1810-1833) worked on the Stockton and Darlington Railway.

Unlike these uncles, John's father, Jeremiah Dixon (1804-1882), lived a quiet life above a Newcastle bank with his wife, Mary.

John Dixon enters the world

Past generations of the Dixon family had been members of the Society of Friends (the Quakers). Jeremiah and Mary Dixon's first child, John Dixon, was born on 2 January 1835, nearly two years after the wedding. The birth was registered at the Society of Friends' Monthly Meeting of Newcastle upon Tyne. The date in the register is written in the Quaker style as '1835 1st mo. 2d' and a note added under the names of the parents that they were not in membership. This was because Mary's mother, Ann Pease, was a Quaker who had married the non-Quaker John Frank. At that time the Society of Friends would not tolerate marriage to non-Quakers and Ann Pease was disowned by the Darlington Monthly Meeting. The children had no birth-right membership of the Society of Friends; even though Mary had a strict Quaker upbringing from her mother, she never applied for membership of the Society.

On 23 January 1835 John Dixon's birth was announced in *The Durham Chronicle* and the *Durham County Advertiser*, but not in the Newcastle press.

Nothing is known about John's earliest years. His first sister, Augusta Ann, was born when he was almost two years old, and his first brother, Raylton, when he was three and a half years old. His mother Mary would probably have been able to count on the support of nearby Newcastle Quaker families to help look after the young John in the later stages of these two pregnancies. By the time her fourth child, Amelia, was born in August

1840, John would be more independent; he might even have started school. By 1855 Jeremiah and Mary employed a servant, nineteen-year old Susannah Blenkinsop, and there may have been a servant when John was an infant.

Life above the bank

John Dixon grew up with his brothers and sisters above the Northumberland and Durham District Bank in Newcastle upon Tyne, where his father was the chief clerk. The bank building still stands as Lloyds Bank, next to the Theatre Royal, although its magnificent interior was gutted in a misguided attempt at modernisation by Lloyds. The windows of their rooms on the top floor can still be seen, but the rooms behind those windows are no more, the interior of the building having been converted into a full-height atrium. From these windows the children would have looked out over Grey Street and Market Street, and the pit door of the Theatre Royal. Augusta Ann remembered that the streets were always busy, more so on the Saturday market days. She also recalled the excitement of the procession of judges and civic leaders for the Assizes and the noisy campaigns preceding elections.

Although Jeremiah Dixon never returned to the Society of Friends after they had refused to accept his marriage to Mary, there is no doubt that life at home was based on Mary's Quaker values. When the youngest son, Waynman Dixon, wrote letters home from Egypt in the 1870s, he still used the traditional Quaker 'thee' and 'thy'. It would have been the normal practice to educate Quaker children from families enjoying a reasonable income at either Ackworth, near Pontefract, or Bootham in York, after which they would begin a career in business and commerce. Engineering was a comparatively rare occupation among 19th century Quakers, although a great many were involved with iron manufacture, starting with Abraham Darby at Coalbrookdale in the 18th century. But several factors combined during the early years of the three Dixon brothers to prepare them for successful engineering careers.

The three brothers, John in particular, had a natural aptitude for practical mechanics, judging from their sister's description of their activities in the upstairs rooms above the bank. Their eldest sister, Augusta Ann, recalled the large rooms at the top of the bank:

> 'One contained a large cold bath, also a joiner's bench and a large and smaller lathe; my father was a clever joiner and made and mended our toys, and my elder brother John, who was then going to Bruce's School, had always many works going on. Modelling, casting, ornamenting boxes with beautiful eccentric turning; snuff boxes were a great subject for ornamentation: then very generally carried by elderly people. Fire works were manufactured, and I was left to watch and dry explosives on the oven top, while John was at school.'

'Grey Street with the Theatre Royal' pen and ink drawing c1840 by J W Carmichael. John Wilson Carmichael (1800-1868) was born in Newcastle upon Tyne but later moved to London. He was a marine artist and was sent to the Baltic by the Illustrated London News to record scenes during the Crimean War. In this drawing the bank can be seen just beyond the Theatre Royal. The Dixon children had the run of the top storey rooms. Reproduced by courtesy of Newcastle City Libraries, reference 025345.

The three boys would come to realise that the livelihoods of their father and grandfather, in banking and in coal ownership respectively, had come to abrupt ends. These experiences would be in stark contrast to the exciting tales told by their railway engineering uncles, John and Edward Dixon. In 1925 Waynman Dixon wrote a pamphlet about the origin of the railways, which he introduced thus:

> 'An octogenarian who in his boyhood was in intimate association with the survivors of the pioneers who promoted and constructed the Stockton and Darlington Railway in the beginning of the last century writes these personal reminiscences of the stories which he had from them at first hand.'

In the text Waynman wrote that he remembered having seen *Puffing Billy* running in front of George Stephenson's cottage at Wylam-on-Tyne, an experience he had no doubt shared with John and Raylton. At this time, Newcastle upon Tyne was a world-renowned centre for engineering, with the works of William Armstrong, Robert Stephenson, and the many shipyards along the Tyne. John, Raylton and Waynman Dixon grew up in an area alive with engineering industry, expertise, and innovation.

School years

John attended the Percy Street Academy at No.80 Percy Street in Newcastle, founded in 1806 by John Bruce and noted for mathematics and sciences. After John Bruce's death in 1834, the school was taken over by his son, Dr John Collingwood Bruce, by all accounts an inspirational teacher. The school enjoyed a high reputation, and its fee-paying pupils came from the families of the middle classes and minor gentry. Railway engineer Robert Stephenson, ironmaster Sir Lowthian Bell and shipbuilders Sir William Gray of Hartlepool and Charles Palmer of Jarrow had all been pupils at the school. Robert Stephenson attended the school between the ages of twelve and sixteen.

When he had reached his eleventh birthday, John Dixon left Bruce's school and went as a boarder to the Friends' School, Brookfield, in Wigton, Cumberland. The school had opened in 1815 for the education of Quakers' children, originally from nine to fourteen years of age, but extended in the 1830s to seven to fifteen years of age. It was quite small, with an average intake of ten girls and ten boys each year. Thomas Richardson, the main benefactor of the Friends' School and the British School in Great Ayton, North Yorkshire, gave money for the purchase of land and a new school building at Wigton in 1825. Later, when Thomas Richardson retired to Great Ayton from his banking career in London, he briefly lived in Ayton House, the house where Waynman Dixon would spend his last thirty years.

Who's who?
John Collingwood Bruce (1805-1892)

After an education at Mill Hill and Glasgow University, John Bruce started his career in the Presbyterian Church but soon joined his parents in the running of their school. On his father's death in 1834, John took over the school, living on the premises with his family, six full-time teachers and around 30 boarding pupils. Unlike his parents, Dr Bruce's main interests were in history and the arts. The school was notable for its visiting art teachers including the landscape painter Thomas Miles Richardson and, later, his three sons in succession. John Dixon become a proficient amateur artist.

Apart from the school John Bruce was an expert on Hadrian's Wall. *The Handbook to the Roman Wall* was first published in 1863 and regularly revised during his lifetime, becoming the standard text on the wall. Another of his interests was the traditional songs of Northumbria, and he collected many in his *Northumbrian Minstrelsy*.

Dr Bruce retired from the school in 1863. Teaching, archaeology and folk music could not compete with the excitement of building railways in foreign lands, and his son, George Barclay Bruce, became the consulting engineer for the Rio Tinto Mine railway and ore-loading terminal, the terminal being built by John Dixon in 1874-76. Dr Bruce's grandson, George Barclay Bruce junior, also worked on the Rio Tinto railway.

Above) Bruce's School, Newcastle' engraving by R P Leitch. Richard Principal Leitch (1827-1882) was a Scottish artist and engraver who worked in London for the Illustrated London News and book publishers. Engraving from The Life of George Stephenson and his son Robert Stephenson by Samuel Smiles, Harper and Brothers, New York. 1868. Reproduced by courtesy of Newcastle City Libraries.

Right) Rev John Collingwood Bruce (1805-1892) was an inspirational teacher. Reproduced by courtesy of Newcastle City Libraries.

John was a pupil at Wigton from April 1846 to June 1849. This was a time of some surprising impropriety at Brookfield. In the summer of 1845, Charles Barnard was appointed as superintendent and headmaster. He had been a teacher at Ackworth, the Quaker School near Pontefract and, as he was about to marry, his new wife was appointed housekeeper at Brookfield. She died in January 1846 and Charles began to pay attention to Mary Ann Ord, the senior teaching apprentice at the school. She had attended as a pupil from November 1835 to May 1844, presumably starting when she was seven, and so must have been barely eighteen when the relationship with Barnard began. Not surprisingly, the school's governing committee disapproved, and Barnard submitted his resignation towards the end of 1847. At their next meeting, the committee members were surprised to receive a letter from seven parents in Newcastle, including Jeremiah Dixon, stating that they felt Barnard's resignation would be a great loss to the school. As a result of the letter, the committee cancelled Mary Ord's indentures and re-engaged Charles Barnard, who promptly married Mary and took up residence in the entrance lodge.

Charles and Mary Barnard's management of the school does not appear to have been very satisfactory, and there were complaints. One concerned the rude behaviour and bad language of the boys. Early in 1851, Barnard resigned for a second time but, on this occasion, he left Wigton.

One of John Dixon's friends at the school was John Mark, and a history of the Mark family records the competition between the two boys John Mark and John Dixon:

> 'In the competition for the honour of possessing the first place in the school, the last to surrender to him (John Mark) was his particular friend and school-chum, John Dixon, now the eminent civil engineer who brought Cleopatra's Needle from Egypt and erected it on the Thames Embankment, and whose name is connected with great engineering enterprises in that country, but more recently as the builder of the new bridge at Hammersmith.'

John Mark was later Mayor of Manchester, and on the occasion of the wedding of his youngest daughter, Florence, to Robert Hutchinson on 29 January 1891 presents were received from Sir Raylton and Lady Dixon, and from Mrs John Dixon (John had died the previous day).

Engineering apprenticeship with Robert Stephenson

After leaving school in the summer of 1849, John became an articled pupil of Robert Stephenson at the Forth Street Works, which was owned by Joseph Pease and Thomas Richardson, both Quakers. Dr John Bruce was a good friend of George and Robert Stephenson. George Stephenson died in 1848, a year before John Dixon started his apprenticeship at the Forth Street Works. It is likely that Dr Bruce, recognising John's engineering talents, facilitated the apprenticeship at Robert Stephenson's works.

By the time John started his apprenticeship, Robert Stephenson was probably the foremost engineer in the country and the MP for Whitby, and would be rarely seen at the works. In 1851 Stephenson started work on the railway from Alexandria to Cairo, which would be used by John's younger brother Waynman some twenty years later. The 1850s were years of great activity at the Forth Street Works, with fabrication of bridges, caissons, dock gates and even ships in addition to its original work on locomotives and engines. In 1848 Edward Pease had written that he saw all his investments sinking, apart from the Forth Street Works; he had loaned Robert £500 to start the business and in 1848 alone had received £7,000 from the concern. By 1859 the Forth Street Works was the largest employer on Tyneside. John could not have wished for a better introduction to practical engineering, and to his fellow Forth Street apprentices who would later own successful engineering businesses. One of these was Thomas Whitwell from Kendal, who started his apprenticeship in 1856 and who would later establish the Thornaby Ironworks with his brother William; they were both Quakers. Another was Jeremiah Head, who married Thomas Wrightson's sister Rebecca, and became associated with the engineering company of Head Wrightson at Thornaby.

'Returning from the Meeting' etching by W H Nutter in Friends' School, Brookfield, Wigton 1815-1953 by David W Reed, published by Wigton Old Scholars' Association 1954. After studying at Cambridge University, William Henry Nutter (1821-1872) became an artist and art teacher in Carlisle. John Dixon attended Brookfield School from 1846 to 1849.

Who's who?
Robert Stephenson (1803-1859)

Robert was the only son of George Stephenson. Although Robert was undoubtedly the better engineer, history often gives more prominence to George, even to the extent of crediting the father with the son's achievements. Robert was taught at the village school in Long Benton, east of Newcastle upon Tyne, and later at the Percy Street Academy in Newcastle. This was followed by an apprenticeship with Nicholas Wood, the mining engineer at Killingworth Colliery where George was an engine-wright. Robert worked with his father on the survey for the Stockton and Darlington Railway and on the Liverpool and Manchester Railway, building the famous *Rocket* which won the Rainhill trials in 1829. Although his involvement with railways continued, Robert Stephenson's engineering genius was perhaps more apparent in his bridges, such as the High Level Bridge in Newcastle in 1849 and the Britannia Tubular Bridge across the Menai Straits in 1850. The design of these bridges demonstrated a thorough understanding of the properties of cast iron and wrought iron, and how the two materials could be used to create unprecedented spans.

In 1823 Robert founded the Forth Street Works, the world's first purpose-built workshop for manufacturing railway engines, with a £500 loan from Edward Pease. Robert was elected Member of Parliament for Whitby in 1847. He was president of the Institution of Civil Engineers from 1855-57 and president of the Institution of Mechanical Engineers from 1849-53. In later life he declined a knighthood. It was perhaps only after his death that the nation fully recognised Robert Stephenson's achievements; his funeral procession and burial in Westminster Abbey was comparable with those of royalty.

'Forth-Street Works, Newcastle' an anonymous engraving in The Life of George Stephenson and his son Robert Stephenson by Samuel Smiles, Harper and Brothers, New York. 1868. Robert Stephenson and Company, established in 1823 at Forth Street in Newcastle upon Tyne, was the first company set up specifically for the manufacture of steam locomotives. Many of the north east engineers started their careers as Forth Street Works apprentices. It is a great pity that what remains of the premises does not seem to be valued by the city.
Engraving from The Life of George Stephenson and his son Robert Stephenson by Samuel Smiles, Harper and Brothers, New York. 1868.
Reproduced by courtesy of Newcastle City Libraries.

Bishopwearmouth Ironworks

After completing his training, probably in 1856, John was appointed engineer and manager of the Bishopwearmouth Ironworks in Sunderland. This had been built in 1826 and consisted of blast furnaces and puddling furnaces. By the time John arrived, it had become part of the Derwent Iron Company and was considerably expanded in the late 1840s.

The Derwent Iron Company was a typical example of the complex business arrangements made by Quaker families. In 1839 the Quaker William Richardson (1801-1879), apparently while taking the spa waters at Shotley Bridge, was shown outcrops of ironstone at Consett. Convinced of its potential, he encouraged a Quaker partnership of William Backhouse (1807-1869), Charles Bragg (1801-1874), John Mounsey (b.1806), the brothers Caleb Richardson (1796-1875) and Edward Richardson (1810-1886), and Thomas Richardson (1800-1872) to establish the Consett Iron Company in 1840. This new company erected two blast furnaces and rolling mills. Caleb and Edward were brothers of Jonathan Richardson (1802-1871), a leading figure in the Northumberland and Durham District Bank. Jonathan had recently purchased lands at Consett and taken leases on extensive royalties on coal and ironstone deposits. He made agreements with the Consett Iron Company for the use of his land and the working of his coal and ironstone deposits, although from 1852 better quality Cleveland ironstone from Pease and Partners, another Quaker business, was used, brought to Consett by the largely Quaker controlled Stockton and Darlington Railway.

Within a few years the Consett Iron Company merged with the Redesdale Iron Works to form the Derwentside Iron Company. Jonathan Richardson was never formally involved with the Derwentside Iron Company although he attended their meetings and took a leading part in the business. But above all, he facilitated a massive loan of £1 million from the Northumberland and District Bank to the Derwentside Iron Company, a loan which was never repaid and led to the collapse of the bank in 1857.

At first sight it would seem unusual that John Dixon, an inexperienced young engineer, should have been placed in this responsible position. But the appointment may well have been arranged by Jonathan Richardson, brother of Caleb and Edward Richardson, who was married to Elizabeth Backhouse. Jonathan took an active interest in the operation of the ironworks, but his primary position was manager of the Northumberland and Durham District Bank in Newcastle where John's father was employed. However, the oft confusing network of Quaker financial and family connections did have its limits. Jonathan Richardson was not directly related to the James Richardson who married John Dixon's sister, Augusta Ann.

The relationship with Jonathan Richardson would prove to be a mixed blessing for the Dixon family. Although Jonathan probably had a hand in John's first appointment, it was the £1 million loan by the Northumberland and Durham District Bank to the Derwent Iron Company that led to the collapse of the bank in the same year, 1857, leaving John's father without employment. At this time, the Derwent Iron Company was said to be famous only for its size and its inability to make a profit! Jonathan Richardson, with his involvement in both the bank and the iron company, was held largely to blame for the financial disaster. It may be that, fearing the worst, Jonathan ensured John's employment just as his father was about to lose his job.

John found the Bishopwearmouth Works in a sorry state. In 1845 a furnace exploded when a quantity of scrap cannon and shells was being melted in a furnace. One of the shells still held its charge and exploded, killing a boy of fifteen. Later in the year a tremendous boiler explosion at the works killed six workmen and seriously injured thirty more. Twelve surgeons from Sunderland spent all day at the works attending to the injured. In 1849 there was yet another explosion when a rolling mill boiler was propelled about 60 feet into the air. This time there was only one fatality, the engineman who died from scalds. Then, in 1855, the Derwent Iron Company decided to transfer all manufacturing to Consett. Just three weeks before Christmas 1856, most of the Bishopwearmouth workforce was given notice. A week later, over 500 men and boys had lost their employment; the season of goodwill proved illusory.

There were press reports that a new company was to be formed to take over the iron works. This seemed possible because about 100 men were retained to keep the site open while a new owner was sought, but nothing transpired over the next few months. Then in April 1857 the entire works was put up for auction with Mounsey, I'Anson and Company of Newcastle acting as agents for the sale. It appears that John Dixon and Jasper Capper Mounsey then took over operations at Bishopwearmouth, with the site now in the ownership of the Derwent and Consett Iron Company, which was formed after the collapse of the Northumberland and Durham District Bank. The site was idle for most of 1857, but by November it was reported to be in partial operation, returning to full production in March 1858 manufacturing iron bars. Jasper Capper Mounsey appears not to have been actively involved with the works, as he remained at Mounsey, I'Anson and Company and lived at Carlton Terrace in Newcastle until 1861.

The reprieve of the Bishopwearmouth Iron Works under John Dixon was short lived, and the works was closed down in August 1861. Mounsey and Dixon must have been thinking of setting up in business on their own account, and now their opportunity had arrived. They purchased the Bedlington Iron Works and hoped to realise their ambitions. It was said that Mounsey had the money and Dixon had the brains, a credible observation given Mounsey's connections with the Backhouse Bank and Dixon's engineering training. John was able to engage some of the men from Bishopwearmouth to work for him at Bedlington.

When Bishopwearmouth closed in 1861 there had been rumours that the North Eastern Railway Company might rescue it. These rumours came to nothing and in August 1863 the site was again put up for auction but did not find a purchaser. It remained idle for a while but, with trade improving, the Derwent and Consett Iron Company re-opened at least part of the works at the end of 1863. Attempts to set it up as a limited company were unsuccessful and in 1866 the site finally closed down.

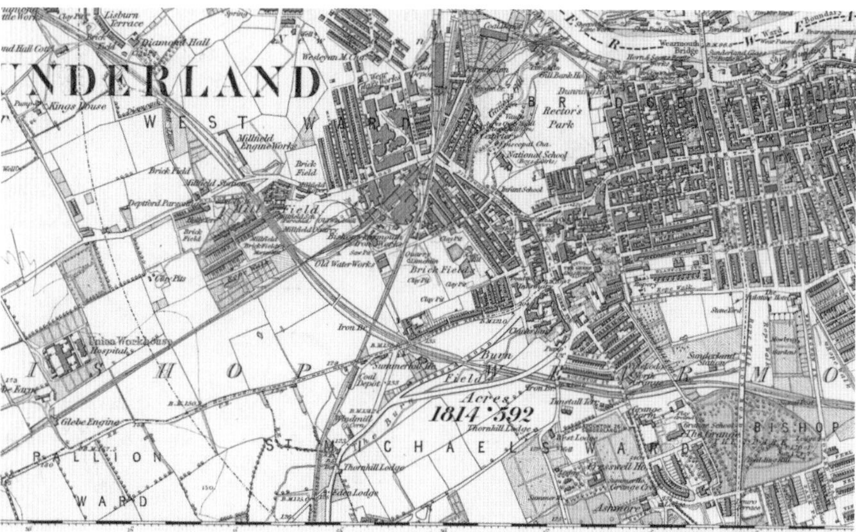

Left) Bishopwearmouth Iron Works around 1850.
Engraving reproduced by kind permission of the SINE Project, The Museum of Antiquities, University of Newcastle upon Tyne.

Right) Bishopwearmouth Iron Works. Ordnance Survey Six Inch Series Surveyed 1855, published 1862, Durham VIII.
Reproduced by permission of the National Library of Scotland.

Who's who?
Jasper Capper Mounsey (1820-1895)

Although fifteen years his senior, Jasper Capper Mounsey was a lifelong friend of John Dixon. In his youth John would have certainly known the Mounsey family as they were all members of the Quaker community in Newcastle upon Tyne. But it was from the time John started work at Bishopwearmouth, when in his early twenties, that their friendship grew. Jasper was the son of Thomas Mounsey (1793-1850), a wealthy farmer, coal owner and a Quaker in Bishopwearmouth. Thomas Mounsey married Mary Capper in 1817; they had six children with three sons (Edward, Jasper and John) and one daughter (Katharine) surviving to adulthood. In the 1840s Jasper and his brother Edward were in business as iron merchants with John and William Cargill, trading as Cargill, Mounsey and Company in Newcastle upon Tyne. In 1848 Jasper left this business to form a partnership with Charles I'Anson, a Quaker from Darlington, while the Cargills and Edward Mounsey continued as Cargill and Company. Mounsey, I'Anson and Company had offices at No.23 Grey Street. From the mid-1860s Edward and John Mounsey were coal fitters, the agents who bought coal from the mine owners and sold it to the shippers.

When Thomas Mounsey died in 1850, his son Jasper, now thirty, was still living in the family home at Hendon Hill in Sunderland. The following year he married Elizabeth Waite, a Quaker from London. With Jaspar working at the Ridsdale Iron Works, he and Elizabeth lived at No.27 John Street, Sunderland. In 1855 they moved back to Newcastle, living at No.10 Carlton Terrace, before going to Bedlington in 1862, when Jasper began his partnership with John Dixon. Jasper and Elizabeth had seven children. In the manner of Quaker inter-family marriages, Jasper developed strong ties with the Backhouse family. In 1847 his brother Edward married Emily Backhouse, and in 1856 his sister Katharine married Edward Backhouse (1808-1879), giving Jasper a connection to the Backhouse Bank. Edward and Emily were children of the Quaker banker Edward Backhouse (1781-1860) and his wife Ann (née Pease). The Backhouse Bank connection would be later important for John's brother Raylton, when he started his own shipbuilding business with Thomas Backhouse.

After the tragic death of his first wife and the sale of the Bedlington Iron Works in 1862, Jasper moved to London. Initially he and John Dixon were in business together as iron merchants at No.27 Leadenhall Street, but within a few years they set up their own businesses, while remaining close friends. Mounsey established himself as an iron merchant, initially at No.118 Cannon Street and later at No.7 Laurence Pountney Hill, close to John Dixon's office at No.1 Laurence Pountney Hill. He was an agent for several northern companies, including the Consett Iron Company and the Stockton Forge Company. In 1879 he was joined by his son Alfred Mounsey and Alfred Russell, and the business moved into Suffolk Lane, just off Laurence Pountney Hill. Jasper retired from the partnership in 1885.

Jasper married Eliza Stanton in 1869 at Whorlton Church, County Durham; she was forty-one and he was forty-nine. Eliza's father, Philip Holmes Stanton, was a solicitor in Newcastle. The family lived at Summerhill Grove, in one of the grand houses built by the wealthy Quaker families of Newcastle. Philip Holmes Stanton was certainly well-connected in Newcastle; the trustees of the Stephenson Memorial Schools, set up in memory of George Stephenson, included Robert Stephenson and his son George Robert Stephenson, Joseph Whitwell Pease, and Philip Holmes Stanton. Dr Bruce had spoken at the laying of the foundation stone. Eliza's brother married a daughter of George Parker Bidder (1806-1878) an eminent civil engineer.

After the wedding Jasper and Eliza lived in Greenhithe in Kent, later moving to South Norwood and finally to Croydon in 1887. Here they were near neighbours of John and Mary Dixon. Jasper and Eliza had one daughter, Beatrice, born in 1872. By the time of John Dixon's death Jasper, now retired, Eliza and Beatrice had moved to Bath.

Bedlington Ironworks

The Bedlington Ironworks was established in 1736, sited in the picturesque Blyth Dene where there was local access to iron ore, coal and water power. It was one of the earliest iron works in the north east of England, specialising in iron goods for the Sunderland shipyards: castings, anchors, chains and nails. Bedlington did not have its own blast furnace, buying in pig iron from outside suppliers. From 1819 to 1853 the works was under the management of Michael Longridge, who was also a partner, along with George and Robert Stephenson and the Quaker banker Thomas Richardson, in the Forth Street Locomotive Works in Newcastle. Bedlington was well equipped, and manufactured patented malleable iron rails, much in demand by the rapidly expanding network of railways. Having started to produce boiler plate, wheels and axles for Robert Stephenson, Michael Longridge opened his own Engine Works at Bedlington in 1837, in competition with Forth Street and much to the consternation of Thomas Richardson. Longridge was in charge of the Forth Street Works during the lengthy absences of the Stephensons and may well have taken design ideas and manufacturing techniques from Forth Street to Bedlington. Notwithstanding this, and in spite of Thomas Richardson's criticisms of the way in which he managed the Forth Street operation, Longridge remained a close friend of Robert Stephenson and asked him to be godfather to one of his children.

The prosperity of Bedlington continued until Longridge retired in 1853, from when the works declined. It was acquired by a Mr Spence, but he gave up after only two years and there was a large sale of plant and material, including barrels of ale brewed in the works' own brewery. Spence was unable to find a buyer for the works, it was closed down and left abandoned for the next six years.

Mounsey and Dixon would have been able to acquire the abandoned Bedlington Ironworks at a much-reduced price, no doubt assisted in the purchase by their Quaker connections to Thomas Richardson and Edward Pease, and by their friendship with Robert Stephenson. It seems that the two blast furnaces had been dismantled after 1856 but the 14 puddling furnaces probably remained; it would have been straightforward to purchase pig iron for the puddling furnaces from elsewhere. Dixon and Mounsey added new rolling mills and saw mills to the existing plant, and started production in January 1862 hoping to manufacture forgings, castings, bars, bolts, bridge and other light rails and angle iron.

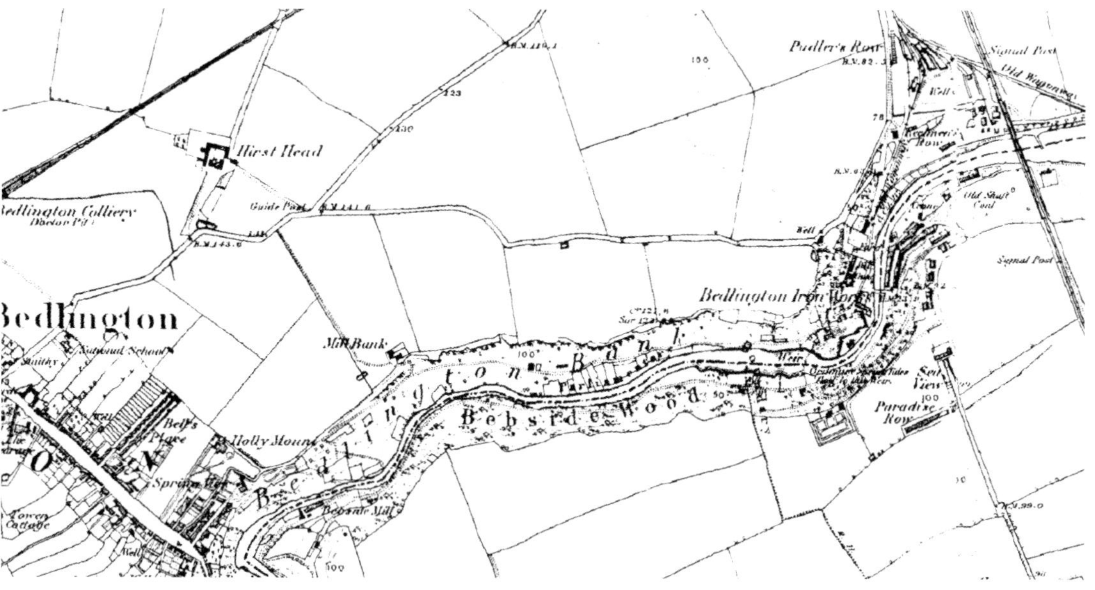

Top) Bedlington Iron Works from the South, 1827. Although an early engraving, the works was still surrounded by countryside when John Dixon and Jasper Mounsey took it over in 1861. The height of the weir shows that ample water power was available at the site.

Left) Ordnance Survey Six Inch Series Surveyed 1858-59, published 1866, Northumberland LXXXII Reproduced by permission of old-maps.co.uk

Tragedies

On the first Friday afternoon after the works opened, Mrs Elizabeth Mounsey, her three eldest children, their governess and two other ladies were being shown around the works by Jasper and John, now in high spirits at the works being returned to full operation. Towards the end of the visit the party was watching the circular saw cutting iron plate. Mrs Mounsey went to step over the saw's rotating drive shaft, which was some six inches above the floor, revolving at great speed and unguarded. Her dress became caught on the shaft, and she was dragged through the narrow gap between the shaft and the floor, where she was partially disembowelled. John grabbed her but could not prevent the lower part of her body being literally torn to pieces in an instant; it was said that she did not even have the time to scream. The full horror of her death, witnessed by her husband and children, is impossible to imagine.

In spite of the best efforts of the partners, the business at Bedlington was not a huge success. Mounsey and Dixon sold out to the Bedlington Coal Company in 1865, from when the works became the Bedlington Iron Company. It could not compete with the newer blast furnaces and iron works of Middlesbrough and closed down in 1868, with the plant and equipment sold and the buildings demolished for building materials.

By this time John Dixon was courting the daughter of George England, who had moved from Newcastle to London where he ran the Hatcham Iron Works. Jasper Mounsey was now a widower with six children. There was little to keep either man in their native north east and they both moved to London, where there was the prospect of more rewarding business opportunities.

Seven years after the appalling death of his first wife, Jasper Capper Mounsey married Eliza Stanton in 1869 and moved to Greenhithe in Kent, then to Croydon. The Mounsey family remained close friends with the Dixon family, Jasper and John both had offices on Laurence Pountney Hill, and at Croydon they lived less than two miles apart. During the 1870s, Jasper Mounsey and two of his sons, Harry and Herbert, visited Waynman Dixon in Egypt. In June 1907 Jasper Mounsey's second wife and his son George, who was then living at Jesmond in Newcastle, visited John Dixon's parents at 'Balla Wray' on Lake Windermere.

THE APPALLING DEATH OF A LADY.—SHIELDS, Saturday Night.—A telegraphic message published in *The Times* of this morning reported the horrible death of Mrs. Mounsey, wife of one of the partners in the Bedlington iron works. These extensive works, formerly belonging to the Longridge family, are situated upon the river Pont, a tributary of the Blyth, and about four miles from that seaport. For some time they had been closed, but three months ago they were taken by Mr. Jasper Mounsey and Mr. Dixon, of Monkwearmouth, gentlemen well known in connexion with the iron trade of the north-eastern counties, and about two months ago Mr. Mounsey and his family took up their residence in Bedlington. The new firm had greatly enlarged the works, adding some new rolling and saw mills to it. The works were opened last week, all except some machinery and a circular saw for cutting iron, which only commenced yesterday. During yesterday afternoon Mr. Mounsey brought his wife, with their three eldest children, and some lady visitors, down to the works, to see them in full operation. They were accompanied by Mr. Dixon and Mr. Nichol, surgeon. Having examined the other portion of the works, the party came into the rolling and saw mills about 10 minutes past 4 o'clock. Having witnessed the circular saw in full operation, the party were about to proceed to another portion of the works. To do so they had to cross a spindle connecting the circular saw with the engine belonging to the rolling-mill by a leather belt, and which spindle, being made of two pieces of iron, was connected together in the centre by nuts. Mr. Dixon and Mrs. Mounsey were the first to go over it, Mr. Mounsey remaining a little behind to assist the young people over. Mrs. Mounsey had stepped over the spindle, which was flying round at a rapid rate, but the bottom of her dress was unfortunately caught by one of the bolts or nuts described. In a moment she was thrown over, and, though Mr. Dixon snatched hold of her, her limbs and the lower part of her person were as instantaneously drawn through an aperture only six inches between the revolving spindle and the ground, and literally crushed out of all form up to her breast. She had not time to scream, and was dead in a moment. The engine was immediately stopped, and the workmen ran from all parts of the factory to help. The poor young ladies and children, who were paralyzed with fright, were taken away as speedily as possible, and the spindle was unscrewed, and the remains of the deceased got out as speedily as possible. They were in a condition too horrible to describe. Mrs. Mounsey was the mother of six children. This shocking occurrence following the Hartley pit accident has caused a most profound sensation throughout the district to-day. Much sympathy is expressed with Mr. Mounsey, who is overwhelmed with sorrow; and the awful accident has caused the most intense grief among the workpeople employed at the factory. A few minutes before 4 yesterday Mrs. Mounsey and her family and visitors passed the houses of the workmen in the highest spirits to witness the works in full operation by the new firm for the first time, and a few minutes after that hour the intelligence ran from house to house, and was carried down to the village, that an accident had occurred, and she was a mangled corpse. Mr. and Mrs. Mounsey were members of well-known families connected with the Society of Friends. The coroner would hold an inquest on the body this evening.

Report of Mrs Mounsey's fatal accident published in The Times of 3 February 1862.
Reproduced by courtesy of The Times / News Licensing.

Acknowledgements

Staff at the Central Library Reference Section, Newcastle upon Tyne, for access to source materials.

Ann Colville, great grand-daughter of John Dixon's sister (Augusta Ann Richardson) for Augusta's reminiscences.

Silvia Gallotti, Lloyds Banking Group archivist, for information about the Newcastle bank building.

Dr Bob Brier of New York for access to Waynman Dixon's letters from Egypt.

References

The Langstaffs of Teesdale and Weardale, Revised Edition
George Blundell Longstaff
Mitchell Hughes and Clarke, London, 1923
In Appendix IX Notes and Wills relating to Dixon and Railton families there are biographical notes on Jeremiah III (1804-1882) and his sons.

Birth
Durham Chronicle, 23 January 1835, page 3
'On the 2[d] inst., at Newcastle, in Mosley Street, the wife of Jeremiah Dixon, Esq., of a son.'

Birth
Durham County Advertiser, 23 January 1835, page 3
'At Newcastle, in Mosley Street, on the 2d inst., Mrs Jeremiah Dixon, of a son.'

Reminiscences of the Dixon Family
Recalled by Mrs Augusta Ann Richardson, 23 June 1911
Transcription owned by Ann Colville (née Richardson)
Contains an account of John Dixon's activities at the top of the bank building in Newcastle.

Intimate Story of the Origin of Railways
W.D.
June 1925
A privately printed pamphlet written by Waynman Dixon.

The Life and Letters of John Collingwood Bruce LL.D., D.C.L., F.S.A. of Newcastle upon Tyne
Sir Gainsford Bruce DCL
William Blackwood and Sons, Edinburgh and London, 1905
Biography of Dr Bruce by his son.

The Handbook to the Roman Wall, third edition
J Collingwood Bruce
Andrew Reid and Company Limited,
Newcastle upon Tyne, 1885
284 pages packed with detail on the wall, clearly demonstrating that its author must have spent many years researching the subject, hopefully not to the detriment of the school.

George and Robert Stephenson, the railway revolution
L C T Rolt
Longmans, London, 1960
The best biography of George and Robert Stephenson.

Friends' School Wigton 1815-1953
David W Reed
Wigton Old Scholars' Association, 1954
The history of the school attended by John and Raylton Dixon, with details of Charles Barnard, his affair with a teaching apprentice, and support for him from Jeremiah Dixon and others. Records Raylton's attendance at the first old scholars' meeting. Unfortunately, the book wrongly credits Raylton with bringing Cleopatra's Needle to England.

Genealogy of the family of Mark or Marke; County of Cumberland
John Mark
Privately printed by Palmer, Howe and Company, Manchester, 1898
John Dixon at Brookfield School, and wedding presents from Raylton Dixon and John Dixon's widow.

The Diaries of Edward Pease
Edited by Sir Alfred E Pease
Headley Brothers, London, 1907
Profitability of the Forth Street Works in 1848.

Biographical Dictionary of British Quakers in Commerce and Industry 1775-1920
Edward H Milligan
Sessions Book Trust, York, 2007
Biographical details of the Mounsey and Richardson families.

Deviating from the Path of Safety: The Rise and Fall of a Nineteenth Century Quaker Meeting
Elizabeth O'Donnell
Quaker Studies, Volume 8, Issue 1, Article 5
George Fox University, Oregon, USA
Covers Jonathan Richardson's role in the Derwent Iron Works and the fall of the Northumberland and Durham District Bank from a Quaker viewpoint.

Ward's Directories for Newcastle and Gateshead, for Northumberland and Durham, and for the North of England
(editions from 1850 to 1863-64)
Robert Ward, Newcastle upon Tyne
Details of Cargill and Company and Mounsey, I'Anson and Company in Newcastle. I'Anson is often incorrectly printed as Jansen.

Analysis of Orders received 1831-62 and 1882-91
Whessoe Papers reference D/Whes 6/50
Durham County Record Office, County Hall, Durham
Orders from Caygill (should be Cargill) Mounsey & Co in 1846 and 1847, with Caygill, Mounsey crossed out in 1848 and replaced by Mounsey, I'Anson & Co. The last entry for Mounsey, I'Anson & Co is in 1857.

Boyd's Inhabitants of London and family units, 1851 and 1869
Details of Jasper Capper Mounsey, his first wife Elizabeth (née Waite) and their seven children, and his second wife Eliza Holmes (or Stanton) and one daughter.

Electoral Registers 1855 to 1887
Details of Jasper Capper Mounsey's addresses.

Fatal accident
The Carlisle Journal, 30 August 1845, page 2
Furnace explosion at the Bishopwearmouth Iron Works when melting down scrap ordnance, one shell containing part of its charge. Fifteen year old boy killed.

Dreadful boiler explosion and loss of life at Bishop-Wearmouth
The Newcastle Journal, 29 November 1845, page 3
Report of the explosion.

Explosion at the Bishopwearmouth Iron Works
The Carlisle Journal, 22 June 1849, page 2
Description of explosion at Mounsey, I'Anson and Company. A rolling mill boiler was blown about sixty feet through the roof of the works. The engineman, Thomas Robinson, was scaled and otherwise injured and died the following morning.

The Consett Iron Works
Durham Chronicle, 2 July 1858, page 7
Account of the start of iron making at Consett and the formation of the Derwentside Iron Company.

The Consett Iron Company Limited, a Case Study in Victorian Business History
A S Wilson
M Phil Thesis, University of Durham, 1973
Full account of the establishment of the Derwentside and Consett works.

By Electric Telegraph
The Newcastle Courant, 11 May 1855
The owners of the Bishopwearmouth Iron Works have given fourteen days' notice of their intention to close the works.

By Electric Telegraph
The Newcastle Courant, 5 December 1856
Upwards of 300 men employed at Bishopwearmouth received a fortnight's notice. All manufacturing operations will be transferred to Consett, but there is an intention to set up a new company next year to carry on at Bishopwearmouth.

Bishopwearmouth Iron Works
The Newcastle Journal, 13 December 1856, page 5
The works now virtually closed with only 100 men remaining. Parties are presently negotiating purchase of the works.

Important Iron Sale at Sunderland
The Newcastle Journal, 21 March 1857, page 4
Advertisement for the auction of the Bishopwearmouth Iron Works, particulars from Mounsey, I'Anson and Company or the auctioneers.

Multum in Parvo
The Liverpool Mercury, 25 March 1858
The Derwent Iron Works at Bishopwearmouth, part of which had been closed for twelve months, was now in full operation.

Untitled paragraph
The Newcastle Daily Journal, 2 October 1861, page 2
Report that the great iron works at Bedlington was to reopen and men from Bishopwearmouth had been engaged. Rumours that the Bishopwearmouth works was to be taken over by parties associated with the North Eastern Railway Company.

Letters from Waynman Dixon to his mother, 19 August 1872 and 12 November 1876
In private ownership (Bob Brier of New York)
Mention of Harry and Herbert Mounsey in Egypt.

Iron Works at Sunderland
The Newcastle Courant, 13 November 1863
The Bishopwearmouth Iron Works, which have been closed for some years, are expected to be sold in a short time and re-opened.

Partnership agreement between J C Mounsey and J Dixon to set up an iron business at Bedlington, trading as Mounsey and Dixon, 30 April 1863
Papers from the Stanton, Croft & Co, Solicitors, collection Reference DT.SC/190, Tyne and Wear Archives, Newcastle upon Tyne
The business was established in 1861, the formal partnership came later.

History of Bedlington Ironworks 1736-1867
Christopher Bergen
G Robinson, Printers, Bedlington
Written in the 1920s or 1930s, a good history with anecdotes from survivors from the works and two illustrations of the site.

Bedlington Iron & Engine Works 1736-1867, a new history
Evan Martin
Northern History Booklets No.52, 1974
Frank Graham, Newcastle upon Tyne, 1974
Comprehensive history of the works from its start in 1736 to the closing years. Includes the ownership of the works by Jasper Capper Mounsey and John Dixon, with details of the fatal accident to Mrs Mounsey. The two illustrations of the works (in 1827 and 1840) are long before the Mounsey and Dixon period but there is a map dated 1858. The

Bedlington Iron Works
The Newcastle Courant, 3 January 1862
Messrs Mounsey and Dixon re-open the Bedlington Works for the manufacture of forgings, castings, bars, bolts, bridge and other light rails, angle iron, etc.

Northumberland Blast Furnace Plants in the Nineteenth Century
T M Hoskison
Transactions of the Newcomen Society for the study of the history of engineering and technology
Volume 25, 1945-46 and 1946-47, pages 73-81
Contains a paragraph on the extensive bar iron works of Mounsey and Dixon. There were two blast furnaces, one built in 1849 and the other in 1854, but these were only in blast until 1855. They may have then been dismantled and sold.

The Appalling Death of a Lady
The Times, London, 3 February 1862, page 9
Messrs Mounsey and Dixon have recently re-commenced the extensive iron works at Bedlington. Mr Dixon and Mr and Mrs Mounsey, with several ladies, were visiting the works when Mrs Mounsey's dress became entangled in machinery and she was literally torn to pieces.

Advertisements and Notices
The Newcastle Courant, 18 September 1868
Preliminary Notice of Sale of the puddling and rolling mills, forge hammers, boilers, etc. at the Bedlington Iron Works.

Obituary of John Dixon
Minutes of the Proceedings of the Institution of Civil Engineers
Volume 104, January 1891, pages 309-311
Biography of John Dixon.

Miscellanea
The Engineer, London, 3 January 1879, page 3
Jasper Mounsey entered into a partnership with Alfred Mounsey and Alfred Russell as agents for Consett Iron Company, John Abbott and Company, Stockton Forge and R Dempster.
Partnership dissolved

The London Gazette, 11 August 1885, page 3719
Jasper Capper Mounsey left the partnership with Alfred Mounsey and Alfred Russell.

Biographical Dictionary of Civil Engineers in Great Britain and Ireland, Volume 2, 1830-1890
Thomas Telford Publishing, London, 2008
Has entries for Edward Dixon (1809-1877), John Dixon (1796-1865), John Dixon (1835-1891) and a rare photograph of John Dixon taken in 1885 for ICE membership.

Balla Wray Visitors' Book 1890-1907
Reference WDX 184 A1543 (11/7/90)
Kendal Archive Centre, Kendal County Offices, Kendal
Records the visit of Mrs Mounsey and George to 'Balla Wray' on 28 June 1907.

2 Early years in London

In 1865, after the failure of the Bedlington Iron Works, John Dixon moved to London. There he set himself up in business in Abchurch Yard but soon took up rooms at No.1 Laurence Pountney Hill, establishing himself as an engineering contractor. Initially he may have been supported by his father-in-law who had his own engineering business in London. John's first two known contracts were for underpinning a wharf near Tower Bridge, and for landing stages by the new Thames Embankment.

John Dixon, civil engineering contractor

It is not known exactly how John came to set himself up as a civil engineering contractor in London. The challenge must have been enormous. Apparently, he had no direct experience of civil engineering contracts and no established network of business contacts, and he was a long way from his home in the north east. The normal route into this profession would have been by spending time with an established engineer to gain experience, before starting an independent business. Prior to the move south, John's experience was all in iron works, although of course the products of such works, particularly wrought iron girders and castings, were used in civil engineering. It seems probable that he was assisted by his father-in-law, George England, who would know many of the engineers and engineering contractors in London.

Street sign at Abchurch Yard. John Dixon would have been familiar with this old sign. Photograph by the author.

Abchurch Yard

Although the 1865 Kelly's Directory lists Mounsey and Dixon at No.27 Leadenhall Street, there were several brokers at this address and therefore this must just have been their representative in London. From 1866, sources give John Dixon's business address as No.5 Abchurch Yard, off Cannon Street. He advertised being in business as a contractor for 'bridges and girder work, iron structures of every description, with or without masonry, delivered or erected' and an iron merchant for 'builders' castings, flitches punched and unpunched, plates, bars, angles, etc.' A flitch was an iron plate for strengthening a timber beam. Not much is known about this business, but it was from Abchurch Yard that John Dixon entered an example of his ironwork at the Paris Exhibition of 1867, although he did not gain an award. The following year it was from Abchurch Yard that he pursued his patent for improvements to floating swimming baths. John kept on the Abchurch Yard premises for some time after taking up the Laurence Pountney Hill office in 1867. As late as 1869 he was listed in the Post Office Directory as 'iron merchant, founder, iron bridge builder and iron manufacturer' at No.5 Abchurch Yard (Harry's Bar, an upmarket restaurant, now occupies the site). In the same year, 1869, Jasper Capper Mounsey was in business as an iron and steel merchant at No.118 Cannon Street.

xvi

BRIDGES, GIRDER WORK,

AND

IRON STRUCTURES,

Of every description, in

CAST OR WROUGHT IRON,

WITH OR WITHOUT MASONRY,

DELIVERED, OR ERECTED,

CONTRACTED FOR BY

JOHN DIXON,

Iron Merchant,

5, ABCHURCH YARD,

LONDON, E.C.

BUILDERS' CASTINGS,

FLITCHES PUNCHED AND UNPUNCHED,

PLATES, BARS, ANGLES, &c.

Advertisement from Laxton's Building Price Book 1868. Laxton's Building Price Book first appeared in 1817 and is still published today and regarded as the estimator's bible. Reproduced from Grace's Guide to British Industrial History at www.gracesguide.co.uk/John_Dixon_(London)

Right) 'Doorways, Laurence Pountney Hill, c.1884' photograph by Henry Dixon & Son, for the Society for Photographing Relics of Old London. Henry Dixon (1820-1893) trained as a printer but developed a successful photography business with his son Thomas J Dixon. He was a master of the carbon process, still held in the highest regard as a photographic printing method. Dixon was commissioned to record buildings that were threatened with demolition and it is believed that these doorways caught his eye simply on account of the Dixon name displayed outside. He was also known for his portraits and photographs of animals in Regent's Park Zoological Gardens. Reproduced by courtesy of the Royal Academy of Arts, London. RA object reference 06/455

Below) Nos.1 and 2 Laurence Pountney Hill today, photograph by author. The premises are now the offices of the highly regarded legal practice QEB Hollis Whiteman, whose sixty-one barristers specialise in all aspects of criminal and regulatory law.

Office at No.1 Laurence Pountney Hill

By the beginning of 1867 John was renting an office at the grand address of No.1 Laurence Pountney Hill, just around the corner from Cannon Street Station. Waynman Dixon later recorded that he joined his older brother in the Laurence Pountney Hill offices on 7 February 1867. Today Nos.1 and 2 Laurence Pountney Hill are considered among the finest surviving merchants' houses in the City of London and are Grade II* listed by English Heritage. Built in 1703, the two properties had elaborate entrances and elegant staircases with spiral balusters. They were the work of Thomas Denning, a master carpenter and builder, who had worked for both Sir Christopher Wren and Nicholas Hawksmoor. John Dixon clearly wished to assert his presence in London.

By the time of John's move to London, No.1 Laurence Pountney Hill had been divided into commercial premises. His fellow occupants were:

- R J and R W Woodcock, architects and surveyors
- Alexander Swanston, merchant and formerly MP for Bandon Bridge, Ireland
- Fred Fatt and Son, wine merchants
- William Green and Company, iron merchants and manufacturers.

Given the size of the building he was sharing with four other businesses, there cannot have been more than a few rooms, perhaps a minimum of a design office and John's own office, no doubt often occupied by his clerk, Herbert Wakeling, during John's lengthy absences.

It is known that some other engineers spent time in the Laurence Pountney Hill office. Reginald Middleton was there around 1872 working on the Ventnor pier, and ten years later Alfred Thorne was working on the Solway viaduct.

At Laurence Pountney Hill, Dixon was surrounded by like-minded men. In 1882 there were six consulting engineers and eighteen iron, steel and metal merchants and agents with premises on Laurence Pountney Hill. And just around the corner in Suffolk Lane was John's long-standing friend Jasper Capper Mounsey, in business with his two sons, agent for the Consett Iron Company and the Skerne Forge Company of Darlington.

Today Nos.1 and 2 Laurence Pountney Hill are occupied by the barristers QEB Hollis Whiteman and are maintained in an immaculate condition. Their outside appearance is virtually unchanged since John's days.

Wharf foundations in London

John Dixon's first known contract was for wharf foundations in 1867. Waynman's description of 'underpinning of the foundations of a large new wharf just below the Tower of London' give clues as to the probable site of this work. The major construction in progress at the time was the Millwall Dock, built between 1865 and 1867. The work was done by John Aird and Company to designs by John Fowler (1817-1898) and William Wilson (1822-1898). As work on the dock progressed, plans for the entrance lock had to be amended, and construction of this lock proved to be the most difficult part of the project. As late as April 1867 a contract for iron lock gates, sluices, capstans and related hydraulic machinery was given to W G Armstrong and Company at Newcastle upon Tyne. It is speculation that the difficulties encountered with the construction of the lock gates necessitated additional piling in 1867 (piling associated with the main dock would have been done in 1865). The Dixon brothers were known to William Armstrong (Waynman had just completed his technical apprenticeship at the Elswick Works), and Armstrong may have recommended them.

Another possible location for the Dixons' piling might have been the Millwall Dock Graving Dock, a dry dock off the main quay for ship repairs. Excavations started there in 1865 and the dock was completed in July 1867 with its caisson, also supplied by William Armstrong, in position by the end of August.

Thames Embankment landing stages

Waynman Dixon noted that his second assignment for his older brother, in 1868, was 'superintending the construction in place of the pontoons for the floating landing-stage on the Victoria Thames Embankment - northside.' Little did he realise at the time, but ten years later John would be on the same site, erecting the obelisk known as Cleopatra's Needle.

The Metropolitan Board of Works had been authorised by an 1862 Act of Parliament to construct embankments along the River Thames. This generally involved piling to stabilise the bank, constructing a carriageway and granite retaining walls, with some steamboat piers and landing stages. The work was sub-divided and let to different contractors. Beneath the Embankment were underground sewers, part of the network designed by the Board's engineer, Joseph Bazalgette. The foundation stone for the first stage (let to Mr. Furness) was laid on 20 July 1864, for the second stage (let to Mr Ritson) on 19 October 1864 and for the third stage (let to Mr. Webster) on 28 July 1866. Although the original estimate for the Embankment works had been £2.5 million, by 1868 the estimated completion costs had risen to £5.5 million.

Building the Embankment caused the demolition of old wooden landing stages. Owners of these stages sought compensation from the Metropolitan Board of Works but were told that the Act of Parliament authorising the construction of the Embankment contained nothing about such compensation. If aggrieved, they could take the matter to court, a response typical of the sometimes high-handed attitude of the Board. Following completion of the Embankment, floating landing stages were commissioned by the more sympathetic Thames Conservancy Commissioners at Westminster Bridge, Waterloo Bridge and Temple. These landing stages were provided with spacious waiting rooms 'highly acceptable in wet or stormy weather' and 'the means of saving lives in cases of emergency.'

John Dixon's contract was only for the construction of the floating pontoons. It is likely that he also tendered for the wrought iron girder bridges between the Embankment steps and the pontoons. Fourteen tenders were received for these bridges, that from the short-lived (1864-1871) London Engineering and Iron Ship Building Company being successful.

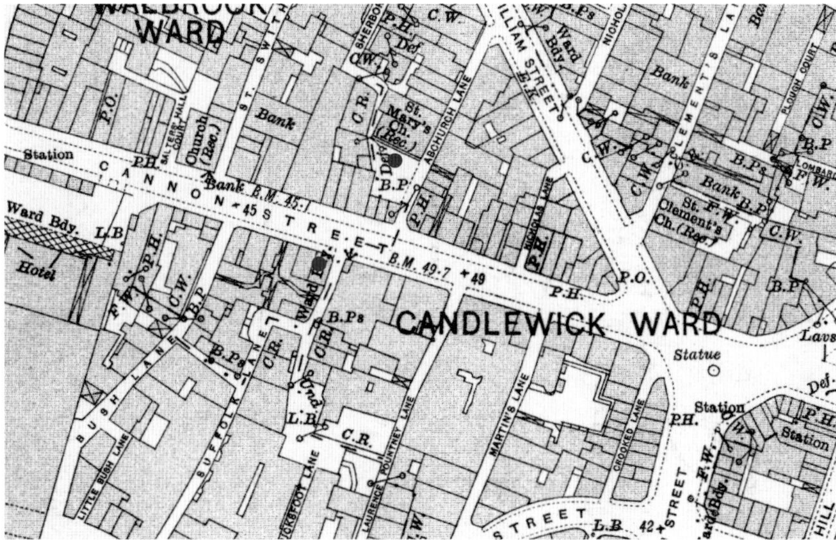

London showing Abchurch Yard and Laurence Pountney Hill. Ordnance Survey 25 Inch Series, Revised 1914, published 1916, London 1915 (numbered sheets) V.11 Reproduced by permission of the National Library of Scotland.

'Cleopatra's Needle and Victoria Embankment' postcard issued to raise money for St Paul's Hospital. If the card was returned with a one shilling postal order it would be entered into a prize draw. The card is from the 1920s or 1930s. The floating landing stages in the foreground are probably those built by John and Waynman Dixon in 1867. Reproduced by courtesy of Norman Emeny.

References

The London Gazette, Supplement, 6 November 1866
Gives John Dixon's address as No.5 Abchurch Yard.

Frederick Kelly's London Post Office Directories

The Millwall Docks: The Docks
Survey of London: Volumes 43 and 44, Poplar, Blackwall and Isle of Dogs
General Editor Hermione Hobhouse
English Heritage 1994
Pages 353-6 chart the construction of the Millwall Dock, possibly the dock work undertaken by Waynman from February 1867, but with so specific mention of either John or Waynman Dixon.

Laying the first stone of the Thames Embankment
The Standard, London, 21 July 1864, page 2
Construction begins of the Metropolitan Board of Works first contract.

The Thames Embankment: Laying the first stone under Contract "No.2"
The Standard, London, 20 October 1864, page 6
Construction begins of the Metropolitan Board of Works second contract.

Thames Embankment: Laying the foundation stone for the Southern Portion
The Standard, London, 30 July 1866, page 3
Construction begins of the Metropolitan Board of Works second contract.

Thames Embankment and Metropolitan Improvement Loans Act Amendment Bill
The Standard, London, 6 June 1868, page 2
Costs more than doubled for the embankment works.

Patents for inventions - Patents Sealed
The London Gazette, 26 May 1868, page 3004
John Dixon of 5 Abchurch Yard in the City of London, contractor, inventor of 'improvements in the construction of floating saloon-baths'.

City of London Election 1868, the Central Committee for securing the return of Charles Bell, Sills J Gibbons and Alderman Philip Twells
The Standard, London, 30 October 1868, page 2
Huge list of names includes Dixon John, 5 Abchurch Yard E.C.

Laxton's Building Price Book 1868
Contains a full-page advertisement for John Dixon at 5 Abchurch Yard.

Patents
The London Gazette, 26 May 1868, page 3004
John Dixon of 5 Abchurch Yard has given notice of his improvements to floating swimming baths.

The Paris Exhibition
The City Press, London, 17 August 1867, page 6
John Dixon of 5 Abchurch Yard exhibited iron at the exhibition but did not gain an award.

Notes written for George Longstaff by Waynman Dixon, 7 March 1918
In private ownership
Includes a note about the construction of the pontoons for landing stages.

A Minor Thames Embankment Contract
The Borough of Marylebone Mercury, London, 18 January 1868, page 3
Contract for the landing stage bridges.

House of Commons - Monday April 27 - The Thames Landing Piers
The Morning Post, London, 28 April 1868, page 2
Question of compensation for owners of old wooden piers.

The Thames Embankment Steamboat Piers
Bell's Weekly Messenger, London, 14 November 1868, page 7
Description of new piers opened at Westminster Bridge and being erected at Waterloo Bridge and Temple.

Opening of the Metropolitan District Railway
The Daily News, London, 25 December 1868, page 5
Steamboats at the Embankment pier land a stone's throw from the station.

3 Floating Swimming Baths

When he was thirty-two, John Dixon took out a patent for a floating swimming bath, and two years later exhibited a model of a floating bath at the Institution of Civil Engineers. In spite of this, there is no evidence that he was involved with the large iron floating swimming bath moored at Charing Cross from 1875 to 1885. However, he was the leading figure in the construction of a wooden floating bath near his house at Surbiton in the 1880s. This project was mired in controversy, initially with the Thames Conservancy over its mooring place, culminating in a pitched battle on the river, and later with Kingston Town Council blaming Dixon for poor construction. He countered with accusations of inadequate maintenance. After an escalating series of angry exchanges, the matter was laid to rest when John moved to Croydon and Kingston Town Council gave up pursuing him.

John Dixon floats the idea of his swimming bath

During his early days in London, while still at Abchurch Yard, John Dixon took out Patent 1868/222 for a floating saloon bath. The wording of the patent was remarkably broad:

> 'This invention has for its object the construction of a floating saloon bath by the use of a tube or pontoon of metal, wood, cork or any other floating material, the sides, ends and bottom of the saloon bath being open or lattice-work, to allow the free flow of water through the same. The inventor also erects cabins or dressing-rooms for the convenience of bathers, likewise a deck or platform around the inside or outside of the bath as a promenade.'

Floating swimming baths could be found on the continent, as at Paris and Berlin, and in the cleaner rivers of England, as in the River Trent at Nottingham, so it is not obvious why Dixon should seek to patent the concept. In the event, he did not proceed with the patent, but must have been taken with the idea of a floating bath. Two years later, in June 1870, the Institution of Civil Engineers held a 'conversazione' when some 1,000 guests viewed a range of exhibits. John Dixon, who was an associate member at the time, contributed several models, including one of a floating bath for river or sea bathing. It was a vessel with gridded sides, and dressing rooms and a gallery running around the perimeter a little above water level.

The first press reports about a floating swimming bath for Londoners, at Crystal Palace, appeared in 1869 but nothing materialised. In 1872 there was a floating bathing house for the use of ladies at 'Athens' on the Thames opposite Windsor Race Course. At 'Athens' Eton College boys bathed without costumes, and the proximity of lady bathers and unclad lads must have raised Victorian eyebrows. Londoners commented that it was strange that further down the Thames there was no such facility when, on a hot day, the city river banks were crowded with juvenile bathers.

London Floating Swimming Bath Company

With the waters of the River Thames becoming relatively cleaner after the completion of Joseph Bazalgette's system of underground sewers, there was talk of mooring a floating swimming bath in the river. The Floating Swimming Baths Company of London announced its prospectus in April 1873, the shares were popular, subscriptions closed nine days later and the shares were soon trading at a premium. Plans for the hull of the floating bath were drawn up by Charles Woodley Whitaker (1837-1884) and Edward Perret (1842-1904). Whitaker had worked for James Brunlees, who would later work extensively with Dixon, and it is probable that Whitaker and Dixon were acquainted. An elaborate superstructure of cast iron and glass was designed by Driver and Kew of Victoria Street. The floating bath was fabricated by the Thames Iron Works and Shipbuilding Company in 1874, and this same company built the *Cleopatra* obelisk vessel for the Dixon brothers in 1877. Although there is no mention of John Dixon in any of the references to the Floating Swimming Baths Company of London, it may be that he had some peripheral involvement in the project.

The bath was launched on 16 May 1874 by Mrs Celia Whitaker, who gave it her name. Fitting out took nine months and in February 1875 *Celia* was towed to her position on the Embankment, at the landing pier by Hungerford Bridge. Bathers were first admitted on 6 July, opening hours being from 6:30am to 8:00pm, tickets cost one shilling.

The wrought iron hull of the vessel was 180 feet x 31 feet, providing a pool of 135 feet x 25 feet, with a depth varying from 3 feet to 7 feet. An elaborate filtration system was installed, with a large settling tank and a series of canvas filters, capable of handling 500 gallons per minute and the water could be heated. Overall cost was not far short of £18,000. Some years later Whitaker and Perret took the company to court for alleged non-payment of their design fees. They claimed 1½% which they said was the custom of their profession. Unfortunately, the judge would have none of that, 1½% was 'absolutely unreasonable' and 'plainly ridiculous'. He awarded them £70.

The floating bath proved popular, and in 1877 some 150,000 people took to its waters. However, in spite of the claimed heated water in the bath, river swimming was unpopular in the winter. In December 1876 the bath was converted into a skating rink for the winter season. The refrigeration equipment was troublesome and the conversion was not repeated the following winter, when the baths were temporarily fitted out as a gymnasium.

For reasons not entirely clear, the London Floating Bath Company went into receivership early in 1885 and the floating bath put up for auction in the April. An optimistic notice of sale stated that annual ticket sales averaged £1,902 and 'a large rate of interest may be relied on.' Potential purchasers were not convinced, and it failed to reach the reserve price. Later the structure was bought by the South-Eastern Railway Company for scrap.

Floating swimming bath at Surbiton

Whatever John Dixon's involvement with floating swimming baths in London, he was certainly involved in the facility at Kingston upon Thames in the 1880s. John was living in Kingston upon Thames from 1867 to 1885. The first mention of a floating swimming bath for the benefit of the residents of Kingston and Surbiton was in August 1875, when it was reported that 'a few gentlemen' were working on the project. John had instigated this group and their initial meetings were held at his house on the Portsmouth Road. Opposition to the scheme came from local rowing and sailing clubs, and there was criticism over the absence of any public meetings. Interestingly, a letter in the local newspaper acknowledged that views differed as to the beauty of a floating object, ranging from a 'taut and trim sailing boat' to the 'Cleopatra Needle sloop'. This comparison with the *Cleopatra* shows that John's involvement with the obelisk was common knowledge.

In February 1880 a well-attended meeting was chaired by the Rev Dawes, who said that John Dixon had come forward in 'a most public and liberal manner to do his best for getting a bath' but had met with opposition, commenting that 'a man who tried to do anything in any neighbourhood which differed from what had been existing would always meet with the opposition of certain persons'. After much debate about the precise location of the proposed bath, a resolution was moved by Frederick Aston that Mr Dixon's scheme be abandoned and that any other scheme should be initiated at a well-advertised public meeting. This resolution was lost and an alternative resolution that a swimming bath was desirable and a committee should be set up to progress it was carried unanimously. John, rarely known for diplomacy, attacked Mr Aston. It was 'a preposterous absurdity' to say that a scheme could only be launched at a public meeting and that he should be quite free to ask half a dozen gentlemen to his house to discuss the idea of a floating swimming bath. He embarked on a lengthy justification for a floating bath in the river, which he contrasted to public baths on land where there was little flow of fresh water into the pool and where he, or his children, would not venture. He was certainly not being philanthropic; his swimming bath was not for 'the great unwashed of Kingston and the small unwashed of Surbiton' but for himself and his friends who wished to swim. John Dixon estimated the cost of the bath at £1,000 to £1,500, clearly a more modest affair than the Charing Cross Floating Bath which had cost £18,000 six years previously (the reason for the low cost was that John Dixon proposed a simple open timber structure rather than the substantial iron vessel covered with an elaborate glazed roof as at Charing Cross). The meeting concluded with the establishment of an eight-man committee, including the protagonists John Dixon and Frederick Aston.

Aston was not going to accept defeat and collected nearly a hundred signatures condemning the proposed site for the bath, although not opposing the concept of the baths. Elsewhere tempers were rising. A swimmer wrote that Mr Dixon should be supported in 'his public-spirited efforts to supply a crying want' and that it was 'nothing short of ridiculous arrogance on the part of the boating men to claim the whole river for their exclusive amusement'. The local Thames Sailing Club defended its position; it was not opposed to the bath but did not want it moored adjacent to its club house where it would interfere with access to anchorages.

By the time of its first meeting, the committee had swollen to twenty-three men, many representing the various vested interests. Still the main question was the siting of the swimming bath, and John Dixon successfully proposed a deputation should press the Thames Conservancy for a suitable site. The expected difficulties between John Dixon and Frederick Aston soon appeared in the committee, Aston claimed he had been purposely omitted from the deputation to the Thames Conservancy and then resigned on the grounds that the bath was not for the benefit of either Surbiton or Kingston, and certainly not for the poor. The Thames Sailing Club members also resigned. Hostile letters were published in the local press.

Over the next year there was little progress as first the Thames Conservancy and then Kingston Town Council dragged their feet, and there were objections to any of the possible sites. However, the floating swimming bath was built to John's plans and specifications by a local carpenter named Lobb. The enclosed swimming area, 150 feet by nearly 40 feet, was carried on pontoons on either side of the bath, with a hand pump to empty any leakage. Dixon would have no doubt preferred iron pontoons, but the additional cost of £250 was denied him. There had been great difficulty in finding anyone to build the swimming bath for the agreed price. Even then the cost exceeded the Council's limit, and John contributed £100 from his own pocket.

When completed, the structure was moored just above 'The Anglers' inn, although there was still no agreed permanent site. This inn stood at the lower end of the Kingston High Street, with one side of the property facing the river. John's house on the Portsmouth Road was a short distance away, and it is easy to imaging John and his family being frequent users of the swimming bath. Today there are apartments, appropriately named 'The Anglers', on the site of the inn. The floating bath was probably moored where the present-day Town End Pier with 'Turk Launches' projects into the river.

In the summer of 1882, the Town Council approved regulations for the baths. Opening hours were 6:00am until dusk, with the bath closed from the end of September until the beginning of May. By setting the admission charge at only tuppence, the Council was going against Dixon's desire for exclusivity, and at least some of the 'unwashed' might be expected to attend.

A pitched battle on the river

The Thames Conservancy, who regarded themselves as proprietors of the river, had not agreed to the site by 'The Anglers' inn. They despatched their Mr Little with instructions to remove the floating swimming bath, by force if necessary. Just before 10:00am on 11 August 1882, aboard the steam tug *Queen* and accompanied by two or three boats, he arrived by the bath to carry out his instructions. The bath was defended by John Dixon and several members of Kingston Town Council. Mr Little managed to board the structure, ordering the anchors to be lifted, but the Borough Surveyor, Captain Macaulay, informed him that he could not instruct his men while on the Council's property, he must retire either to *Queen* or the river bank. After a struggle with the Council's men, the hapless Mr Little returned to the tug. At this the boats accompanying *Queen* came alongside the bath and made several attempts to cut the anchor chains, but each time were resolutely fended off by the Council's men, to loud cheers from the large crowd of spectators on the shore.

Before there was a serious breach of the peace, Alderman Gould allowed a symbolic lifting of the anchors (the bath was still secured to the shore) and endeavoured to persuade Mr Little to retire. But at this juncture another Conservancy agent, appropriately named Mr Payne, shouted out that the bath would be removed, piece by piece if necessary. His incendiary speech was recorded in shorthand by a reporter from *The Surrey Comet* who was with John Dixon and the Council party. Payne snatched the paper from the reporter, tore it up and hurled it into the river. The Conservancy men then tried to cut through the mooring chains to the shore with a hammer and chisel. Alderman Gould, by now on the shore, bravely grabbed the man with the chisel and hauled him out of his boat. Another Conservancy man on the boat threw a boathook at the Alderman, cutting his thigh, and more Conservancy men attacked Mr Lobb, who was standing alongside Alderman Gould. Superintendent Digby of the Metropolitan Police, who had been present with some constables throughout, then stepped in before further bloodshed ensued. Around 11:30am Little and the Conservancy men retreated, much to the pleasure of the spectators.

After this extraordinary fracas, the bath opened and saw 200 lads using it every night. At the end of September, the Thames Conservancy admitted defeat, allowing the bath to remain on its existing site.

Alleged defective construction of the Kingston bath

Less than a year after the swimming bath was opened, the Mayor of Kingston, J Thrupp Nightingale, somewhat mysteriously proposed that a select committee from the Town Council should 'inquire into the circumstances attending the construction of the swimming bath' but would not go into any details. A letter had been received from Mr Dixon but was left aside for the select committee to deal with.

It turned out that the bath was in a dangerous state, the pontoons were virtually submerged, and the wooden structure damaged in several places. Additionally, when the winter floods had subsided, it was revealed that one of the pontoons had settled over an old pile in the river and had been punctured. A furious argument then ensued between John Dixon and the Council as to who was responsible. Dixon's case was that he had provided free plans and specifications, but penny-pinching had made the structure less durable than he would have wished, using timber instead of wrought iron. A timber structure was more susceptible to wear and tear from the wash of passing steamers and smaller boats knocking into it, but there had been no proper maintenance since the bath was opened. Rubbish had accumulated on the pontoons and they had not been pumped out, consequently they were now dangerously low in the water.

In spite of having originally approved the plans and specifications, the Council now claimed that the design was inadequate and that John himself was incompetent and should appear before the committee. His response was predictable. He was not going to appear before a committee which was 'composed largely of the very men who had the indecency to air their engineering opinions without first taking the trouble to ascertain the facts'.

The Council's committee then sought out Mr Lobb. He explained that his contract had not been with the Council but with none other than Alfred Thorne, the engineer who had worked with John Dixon in Brazil and would later collaborate with him on the rebuilding of the Hammersmith suspension bridge. Thorne's involvement in the swimming bath is unclear. At the time he was living in Hampstead and working in John's office at No.1 Laurence Pountney Hill, probably looking after local matters while John was away on other work. Lobb stated that he had pointed out defects in the construction and that he had been asked to bear half the excess cost over the sanctioned £1,000. It had been suggested to him when he agreed to do the work that there might be a profit of £200 within the £1,000, although any profit would have to be divided 20-80 between himself and Thorne.

Repairs were commissioned from a Mr Stocker, who was of the view that the pontoons' internal framework was not sufficiently robust and, as some of the joints between the planks forming the sides of the pontoons were underwater, leakage was inevitable.

There was an angry exchange of letters in the press between Mayor Nightingale and Dixon. While the Mayor was generally restrained in his words, John was scathing, writing 'I can afford to treat the opinion of such with contempt, and certainly shall not discuss it.' The Council thought Dixon 'was discourteous in every way, and had treated the Corporation in a contemptuous way, as nobodies, and as if he could say anything he liked against them.' According to the councillors, failure of the bath was clearly due to imperfect materials obtained by Dixon's own men. John apparently only had one ally on the Council. At a later meeting, when his letter of 12 September 1883 was read out, it was reported that thirty-one out of the thirty-two members had had quite enough of Mr Dixon. The identity of his single supporter is unknown.

By now John was at St Helier, hoping the climate would chase away the first signs of what would prove to be a fatal illness. He wrote to the Council repeating his case. The bath was not a Thames barge that could be roughly handled, yet it had withstood the floods of the last winter. All it required was reasonable care and attention, which it was not receiving. It would not have been possible to obtain a bath of its size for the specified £1,000 had more extravagant materials been used. He concluded:

> 'I knew from experience some few narrow-minded men would certainly find fault; but a bath was wanted, and having got that, I am quite satisfied to have served to the best of my ability the contented majority of both the Corporation and the public. I shall say no more.'

In retrospect

The fundamental problem with the floating swimming bath at Kingston was surely that it had been built at the lowest possible cost and would have required careful construction and regular maintenance to maintain its integrity. Was John Dixon to blame for the failings in the Kingston Swimming Bath? He could be accused of letting his enthusiasm for the project produce a design that was barely adequate, and not foreseeing that regular maintenance might be neglected. Timber floating baths needed proper maintenance. At Nottingham a similar floating bath had cost much the same as the Kingston bath, but annual maintenance was £90 and a competent attendant was employed. Virtually no maintenance had been carried out at Kingston, and the comparison goes a long way to exonerate Dixon. Unfortunately, his combative style when his engineering abilities were challenged certainly stood in the way of finding a satisfactory outcome to the difficulties and to keeping his local reputation intact.

It is not known what happened to the floating swimming bath but it probably fell into disuse through continued neglect, and the introduction of local land-based swimming pools with much better facilities.

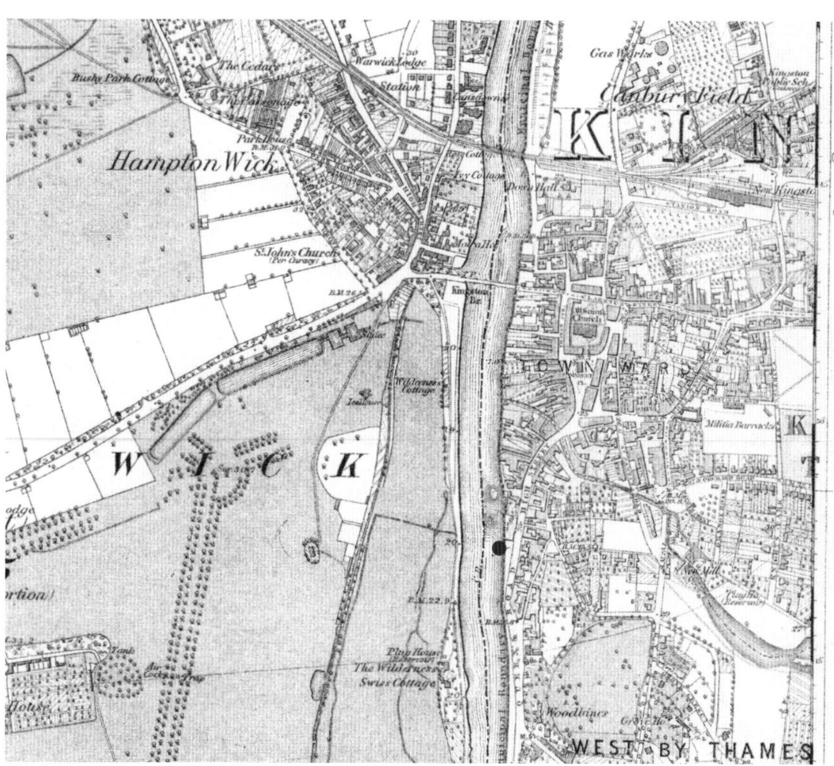

Site of the floating swimming bath at Kingston on Thames.
Ordnance Survey Six Inch Series Revised 1894-95,
published 1898, Middlesex XXV.SE
Reproduced by permission of the National Library of Scotland.

References

Miscellanea
The Engineer, London, 12 July 1872, page 19
Floating bath-house for ladies at Athens, the famous bathing place for nude Etonians.

222, J Dixon, Abchurch Yard, London "Floating Saloon Baths" dated 22nd January 1868
The Patent Journal - Class 10 - Miscellaneous
The Engineer, London, 21 August 1868, page 254
The patent for a floating swimming bath which was not proceeded with.

The Conversazione at the Institution of Civil Engineers - Docks Harbours and Bridges
Engineering, London, 3 June 1870, page 398
John Dixon's model of a floating swimming bath exhibited.

The Floating Swimming Baths Company (Limited)
Pall Mall Gazette, London, 16 April 1873, page 16
Share prospectus with ambitious plans for floating baths on the Thames, Mersey, Clyde and Tyne.

Floating Swimming-Baths on the Thames
The Building News, 3 July 1874, page 8
Description and illustration of the baths.

The Thames Swimming-bath at Charing-Cross
Illustrated London News, 17 July 1875, pages 11-12
Full description with illustration of interior of the baths on page 12.

The Thames Iron Works 1837-1912: A Major Shipbuilder on the Thames
Daniel Harrison
Museum of London Archaeology and Crossrail Limited, 2015
History of the works but no mention of the floating swimming bath.

Metropolitan News
Illustrated London News, 11 October 1873, page 335
Metropolitan Board of Works consent for floating swimming bath at the west side of Charing Cross.

Metropolitan News
Illustrated London News, 23 May 1874, page 487
Floating Swimming Baths Company's first bath launched last Saturday.

The Floating Glaciarium
The North London News and Finsbury Gazette, 30 December 1876, page 4
Successful conversion to skating rink.

Christmas Entertainments
The Globe, London, 24 December 1877, page 7
Charing Cross Floating Swimming Bath now fitted up as a gymnasium.

Common Pleas Division - Whitaker and another v The Floating Swimming Bath Company
The Times, London, 21 April 1880, page 4
Claim for 1½% thrown out by the judge, award of only £70.

The Times, London, 21 March 1885, page 19
Notice of sale by auction of the floating bath on 17 April.

The Floating Swimming Bath
The Globe, London, 18 April 1885, page 2
Baths put up for auction by order of Court of Chancery.

Floating Swimming Baths
The Surrey Comet, 7 August 1875, page 5
It was reported that a few gentlemen were working on the project.

To the Editor
The Surrey Comet, 14 February 1880, page 5
Letter expressing opposition to the plans for a floating swimming bath.

The Bath Question at Surbiton
The Surrey Comet, 21 February 1880, page 3
Lengthy report of meeting where John Dixon clashed with T F Aston.

To the Editor
The Surrey Comet, 21 February 1880, page 3
Letters from a swimmer and the secretary of the Thames Sailing Club.

The Proposed Swimming Bath
The Surrey Comet, 6 March 1880, page 5
First committee meeting, resignation of Frederick Aston and the Thames Sailing Club. Angry letters from Aston.

Town Council Meeting - July 20 - The Floating Swimming Bath
The Surrey Comet, 22 July 1882, page 4
Approval of opening hours and regulations for the bath.

Town Council Meeting - Aug 3 - The Floating Swimming Bath
The Surrey Comet, 5 August 1882, page 4
Still no agreement between the Thames Conservancy and the Town Council over the site.

Attempted Forcible Removal of the Floating Swimming Bath - Extraordinary Proceedings
The Surrey Comet, 12 August 1882, page 4
Graphic description of the battle between the Thames Conservancy men and the Kingston Council men.

Town Council Meeting - Sept 28 - The Floating Swimming Bath
The Surrey Comet, 30 September 1882, page 4
Thames Conservancy admitted defeat.

Town Council Meeting - May 3
The Surrey Comet, 5 May 1883, page 4
Matter of the construction of the swimming bath raised by the mayor.

Town Council Meeting - August 2
The Surrey Comet, 4 August 1883, page 4
Acrimonious exchange of letters between Dixon and the Council.

Editorial
The Surrey Comet, 11 August 1883, page 4
The construction of the bath was discreditable, the Council put too much faith in Dixon's advice but further explanation was needed from John Dixon.

The Swimming Bath - To the Editor
The Surrey Comet, 18 August 1883, page 4
Letter from John Dixon at St Helier.

Town Council Meeting - October 25
The Surrey Comet, 27 October 1883, page 4
31 out of the 32 members had had enough of Mr Dixon.

Swimming Baths - To the Editor of *The Times*
The Times, London, 6 November 1874, page 11
Letter in support of the floating swimming bath in London, and details of the similar bath at Nottingham.

4 Southport Pier extension

The original Southport pier was opened in 1860, but barely reached the sea at low tide. It was extended in 1864 and again in 1867. This later extension included an enlarged pier-head with landing stages, design and construction being by John Dixon. The supporting columns in both the original pier and in Dixon's extension were sunk using the 'sinking pile' method developed by James Brunlees, in which water was pumped down the inside of the column to fluidise the sand around its base. John Dixon's pier-head was destroyed by fire in 1933.

Seaside piers

Piers, as a place to promenade and take the sea air as opposed to just providing access to sea-going vessels are, with a few exceptions, only found around the coasts of England and Wales. Of the nearly ninety piers, all save one were constructed before the First World War and are an intrinsic part of the development of the Victorian seaside resort. Given their vulnerability to storms, errant shipping and fire, it is not surprising that fewer than half of them survive today, some in a sorry state of repair.

The usual method of construction was to drive cast iron columns into the sand, with wrought iron girders carrying the wooden decking and cast iron balustrades. This basic structure could be adorned with all manner of refinements, from simple seating to an entire concert hall. Because the construction was so similar to that used in railway viaducts and in jetties, it was relatively straightforward for a civil engineer experienced in these fields to work on piers. John Dixon was such a man, with experience in the manufacture of iron components, and of building jetties. Although primarily a contractor, he carried out design work for his first two piers: the extensions at Southport and the pier at Douglas, Isle of Man. His final pier, at Llandudno, is probably the best example of a Victorian seaside pier in Britain.

With the completion of Llandudno pier, John Dixon seems to have ended his association with British seaside piers. He had a large engineering contracting business and it may have been simply that these piers were too small to interest him. However, he continued to work on structures based on the driven-pile design, such as loading facilities, wharves and bridges.

Southport Pier

Southport, well known for the great distance between high and low water marks, had the first pier built purely for pleasure. Earlier piers were mainly along the Channel coastline, to provide convenient access to shipping. Southport saw its potential as a holiday resort within easy reach of Lancashire's factories and mills but there was a large expanse of sand between the town and the sea. The Southport Pier Company was set up to construct a pier because 'as the water will not come up for the visitors, an attempt has been made to facilitate the visits of the people to the sea.' In 1852 nineteen local worthies formed themselves into a management committee and published a share prospectus. It was intended to build a jetty or pier out from the promenade with facilities for bathing and access for pleasure vessels. In the words of the prospectus:

> 'The want of a convenient and ready access to low water has long been felt to be a serious inconvenience to the visitors and inhabitants of Southport, and the rapid increase of the town renders the

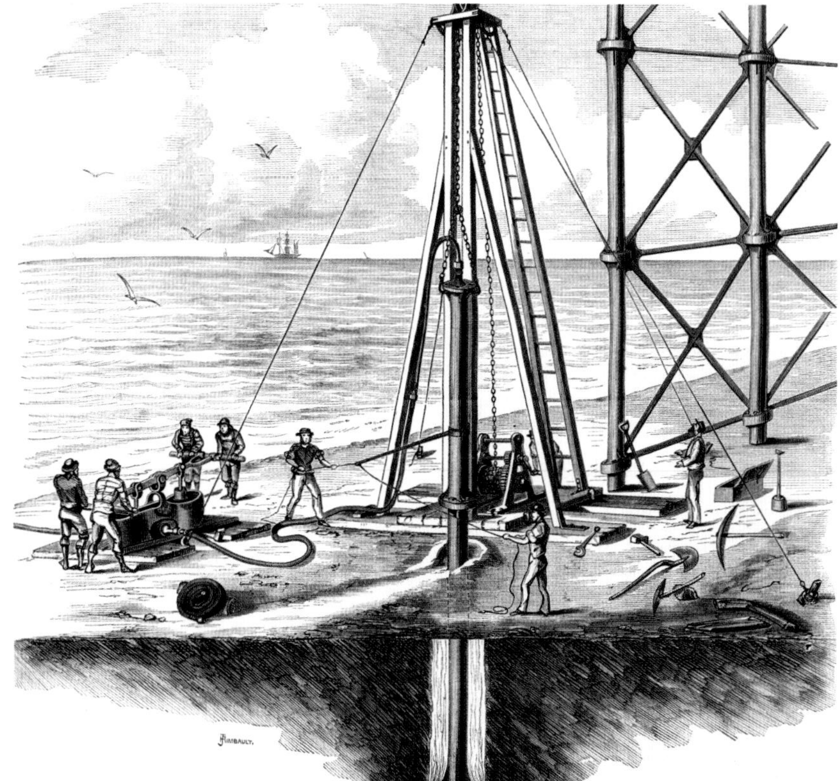

'Sinking piles at Southport pier' engraving by J H Rimbault. John Henry Rimbault (1820-1888) was an artist and engraver. In his early days he was also the tenant of 'The White Hart' inn in the St Anne district of London. Seriously injured when he was run over by an omnibus on 1 September 1888, he died five days later. This engraving was from a sketch taken on the shore at Southport. Engineering, London, 1 May 1868, page 411.

construction of a pier for that purpose almost a matter of necessity, and, at the same time, holds out a fair prospect of its forming a safe and lucrative investment.'

Southport's inhabitants were not convinced that, in the days of unlimited liability of shareholders, the pier might be a safe and lucrative investment and nothing came of the proposal. The idea of a pier was revived with more success in 1859 by the Southport Pier Company, now re-established as a limited company. Within two months the shares were fully subscribed. William Fairburn was appointed as consulting engineer, with James Brunlees as resident engineer, assisted by Henry Hooper. Contractors were W and J Galloway and Sons, who also cast the columns for the piles. Based in Manchester, they produced iron castings, boilers and steam engines. Civil engineering contracting, such as the Leven Viaduct and the Southport pier (both for James Brunlees), was a relatively minor part of their business. The cost of the Southport pier was estimated at £6,900 although the final sum was £8,700.

Who's who?
James Brunlees (1816-1892)

James Brunlees was an example of Victorian social mobility, achieved through technical skills. His father was a gardener on the estate of the Duke of Roxburgh and thought that his son might aspire to be a landscape gardener. Young James offered his assistance to Alexander Adie, a surveyor who was working on the estate, and made such a good impression that, when James was twenty-two, Adie engaged him on the Bolton and Preston Railway. Other railway work followed. From his first experience of surveying, James Brunlees had devoted most of his spare time to study and by his early thirties was recognised as a competent civil engineer.

He was appointed engineer on the Londonderry and Coleraine Railway, and then on the Ulverstone and Lancaster Railway, which involved crossing estuaries in Morecambe Bay. Here he developed his innovative 'sinking pile' method for the Leven Viaduct.

After working on railways in Brazil and Italy, he returned to England where he was engineer for the construction of many railways. James Brunlees was the engineer for the Solway Junction Railway in the 1860s, which involved the design of a viaduct across the 1¼ mile wide Solway Firth. His use of cast iron columns to support wrought iron girders was criticised when ice floes damaged the structure in 1881, although this had little effect on his subsequent reputation. John Dixon rebuilt the viaduct using wrought iron for the outer columns.

Apart from his work on railways, Brunlees was involved with dock improvements and seaside piers. He designed the piers at New Brighton and New Ferry on the Mersey, and at Rhyl, Llandudno and Southend. With Sir John Hawkshaw he was the design engineer for the Channel Tunnel proposed in 1872, and with Douglas Fox he was engineer for the Mersey Railway, including a tunnel under the river between Birkenhead and Liverpool. He and Douglas Fox were both knighted for this work in 1886.

James Brunlees was president of the Institution of Civil Engineers 1882-83. He died after a long illness at the age of seventy-six.

'Southport Pier from Victoria Hotel 2938 JV' photograph from the 1880s. Steamer services are advertised, and here at low tide the necessity for John Dixon's pier extension of 1868 is all too apparent. There are comparatively few people on the beach, but the promenade and pier are busy. Notice the pony rides under the pier and the sailing ship beached on the sands. The tramway installed in 1864 can be seen on the left side of the pier. Reproduced by courtesy of SouthportWorld (www.southportworld.co.uk)

Construction of the pier

The pier was supported on 7 inch diameter cast iron columns, with wrought iron girders of 50 feet span between the columns. At the seaward end the 15 feet wide walkway opened out onto a platform 100 feet long and 30 feet wide, with twin staircases leading down to the sea or, at low tide, the sands.

Construction began on 1 August 1859, with the 237 piles all being driven into the sands within six weeks. Columns were embedded in the sand using the 'sinking pile' technique recently developed by James Brunlees and the Galloways on the Leven Viaduct for the Ulverstone (now Ulverston) and Lancaster Railway. The cast iron piles supporting a pier would have conventionally been driven into the sand using a pile driver, or by screwing the piles down into the sand using a hydraulic drive. Both methods were slow, and required stronger piles, with a larger cross-section, than would be needed to carry the completed pier. With James Brunlees' method, water under pressure was pumped down a 2½ inch diameter tube inserted inside the hollow pile, fluidising the sand around the bottom of the pile and allowing it to sink under its own weight. With the columns in place, the contractors began mounting the wrought iron girders but, at the turn of the year, work was brought to a sudden halt. It had been found when testing the spans that the girders failed at half the test weight due to an error in the calculations. William Fairburn was consulted and specified remedial work. The spans already installed were taken down, and replacement girders fabricated at a cost of about £1,840.

Grand opening

The grand opening ceremony took place on Thursday 2 August 1860. A procession from the Town Hall, accompanied by two military bands, arrived at the pier where the chairman of the Pier Committcc gavc a 'lengthy and able inaugural address' including the claim that the pier, the largest in the kingdom, would make Southport 'the Montpelier of England'. Although lacking a pier, Montpellier was famous for its healthy climate and its name was adopted for fashionable areas in several British towns, mysteriously spelled with only one 'l'. After a short cruise in a Liverpool steamer, the procession reformed and returned to the Town Hall for lunch and more speeches. The matter of the calculation error was referred to by the chairman of the Pier Committee, with William Fairburn going to some lengths to explain that the structure was very strong and safe. Not only had he checked the calculations, but he had tested the spans to 90 tons, far in excess of the anticipated loading of 25 tons. James Brunlees could not be present at the opening as he was on his way to Brazil, perhaps expediently since the error appears to have been his.

In spite of its length of 1,200 yards, the iron pier did not reach the sea at low tide so, while it provided a breezy walk along its deck, its potential as a shipping jetty was limited. A light tramway track was laid along the decking for those averse to the breezy walk to the end of the pier.

The first extension 1863-64

Southport pier was an instant success, attracting over 122,000 visitors in its first six months and paying the shareholders a 10% dividend, rising to 14% by 1863. But by then its limitations were all too obvious and in 1863 the directors of the company agreed to extend the pier by 800 feet (many press reports at the time incorrectly stated by 800 yards). Work was soon underway. At the end of the year it was decided to also widen the existing pier by 8 feet. The tramway rails would be repositioned onto this extension, giving pedestrians sole access to the original decking, and other improvements made. All of this work was completed by 1864, again by the Galloways.

1867 improvements

In 1866 there were proposals to build a second pier at Southport, its supporters claiming that the original pier was defective and did not meet the town's needs. Their new Alexandra Pier was to be to a design by Eugenius Birch (1818-1884) and would cost £50,000, a price which makes the original pier a real bargain. Birch was a competent pier designer and invented the screwed pile technique on his first pier, at Margate, where the first pile had been driven in May 1853. After Margate, Birch built thirteen more piers before his death in 1884, the most famous being

'Southport Pier Head 1932' photograph taken just before the fire the following year. This shows the end of the extension built by John Dixon. Reproduced by courtesy of SouthportWorld (www.southportworld.co.uk)

the West Pier at Brighton. In passing it should be said that Eugenius Birch toured Italy, Nubia and Egypt over the winter of 1874-75, where he made many water colour sketches. John Dixon's brother, Waynman, lived in Egypt from 1871 to 1877 and by the time of Birch's visit was prominent in the ex-patriate English community. Waynman, like his brothers John and Raylton, was a talented amateur artist. Perhaps Eugenius Birch would have met Waynman, although he was briefly in Spain in the late autumn of 1874 in Spain and may have missed Birch's visit.

No doubt spurred into action by the prospect of competition, the Southport Pier Company set about implementing improvements to the pier suggested by James Brunlees, who presented a model of the improved pier to the shareholders' meeting in January 1867. There would be an enclosed incline from the higher level to the lower pier to replace the existing steps, an early example of provision for disabled access since the steps were 'a great nuisance to invalids and tend to prevent parties in bath chairs from going to the furthest pier-head'. The pier-head itself was to be enlarged with outside steps and landing stages, all at an estimated cost of £4,000. The contract, for detail design and construction, was awarded to John Dixon, and in May 1867 he was placing advertisements in the local press for pile drivers and carpenters to work on the project. As events turned out, the Southport Pier Company need not have been concerned. Whereas the original Southport pier had been built without Parliamentary approval, the proposed Alexandra Pier required an Act of Parliament. To the relief of investors in the existing pier, the Bill to initiate the Act was not approved.

John asked his younger brother, Waynman, then only twenty-three years old, to supervise the final stages of work, and he arrived at Southport on 21 August 1867.

In spite of what would have been John's careful preparations, not all went to plan. In April, severe storms brought a quantity of timber, presumed from a shipwreck, crashing against the pier. A good deal was cut away, but a 40 feet length became jammed in the structure and fractured a girder. The tide turned at 9:30pm, bringing the timber against the pillars of the new extensions, close to the point where it joined the original pier. Some pillars 'though of great strength' gave way, and twenty or thirty yards of the pier came down. There were no serious injuries to the several men who were trying to clear the timbers from the pier, although two very nearly fell into the sea.

John Dixon used the 'sinking pile' method, successfully used by James Brunlees for the original Southport pier, although there is some disagreement over the details. In *Engineering* an illustrated article shows four men operating a pump to deliver the pressurised water to the top of the cast iron pile. However, *The Illustrated London News* claimed that the water was delivered via a direct connection to the town's water mains at a pressure of 50 lb/in^2. Given the length of the pier, and that the *Engineering* illustration has men working on the sand right at the edge of the sea, it is probable that mains water was used for the piles near the land, with pumped water taking over at some distance away. Certainly the piles at the extreme end of the pier were sunk using a pontoon-mounted pump as the shore was only exposed briefly at low tide.

Each of the slender 9 inch diameter cast iron piles had an 18 inch disc at the lower end. Piles were sunk to depths of 15 to 20 feet, taking between twenty and thirty minutes each. John Dixon was clearly impressed by the ease with which the pile descended into the sand and carried out some of his own experiments using a smaller diameter disc, sinking a pile to a depth of 26 feet in under twenty minutes. Unfortunately, the experiment had to be terminated when there was an accident in fitting one of the column sections, otherwise it was believed that a depth of 50 feet might have been achieved in half-an-hour.

Following the success of the 'sinking pile' method it was suggested that James Brunlees and John Dixon might use the same method to erect a lighthouse on the treacherous Goodwin Sands to replace the lightship, but nothing came of the idea.

Re-opening of the pier

Southport's modified pier was opened on Monday 23 March 1868, with an incoming tide and a strong north-west wind blowing. The Pier Company directors examined the structure, which showed not the slightest vibration, but quickly retired to the shelter of the waiting room. With three cheers for the Queen and one for the pier, the structure was declared open to the public.

John Dixon was presented with a certificate, embellished with a large red seal, from the Southport Pier Company Limited, dated 28 March 1868, thanking him for the satisfactory manner in which he completed the work.

Southport pier in later life

Remarkably, given its history, Southport Pier still stands. A serious storm in 1889 wrecked the foundations of the refreshment rooms, in 1894 part of the pier collapsed as construction work on Marine Drive had resulted in sea water scouring the sand away from the pier supports, and in 1897 fire destroyed the pavilion at the pier entrance. Repairs were made after the first two incidents, and after the fire a new pavilion was built. John Dixon's pier-head was not so fortunate. On the night of 3 July 1933 his pier-head was ablaze, the fire even visible in Blackpool. This time the damage was too extensive for repairs, and the Southport pier lost 747 feet of its length. Rumours of arson were set aside by the Southport Fire Brigade, the dropping of a lighted cigarette end being the likely cause. John Dixon's pier-head was not the only loss due to the fire. Miss Blanche Laughton lost the instruments played by her ladies' orchestra and her lifetime collection of orchestral scores. Professor Pearson, the high diver, lost his pitch and Le Hurst, the ventriloquist, lost his doll 'Jimmy'.

In 1936 the pier was sold to Southport Corporation. After the Second World War another fire, storm damage and falling revenues put the future of the pier in jeopardy. In 1990 a motion to demolish the pier was defeated by only one vote at Sefton Metropolitan Borough Council. Fortunately, European and Heritage Lottery grants have enabled the pier to be restored, although not entirely to its original state as the pier-head pavilion is now a contemporary design.

Southport Pier Company Limited

At a Meeting of the Board of Directors
OF THE
Southport Pier Company Limited
held at the Scarisbrick Hotel, Southport,
on 28th March, 1868.

It was resolved
That the best thanks of the Company be presented to
John Dixon Esqre.
Contractor, for the highly satisfactory manner in which he has completed his Contract with the Company to erect the Extension Pier; the materials used, the work done, and the time consumed having our unanimous approval.
That a Copy of the above resolution be engrossed, signed by the Directors, have the Common Seal of the Company attached, and be presented to that Gentleman.

Chairman

Above) 'Pier Fire, Southport 1933' photograph. The scene after the disastrous fire of 3 July 1933. Curious spectators are being held back by a barrier while a solitary official stands guard at the very end of the surviving structure.
Reproduced by courtesy of Martin Easdown from his Marlinova Collection.

Left) Certificate dated 28 March 1868, presented to John Dixon on completion of the pier extension by the Board of Directors of the Southport Pier Company Limited.
Reproduced by courtesy of Beth Porteous, great grand-daughter of John Dixon, and photographed by Neil Crick ARPS of Smart-Ideas Photography.

Acknowledgements

Beth Porteous, great grand-daughter of John Dixon, for information about the certificate presented to John Dixon by the Southport Pier Company Limited.

Martin Easdown for additional information on the pier and for photographs.

Gillian Morgan of Crosby Library, Sefton and Andrew Brown of the *Southport Visiter* for assistance in locating possible illustrations.

References

Lancashire's Seaside Piers, also featuring the piers of the River Mersey, Cumbria and the Isle of Man
Martin Easdown
Wharncliffe Books, Barnsley, 2009
Includes a comprehensive history of Southport Pier up to the present day.

Southport Pier Company
The Liverpool Mercury and Lancashire, Cheshire, and General Advertiser, 10 December 1852, page 5
Prospectus for a jetty or pier.

Southport Pier Company
The Liverpool Mercury and Lancashire, Cheshire, and General Advertiser, 20 May 1859, page 1
Revised prospectus for the pier.

Obituary of Sir James Brunlees
Proceedings of the Institution of Civil Engineers,
Volume III, 1893, pages 367-371.

The Opening of the Ulverstone and Lancaster Railway
The Lancaster Gazette, 29 August 1857, page 6
Description of James Brunlees' novel method for sinking piles on the Leven Viaduct.

Description of the iron viaducts erected across the tidal estuaries of the rivers Leven and Kent, in Morecambe bay for the Ulverstone and Lancaster Railway
James Brunlees
Proceedings of the Institution of Civil Engineers, volume 17, 1858, pages 442-447

Ormskirk and Southport - New Pier
The Preston Chronicle and Lancashire Advertiser, 9 July 1859, page 6
The whole of the shares, £8,000, were taken up and construction soon to be commenced.

Domestic News
The Bolton Chronicle, 16 July 1859, page 6
Contract for construction finally let to W and J Galloway, estimated cost £6,900.

The Southport Pier - Engineering Error
The Manchester Courier and Lancashire General Advertiser, 11 February 1860, page 9
Mistake in the engineering calculations discovered when girders failed under half the required test loading.

Opening of the Southport Pier
The Preston Chronicle and Lancashire Advertiser, 4 August 1860, page 6
Full description of the opening ceremony of the original pier, and people involved in the construction: designer, James Brunlees; contractors, Messrs W & J Galloway.

Opening of the New Pier at Southport
The Daily Post, Liverpool, 3 August 1860, page 8
Full account of ceremony and engineering details, including William Fairburn's comments about the strength of the girders.

Southport Pier
Illustrated London News, 18 August 1860, page 20
Description of the pier and its construction, with an illustration of the opening day.

Description of the Pier at Southport, Lancashire
Henry Hooper
Minutes of the Proceedings of the Institution of Civil Engineers, Volume 20, 1861, pages 292-297
Full technical description of the pier.

The Southport Pier
Supplement to the Preston Herald, 4 February 1865, page 10
Annual meeting told that the extension and widening were both complete.

Historical Development of Iron Screw-Pile Foundations: 1836-1900
Alan J Lutenegger
University of Massachusetts, USA International Journal for the History of Engineering and Technology, volume 81 No. 1, January 2011, pages 108-128
A history of screw piling for lighthouses, piers and similar structures, with lists of such structures around the world, but does not mention John Dixon.

Society of Engineers
The Engineer, London, 12 March 1875, page 185-6 with illustrations on page 182
A comprehensive article on the construction of piers. John Dixon's method of driving cast iron piles is described. Details of twelve piers are included with dimensions and construction costs.

Ormskirk and Southport - New Pier
The Preston Chronicle, 20 October 1866, page 6
Proposal for a new pier being aired in the town.

Southport Pier Company
The Preston Chronicle and Lancashire Advertiser, 2 February 1867, page 7
Report on half-yearly meeting. The directors wish to improve the pier and Mr Brunlees had provided a model showing the improvements. These included an enclosed platform from the higher to the lower pier, and an enlarged pier-head with outside steps and landing stages. Cost about £4,000.

Serious Accident to Southport Pier
Liverpool Mercury, 19 April 1867, page 3
Report on the incident.

Local Bills in Parliament - The Southport (Alexandra) Pier
Liverpool Mercury, 17 May 1867, page 7
Failure of Bill for a second pier at Southport.

Advertisements and Notices
Liverpool Mercury, 23 May 1867, page 3
Small advertisement placed by John Dixon for pile drivers and carpenters – A few good hands can find employment on the Southport Pier Extension Works. Apply to John Dixon, 5 Abechurch-yard, London, E.C. The advertisement was repeated in two subsequent issues.

Notes received in 1921 from Ralph Longstaff, Elder, son of Geo. B. Longstaff
Waynman Dixon, 4 October 1921, private collection.
George Longstaff had extensively researched the Dixon genealogy. In these notes, Waynman wrote 'Then on 21 VIII 1867 went to Southport to erect an iron pier extension. On 9.II.1869 went to Douglas, Isle of Man, to erect iron promenade pier.'

Opening of the Southport New Extension Pier
The Ormskirk Advertiser, 26 March 1868, page 3
John Dixon's extension opened to the public.

Sinking piles at Southport pier
Engineering, 1 May 1868, page 411
James Brunlees' novel method of sinking plies into sand.

The Aquarium
The Brighton Guardian, 4 July 1877, page 5
Review of concerts at the Brighton Aquarium with a note about collection of water colours by Eugenius Birch 'made during a recent tour of the East; they embrace a large area and cover a considerable variety of life and character.'

Southport undaunted by Pier Fire
The Lancashire Daily Post, Preston, 27 July 1933, page 5
Property lost in the fire belonging to Miss Blanche Laughton and the ventriloquist Le Hurst.

Southport Pier Fire and Incendiarism
The Lancashire Daily Post, Preston, 29 July 1933, page 5
Theory that the recent fires at Southport, Llandudno and Colwyn Bay piers were the work of incendiaries dismissed by Deputy Superintendent Appleton' cigarette end more likely.

5 Isle of Man

The pier at Douglas, Isle of Man, designed and constructed by John Dixon, opened in 1869. It was the first of several piers which he constructed. The design was entirely conventional, with wrought iron girders supported on cast iron columns driven into the sand. John's brother, Waynman, was the resident engineer. Sadly, the pier declined in popularity and the pier company was wound up in 1891 with the structure sold as scrap metal. The oft-quoted story that it was reassembled at Rhos-on-Sea, North Wales, is without foundation. Following the completion of the pier, John Dixon was involved in plans for harbour improvements at Ramsey, but these came to nothing.

The Iron Pier at Douglas

With an ever-increasing number of holiday visitors to the Isle of Man, the Douglas Iron Pier Company was established in 1868 to erect a promenade pier on the sea front. By that time most of the major resorts, apart from Bournemouth and Llandudno, boasted piers, with more than twenty-five built around the coast. The share prospectus expressed justifiable concern that Douglas was falling behind as a seaside resort:

> 'The promoters of the Douglas Promenade Iron Pier Company, Limited, have observed with regret that Douglas as a watering place is being left behind in the race of progress, making little or no exertion to increase its attractions for residents and summer visitors. Almost every watering place in England of the slightest pretension has its iron promenade pier, and, with hardly a single exception, these piers have been a signal success, both as an attraction for visitors and in a financial sense, paying large dividends to shareholders.'

From the seven proposals received, in December 1868 John Dixon's plans were selected. He proposed a 1,000 foot long pier with an entrance booth and a refreshment house at the far end. Initially the cost of the pier was estimated at £8,000, so it is easy to see why they accepted John's quotation of only £6,000. John's brother, Waynman, was to act as resident engineer and, on 9 February 1869, he arrived at Douglas. The site foreman was Mr Smith. The first pile was driven on 17 March 1869, and the pier was completed within the short space of five months and within the contract price of £6,000. The local press reported 'Mr. Dixon has been exceedingly liberal in his interpretation of the agreement, having, we understand, spent some hundreds of pounds more than the strict letter of the specification required.' In fact, the total cost had been £6,500.

Construction was conventional with seventy-eight cast iron piles, of 10 inch diameter, supporting wrought iron girders with timber decking. The 17 feet wide promenade widened to 40 feet at the seaward end, where there was a refreshment saloon with an open smoking gallery above. Steps led down to the water level to enable boats to land passengers. At the land end, tolls were collected from a small Chinese pagoda and turnstile. The advertisement for a gatekeeper resulted in thirty-one applications, suggesting local enthusiasm for the pier, or possibly few job opportunities. Before it was opened to the public, the directors invited the local Artillery Volunteers, who were 'always ready to risk their lives in scenes of danger', to march up and down the structure to test its solidity. There was no trace of vibration. The load bearing capacity of the pier was thoroughly tested on 16 September 1869, the day of the Isle of Man Races, when it was crammed with fully 1,000 people. At the beginning of the following month, high tides breaking against the promenade wall made plumes of spray thirty feet high. People gathered on the promenade, some of them half-expecting to see the iron pier washed away, but they were disappointed. John knew that his pier was secure; the piles had been driven into solid bedrock under the sand, even with a twenty-five hundredweight monkey and a fall of ten feet it had been a difficult task. The high tides demonstrated the effectiveness of his timber breakwater which had been added a few weeks after the opening of the pier. This well-designed structure, placed diagonally across the sand under the pier, took the force out of the incoming waves and prevented them breaking under the decking.

The opening of the pier

The Douglas Iron Pier opened on 19 August 1869. John Dixon's water colour painting, done on the opening day, shows throngs of holiday-makers in front of the pier. A week earlier, during the Douglas Regatta, Waynman had unofficially opened the pier while it was still being painted and donated the £10 takings to the Isle of Man Hospital, an example of his life-long interest in hospital provision.

At the opening ceremony the directors were full of praise for John Dixon:

> 'The directors take this opportunity of publicly stating that the contractor his done his work well, and has not from the first put a niggardly construction upon the contract; but, on the contrary, has put a liberal interpretation on any doubtful point, and has thus saved the directors much trouble.'

In his reply, John pointed out that the construction had been free from accidents. The directors, he said were 'an honourable, straightforward, and business-like body of gentlemen.' There were cheers for both John and Waynman Dixon.

Initial success

At first the pier was a great success. The refreshment house at the end of the structure was 'let to a suitable tenant and comfortably furnished for visitors' and in the first two months 44,000 tickets were sold for the pier. At the first annual meeting of shareholders a dividend of 5% was announced, and the directors of the pier company optimistically predicted that within two years shareholders would receive 'a dividend not much under 20%.'

The shareholders' meeting of 1872 was informed that two waiting rooms for ladies and gentlemen had been erected. If Douglas had been slow to build its pier, there were now plans for the resort to be one of the first with a large aquarium. Following the success of the aquarium at the Crystal Palace Exhibition, Brighton was already constructing a very large aquarium at a cost of £40,000. The attraction of an aquarium was agreed, although there was uncertainty as to its siting. Placing the aquarium underneath the pier would allow the refreshment room to remain in its present position and 'would thus avoid the immense heat that would prove fatal to the inhabitants of the aquarium'. The summer sun at Douglas in those days must have been powerful indeed. There was also discussion about the possible sale of alcohol and tobacco in the refreshment room. It was noted that other piers sold beer; one of those present had been to Ryde Pier, where beer was sold, and that 'he had not seen any abuse of the privilege there and had not seen any persons make beasts of themselves'. However, a director's closing remark was that, as both alcohol and tobacco were evils, the wisest plan would be to have nothing to do with either.

The local poet James Sutherland was quite taken with John Dixon's pier. In 1873 he published a book of poems opening with a lengthy recitation of the charms of Douglas, including a verse on the pier.

'There runs into the middle of the bay
A long and pleasant promenading pier,
And many here resort throughout the day
To breathe the freshness of the waters clear.
On summer evenings hundreds here repair
To see the fashions and themselves be seen;
To hear the music, and escort the fair,
And watch the rowers skim the wave serene,
Or gliding through the space the iron piles between.'

He went on to write a ten-verse poem ostensibly entirely dedicated to the Douglas Iron Pier, although he seems to have been more interested in young ladies than engineering construction, as shown in the first four verses.

'Here stands in lovely Douglas Bay,
An Iron Pier so grand for walking,
Where hundreds promenade every day,
So gaily dressed and lively talking.'

'But chief at eve, at eight about,
After th' arrival of the steamers,
The Pier looks best, for then come out
The ladies decked with flowers and streamers.'

'And sweet it is these belles to see
Of Mona's Isle and other places,
All promenading in their glee,
With beaming eyes, and oh! what faces!'

'The aptest language ne'er could tell
The beauties of these charming creatures,
So fair, they seem to have a spell,
They have such pleasing forms and features.'

The Victoria Pier

Whilst John Dixon was working on the iron pier, improvements were taking place in the harbour at Douglas for the Harbour Commissioners. One of the masonry harbour walls, later known as the Victoria Pier, was constructed specifically for the transfer of passengers and goods to and from steam ships. Previously such transfers were done using small boats, with much inconvenience to passengers. In some references there is confusion between the construction of the iron pier and the Victoria Pier. The Commissioners appointed Robert Casement, described as 'a practical although not a professional engineer', to supervise their work but some press reports at the time incorrectly state he was the foreman on the iron pier. Incidentally, Casement's appointment was vigorously opposed by John Coode, the eminent civil engineer who was advising the Harbour Commission. In an example of the disdain with which some professionally qualified engineers viewed men with only practical training, Coode considered him not to be properly qualified for the position. This issue would occupy the Institution of Civil Engineers towards the end of the 1870s, when John Dixon made his views known in the engineering press, and indeed continues today with the sometimes pedantic distinctions between engineer, technician, tradesman and mechanic.

Within weeks of opening on 1 July 1872, the pier had been named after Queen Victoria. Although not conceived as a rival to John Dixon's promenade pier, since it was nearer the town centre and cost nothing to walk along, it soon became more popular. Jostling with the steamer passengers were sightseers and entertainers such as 'singing men and singing women, and minstrel boys'.

'Douglas Promenade Pier' 19 August 1869, pencil and water colour by John Dixon. It is possible that John put himself in the picture. Is he the gentleman in the top hat, with his wife Mary in blue, George age five and Cornelia age four? The lady in white could be a servant to look after the children. Little ones Nora and Maud would have been left at home in Kingston upon Thames.
Reproduced by courtesy Manx National Heritage (Isle of Man) reference 1958-0219 and Bridgeman Images, reference MNX3657357

'1504 Douglas, the Iron Pier' photograph. From the booklet Six Photographs of the Isle of Man by Brown and Son, Athol Street, Douglas. There are some interesting differences between this photograph and John Dixon's painting. The photograph has ornate stone pedestals at the lower ends of the curved steps, one with a lamp, which are absent in John Dixon's view. However, Dixon's single lamp has a glass cover and finial, features missing from all the lamps in the photograph.
Reproduced by courtesy Manx National Heritage (Manx Reference Library) reference M08479/1 and Bridgeman Images, reference MNX3657585

Gradual decline of the Iron Pier

Unfortunately, the initial popularity of the iron pier did not last. Young men loitering at the entrance were annoying ladies and putting them off visiting the pier. The proprietor of one of the pier shops was charged with fraud. Arguments arose about the sale of alcohol; the directors believed that respectable people would shun the pier if compelled to mix with persons attracted by the sale of liquor but passed the question over to shareholders.

The pier company seems to have lacked ambition, and for the structure remained a simple walk-way with none of the additional amenities which increasingly became expected on a seaside pier. A year after the opening of the pier a new landing jetty was completed in the harbour at Douglas. Extensions to the coastal promenade further reduced the pier's appeal. Seven years after the opening of the pier, the £5 shares were trading at £4 15s, three years later their value had fallen to £3 15s. There were complaints about the abusive manner of the gate keeper, swearing at visitors and kicking angler's tackle about the pier. No action was taken against him other than the advice to visitors that he should be ignored, but after many months advertisements appeared for an active and trustworthy man, with character testimonials to accompany applications. The new gate keeper, Mr Green, earned much praise and was said to look after the pier as if it were his own property.

In spite of Mr Green's efforts, the decline in popularity of the pier continued. No dividend was forthcoming in 1886, the directors wishing to use profits to make improvements, including 'accommodation for entertainments of a better class than hitherto given on the pier'. At the end of the year, shares offered at £2 remained unsold. A report that the Manx Line was proposing to purchase the pier and convert it into a landing for shipping was dismissed in the press as 'an absurd notion'. By April 1887 shares were selling at just sixteen shillings and at the shareholders' meeting it was suggested that the need for the pier had passed and the structure should be sold. The end of the pier was in sight.

The end of the pier

By 1889, twenty years after its opening, the local newspaper commented on the Iron Pier Company's want of enterprise, with no dividend and little hope for the future. A year later the same paper was of the opinion that the Douglas Iron Pier Company had 'gone to the dogs' as an investment. By this time John Dixon had built the magnificent pier at Llandudno, and it was said that its substantial profits would make mouths water in Douglas. In 1891 the shareholders unanimously decided to wind up the company and in the following year the structure was sold to a Birmingham business for £1,600. They promised to turn the pier into a going-concern, with structural extensions at the end of the season, but these were just dreams. Within two months the Douglas Commissioners bought the pier from them for £1,650, with a view to demolish it. They tried to sell the ironwork for £1,200, suggesting that other towns on the Isle of Man, or elsewhere, might be interested. The directors of the Pensarn (Abergele) Pier Company looked at it, but there were no takers. Eventually it was demolished by a Manchester scrap merchant in 1894.

Several authors of publications on the history of piers state that John Dixon's pier at Douglas was dismantled and rebuilt by him at Rhos-on-Sea, North Wales, in 1893, or even as late as 1896. Pier historians Martin Easdown and Darlah Thomas have pointed out the absurdity of this, since John Dixon died in 1891. They suggest that the confusion perhaps partly stemmed from the liquidator, appointed when the Rhos pier concern was bankrupt in 1896, a Board of Trade official named John Caister Dixon. This is not the only instance of John Dixon being credited with work which was not his. Two years after the opening of the Douglas pier, the Manx press reported that John Dixon of London had been engaged to construct a tunnel under the Mersey; in reality this was the notorious John Dickson (1819-1892) and the tunnel work succumbed to one of his three bankruptcies. In another example of careless reporting, in 1888 it was stated that the handsome pavilion for the Injebreck Pleasure Grounds, in the centre of the Isle of Man, was purchased from 'the firm of Dixon and Co, of Liverpool, the builders of the Douglas Iron Pier.' In fact this was Isaac Dixon and Company, no relation to John Dixon.

There is a postscript to John Dixon's work at Douglas. Some years later there was a proposal to build a sea wall enclosing the south sands at Douglas to provide a new thoroughfare. Sceptics claimed the wall would be washed away. John Dixon heard of the controversy and wrote to the local paper explaining how a secure wall might be constructed for modest cost, quoting other more exposed locations where similar sea walls had withstood the elements. He concluded his letter with a PS: 'If they give me the land reclaimed I will very soon make the embankment.'

Ramsey harbour improvements

Whilst work was proceeding on the Douglas pier, John Dixon was asked to investigate a proposed low-water landing and iron breakwater for Ramsey Bay. The people of Ramsey, on the north eastern Manx coast, had been watching tourist vessels pass by on their way to Douglas, and they wanted their own landing facility and, for good measure, an extension to the sheltered waters of the harbour. The Manx government at Tynwald sanctioned expenditure and offered a grant of £28,500. John Coode, an experienced civil engineer who would shortly be knighted for his work on Portland Harbour, submitted plans for a solid masonry pier. However, the Tynwald authorities, alarmed at the cost estimate and realising that an iron pier would be cheaper, asked John Dixon to submit proposals. His report, dated 15 April 1869 and sent from his London office, started a long-running controversy. Local people at Ramsey favoured the traditional masonry pier; they were greatly suspicious that an iron pier would not provide adequate shelter for shipping, would corrode, and would cause silting in the harbour. In August 1869 a Committee of the Tynwald Court sat to consider the rival proposals but had to be adjourned as it was realised that neither John Coode nor John Dixon had been invited to explain their respective plans! Later, and in typical fashion, John Dixon robustly defended his design by seeking the opinions of no fewer than twelve engineers with a wide experience of iron piers and harbours, including Captain Calvert (surveyor to the Admiralty), James Brunlees (the experienced pier designer), James Douglas (engineer to Trinity House), and Edwin Clark (Robert Stephenson's resident engineer on the Britannia Tubular Bridge).

Meanwhile two more schemes had been put forward, based on a compromise of masonry breakwaters with iron or timber extension, and a series of vague sketches and suggestions from others. A committee was appointed by the Tynwald Court but was unable to agree on the best scheme and, in November 1869, submitted two rival reports. Three members of the Committee favoured John Coode's masonry pier, which would cost about £58,000 or about £48,000 if part of the structure was in timber. They were suspicious of an iron landing pier as part of the harbour but thought that one could be constructed in a different location. John Dixon had given them plans for such a structure at a cost of £25,000, and they thanked Mr Dixon for the great trouble he had taken in preparing and laying before them his plans. However, their confidence in John Dixon was tempered by their suggestion that if the iron pier was adopted 'some engineer of eminence who has given special attention to such works should be consulted'. The Committee chairman and one other member submitted the alternative report. John Coode's masonry breakwater with timber extension would cost £48,000. John Dixon's original iron pier would cost £40,000 and his modified scheme would cost £25,000. Two other schemes put forward were estimated at £15,000 and £44,480. Their minority report did not recommend any of the schemes put before them, but suggested the existing harbour be extended and consideration given to an entirely separate iron pier. Faced with this dilemma, the Tynwald Court merely agreed to circulate copies of each report for further consideration, displaying the not unusual reticence of committees to commit themselves.

The arguments raged for over three years; Ramsey holding out against an iron pier, Tynwald refusing the additional expenditure for a masonry structure. One non-Ramsey representative, concerned at the cost of a stone pier, was quoted as saying it was 'more than north-side people were entitled to.' Eventually the head of the Manx government, the Lieutenant-Governor, went to Ramsey to listen to local concerns and make a decision. His decision was to dismiss both Coode's and Dixon's plans, and to suggest extending the existing South Pier.

Acknowledgements

Matthew Richardson and staff at Manx National Heritage, Douglas, Isle of Man

References

Seaside Piers
Simon H Adamson, B T Batsford Ltd, London, 1977
A general history of British piers. John Dixon is said to be 'perhaps the most notable engineer/contractor' involved in pier construction, but is credited with re-erecting the Douglas pier at Rhos in 1896, five years after his death!

Pavilions on the Sea, a History of the Seaside Pleasure Pier
Cyril Bainbridge, Robert Hale Limited, London, 1986
Another general history. Bainbridge states that the Llandudno pier 'was built with a turn of approximately 45 degrees about a third of the way down its length.' This is incorrect; the original pier had an extension, incorporating the 45 degree angle, seven years after John Dixon's pier had been opened. Bainbridge also repeats the fiction about the pier at Rhos, with the assertion that, in 1896, John Dixon was re-erecting piece by piece the pier which thirty years earlier he had built at Douglas, Isle of Man.

Lancashire's Seaside Piers, also featuring the piers of the River Mersey, Cumbria and the Isle of Man
Martin Easdown, Wharncliffe Books, Barnsley, 2009
Has a brief description of the Douglas pier, pages 169-172. Written before Martin Easdown and Darlah Thomas dismissed the myth of the pier being rebuilt at Rhos, see below.

Piers of Wales
Martin Easdown & Darlah Thomas
Amberley Publishing Plc, Stroud, 2010.
An excellent history, which exposed the myth of John Dixon re-erecting the Douglas pier at Rhos. Contains a detailed account of the pier at Llandudno, its construction and history, with many photographs. Llandudno pier pages 104-119, Rhos pier pages 120-136.

National Piers Society website at www.piers.org.uk/pierpages
Includes Douglas in its list of lost piers and includes the repudiation of the Rhos pier story by Easdown and Thomas.

Legal notices - Douglas Promenade Pier Company Limited
The Liverpool Mercury, 19 August 1868, page 4
Offer of £5 shares to the public.

The Promenade Pier at Douglas, Isle of Man
Engineering, 11 December 1868, Volume 6, page 524
List of firms submitting tenders. John Dixon's tender was selected on the previous Tuesday (8 December).

The Manx Sun, Douglas, 14 August 1869, page 4
During the regatta the Iron Pier, which was then being finished by painters and decorators, was opened on Thursday by Mr. Waynman Dixon. Three pence was charged with all the proceeds going to the Isle of Man Hospital. With 800 visitors, £10 was donated to the hospital.

The Iron Promenade Pier, successful opening
The Isle of Man Times and General Advertiser, Douglas, 21 August 1869, page 5
Pier opened on Thursday 19 August. Article contains a full description of the pier and praise from the directors for John Dixon.

The Douglas Promenade Pier
The Illustrated London News, 18 September 1869, page 285
Description and illustration of the pier.

Isle of Man Races
The Isle of Man Times and General Advertiser, Douglas, 18 September 1869, page 5
The pier crammed on the day of the horse races.

The High Tide
The Isle of Man Times and General Advertiser, Douglas, 9 October 1869, page 5
Pier withstood the high tides and the effectiveness of the breakwater.

The Manx Sun, 5 March 1870, page 4
Report on the Half-yearly General Meeting of Shareholders of the Douglas Iron Pier Company. The directors had received seven plans and designs for the pier and selected that of John Dixon. 'In the short space of five months he has fulfilled the terms of his contract in a very satisfactory manner under the personal superintendence of Mr Waynman Dixon.' The pier was formally opened on 19 August 1869 by His Excellency the Lieutenant-Governor and Mrs Loch. The refreshment house had been let to a suitable tenant and was comfortably furnished for visitors. There were 44,000 visitors during the two months ending 19 October 1869.

Douglas Iron Promenade Pier
The Daily Courier, Liverpool, 5 March 1870, page 7
First annual meeting, total cost had been £6,500. 5% dividend declared.

Opening of the New Landing Pier
Engineering, London, 8 July 1870, page 24
Opening of the new landing pier means that Douglas is no longer a tidal harbour.

The Iron Pier Company, Limited - proposed aquarium, the licensing question - drinking v smoking
The Isle of Man Times and General Advertiser, Douglas, 24 February 1872, page 6
Annual General Meeting with discussion of a possible aquarium and the sale of beer.

Douglas and other poems
James Middleton Sutherland
Brown and Son, Douglas, 1873
Contains the poem 'Douglas' and 'The Douglas Iron Pier'.

Letters to the Editor - A hint to the Douglas Iron Pier Company
The Isle of Man Times and General Advertiser, Douglas, 30 May 1874, page 3
Young men were deterring ladies from visiting the pier.

(Small news item)
The Isle of Man Times and General Advertiser, Douglas, 6 June 1874, page 8
Shop proprietor charged with intent to defraud.

The proposal to licence the Iron Pier
The Isle of Man Times and General Advertiser, Douglas, 28 November 1874, page 5
Decision on sale of alcohol passed over to shareholders.

Great Sale of Shares
The Isle of Man Times and General Advertiser, Douglas, 20 May 1876, page 5
Twenty £5 shares in the Douglas Iron Pier Company sold for £4 15s.

Editorial
The Isle of Man Times and General Advertiser, Douglas, 30 December 1876, page 4
No action taken over the abusive nature of the gate keeper.

Sale of shares belonging to Major Bacon's estate and others
The Isle of Man Times and General Advertiser, Douglas, 3 May 1879, page 4
Thirteen shares sold at £3 15s.

Douglas Iron Pier
The Isle of Man Times and General Advertiser, Douglas, 17 March 1883, page 2
At the annual meeting of shareholders the toll keeper, Mr Green, was commended.

Summary
The Isle of Man Times and General Advertiser, Douglas, 17 April 1886, page 4
No dividend, improvements to be made to the pier.

Mr Craige's share sale
The Isle of Man Times and General Advertiser, Douglas, 11 December 1886, page 5
Shares offered at £2 were unsold.

An Absurd Notion
The Isle of Man Times and General Advertiser, Douglas, 15 January 1887, page 5
Report that the Manx Line was to purchase the pier.

Mr Craige's share sale
The Isle of Man Times and General Advertiser, Douglas, 16 April 1887, page 5
Shares sold at 16s.

Summary and notes
The Isle of Man Times and General Advertiser, Douglas, 30 April 1887, page 4
Annual meeting told that the structure should be sold.

Summary
The Isle of Man Times and General Advertiser, Douglas, 24 September 1890, page 2
The pier company had gone to the dogs while the new pier at Llandudno was making huge profits.

Douglas Improvements
The Isle of Man Times and General Advertiser, Douglas, 16 November 1872, page 8
Letter from John Dixon pointing out that the ground below the shore was quite solid. When he built the Iron Promenade Pier he had great difficulty driving in the piles, which were 10 inch diameter, even with a 25 hundredweight monkey and a fall of 10 feet.

Letters to the Editor: The New Street Question
The Isle of Man Times and General Advertiser, Douglas, 23 November 1872, page 4
John Dixon's letter giving his opinion on the durability of a sea wall, suggesting a suitable design and offering to build it if he could have the reclaimed land.

The New Pleasure Resort
The Isle of Man Times and General Advertiser, Douglas, 3 March 1888, page 4
The Injebreck Pleasure Grounds have purchased a very handsome pavilion from the firm of Dixon and Co., of Liverpool, the builders of the iron pier.

Summary and Notes
The Isle of Man Times and General Advertiser, Douglas, 4 May 1889, page 4
The Iron Pier Company would not pay a dividend, suggestions that entertainments should be provided or the pier should be disposed of.

Douglas Iron Pier Company
The Isle of Man Times and General Advertiser, Douglas, 8 May 1889, page 3
Article sub-headed 'The Company's want of enterprise, no dividend, little hope.'

Douglas Iron Pier Company
The Isle of Man Times and General Advertiser, Douglas, 18 July 1891, page 4
The promenade extensions have led to dwindling traffic on the pier, and the shareholder decided unanimously to wind up the concern.

The Douglas Iron Pier - Structure Sold
The Isle of Man Times and General Advertiser, Douglas, 16 August 1892, page 2
The liquidator of the Douglas Iron Pier Company sold the structure to a Birmingham concern for £1600. They intend to open the pier with swimming and other galas and that, at the end of the season, they will enlarge the structure.

Purchase of the Iron Pier by the Town
The Isle of Man Times and General Advertiser, Douglas, 8 October 1892, page 4
The Douglas Commissioners purchase the pier from the above Birmingham concern for £1650, with a view to demolish it.

The Manx Sun, 29 May 1869, page 1
Report of the Proposed Iron Pier and Deep-water Landing Stage at Ramsey by John Dixon. The report was dated 15 April and addressed to H E H B Loch Esq and was sent from 1 Laurence Pountney Hill.

The Manx Sun, 28 August 1869, page 4-5
Debate over how much stilling of the water would be offered by an iron pier. Proponents included the Admiralty Surveyor and Brunel's maritime assistant for fifty years. Coode's plans were too expensive. The people of Ramsey were in favour of combining the plans of Coode and Dixon. There was an alternative plan suggested by E C Farrant (he was a local farmer and Member of the House of Keys for Ayre) for a stone pier to low-water mark with an iron extension.

Mr. Dixon's Report
The Isle of Man Times and General Advertiser, 23 October 1869, page 6
Long article of John Dixon's report on the proposed Low Water Landing and Iron Breakwater for Ramsey Bay. Access to steamers would be by a light open viaduct resting on light iron columns, somewhat after the style of the new Promenade Pier at Douglas.

Mr Dixon's Report
The Isle of Man Times and General Advertiser, Douglas, 30 October 1869, page 6
Correspondence sent by John Dixon in which twelve eminent engineers express their view that an iron structure for the Ramsey pier would be suitable and durable.

Tynwald Court, Douglas, Thursday November 25, 1869
The Isle of Man Times and General Advertiser, Douglas, 27 November 1869, page 5
Report of the Committee to consider the Ramsey schemes and their failure to agree.

The Manx Sun, 9 April 1870, page 4
Long report on the debate over the Ramsey plans for the iron pier. Mr. Coode's Plans had found favour over John Dixon's. Coode's Soundings were thought to be more accurate, the lifeboat coxswain was worried about the safety of vessels with an open iron-work pier as opposed to a solid stone structure, and corrosion of the iron would be a problem.

The Manx Sun, 28 October 1871, page 4
Mr. John Dixon on London has been engaged to construct a tunnel under the Mersey from Liverpool to Birkenhead. This is not John Dixon, but John Dickson (c1819-1892), the notoriously unreliable contractor who was bankrupt three times over.

The Manx Sun, 27 January 1872, page 4
The Tynwald Court had substituted an iron pier for a solid one and made a grant of £28,500. The iron pier had been adopted for reasons of economy. However, now the cost of iron had increased and there were concerns about the effectiveness of an iron pier in poor weather.

The Manx Sun, 7 September 1872, page 4
Comments about delays after delays with the Ramsey pier project.

The Manx Sun, 26 October 1872, page 4
Public Meeting at Ramsey passed three resolutions: that a pier should be built, that it should be a low-water landing and that it should be a stone structure.

The Manx Sun, 16 November 1872, page 4
Tynwald Court in Douglas on 15 November had received a petition from Ramsey. They would consider this and make a decision on 26 November. His Excellency Loch would visit Ramsey to listen to their concerns. Other Tynwald members were worried about costs which were 'more than northside people are entitled to.'

The Manx Sun, 30 November 1872, page 4
Tynwald Court meeting on 26 November. The Lieutenant-Governor proposed an extension to the existing south pier rather than construct an iron pier.

The Manx Sun, 14 November 1874, page 2
Work was again postponed on the South Pier extension at Ramsey.

6 Windermere Ferry

John Dixon's brother-in-law, James Richardson, built a splendid country house named 'Balla Wray' on the western shore of Lake Windermere. In 1870 John Dixon replaced the old rowing boat ferry from Bowness with a steam powered vessel, probably as much from sensing a business opportunity as being motivated to improve his sister's travel arrangements. The ferry operation was dogged with problems and John abandoned it after failing to prevent the lake steamer, as he saw it, poaching his potential clients.

'Balla Wray'

John's sister, Augusta Ann Dixon, married James Richardson in 1857. James was a partner in E and J Richardson at Elswick, Newcastle upon Tyne, the largest leather tannery in the north east of England. Their family home was at No.3 Summerhill Grove, just half a mile west of the Central Station which had opened in 1850. James wanted somewhere away from the polluted air of Newcastle for his family to take holidays and decided to build a house in the Lake District. Following the arrival of the railways, the Lake District had become a much sought-after location for grand country houses for the nouveau riche of Victorian society. It was possible for the Richardsons to travel by train from Newcastle to Windermere. The Newcastle and Carlisle Railway, taken over by the North Eastern Railway in 1862, covered the sixty miles across the Pennines to Carlisle. From here it was a fifty mile journey south on the Lancaster and Carlisle Railway to Oxenholme Station, with the final ten miles from Oxenholme to Windermere on trains operated by the London and North Western Railway. The entire journey could be accomplished in under six hours.

In March 1870 John, who was no stranger to contract law, drew up an agreement for his brother-in-law James Richardson to lease of a plot of land on the shores of Lake Windermere. Here James built the fine house which became known as 'Balla Wray'. John contemplated building on an adjacent plot on his own account but decided against the idea. However, he did construct a steam-powered ferry across the lake and briefly toyed with the notion of taking over the Ferry Hotel.

To James Richardson's dismay 'Balla Wray' later became the home of his parents-in-law, Jeremiah and Mary Dixon. What had started as an arrangement whereby they could rent part of the house when James and Augusta were in Newcastle became virtually permanent residence over most of the house; so much so that his father-in-law became known as 'Jere Dixon of Balla Wray'. Regardless of whether it was considered a Richardson house or a Dixon house, members of both extended families often visited the house, especially at New Year and Easter, as did members of other Quaker families from the north east.

The Windermere ferry

There had been a ferry across Lake Windermere since the 16th century, using rowing boats. By the 18th century the rights to operate a ferry were owned by the Curwen family of Belle Isle. In May 1870 John Dixon agreed a lease with the Curwens for the right to operate a ferry across the lake for twenty-one years, at an annual rent of £100, with the important proviso that no opposition ferry could use the landing stage. The lease specified that Dixon would construct, work and maintain the ferry.

John's ferry boat was an open vessel with a ramp at either end. It hauled itself across the lake by means of a chain laid across the lake bed, with sufficient slack to allow it to be looped round three outboard winding wheels. These winding wheels were driven by a steam engine, mounted along with the boiler on one side of the vessel. Although there were some counterbalance weights on the opposite side, the craft had a pronounced list in its unladen state. Permission to lay the chain was obtained from Lord Lonsdale and the ferry service began. Capacity was limited to a coach and four horses, or two coaches provided the horses were detached.

It might have been supposed that John would have asked his brother, Raylton Dixon, to build the ferry boat at his shipyard in Middlesbrough. However, the vessel does not appear to have been professionally designed, rather something put together from whatever materials were to hand locally, probably using a second-hand boiler and engine. It was certainly not the graceful design that would have been expected from the Cleveland Dockyard.

Several modifications were made during the life of the ferry. The chain was replaced by a wire cable, and later a second guide cable was installed. The engine controls, originally open, were later enclosed in a simple wooden hut to provide some shelter for the ferry operator.

The first two years

John Dixon found that operating the ferry was far from plain sailing. Right from the start he had arguments with the Curwen Estate, so much so that in April 1870 Henry Curwen withdrew the lease and contemplated running a ferry himself. The two men overcame their quarrel, and the new steam ferry service started later that year. It was acclaimed as a welcome improvement, as shown by the local press from November 1870:

Painting of 'Balla Wray' by John Dixon in 1875. The elderly gentleman in the foreground is John's father, Jeremiah Dixon, known as 'Jere Dixon of Balla Wray', with John's family in the distance. John and Mary, with their nine children, are recorded in the Visitor's Book for 'Balla Wray' in July 1875. Reproduced by courtesy of Beth Porteous, great grand-daughter of John Dixon, and photographed by Neil Crick ARPS of Smart-Ideas Photography.

'This beautiful but hitherto inconvenient crossing place on Lake Windermere has now been greatly changed for the better. The steamer and chains, which have taken the place of the old lumbering row boat, complete the crossing and return in much less time than the old boat took to go one way. The men employed are also prompt and obliging, so much that they hurry across the lake on hearing the first intimation of a passenger.'

Indeed, the men employed were so assiduous that, on more than one occasion, they were reported to have responded to an evening call from the opposite shore only to find that it was an owl hooting in the darkness! John was obviously concerned about the character of his ferryman. In August 1871 he advertised for a new ferryman in the London press only, presumably because he wanted to interview applicants himself:

'Man wanted at Windermere Steam Ferry; wages 22s per week, house, and firing; must be accustomed to machinery; no one need trouble himself or me by applying, who has not a very long and unexceptionally good character.
J. Dixon, 1 Laurence Pountney-hill, E.C.'

There was a curious incident in June 1872 when William Waite, a labourer, attempted to set fire to the ferry early one morning. Dixon's requirement for a man of good character proved wise because the new ferryman saw the fire from his cottage window, rushed out with a bucket of water and extinguished the blaze before any real damage was done. When Waite appeared at the Appleby Assizes it transpired that he had escaped from the workhouse where he was considered 'not fit to be at large.' In court he said that he wanted to burn the ferry so that a bridge would be built across the lake. He was sentenced to a month's imprisonment with hard labour; in those days there was little regard for mental health issues save for the judge's vague recommendation that his friends should take care of him when he was released.

Dixon v Curwen

Unfortunately, relations between John Dixon and the Curwen Estate again deteriorated. The Curwen Estate built a new pier at the Ferry Hotel, whereupon lake steamers started to pick up passengers who, John claimed, would have otherwise used the ferry. Reacting to Dixon's complaints, the Estate at first prohibited lake steamers from using the pier, but in May 1872 they relented. In June 1872 the Curwen Estate received a letter from John Dixon at his Laurence Pountney Hill office. He had instructed his solicitor to procure an injunction to compel the estate to abide by the terms of the agreement. Throughout his career, John readily took recourse to legal action if he believed that he had been wronged; it was a matter of principle rather than a decision arrived at after balancing costs against likelihood of victory. At last, in 1877, the case was heard in the Court of Chancery. Dixon's case was dismissed by the judge, who ruled that the lake steamers were not 'opposition ferries' on the basis that their landing points on the eastern shore were different. Ferry passengers disembarked on the highway to Bowness, a mile or more from the steamer pier, therefore the steamers were not a direct alternative to the ferry. John had to pay the Curwen's legal costs. Characteristically, he appealed, but the appeal was dismissed in June 1877.

John also quarrelled with Mr Borthwick, who was the tenant of the Ferry Inn. Prior to the introduction of the steam ferry, the ferry lease had generally been given to the tenant of the Ferry Inn. When John Dixon signed his lease for the steam ferry, an aggrieved Borthwick would have experienced a loss of income. Furthermore, there were arguments between Dixon's ferry operators and the hotel over the building of the iron pier to facilitate steamer access, and the subsequent competition for passengers. At one point John thought of taking over the lease of the Ferry Inn himself, as a means of resolving the dispute, but this came to nothing.

With the loss of Dixon v Curwen, John abandoned his interest in the lease of the ferry rights, which reverted to the tenant of the Ferry Inn who continued the service using John's steam ferry. In 1915 this vessel was replaced by a new steam-driven ferry boat, which was in turn replaced in 1954 by the *Drake*. Initially steam-powered, *Drake* was converted to diesel engines in 1960. The current ferry *Mallard* entered service in 1990.

John's family visits to 'Balla Wray'

The 'Balla Wray' visitors' books record visits of John, Mary and their children from 1871 onwards. John made infrequent visits to 'Balla Wray', his business interests taking first call on his time. He and Mary visited the house together on five occasions, Mary on her own three times and John on his own twice. Perhaps indicative of the little time John spent with his own family, in the earlier visits John and Mary together gave their home address, but after 1875 John gave his business address. In the earlier years they would see John's parents, later they would be entertained by John's sister Augusta Ann Richardson; her husband James found business pressures made it difficult for him to spend much time in his country house. Some of John and Mary's children might accompany them, and young George came by himself on two occasions, once when he was only seven years old and once when he was nearly eleven years old. It is likely that one of John's domestic servants accompanied him, but servants' names did not appear in the visitors' book. On Good Friday 1881, John, Mary and all nine of their surviving children arrived at 'Balla Wray'. John left one week later but the rest of the family stayed for three weeks. By now John's family ties to the house on the shore of Windermere were coming to an end. His mother had died in 1877 and his father only had one more year to live. He would have found the last part of the journey irksome. Since relinquishing ownership of the ferry, he would have grudgingly been required to pay the fare for the crossing, even though it was in the vessel he had built himself.

Top) 'Windermere Steam Ferry' photograph by Chronicle. This carefully hand-tinted photograph from the end of the 19th century shows John Dixon's ferry in operation. The vertical boiler, mounted on one side of the ferry, gave the vessel a pronounced list unless it was fully laden.
© Alamy Images reference ER75ET

Right) 'The Ferry Crossing, Windermere' hand-tinted postcard. This clearly shows the list due to the boiler and engine being mounted on one side of the vessel. The wooden shelter for the ferry operator was a later addition. Reproduced by courtesy of Bill Clark from www.south-lakes-uk.co.uk

More Dixon confusion

A letter appeared in the *Westmorland Gazette* in 1915, when John Dixon's vessel was replaced by the new ferry, with an old poem reciting that the designer of the ferry had later brought Cleopatra's Needle to London:

'My six and forty years of running,
Attest the engineering cunning
And genius of that master mind,
By which I was at first designed.
His was the Herculean fame,
Of bringing to the banks of Thame,
That mighty monolith we see,
Raised to the Queen of Anthony.'

This was sent in by a George Dixon of Howe End, Far Sawrey, so it might reasonably be supposed that he was a relative of John Dixon. However, this is not the case; this George was the youngest son of the George Dixon, the first superintendent of the Quaker North of England Agricultural School in Great Ayton, North Riding of Yorkshire. There is no documentary evidence that these Dixons, known as the Dixons from Staindrop, were from the same family as the Dixons from Raby and Cockfield. Dixon family genealogists have tended to believe that they were part of the same family, but on a branch that divided in the distant past.

This letter probably gave rise to the incorrect assumption that a George Dixon had designed the ferry.

Acknowledgements

Dick White for his kind assistance with information on the ferry and the Curwen family.

Staff at the Kendal Records Office for access to records.

The North Eastern Railway Association for information on train timetables.

Bill Clark (www.southlakes-uk.co.uk) for providing images of the ferry.

References

The Great Age of Steam on Windermere
George H Pattinson
Windermere Nautical Trust, Windermere, 1981
Describes John Dixon's ferry but wrongly attributes it to 'George Dixon of *Balla Wray*'.

The Windermere Ferry, history, boats, ferrymen and passengers
Dick White
Helm Press, Kendal, Cumbria, 2002
A good history of the ferry, although there is some confusion about the identity of George Dixon.

Westmorland Gazette, 12 November 1870
Article in praise of the improved service offered by the new ferry and the men employed who were 'prompt and obliging'.

Mechanics, &c., Wanted
London Daily Chronicle and Clerkenwell News,
26 August 1871, page 3
John Dixon's advertisement for a ferry operator

General News - Setting fire to the Windermere Ferry Boat
The Yorkshire Post and Leeds Intelligencer, Leeds,
27 July 1872, page 7
Report on the hearing at Appleby Assizes.

The Curwen Family of Workington Hall
Reference D Cu /3/191Correspondence from 1870
Reference D Cu/3/193 Correspondence from 1872
Whitehaven Archive Centre, Cumbria Record Office and Local Studies Library
Letters concerning the start of the steam ferry operation, the lease of the hotel and the dispute over the lake steamers picking up ferry passengers.

A Windermere Ferry Case
Lancaster Gazette and General Advertiser for Lancashire, Westmorland and Yorkshire,
17 January 1877
Court case between John Dixon and the Curwen estate, John Dixon claiming that 'opposition ferries' were not to be allowed, whereas the Curwens had allowed lake steamers to take passengers to Bowness.

Law Intelligence - Notices this day - High Court of Justice
The Morning Post, London, 19 June 1877, page 7
John Dixon's request to appeal: Chancery Division, Rolls Chambers, Chancery Lane, before Mr. Church, Chief Clerk, at 12 - Dixon v Curwen.

Law Notices - this day - High Court of Justice, Chancery Division
London Evening Standard, 15 February 1879, page 6
Dixon v Curwen, opposed petitions.

Letters
Westmorland Gazette, 30 January 1915
Letter from George Dixon of Howe End, Far Sawrey, with an old poem stating that the designer of the ferry had later brought Cleopatra's Needle to London. In fact this was George Dixon junior (1846-1923) the youngest son of George Dixon (1812-1904) who was the first superintendent of the large Quaker school in Great Ayton. Although there is no direct evidence, it is generally supposed that this Dixon family branch, from Staindrop, shared common ancestors with the Cockfield Dixons. George Longstaff and Waynman Dixon both believed this to be more than likely.

Balla Wray Visitors' Book 1871-90 and 1890-1907
Reference WDX 184 A1543 (11/7/90)
Kendal Archive Centre, Kendal County Offices, Kendal
Lists visitors from the Richardson and Dixon families, with some sketches and diary entries.

7 Isle of Wight

Among the twelve seaside piers built around the coast of the Isle of Wight are piers at Ventnor and Shanklin. There is no direct evidence for John Dixon's involvement with the pier at Ventnor, although the obituary of Reginald Middleton implies that he was engaged in its design and construction. In the early 1870s Middleton spent some time in Dixon's offices at No.1 Laurence Pountney Hill as an assistant engineer. John did construct the pier at Shanklin in 1888, along with his colleague Alfred Thorne. In view of his poor health at the time, it is probable that Alfred Thorne carried out most of the work.

Ventnor Pier

Ventnor had debated the desirability of building a pier and breakwater since 1846, when a public meeting was called to consider the matter. The next year a detailed proposal for financing a pier with a competition for its design was published and generated much interest. A committee was set up to further the proposals and there was talk of setting up a company, but the scheme came to nothing.

Fifteen years later, in 1861, the Ventnor Pier and Harbour Company issued its prospectus to raise £15,000 for building two masonry breakwaters, some 700 feet apart, to form a harbour. Mr Saunders, engaged as the company engineer, was probably Theodore R Saunders, who would later be the resident engineer for the Royal Victoria Pier at Ventnor. The prospectus was extremely vague about the pier, other than to be optimistic about the potential tolls from shipping; there was no mention of its use for promenading. The editor of *The Isle of Wight Observer*, published in Ryde which, in 1814, had the first pier in the country, was unimpressed. The depth of water in the harbour at low tide would be insufficient, and he recalled the past attempts to give Ventnor a pier:

> 'The greatest drawback, however, which we see against this scheme is the narrow-minded and culpable apathy of the inhabitants with regard thereto; and if they do not take the initiative in their local matters, and subscribe liberally for shares, it is grossly childish on their parts to pray to Hercules to help them.'

In spite of his pessimism, April 1863 saw construction begin on the two breakwaters, with sixty men driving parallel lines of timber piles into the seabed, boarding them across and in-filling with hard core, rocks and soil. There was no pier as such but, confusingly, press reports often referred to the two breakwaters as piers. Within two months 260 feet of the planned 300 feet of the western breakwater were completed and opened to the public. At the beginning of July, the paddle-steamer *Chancellor* began a service between Ventnor harbour and Ryde, using the partly completed western breakwater. On the first day the vessel moored alongside the breakwater at high tide without any trouble. But the next day, with a falling tide, the captain was suspicious of approaching the breakwater. He was encouraged to do so by the assembled crowds shouting that there was plenty of water. *Chancellor* duly tied up, but as the tide receded, she became stranded on a rock. Next morning, she began to take in water before a heavy swell lifted the vessel, causing her to break in two amidships.

Work on the two breakwaters was completed in late spring 1864. Belatedly recognising the potential as a promenade pier, railings and seats were installed along the western breakwater, with a charge for admission. Poor construction of the breakwaters led to damage on several occasions, culminating in 1867 when winter storms carried away a good section of the structures and the project was abandoned. The remains of the two breakwaters were sold by auction.

A new proposal for Ventnor pier

Undeterred by the ever-present likelihood of Channel storms, in 1870 local businessmen George Mead Burt and Fletcher Moor set up the Ventnor Pier and Esplanade Company with a capital of £35,000. Their intention was to build an iron pier extending seawards for about 700 feet from the site of the previous western breakwater, with an embankment and esplanade along the shoreline. Board of Trade approval was granted, over-riding objections from a householder living above the site that smoke from the buildings on the pier would affect his property.

The take-up of shares was extremely slow, and only one tenth of the authorised £35,000 was raised. In spite of reluctance by potential shareholders to commit to the project, work began in December 1871. It was said that the promoters were keen to keep all the shares within the town, and to exclude 'metropolitan speculators'. Contractors were Roe and Grace of Southampton, who were well-regarded for their work on piers. By the following year, 478 feet of the proposed 700 feet had been completed and this section of the pier was opened to the public. The cost of £3,500 had exhausted the available funds, which included a loan from the Capital and Counties Bank. However, there was public enthusiasm for the pier, with praise from a town guide:

> '… a new pier which is its favourite promenade, the charge for admittance is 2d per person, periodical tickets are also issued. A band of music usually plays at the end of the pier during summer months. Should the tourist be so fortunate as to visit the spot on a beautiful moonlight night, he will be entranced by the lovely fairy-like scene, the lights from the houses dotted on every hand …'

However, as had been the case at Southport, the pier was of insufficient length to enable vessels to moor at the end, and passenger traffic was essential to its financial viability. An extension of 120 feet was added a few years later at a cost of £1,200. Difficulties were then experienced in finding the £1,000 needed to construct a landing stage at the end of the pier. By the summer of 1879 only £345 of the necessary £1,000 was forthcoming, but the work was eventually completed two years later.

Disaster befell the pier in 1881. At 2:30pm on Sunday 27 November a violent gale carried away about one third of the structure. First to be washed away was the recently-completed landing stage, soon followed by the entire pier head with the bandstand, together with about 40 feet of the pier structure. Damage was estimated at £3,000 and led to the winding up of the Ventnor Pier and Esplanade Company.

Ventnor Pier' photograph. The possible involvement of John Dixon and Reginald Middleton in the design of the pier at Ventnor is open to doubt. The pier was largely destroyed by storms in 1881. Reproduced by courtesy of Martin Easdown from his Marlinova Collection.

Who designed the pier?

It is not certain who designed the pier. Records gathered by the late Faye Brown, and now with the Ventnor Local History Society, contain a reference to a shareholder meeting of December 1870 in which an estimate was received from John William Grover (1836-1892). Grover, a civil engineer, worked with Richard Ward on the design and construction of the iron pier at Clevedon, Somerset, in 1868, and he designed an iron pier for the Royal Arsenal at Woolwich in 1870. However, his obituaries did not mention the pier at Ventnor.

There is evidence that a design for the pier originated in John Dixon's office. Reginald Empson Middleton was a civil engineer who briefly worked for John at the Laurence Pountney Hill office in the early 1870s. Middleton's obituary stated that, when working for John Dixon, he was 'engaged on the designing and construction of piers and viaducts at Ventnor, Whitby, and other places'. The reference to viaducts is to those on the Whitby to Loftus railway. The pier at Ventnor must surely be the pier built in 1872-73. In spite of searching contemporary newspapers, no specific reference to John Dixon and the Ventnor Pier has been found. Of course, it maybe that Dixon and Middleton unsuccessfully tendered for the pier.

The excellent book, *Piers of Hampshire and the Isle of Wight,* credits Roe and Grace with the pier, but they were primarily engineering contractors rather than designers. Is it possible that they contracted out the design to John Dixon's office?

Who's who
Reginald Empson Middleton (1845-1925)

Reginald Empson Middleton was born at St Bees in 1845, the son of the local curate, Joseph Empson Middleton. He was educated at St Bees Academy, followed by Charterhouse School from 1858 to 1861. Rather than go on to university, Reginald took an apprenticeship at the Robert Stephenson Works in Newcastle upon Tyne from 1861 to 1865. It seems more than likely that this was arranged through the Dixon family.

George Dixon (1820-1876) was born in Cockfield and worked for many years as a colliery viewer around Cockfield. He and John Dixon were both great grandsons of George Dixon (1731-1785). At some time in the 1850s this George Dixon and his wife Isabella moved to Whitehaven; Isabella had been born in St Bees in 1821. George was employed by the local ironstone mines and trained his young step-brother John Alexander Dixon (1847-1888) as a mining engineer. After Isabella's death, George married Bridget Noble, who had been born in 1835 at St Bees. The Middleton family would certainly have known George Dixon, who would have no doubt fostered Reginald Middleton's interest in engineering. Of course, John Dixon had also been a Robert Stephenson apprentice from 1849 to 1856.

After completing his apprenticeship, Reginald gained experience on the Whitehaven, Cleator and Egremont Railway and in 1870 worked with James Brunlees on the Solway Junction Railway (John Dixon rebuilt the Solway Viaduct in 1882-83). It seems that John assisted Reginald in the early stages of his engineering career by giving him work on the Southport Pier extension in 1867. After a period in Spanish Honduras on the Honduras Inter-Oceanic Railway, Reginald returned to England and became an assistant to John at No.1 Laurence Pountney Hill, sometime in the early 1870s. While there he must have been engaged on the design of the Whitby to Loftus railway viaducts and the pier at Ventnor, if his obituary is correct.

Reginald Middleton left No.1 Laurence Pountney Hill to become resident engineer at the Cadiz Water Works, then in 1876 set up his own consultancy in Westminster, specialising in bridges, drainage and piers. In 1883 he was in charge of setting out measurements for the Forth Railway Bridge, on which work he published a book in 1887. He also published works on surveying and water supplies. In later life he concentrated on water supplies, was appointed Assistant Commissioner to the Royal Commission on Metropolitan Water Supply in 1892 and was extensively consulted on water supplies.

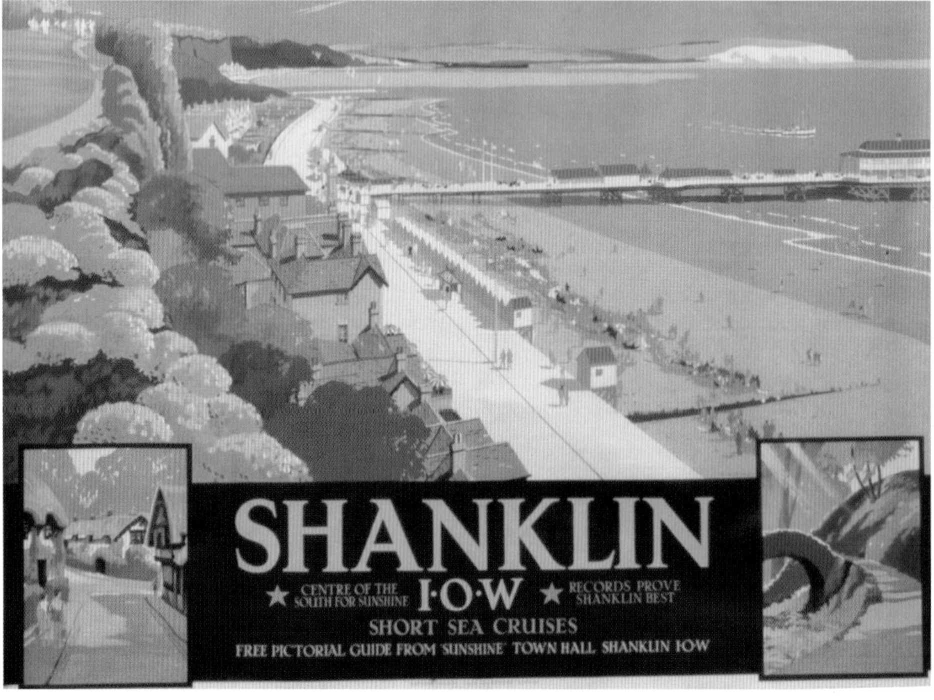

Above) 'Isle of Wight, The Pier, Shanklin' postcard. The pier as built by John Dixon, before the addition of the central pavilion in 1909. By this time the active use of bathing machines was declining, and those shown may have been used as stationary changing rooms, rather than for transporting bathers, anxious to preserve modesty, into the water.
Reproduced by courtesy of Ian Boyle of Simplon Postcards at www.simplonpc.co.uk

Right) 'Shanklin I·O·W' Southern Railway Trade Advertising Service poster. A 20th century image of the pier with the central pavilion. The poster emphasises the importance of a pier, particularly one offering sea cruises, to resorts eager to attract visitors.
Reproduced by courtesy of Dave Jones of Grand Central Railway Auctions.

The pier rebuilt

Following the damage to the pier in the storms of 1881, the Ventnor Local Board purchased the remains and proposed to build a replacement. A new pier company was established. Henry E Wallis drew up plans, and promptly spent his honeymoon at Ventnor. But the question of the new pier revived the caustic comments about the townsfolk of Ventnor made in *The Isle of Wight Observer* in 1885. Should the old pier be rebuilt, or should there be a new structure? Public disagreement, accusations of press censorship and a Board of Trade enquiry ensued. Eventually Wallis submitted revised plans, incorporating rebuilding part of the existing pier, to a length of 650 feet. The contract for construction was given to Mr Trehearne at the end of 1885; Theodore Saunders was his resident engineer. The new pier was completed by October 1887 at a cost of £8,600 and named 'The Royal Victoria Pier' although the opening ceremony was by the Attorney General and not Her Majesty.

The rebuilt pier fared much better than its predecessors. In 1939 a section was removed as it was feared it could be used as an enemy landing site, but the structure was restored and reopened in 1955. Although popular with holiday makers, little was spent on maintaining the pier, and following a fire in 1985 and further storm damage it was declared unsafe. It was finally demolished in 1993.

John Dixon's tenders for work on the Isle of Wight

John Dixon submitted tenders for three contracts on the Isle of Wight in the period when the building of an iron pier was under discussion in Ventnor. He tendered for the supply of cast iron pipes for a new reservoir at Cowes in 1867, and the following year he unsuccessfully tendered for the supply of cast iron pipes for an outfall at Ventnor, and separately for their installation. This does not imply any particular interest in the Isle of Wight on Dixon's part, since lists of calls for tender were available within civil engineering, building and contracting circles.

Shanklin Pier, two false starts

In common with many other seaside towns, Shanklin saw optimistic pier companies announce plans but fail before any construction could begin. In November 1864 the Shanklin Bay Pier Company Limited announced that it was to apply to the Board of Trade for an order to construct a promenade pier, 1,200 feet long or thereabouts, near the Coast Guard House. The application trundled through the laid down procedure, and a provisional order obtained in April 1885 for the pier, which it was estimated might cost an exorbitant £24,000. Nothing further happened until 1883 when the company was dissolved.

In 1877 a group of local gentry, concerned that the frequent pleasure boats cruising round the Isle of Wight could not stop at Shanklin, revived the idea of a pier. After many private meetings, the Shanklin Pier Company emerged in mid-1878, with a capital of £8,000. A pier of 1,250 feet length was proposed, which would allow steamers to land at any state of the tides. Cost estimate was a more realistic £7,000. It proved difficult to reach agreement with the Lord of the Manor and the Local Board, who wished to prevent the pier company using it to transfer goods which might conflict with pleasure use (the nature of such goods was left to the imagination). Eventually an application was submitted to the Board of Trade and approved in June 1881. Plans were drawn up by the London partnership of Henry David Davis and Borrow Emanuel, architects and surveyors, but the necessary capital could not be raised. Perhaps the violent gales of April 1882 deterred potential investors.

Construction of Shanklin Pier eventually starts

In 1885, by which time most of the island's resorts had pleasure piers, there was a more determined effort to build a pier at Shanklin, and this time the promoters were fully supported by the Lord of the Manor and the Local Board. The 1,200 feet long pier was to be constructed near the centre of the Esplanade. The Shanklin Esplanade Pier Company was set up, with a share capital of £12,000 in £2 shares. Parliamentary approval was given, but anticipated costs had risen and the share capital was increased to a surprising £30,000. The pier was designed by F C Dixon (whose identity remains a mystery) and Martyn Noel Ridley. John Dixon and Alfred Thorne were awarded the construction contract and work began in August 1888. Thorne had frequently worked with Dixon, the latest being the previous year's rebuilding of the Hammersmith Suspension Bridge. Given John Dixon's deteriorating health, Alfred Thorne took the leading role in the pier's construction. Raising sufficient finance soon became a problem. In February 1889 a revised contract was agreed with Alfred Thorne at a cost of £23,240, part of which would be paid in company shares. Work proceeded slowly, dictated by the availability of funds. It seems that the partially completed pier was in use from early in 1890, although it was not officially opened until 18 August, and even then it was not completely finished. On Whit Monday, when the Shanklin Rowing Club held races off the pier, more the 1,100 visitors passed through the turnstiles to watch the events and listen to the Shanklin Town Band.

A guide to the holiday attractions on the Isle of Wight, published in 1890, noted that at Shanklin 'bathing good, pier long and unfinished, shops good but dear, lodgings excellent and sanitarily certified.'

Financial woes

By September 1890 the directors were reported to be almost in despair at raising the capital needed to complete the pier. Only 1,886 of the authorised 6,000 shares had been taken up. William H Willis, a prominent local figure, then offered a loan of £6,000 in addition to his £2,000 worth of shares. Even this was insufficient, and a further £450 was needed to complete the pier head and enable steamers to come alongside. Mr Willis announced that he would purchase more shares to cover this work, to great cheers at the directors' meeting.

Financial woes continued, not helped by the storms of March 1891 which washed away the landing stage at the end of the pier although it was rebuilt by the summer. Interest on Willis's loan was unpaid; his patience was exhausted by February 1892 and the receiver was called in. There were no purchasers when the receiver put the pier up at auction, so it was kept open and some improvements made with additions of a bathing stage, shelters, lavatories and a bandstand. Finally, in 1900 the Extension Pier (Shanklin) Company was formed and bought it from the receiver for £12,500.

Under its new ownership the pier was more successful, and in 1908 Alfred Thorne was engaged to build a pavilion on the central section of the pier. Unfortunately, this was destroyed by fire in 1918, but rebuilt in 1927. The pier remained popular until the Second World War when a section was blown up to prevent it being used as an enemy landing. In 1944 one of the PLUTO (Pipe Line under the Ocean) lines was laid along the pier but never used. With the wartime gap bridged with a concrete structure, the pier was restored as a holiday attraction until the great storm of 1987 destroyed most of the structure. An attempt to rebuild it failed, and it was finally demolished for scrap in 1993.

John Dixon, recognised pier constructor

A paper on piers was presented to the Society of Engineers in 1875, in which John Dixon's contributions to pier construction were featured. By the mid-1870s, Dixon was a recognised exponent of pier construction using a pile-driver to sink the columns into the sand. He favoured columns of 8 inch internal diameter and 1 inch thickness, with four projecting ribs running the length of the column. Fracture of the casting when piling was avoided by inserting a wooden dolly above the head of the column, with a ring of rubber between the dolly and the upper flange of the column.

The same paper detailed dimensions and costs of twelve piers. Construction costs per foot ranged from £5 to £14, partly dependent on the overall design but no doubt partly reflecting the efficiency of the contractor. Dixon's Douglas pier was a creditable £6 per foot, his Southport pier extension came out at £7 18s 4¾d per foot.

Acknowledgements

Martin Easdown, probably the most knowledgeable authority on British piers.

Lesa Davies of the Isle of Wight Heritage Service.

Michael Freeman for information on the Ventnor pier, in particular searching for any reference to its designer in the files of the late Fay Brown, an expert in Ventnor local history.

References

Piers of Hampshire and the Isle of Man
Martin Easdown and Linda Sage
Amberley Publishing, Stroud, 2011
A comprehensive work with many references from the National Archives at Kew; includes the piers at Shanklin and Ventnor.

Piers of the Isle of Wight, a nostalgic review
Marian Lane
Isle of Wight Council, Newport, Isle of Wight, 1996
Includes a detailed history of the Ventnor pier but with no mention of John Dixon.

Classified advertising
The Times, London, 5 October 1846, page 3
Public meeting to consider a new pier and breakwater at Ventnor.

Pier at Ventnor
Isle of Wight Observer, Ryde, 12 September 1857, page 3
Letter to the editor detailing how a pier at Ventnor might be financed and designed.

Ventnor
Hampshire Telegraph and Sussex Chronicle, and General Advertiser for Hants, Sussex, Surrey, Dorset and Wilts, Portsmouth, 5 October 1861, page 8
Prospectus issued by the Ventnor Pier and Harbour Company to raise £15,000.

Ventnor Pier and Harbour Company
Isle of Wight Observer, Ryde, 2 November 1861, page 4
A proposal to build two masonry breakwaters to form a harbour, with a pier extending from the eastern breakwater. Accompanying editorial cast scathing remarks about the lack of enterprise among the inhabitants of Ventnor.

Total wreck of the Excursion Steamer Chancellor
The Hampshire Advertiser, Portsmouth, 4 July 1863, page 4
Steamer *Chancellor* moored alongside the new pier but grounded at low tide, becoming a total wreck.

Cowes
The Isle of Wight Observer, Ryde, 6 April 1867, page 3
Three tenders received for water pipes, one from John Dixon and Company, Abchurch Yard, London. The Cowes Board of Health engineer is to decide which to accept.

Ventnor Local Board
The Isle of Wight Observer, Ryde, 9 May 1868, page 3
Tenders for outfall works: Contract 7 for supply of cast iron pipes, eight tenders received including John Dixon, Contract 8 for installation, five tenders including John Dixon.

Piers and Harbours in the Isle of Wight
Hampshire Telegraph and Sussex Chronicle, and General Advertiser for Hants, Sussex, Surrey, Dorset and Wilts, Portsmouth, 9 March 1870, page 4
Board of Trade proposes to proceed with orders for piers at Alum Bay and Ventnor. Mr Richards' objections insufficient to prevent pier at Ventnor.

Shareholder meeting of December 1870
Files of the late Fay Brown, Ventnor and District Local History Society
Reference to an estimate received from a civil engineer by the name of Mr Grover, described as 'connected with Clevedon, Woolwich and other piers'.

Proceedings of the Institution of Mechanical Engineers, December 1925, page 1287-88
Memoirs - Reginald Empson Middleton
Obituary of Reginald Middleton with a list of his works, including his work with John Dixon at Laurence Pountney Hill where he was 'engaged on the designing and construction of piers and viaducts at Ventnor, Whitby, and other places'.

Proceedings of the Institution of Mechanical Engineers, Volume 112, 1893
Obituary - John William Grover
Comprehensive obituary which makes no mention of the pier at Ventnor.

Piers and Harbours in the Isle of Wight
Hampshire Telegraph and Sussex Chronicle, and General Advertiser for Hants, Sussex, Surrey, Dorset and Wilts, Portsmouth, Portsmouth, 9 March 1870, page 4
Messrs Burt, Moor and others were setting up The Ventnor Pier and Esplanade Company with a capital of £35,000.

A Pier for Ventnor
The Hampshire Advertiser, Southampton, 1 March 1871, page 4
Work to begin soon on the iron structure.

Ventnor - the new pier
Hampshire Telegraph and Sussex Chronicle, and General Advertiser for Hants, Sussex, Surrey, Dorset and Wilts, Portsmouth, 11 May 1872, page 9
Difficulties in obtaining iron. Contract let for only £7,000, but only £3,500 raised so far.

Ventnor - The Pier Company
The Isle of Wight Observer, Ryde, 20 September 1873, page 6
Directors' first report. The pier was complete at 478 feet in length and a cost of £3,500. They obtained possession from the contractor in April 1873. The pier required an extension of 120 feet to enable steamship traffic, for which the pier depends if it is to be a sound investment. The extension should cost about £1,500 (this was later increased to £2,000).

Ventnor Pier Company
The Isle of Wight Observer, Ryde, 21 February 1874, page 6
Shareholders' meeting told that after eight months the portion of the pier completed had made a profit. £2,000 was needed to extend and complete the pier.

Ventnor Pier and Esplanade Company
The Hampshire Advertiser, Southampton, 24 September 1879, page 4
Bank loan to be paid off, only £345 of the necessary £1,000 for the landing stage raised.

Violent storms - Stranding of a turret ship, Destruction of Ventnor Pier
The Hampshire Advertiser, Southampton, 30 November 1881, page 7
Severe storms on Sunday 27 November destroyed half of the pier.

Ventnor - Terrific gale
The Isle of Wight Observer, Ryde, 3 December 1881, page 6
At 2:30pm on Sunday 27 November the gale carried away about one third of the Ventnor Pier. The landing stage, recently constructed at a cost of £1,200, was first washed down, tearing down several iron girders, followed by the entire pier head with the bandstand, together with about 40 feet of the pier structure. Damage estimated at £3,000. This was the second pier at Ventnor to have succumbed to the violent seas at Ventnor.

Ventnor - The Pier Company
The Isle of Wight Observer, Ryde, 22 September 1883, page 6
Pier Company to be wound up (the pier was later rebuilt).

Ventnor
The Isle of Wight County Press and South of England Reporter, Newport, 28 February 1885, page 8
Mr H Wallis designed new pier and spent his honeymoon at Ventnor.

Ventnor - The latest phase of the pier question
The Isle of Wight County Press and South of England Reporter, Newport, 9 May 1885, page 8
Disagreements over the new pier.

The Ventnor Pier - Board of Trade Enquiry
The Isle of Wight County Press and South of England Reporter, Newport, 29 August 1885, page 7
Debate about the height of the pier, whether to rebuild the existing pier or build a new pier, etc.

The Royal Victoria Pier, Ventnor
The Isle of Wight County Press and South of England Reporter, Newport, 29 August 1885, page 7
The opening ceremony described.

Shanklin Bay Pier
The Isle of Wight Observer, Ryde, 19 November 1864, pages 2-3
An application was to be made for a promenade pier 1,200 feet long.

Abstract of the Provisional Order for Sandown (sic) Bay Pier
The Isle of Wight Observer, Ryde, 28 January 1865, page 3
Further details of the Shanklin pier, including estimate of £24,000.

Shanklin, Sept 19 - A Pier for Shanklin
The Hampshire Advertiser, Southampton, 19 September 1877, page 4
Proposal to set up a pier and landing stage company.

Shanklin, June 19 - A Pier for Shanklin
The Hampshire Advertiser, Southampton, 19 June 1878, page 4
Determination to set up a company to build the pier.

Shanklin - The Local Board and the Pier Company
Hampshire Telegraph and Sussex Chronicle, and General Advertiser for Hants, Sussex, Surrey, Dorset and Wilts, Portsmouth, 16 February 1881, page 4
After lengthy objections, agreement reached to apply for a provisional order to erect the pier.

Shanklin - The Pier
The Evening News, Portsmouth, 16 November 1885, page 3
A real effort was being made to promote a pier company.

"Piccadilly" and the Isle of Wight
The Isle of Wight County Press and South of England Reporter, Newport, 16 August 1890, page 5
Quotes from a guide to the Isle of Wight published in *Piccadilly* magazine, pier long and unfinished.

Isle of Wight - Shanklin - Pier Company
The Evening News, Portsmouth, 13 September 1890, page 2
Directors in despair when Mr Willis offered a loan of £6,000.

Aquatic Sports
The Isle of Wight County Press and South of England Reporter, Newport, 31 May 1890, page 8
Over 1,100 visitors to the pier on Whit Monday for the races.

Tremendous storm and great snowfall in the island
The Isle of Wight County Press and South of England Reporter, Newport, 14 March 1891, page 5
Pier landing stage washed away.

8 Egypt and Cleopatra's Needle

John Dixon gained national recognition through the transportation of the obelisk known as Cleopatra's Needle from Alexandria to London, and its erection on the Thames Embankment in 1878. John's association with Egypt had begun in 1870 when he built a bridge over a channel in the Nile at Cairo, employing his young brother, Waynman, as resident engineer. John and Waynman were later engaged by the Scottish Astronomer Royal, Charles Piazzi Smyth, to carry out a survey of the interior of the Great Pyramid. They discovered two passages leading upwards from the Queen's Chamber, the so-called 'air shafts' or 'ventilation passages' which have since been the subject of much speculation and attempted exploration. While Waynman's name is generally associated with these two passages, John's name is linked with three relics retrieved from the foot of the two passages his brother and taken back to London.

Egypt in the 19th century

For centuries Egypt had been part of the Ottoman Empire, but by the end of the 18th century it had assumed strategic importance to Great Britain because of its key position on the route to India, the treasure of the British Empire. In France, Napoleon had ambitions to challenge British supremacy in the east and launched a successful invasion of Egypt in July 1798. His troops were soon followed by an army of administrators, scientists and scholars who attempted to introduce the principles of the age of enlightenment to the lands around the Nile. French historians and archaeologists started a systematic study and recording of the remains of ancient Egypt, notably discovering the Rosetta Stone.

Among British politicians there was increasing alarm at the intentions of their arch-enemy in the Near East. Napoleon's fleet, which hitherto had managed to evade the attention of the British Navy, was routed by Nelson at the Battle of the Nile in August 1798. In spite of this disaster at sea, Napoleon's campaign on land continued over the next three years and it was not until the British victory at the Battle of Alexandria in August 1801 that he was forced out of Egypt.

The departure of Napoleon led to a civil war, which opened up the opportunity for Muhammad Ali to take control of

'Copper Smiths' Bazaar, Cairo 1871' by E A Goodall. Edward Angelo Goodall (1819-1908) was one of a family of artists. His father was an engraver, his brothers Frederick and Walter, and his sister Eliza, were artists, as were Frederick's sons Howard and Trevelyan. John Dixon was a good friend of Edward Goodall and was present at a dinner party at his house when the possibility of bringing Cleopatra's Needle to London was discussed. Edward and Frederick visited Egypt in 1870.
Painting reproduced by courtesy of Richard Goodall of Canada at www.goodallartists.ca

Egypt, nominally still part of the Ottoman Empire, in 1805. Muhammad Ali, born in what is now Greek Macedonia to Albanian parents, ruthlessly established himself as the undisputed ruler of Egypt, the self-styled 'Khedive'. He shared many of Napoleon's ambitions for Egypt, with state functions based on European practice and with his position supported by military and economic strength.

After Muhammad Ali's death in 1849 his descendants attempted to take control of the country. First was his nephew Abbas I, murdered in 1854, and then his son Said. Both proved to be weak leaders and it was not until his grandson, Ismail, became Khedive after Said's death in 1863 that the former authority of the Khedive was restored. Ismail had grand plans for the modernisation of Egypt. The country was opened up to European ideas, expertise and investment. French influence was still alive and it was French and Egyptian money that realised the dream of the Suez Canal between 1859 and 1869; Britain had regarded the idea as impracticable. During Ismail's reign, British, French, German, Italian and American nationals came to Egypt, reorganising the army and navy, setting up postal and telegraph systems, railways, new industries, irrigation projects, lighthouses, harbours and breakwaters.

Egypt's economy eventually collapsed under the ever-increasing tax burden imposed by Khedive Ismail to finance these grand designs. The situation was retrieved by Disraeli, who stole a march on the French through buying out the Egyptian share of the Suez Canal. Long-standing mutual suspicion between France and Britain was then put aside amid increasing European concern for the future of Egypt. They connived with the Ottoman authorities to have Ismail replaced by his son Tewfik in 1879. An anti-European and anti-Ottoman revolt ensued, led by some elements of the army, and with popular support among the peasants. France and Italy declined to join Britain in military action, and the insurrection was suppressed by the British naval bombardment of Alexandria, followed by a land invasion, in 1882. These actions gave Britain effective control over Egypt, a situation which continued until the 1950s and the Suez debacle.

The British fascination with Egypt

During Ismail's reign, countess travellers boarded a train at Waterloo Station, crossed the Channel and continued their rail journey across Europe to Brindisi, where they took the ferry to Alexandria. This was the first part of the journey for the civil servants and military officers required by the British administrations in India and the Far East. Alexandria was the destination for the entrepreneurs and engineers wishing to do business in Egypt, and for the growing number of tourists. Those who could afford the journey were lured to Egypt by many attractions. There were the archaeological sites, especially those with Biblical associations which were enthusiastically promoted by local guides or dragomans, such as the actual bulrushes where the baby Moses was found. There was the promise of an exotic culture entirely different to the European experience, and without the constraints of European society. There was a hot and dry atmosphere which was believed to provide respite for the many chest complaints brought on by the damp climates and industrial pollution of English towns and cities.

The Nile bridges

In the 17th century a barge laden with stone sank in the Nile, west of Cairo. Over the years a sandbank built up, which later became the island of Geziret. A crossing of the Nile was made via a pontoon bridge from Cairo to the island, followed by a track on top of an earth dam in the channel to the west of the island. Keen to expand trade and tourism, the Khedive Ismail commissioned a programme of improved bridges. The pontoon bridge was replaced by the Kasr el Nil bridge, built by the French Compagnie de Fives-Lille. Construction started in 1869 and the bridge opened in 1872. Pedestrian, ass and camel traffic crossing this bridge was captured in one of the early cine films produced by Auguste and Louis Lumière in 1898. The original wooden deck was replaced with concrete in 1913 by the Cleveland Bridge Company of Darlington. Then in 1933 the Kasr el Nil bridge was replaced by a new structure, built by Dorman Long of Middlesbrough, but retaining the splendid statues of lions on either side of the east and west approaches to the bridge.

When construction had started on the first Kasr el Nil bridge, the dam on the west side of Geziret was still used as the crossing, but it caused restrictions to the flow of the Nile and was at best a rough and ready form of crossing. In 1870 the Egyptian government awarded a contract to Shaw and Thomson for a bridge from Geziret to the west bank. James Shaw engaged John Dixon to carry out the work.

'Le Pont des Anglais'

John Dixon probably carried out most of the design work for this bridge himself. His plans would have been approved by John Fowler (1817-1898), who was advising the Khedive on civil engineering matters, and who would later design the Forth Bridge with Benjamin Baker. Dixon's design was a wrought iron girder bridge supported on cast iron columns, with a swinging section at the west end to allow passage of river vessels. Sixteen cast iron columns, each 88 feet high and 8 feet 6 inches in diameter were sunk into the river bed in pairs, carrying eight wrought iron girder spans. The swinging section of the bridge, forming the final two spans of the bridge, was carried on a group of four smaller cast iron columns. Remarkably it could be swung open by one man.

Construction was managed on site by John's younger brother. On 7 January 1871, then twenty-six years old, Waynman Dixon landed in Egypt to supervise the building of the bridge, which became known as 'Le Pont des Anglais' to distinguish it from the French-built 'Kasr el Nil'.

He had with him a small team of British workers, led by Bill Grundy. The 1,700 tons of ironwork was supplied by Shaw and Thomson and shipped to Egypt.

A tented construction camp was established on site, referred to by Waynman as the 'Ghizah Bridge Works'. A small army of local labourers was recruited. In April 1872 Waynman wrote 'the bell has just rung and the men are coming surging up for their pay, making a perfect babel of talk in Arabic, Turkish, Greek, Maltese, German, French and English.' Managing this workforce must have been a challenge.

The bridge was completed in the autumn of 1872, with John Dixon travelling to Egypt at the end of September to wind up the bridge construction site. 'Le Pont des Anglais' was opened in November 1872 by Prince Hussein Kamel (1853-1917), the son of Khedive Ismail and the Minister for Public Works.

After the opening of 'Le Pont des Anglais', Waynman Dixon remained in Egypt for five years, working on engineering contracts with Fred Dixon. Fred Dixon, unrelated to John and Waynman, was the son-in-law of Henry McKillop (1822-1879) who was in charge of the Egyptian harbours and lighthouses, and later Admiral of the Egyptian Navy. Many of their contracts came from James Shaw, still living in London but a frequent visitor to Egypt, contracts which Waynman modestly described as 'fairly profitable'. One of these contracts was for the construction of an iron lighthouse at Berbereh. The involvement of his older brother John in these contracts is unknown, but later Waynman entered into an agreement on his own behalf with James Shaw to import engines and other machines. When Shaw faced financial collapse in 1875, he attempted to declare his Egyptian ventures bankrupt, which led to acrimonious letters between him and his creditors, including Waynman. Waynman had to sell the stock of engines and machines valued at £20,000 but managed to escape personal loss.

In 1913 the original bridge was replaced with a steel structure on concrete piers, built with Belgian assistance. 'Le Pont des Anglais' was renamed Kobri el Galaa (Evacuation Bridge) after the last British soldier to leave Egypt crossed it in 1955 in the wake of the Suez crisis.

Who's who
James Shaw (1836-1883)

James Shaw was born in Aberdeen in 1836. When he was fifteen he left, penniless and friendless (as he later claimed) to become a junior clerk in a Glasgow metal brokers. Turning twenty-one, and now with a developed business sense, he went into partnership with James Thomson. They traded as iron merchants Shaw and Thomson, from 1858 to 1866, in Queen Street, Glasgow. Moving to London, they continued from offices at No.150 Leadenhall Street. Thomson died in 1870, leaving Shaw as the sole owner. James Shaw was undoubtedly more of a shrewd businessman, sensing any opportunity to make a profit, rather than a practical engineer.

Shaw developed extensive business interests in Egypt, where he counted the Khedive (the governor of Egypt) among his friends. He supplied the iron rails for 150 miles of railways, and also obtained the stores contract from the Egyptian Government. By 1874 he could claim that he had made no less than nineteen visits to Egypt and that every difficulty had been met cordially and honourably by the Khedive's officials. In addition to the work in Egypt, he was supplying iron rails to many foreign governments and obtained other extensive contracts. He had financial interests in two iron works at Stockton on Tees (Stockton Rail Mill Company and Moor Works of Shaw, Johnson and Reay) supplying rails. Shaw became very wealthy and was elected Sheriff of London and Middlesex in 1874. A staunch Conservative, he unsuccessfully stood for Parliament at Aberdeen on three occasions.

This good fortune came to an end in 1875, with the collapse in the iron trade following the introduction of steel rails. James Shaw faced serious financial difficulties. He largely settled with his creditors at home, but his situation in Egypt was more troublesome. In December 1875, Waynman complained about Shaw's behaviour in a letter to his mother. He had received some unpleasant letters, but Waynman excused his behaviour since 'he has had much to try his temper and upset his equanimity, so I make many excuses for him but at the same time have written my sentiments pretty clearly.' There were moves in Egypt to have Shaw declared bankrupt, but Waynman managed to head these off. Shaw's bankruptcy would have had serious implications for Waynman as he held, jointly with Shaw, some £20,000 stock of engines and machines.

Back in England, Shaw recovered from his financial woes and took over the CwmAvon Works, South Wales, in 1877. John Dixon invested capital in this business, which proved highly profitable. By 1881 James Shaw's health had deteriorated and he sold the CwmAvon Works. Two years later, he died.

DETAILS OF BRIDGE OVER THE NILE AT GIZEH.

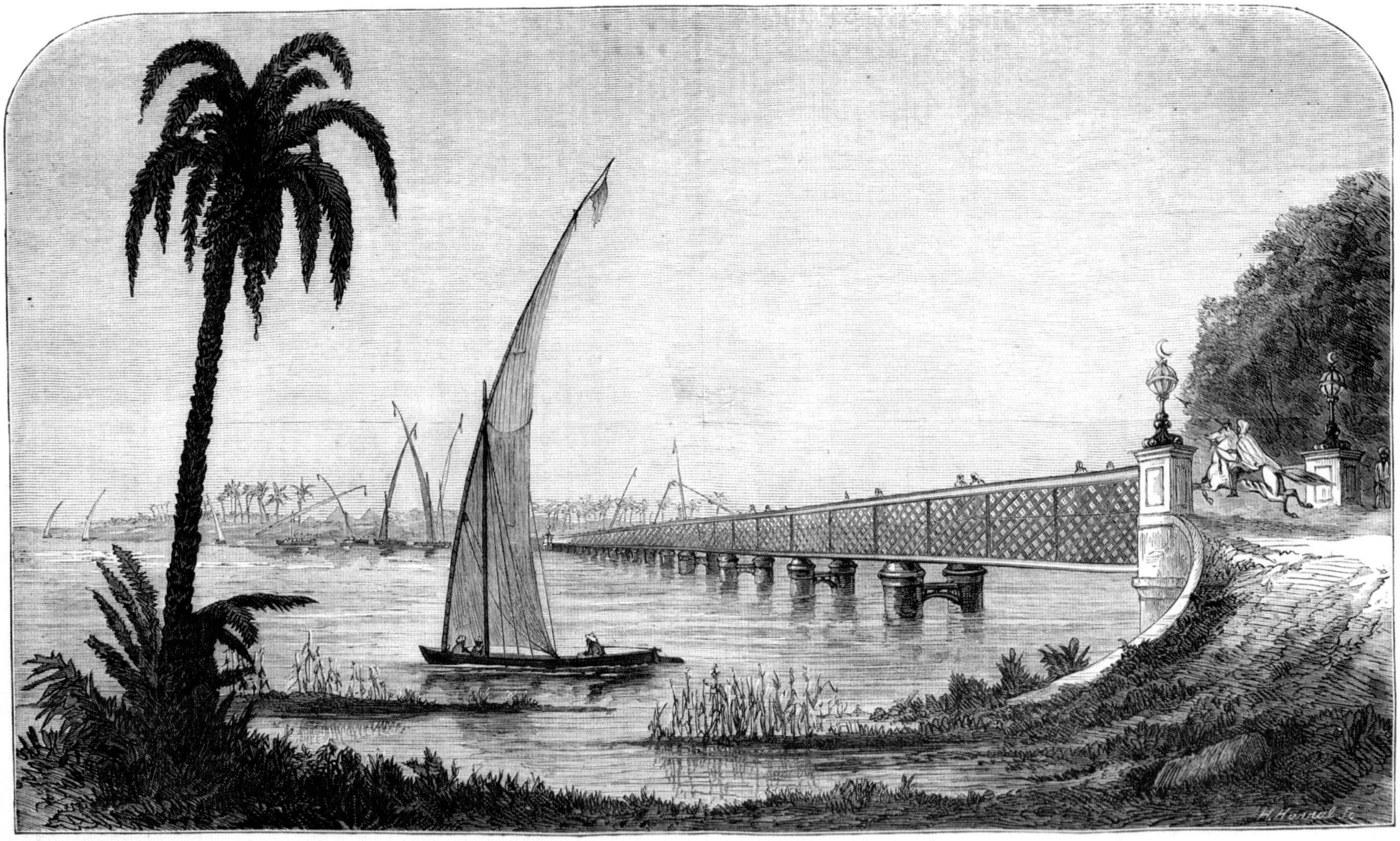

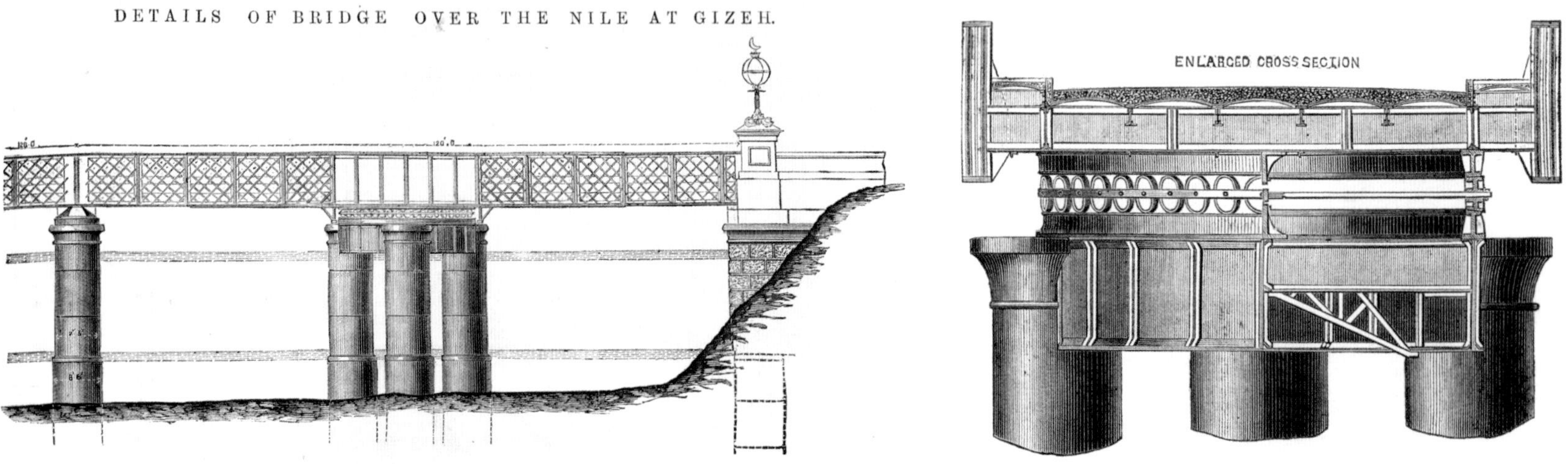

Top) 'Bridge over the Nile at Gizeh' engraving of 'Pont des Anglais' looking west from the island of Geziret towards the pyramids. In this view the opening section is at the far end of the bridge, hence the concentration of vessels near the distant bank.
The Engineer, 6 December 1872, page 379.

Above and right) 'Details of Bridge over the Nile at Gizeh' engravings showing the section of the bridge that could be swung open to allow for river traffic.
The Engineer, 6 December 1872, page 377.

Engineers working in Egypt

With the Khedive's desire to modernise his country, there were many European engineers working in Egypt in the 1870s. Many took their own skilled men, although there were some Egyptian joiners and blacksmiths. Local labourers could be hired cheaply, but they did not enjoy a reputation for hard work. The best accommodation was in Alexandria, where the sea air balanced the excessive heat, and it was at Alexandria that Waynman settled for his seven years in Egypt. Good drinking water was readily available, and food, especially fruit, plentiful and cheap. Foreigners were advised to restrict alcohol consumption to French wine diluted with water, but this warning was ignored by many, leading to a prevalence of liver complaints among the European community. Medical treatment could be a problem, particularly outside Cairo and Alexandria. John and Waynman would have been relieved that they could rely on their good friend Dr Grant for medical advice; Arab barbers acted as doctors, but their interventions were apparently confined to bleeding or applying leeches.

Charles Piazzi Smyth

Charles Piazzi Smyth (1819-1900) was the Scottish Astronomer Royal from 1846 to 1888. Charles's destiny was surely in the stars; his father was a highly regarded amateur astronomer, and his godfather was a famous Sicilian astronomer. As a young man he spent ten years in Southern Africa working at the Royal Observatory at the Cape of Good Hope. He was then appointed Scottish Astronomer Royal and moved to Edinburgh, where he married Jessie Duncan in 1855. The following year Robert Stephenson lent them his yacht for a voyage to investigate the potential of Tenerife for astronomical investigations. From the mid-1860s, Piazzi Smyth became increasingly fascinated by the Egyptian pyramids. This interest started with the romantic conjecture that the standard inch was somehow related to the Biblical cubit, and that the geometry of the Great Pyramid at Giza had been set out by divine guidance. Such theories were propagated by John Taylor (1781-1864), a writer and publisher with no scientific background, who believed that the mathematical pi and golden mean were incorporated into the dimensions of the Great Pyramid.

All of this lured the Piazzi Smyths to Egypt where they spent four uncomfortable months trying to survey the Great Pyramid. From these investigations Charles published his book *Our Inheritance in the Great Pyramid* in 1864, which became hugely popular. He was convinced that modern measurement systems derived from ancient Egypt and the hand of God, with the 'sacred cubit' equivalent to 25.02 inches and the 'pyramid inch' equivalent to 1.001 inches.

Piazzi Smyth's increasing involvement in 'pyramidology' not surprisingly resulted in his rejection by the scientific community. He retired from Edinburgh in 1888 and moved to Ripon in Yorkshire. He and his wife are buried, appropriately, under a pyramid-shaped tombstone at Sharow, near Ripon.

Correspondence between Piazzi Smyth and the Dixons

Charles Piazzi Smyth knew that he needed an accurate survey of the Great Pyramid in order to advance his theories about its design and measurements, but he also knew his personal limitations as a surveyor. In 1871 he became acquainted with John and Waynman Dixon, who were working on Le Pont des Anglais, through Dr James Grant. The Dixons struck up a friendship with Piazzi Smyth and were both enthusiastic about the idea of a survey of the Great Pyramid, particularly Waynman.

The brothers then corresponded with Charles Piazzi Smyth, and their letters are preserved in the Royal Observatory Library in Edinburgh. From 1871 to the end of 1872 the letters were written by John, but thereafter by Waynman. They provide a good illustration of their different personalities. John's letters are always brief and to the point, none more so than one written on 27 September 1872:

> 'Dear Sir,
> Can you tell me what is about the temperature of the Delta water close inshore about halfway between Suez & Aden? I'm asked about a condensing apparatus for fresh water at Jeddah, the port of Mecca, to supply the Pilgrims. I'm off to Egypt beginning of week.
> Yours truly, John Dixon'

At the end of 1872, when the survey and the bridge were complete, John's letters ceased. From then Waynman took over the correspondence, developing an apparently close friendship with the Smyths and an interest in the pyramid theories. His letters are much longer, often with greetings to Mrs Smyth, and continued until 1882, ten years after John's last correspondence.

The work on the Great Pyramid

It would appear that John was in Egypt in November 1871, and he was certainly there for several weeks in March 1872, returning in September for the opening of the bridge and again in November on a hurried visit. The remainder of the time he was relaying information to Piazzi Smyth from his brother's letters. Whereas Waynman was fascinated by Egypt and became a recognised Egyptologist, John's interest was fleeting. As he explained in a letter of April 1872, prompted by finding a lengthy letter from Piazzi Smyth waiting for him on his return to London:

> 'I am too busily occupied discharging the accumulation of business matters to have time for a few days to devote any attention to its contents which I doubt not I shall find interesting and for the same

reason will not report to you our Pyramid matters and research until I can give it due leisure.'

As if to prove the point, Piazzi Smyth had to wait five months for John's next letter.

John was keen that the piles of stones surrounding the Great Pyramid should be cleared away. He had thought of using these stones as rubble in the supports of 'Le Pont des Anglais', but the distance between the two sites made this impracticable, given the primitive transport arrangements. He then suggested to Piazzi Smyth that money could be raised to get the job done. He would put in £50 himself and he was sure that the Duke of Sutherland and John Fowler would each contribute £250. The Duke of Sutherland had accompanied the Prince of Wales on his visit to Egypt in 1869 and John Fowler had been advising the Egyptian government on various civil engineering projects. Nothing came of these thoughts.

Piazzi Smyth was keen to investigate the possibility of shafts leading off the Queen's Chamber, similar to the twin shafts from the King's Chamber discovered by Howard Vyse in 1837. When Waynman did indeed discover two passages leading from the Queen's Chamber, John reported this to Piazzi Smyth. Smyth thought they were ventilating shafts, but John pointed out that this theory was rather upset by the fact that they were sealed off from the main chamber by five inches of stone. There was also the thought that passages from the King's Chamber might be connected to passages from the Queen's Chamber. To test this theory John suggested firing a pistol into one passage while holding a lighted candle in the other and looking for any movement in its smoke. Waynman and James Grant carried out this experiment but saw no movement in the candle flame.

John was convinced that there was another passage beneath the entrance passage, and they had drilled down in the floor of the entrance passage without result. At this point John, ever a man to confront problems directly and with little regard for antiquity, thought of breaking into the lower level of the pyramid from the outside. There was a precedent for such brutal attack. In the ninth century Caliph Abdallah al-Mamun, unable to achieve his dream of destroying the Great Pyramid, had settled for opening up a breach in the outer masonry, leading to the Ascending Passage, after six weeks of hard labour. At this time there was little protection for the ancient monuments, although Waynman Dixon and James Grant were later admonished by the French archaeologist Auguste Mariette (1821-1881) who had been placed in charge of Egypt's monuments by the Khedive.

During John's hurried visit to Egypt in November 1872, Waynman and James showed him the interior of the Great Pyramid. John was all for calling the newly-discovered passages 'Dixon's Passages' but, sadly, this name never caught on. He visited the Petrified Forest between Cairo and Suez, where he collected some samples of fossilised pine. Waynman handed over three relics to his brother, which John brought back to England packed in a cigar box.

The three relics

In the course of creating openings into the twin passages Waynman came across three items which had lain undisturbed since the pyramid was sealed over four thousand years ago:

- A small double hook of bronze, some two inches across the tips of the hooks, with riveted pins securing it to a fragment of wooden handle, at the foot of the ascending channel of the southern passage.
- A stone ball with average diameter 2¾ inches and weighing 1 pound 3 ounces, at the foot of the ascending channel in the northern passage. Usually said to be granite, Piazzi Smyth thought it of green stone rather than granite and immediately assumed that it was an old Mina weight.
- A length of cedar wood, 5 inches long and with a rectangular cross section of ½ inch width, was found alongside the granite ball. Piazzi Smyth noted that there were two small tooth-like stones set into one surface.

John first sent the three items to Charles Piazzi Smyth in Edinburgh, where they arrived on 26 November 1872 and were recorded in Smyth's journal. They were then returned to John, who arranged for them to be illustrated in *Nature* magazine the following month, with an accompanying article by Henry Williams Chisholm (1809-1901). Chisholm, the Warden of Standards at the Board of Trade, was particularly interested in the possibility that the granite ball was a weight. After questioning several experts of the day, Chisholm concluded that it might indeed be equivalent to the ancient Egyptian Mina weight. Waynman later criticised the article for being 'full of many egregious errors'. One such error, pointed out by Smyth, was an incorrect base length of the pyramid, but the nature of other errors is not clear.

The article in *Nature* was picked up by the popular press, and there was further speculation as to the purpose of the three items. Suggestions included the ball being used as a hammer or as a plumb bob; further evidence for use as a plumb bob was the presence of small white spots on its surface, which may have been from mason's chalk marks. The article appearing in *The Graphic* and in the American *Harper's Weekly* included a sketch by John Dixon of the three items along with the two foot long casing stone, found separately by Waynman in a heap of debris on the northern side of the pyramid. He saved it from being broken up for building stone and sent it to a delighted Piazzi Smyth, who was able to use it to determine the exact base length of the pyramid. The inclusion of the huge casing stone in this drawing has misled some to think it was found in the Queen's Chamber 'ventilating shafts' along with the other three items.

The Graphic article included two drawings of the pyramid interior, which it attributed to John Dixon in spite of the artists name 'H Hassan' clearly inscribed on each drawing. Waynman criticised his brother for allowing Hassan's popular sketches to appear with the detailed drawings of the relics and casing stone.

The fate of the relics

The cedar rod was donated to the University of Aberdeen by Dr James Grant. An old catalogue in the library of the University of Aberdeen recorded that the cedar rod had arrived in a glass tube and that it had disintegrated when removed from the tube. The stone ball and the metal hook, in their cigar case, were eventually inherited by John Dixon's great grand-daughter, Beth Porteous, in 1970. Although there was a third item in the case it was not the cedar rod but a small stone, quite possibly one of the small stones originally set into the surface of the cedar rod. Mrs Porteous presented the case and contents to the British Museum in 1972. After a period when they were mislaid, they were rediscovered in 1993 due to the efforts of the author Robert Bauval after a false rumour that they might have been buried under Cleopatra's Needle on the Embankment.

The British Museum describes its two items in mundane terms. Disregarding the speculation that the stone ball was an ancient Egyptian Mina weight, as postulated by Piazzi Smyth and Chisholm, it is merely a 'spherical pounder'. The double bronze hook is a 'metal tool or implement'. Robert Bauval became excited at the possibility of using carbon dating techniques on the length of cedar wood in order to determine the age of the pyramid. Apart from the fact that the cedar wood length no longer exists, the age of the pyramids is known from other sources to within the limits of carbon dating.

The flooring of Sir Henry James

Major General Sir Henry James (1803-1877) was the Director General of Ordnance Survey and had a reputation for being eccentric and egotistical. He was deeply involved in the debates about the significance of the pyramid's dimensions and had published a series of notes on the matter. In these notes he had included a fanciful theory to explain grooves found in the stonework near the 'portcullis block' or 'granite leaf'. The grooves would support the ends of rollers which formed part of an elaborate system of ropes and pulleys, either to have carried the King Cheops, in a truck, to inspect the progress of his pyramid's construction or to lower the 'portcullis block'. When John Dixon published drawings of aspects of the interior of the pyramid in *The Graphic* magazine in December 1872, James enthusiastically sent him a drawing of his ideas. John was contemptuous of James's ideas, pointing out that the rollers would only have supports at one end since there were no corresponding grooves for the opposite ends. John wrote to Piazzi Smyth telling him how he had 'floored Sir H James and his stupid theory' and that this was an example of how one should beware 'haste and inconsiderate hurry on which never accept to jump to conclusions.'

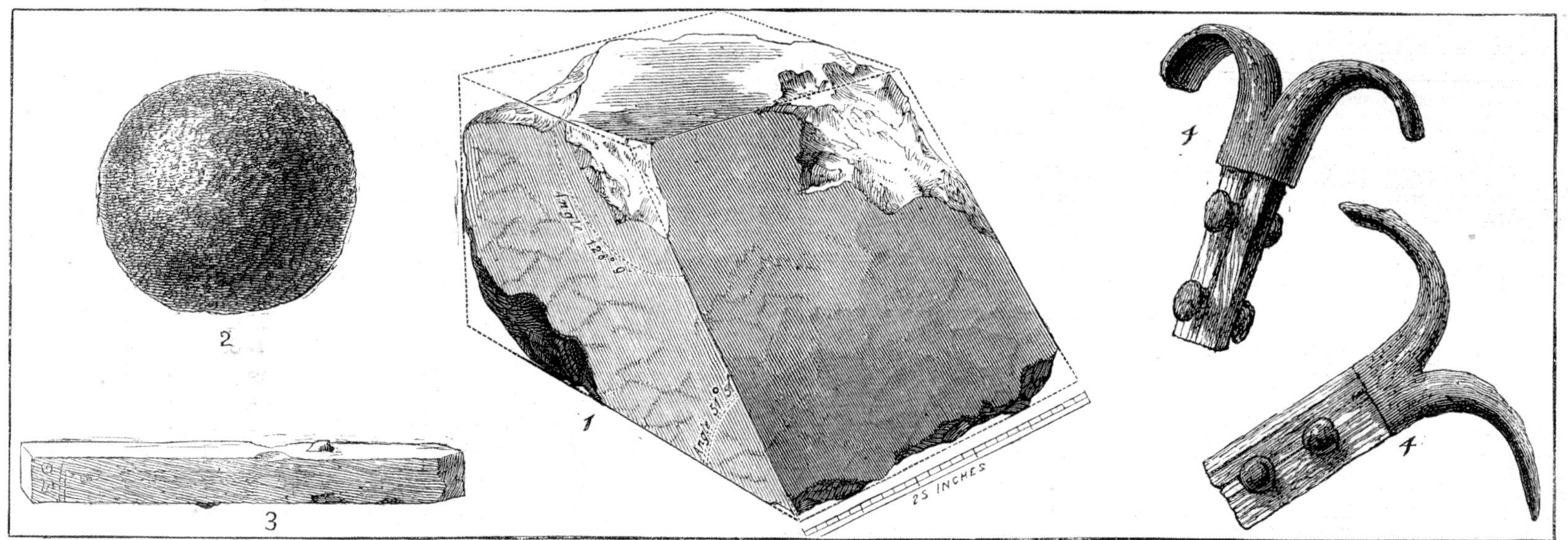

1. Original Casing Stone from North Side—2. Granite Ball, 1 lb. 3 oz. weight—3. Piece of Cedar, apparently a Measure—4. Bronze Instrument with portion of the Wooden Handle adhering to it

DISCOVERIES IN THE GREAT EGYPTIAN PYRAMID

'Discoveries in the Great Egyptian Pyramid' engraving taken from sketches by John Dixon. The granite ball, piece of cedar wood and the bronze hook were found by Waynman Dixon while he and Dr James Grant were carrying out the survey inside the pyramid for Charles Piazzi Smyth. Waynman discovered the casing stone amid piles of stones in the vicinity of the pyramid.

The Graphic, 7 December 1872, page 545 © Illustrated London News Limited/Mary Evans.

Dahabeya cruise up the Nile

At the start of 1873 a party of John Dixon's friends arrived in Egypt. They seem to have been family friends rather than business associates. Waynman was asked to join them and he chartered the dahabeya *Griffin* (a dahabeya was a luxury sailing craft) for a leisurely cruise up the Nile over the following three months. John was not with the party, and only two members of the party are named in Waynman's surviving letters written during the cruise, Tommy Richardson and Mr Waite. This Mr Waite was more than likely a relative of Elizabeth Mounsey (née Waite) the wife of John's partner in the Bedlington Iron Works, Jaspar Capper Mounsey. Elizabeth had been killed in a tragic accident at the Works in 1862, leaving six children. Some of the older children may well have been in the party on the dahabeya. Tommy Richardson's identity is not known, although he does not seem to have been related to John's brother-in-law, James Richardson. On the other hand, there were many Richardsons in Newcastle.

The dahabeya *Griffin* would have been similar to the four dahabeyas used by John Fowler's team of eighteen men led by F Graham, for their survey of the route of the Soudan Railway in 1871-72, indeed *Griffin* may well have been one of these four vessels. A typical dahabeya was about 100 feet long, with cabins, lavatories and a saloon over the rear two-thirds of its deck, with a sun-deck above. The sun deck and the forward part of the main deck were covered by awnings. Food was prepared in the open on the front deck. The dahabeya carried a crew of about six sailors captained by a reis.

Cleopatra's Needle

John and Waynman Dixon are undoubtedly best-known for bringing the obelisk 'Cleopatra's Needle' from Alexandria to London, where it was erected by John on the Thames Embankment. Since this work has been extensively described in other publications, and since the project deserves more space than is possible here, only a brief summary will be given below.

Two ancient obelisks were moved to Alexandria as part of the *Caesareum*, Cleopatra's monument to her lover Julius Caesar. At some later time, one of the obelisks fell to the ground. Immediately after the Battle of Alexandria in 1801, the victorious British troops decided that this fallen obelisk should be transported to England to commemorate the defeat of Napoleon at sea in the Battle of the Nile and on land at the Battle of Alexandria. There was no objection from the Egyptian authorities to its removal, but the British

'Steamer and dahabeahs moored for the night' engraving by J H Rimbault. John Fowler was commissioned by the Khedive to survey a railway between Upper and Lower Egypt. In 1871 his surveying party travelled up the Nile in four dahabeyas and a paddle steamer. This engraving was made from a sketch by G F Jones, one of the surveying party. The dahabeya Griffin chartered by Waynman Dixon may well have been one of the vessels illustrated here. Engineering, 28 February 1873, page 147.

Government steadfastly refused to finance its transportation from Egypt. Nothing was done until the 1870s, when General Sir James Alexander (1803-1885) vigorously campaigned for the obelisk to be brought to England. Apart from the lack of finance, it had not been obvious how to transport the 224 ton granite monolith; the only real precedent had been the obelisk erected in the Place de la Concorde in Paris 1836, which was carried in a specially built ship. When John Dixon was in Egypt for the opening of 'Le Pont des Anglais', Waynman took him to see the fallen obelisk at Alexandria. Waynman designed the wrought iron vessel *Cleopatra* to encase the obelisk, and John had it fabricated in London. John briefly went out to Egypt for its assembly around the obelisk in 1877 and arrangements were made to have it towed to England.

Cleopatra's Needle on the Thames Embankment.

The steamship *Olga* sailed from Alexandria in September 1877 with Waynman on board and the obelisk vessel *Cleopatra* in tow. All went well until the Bay of Biscay, when a ferocious overnight storm necessitated cutting *Cleopatra* free, lest she should collide with *Olga*. In an attempt to rescue the crew aboard *Cleopatra*, six sailors from *Olga* tragically lost their lives. The following morning there was no sight of *Cleopatra* and it was assumed she had sunk to the sea bed. *Olga* proceeded to Falmouth, unaware that *Cleopatra* was still afloat. She was later found by the steamship *Fitzmaurice* and towed into the Spanish port of Ferrol. After repairs she was safely brought to London where John Dixon devised an elegant apparatus to lift the obelisk into the vertical position and lower it down onto the pedestal.

The surgeon Professor Erasmus Wilson had offered to donate the £10,000 estimated cost of bringing the obelisk to London, but on the condition that it arrived safely. He did hand over the £10,000 but then went out of his way to claim credit for the venture. Even more unchivalrous was William Burrell of Glasgow, owner of the *Fitzmaurice*, who hounded John Dixon through the courts for salvage money. This cost Dixon the best part of £10,000 from his own pocket. In spite of talk of a knighthood, John Dixon received little official recognition. Plaques at the foot of Cleopatra's Needle give more prominence to Erasmus Wilson, with not even a mention of Waynman Dixon or Sir James Alexander. Such are the distortions of history.

Waynman was weighed down by the imagined loss of the obelisk and the only too real loss of the six sailors. After *Olga* landed at Falmouth he ceased to work with his brother John and moved to Middlesbrough, where he spent the rest of his working life managing the shipyard on the River Tees owned by his other brother, Raylton.

Acknowledgements

Karen Moran, Librarian at the Royal Observatory, Blackford Hill, Edinburgh for access to the Charles Piazzi Smyth archive.

Shona Elliott at the University of Aberdeen Library for access to Dr Grant's archive and information on the fate of the cedar wood rod, which was donated to the Marischal Museum collection as item ABDUA:24358.

Dr Julie Anderson at the Department of Ancient Egypt and Sudan in the British Museum for information on the current location of the granite ball (their catalogue EA67818 described as a spherical pounder) and the bronze double hook (their catalogue EA67819 described as a metal tool/implement).

Beth Porteous, great grand-daughter of John Dixon, who inherited the cigar box with the stone ball, metal hook and a piece of stone (possibly one of the two stones originally set into the surface of the cedar rod) and donated them to the British Museum.

Dr Bob Brier of New York, who secured much of the Waynman Dixon archive when it was auctioned, including Waynman Dixon's letters home.

References

Details of Bridge over the Nile at Ghizeh
The Engineer, 6 December 1872, page 377 with a full-page illustration on page 379
Description of the bridge known as Le Pont des Anglais, with Illustrations.

The English Consul at Cairo, letter to the Editor
The Times, London, 6 May 1874, page 5
James Shaw expresses regret at the removal of Mr Rogers as consul. Shaw explains that he has been involved in the extension of the Egyptian railways, has made 19 visits to that country and has always found the Khedive's government helpful.

Memoirs of James Shaw
Minutes of Proceedings of the Institution of Civil Engineers, Volume LXXII, Part II, 1882-83, pages 320-323
James Shaw, as Shaw and Thomson, supplied the ironwork for the bridge at Ghizeh. Shaw's close association with the Khedive led to John and Waynman Dixon obtaining several profitable contracts in Egypt, but in 1875 Shaw's financial difficulties brought this to an end.

The First Stockton Ironworks
Alan Betteney
The Cleveland Industrial Archaeologist No.38, 2018
Includes James Shaw's involvement with iron works in Stockton.

A Bridge Misunderstood, and other Cairo crossings
Samir Raafat
Egyptian Mail, Cairo, 29 April 1995
History of the bridges across the Nile at Cairo.

The Industrial Classes in Egypt
The Engineer, London, 22 December 1871, page 432
Article reproduced from the *Pall Mall Gazette*, with much of the content identical to C H Johnson's letter below.

Letters to the Editor - Engineers in Egypt
The Engineer, London, 19 January 1872, page 42
Letter from C H Johnson describing conditions for European engineers in Egypt.

Charles Piazzi Smyth's Journals
Reference ROE 15, 25 and 26
Royal Observatory Library, Blackford Hill, Edinburgh
Cover the investigations in Egypt, the arrival of the casing stone sent from Waynman Dixon, and a visit by Waynman Dixon to Edinburgh.

The Peripatetic Astronomer, the life of Charles Piazzi Smyth
H A Brück and M T Brück
Adam Hilger, Bristol and Philadelphia, 1988
Detailed biography with a description of the four months Charles and Jessica spent in tents by the Great Pyramid in 1864-65.

Letters from John Dixon to Charles Piazzi Smyth 1871-1872
Reference ROE A11-48
Royal Observatory Library, Blackford Hill, Edinburgh
Ten brief letters from John Dixon over the period 25 November 1871 to 26 December 1972. It is typical of John Dixon that he was in his office working on Boxing Day.

Letters from Waynman Dixon to Charles Piazzi Smyth, 1873-1882
Reference ROE A12-50
Royal Observatory Library, Blackford Hill, Edinburgh
Nine letters from Waynman Dixon over the period 4 August 1873 to 13 September 1882.

Notes on the Great Pyramids and the Cubits used in its Design
Colonel Sir Henry James
Thomas G Gutch and Company, Southampton, 1860
Note 8 included details of his supposed wheel and pulley transport arrangements.

Our Inheritance in the Great Pyramid, new and enlarged edition, including all the most important discoveries up to the present time
Charles Piazzi Smyth
W Isbister and Company, London, 1874
Piazzi Smyth's celebrated book, dedicated to the memory of John Taylor and first published in 1867. The 1873 revised edition contains many references to work by John Dixon and by Piazzi Smyth's friends Dr Grant and Mr Waynman Dixon C.E., particularly as follows:
Was robbed casing stone used in other buildings, such as the Sooltan Hassan mosque? (page 16)
Revision to section on the measurements of the coffer in the King's Chamber (pages 134-141).
Sir H James ideas to explain three grooves (pages 155-156)
Waynman's plaster cast of the boss on the granite leaf (page 191)
Discovery of the 'air channels' and relics, and design of masonry in the first ascending passage (pages 363-367)
Measurement of distance between ruled lines in entrance passage (pages 395-402)
Casing stone sent to Piazzi Smyth by Waynman (pages 489-492)

Journal entry for 26 November 1872
Charles Piazzi Smyth's Journal from 15 April 1872
ROE reference number 25
Royal Observatory Library, Blackford Hill, Edinburgh
Description of the three relics by received from John Dixon. Smyth wrote that the ball was described as of granite, but it was green stone.

Waynman Dixon at the Great Pyramid of Giza
Bob Brier
KMT a Modern Journal of Ancient Egypt, volume 23, number 4, Winter 2012-13
KMT, Sebastopol, California
Bob Brier has many letters, drawings and photographs from Waynman Dixon's time in Egypt.

The Pyramids of Giza, Facts, Legends and Mysteries
Jean-Pierre Corteggiani
Thames and Hudson, London, 2007
Translated from the original French, an excellent concise guide to the pyramids.

Carbon-14 Dating the Giza Pyramids? The small relics found inside the pyramids
Robert G Buaval and Javier Sierra
Discussions in Egyptology, Oxford, Volume 49, 2001, pages 6-21.
Robert Buaval has written books of the supposed relationship between the location of the pyramids and the alignment of stars in Orion's belt, artificial structure on Mars and the lost city of Atlantis. In 1993 he initiated the search for the relics at the British Museum, where they were rediscovered having been misplaced since they had been donated to the Museum in 1970 by John Dixon's great grand-daughter Beth Porteous.

Recent Discoveries in the Great Pyramid of Egypt
Nature, volume 7, number 165, 26 December 1872, pages 146-149.
Detailed account on the circumstances of finding the relics in the newly-opened passages, with a description of the three articles and speculation on the use of the granite ball as a standard weight.

Relics of the Pyramids, Letter from E H Pringle
Nature, volume 8, number 196, 31 July 1873, page 263.
Suggested all three objects could have been a plumb line; the cedar wooden handle for the hooks, with the plumb line weighted with the granite ball being suspended from the hooks.

Egyptian Antiquities
The Graphic, London, 7 December 1872, page 527
Description of the three relics found in the recently-opened passages by Mr John and Mr Waynman Dixon, assisted by the English (he was Scottish) physician in Cairo, Dr Grant. Also mentions the casing stone found in a mound of debris and rescued just before it would have been broken up for building material. The three accompanying sketches are all said to be by John Dixon:
Page 544 Discoveries in the Great Egyptian Pyramid 'The Grand Gallery' and 'The Entrance'. Note these are signed 'H Hassan' and not John Dixon. These two illustrations almost seem added as make-weights, 'not inappropriately added' as *The Graphic* puts it.
Page 545 Discoveries in the Great Egyptian Pyramid 'Original Casing Stone from the North Side' 'Granite Ball, 1lb 3oz weight' 'Piece of Cedar, apparently a Measure' and Bronze Instrument with portion of the Wooden Handle adhering to it'

The Great Pyramid
Harper's Weekly, New York, 11 January 1873, page 36
Brief description of the three items accompanied by the casing stone found by Waynman and transported to Piazzi Smyth in Edinburgh, with John Dixon's sketch.

Sacred Egyptian relics said to lie under the Needle
David Keys
The Independent, London, 6 December 1993
A speculative article, based on material from Robert Buaval, suggesting that the three relics might have been buried beneath Cleopatra's Needle.

Letters to the Editor: Belated recognition for the Great Pyramid relics
The Independent, London, 11 January 1994
In which Mrs M Elizabeth Porteous explains how she inherited the cigar box and handed it over to the British Museum in 1972.

Waynman Dixon's letters written from on board the Griffin, January to March 1873
In Bob Brier's collection.

The Soudan Railway Expedition
Engineering, London, 28 February 1873, page 146-7
Description and engravings of dahabeyas on the Nile.

Cleopatra's Needles
Aubrey Noakes
H F and G Witherby, London, 1962
An early book on the London and New York obelisks, largely based on reports in *The Times*.

Cleopatra's Needles
Ron Hayward
Moorland Publishing Company, Buxton, 1978
Similar in layout to the above, with more illustrations. Makes no mention of Aubrey Noakes's book.

Egypt in England
Chris Elliott
English Heritage, Swindon, 2012
Surveys the range of Egyptian influence in English architecture and design, with an accurate and comprehensive account of the journey of Cleopatra's Needle from Alexandria to London. Does reference previous books by Noakes and Hayward.

Cleopatra's Needles, The Lost Obelisks of Egypt
Bob Brier
Bloomsbury Academic Plc, London and New York, 2016
Excellent accounts of the obelisks removed from Egypt, Chapter 5 is on the London obelisk.

9 Works in Brazil

John Dixon's obituary by the Institution of Civil Engineers states that the bridge at Cairo was 'followed by extensive drainage and sanitary works at Rio de Janeiro, and piers in Mexico and Parà on the Amazon.' John was one of two contractors to be involved with Rio de Janeiro drainage works. After Rio he moved on to Campos dos Goytacazes, where he constructed a system of sewers and water supplies. At Campos he was joined by Alfred Thorne, who continued to work with him on several projects afterwards, probably including the loading pier at Pará.

Drainage and sanitary works in Rio de Janeiro

The Empire of Brazil was an independent state, roughly the present-day Brazil and Uruguay, which had broken away from Portuguese rule in 1822. For most of the 19th century it was democratic, politically stable, and with a booming economy based on agriculture. Principal exports were coffee, rubber, sugar, cacao and cotton; the value of exports tripled between 1820 and 1840. Brazil rapidly adopted railways, with the first line opening in 1854, well before railways appeared in many European countries. The growth of cities and factories led to a requirement for modern facilities, and in the second half of the 19th century the country made huge investments in modern sanitation, gas and electricity distribution, communications and transport systems. It is claimed that it was the fifth country in the world to have city sewers and the third to have sewage treatment works.

The burgeoning population of Rio de Janeiro suffered from a variety of bacterial, parasitic and viral diseases. In 1855 the Emperor of the Brazils entered into an agreement with Vianna de Lima and John Frederick Russell, two Brazilian entrepreneurs, to install a drainage scheme in Rio de Janeiro. Lima and Russell engaged Edward Gotto to design the works, and he set up a company in Brazil with John Charretie. Sir Edwin Pearson, who had been the chairman of the Westminster Improvement Commission in London from 1845 until 1852 when he resigned over financial irregularities, was invited to join the company for a fee of £1,500. The Rio de Janeiro Drainage Company was established in 1860 with Gotto as its resident engineer in Rio, and shares offered to the public with a promise of income from the Brazilian government for ninety years. It appears that the company engaged two English contractors, the partnership of Brassey and Ogilvie, and John Dixon. Thomas Brassey was one of the foremost contractors of the time and entered into partnerships with several other contractors at various times. The association with Alexander Ogilvie was said to date from the 1830s when they were competing for a tender. Brassey said 'It's no use making two bites of a cherry; let's go together or one of us retire.'

Sir Edwin Pearson's role seems to have been minimal, but that didn't stop him taking out an unsuccessful court action when his payment of £1,500 failed to materialise. Meanwhile Brassey and Ogilvie began work and connected some 16,000 properties to the sewers, with filtered water piped to 2,000 houses and 670 street corner stand pipes.

Who's who?
Edward Gotto (1821-1897)

Edward Gotto was a railway surveyor before being appointed assistant engineer to the Metropolitan Commission of Sewers in London. Based on this experience, he established his own consulting business concerned with water supplies and drainage in 1852. In 1860 he went into partnership with Frederick Beesley (1836-1902), who also worked for the Metropolitan Commission of Sewers. Over the next thirty years Gotto and Beesley designed drainage schemes in Brazil (Rio de Janeiro and Campos) and many English towns. At the end of the partnership Edward Gotto was appointed General Manager of the Rio de Janeiro City Improvements Company Limited, a position which he held until his death. His many other business interests included collieries and gas works in Brazil, banking in Brazil and West Africa, railways in Africa and mining in Spain and Wales.

City of Rio de Janeiro, 1889.
LAGO, Pedro Correa do. Coleção Princesa Isabel: Fotografia do século XIX. Capivara, 2008

The extent of John Dixon's work in Rio is uncertain, but he was certainly familiar with the sewage system suggesting that he was actively involved. In a lengthy letter to *The Surrey Comet* from his house beside the River Thames at Surbiton, following three serious floods during the winter of 1882-83, he compared the lack of treatment of sewage in England to the situation in Rio de Janeiro. For a capital cost of about £2 10s per head, a proper drainage scheme had been provided for half a million inhabitants, making it one of the healthiest cities in the tropics. An annual charge of £5 10s per house covered all costs. After chemical treatment some of the resulting sludge was made into cement, some used as fertiliser, but the bulk was used to reclaim waste land. There was a reply to John's letter from Gotto and Beesley which gave some details of the Rio scheme. Not only did every street have a sewer, but every house had a drain, a water closet and a yard sink.

In his comprehensive gazetteer of Brazil published in 1866, William Scully reported that, under the practical skill of Edward Gotto, the magnificent sewerage system was already partially complete, although there was no sign of a water supply system. By 1872, some 30,000 properties had been connected to the sewers, about 42% of the buildings in Rio. By 1890 this had grown to almost 60%. However, the Rio de Janeiro Drainage Company was criticised for shoddy workmanship and insufficient capacity. Problems no doubt arose because the sewers were installed before there was a reliable water supply to the city, so there was little flow to keep them flushed out, and because far more dwellings were connected than had been envisaged at the design stage.

John Dixon was definitely in Brazil in 1879. There were press reports of him raising the case of eighty-two virtually destitute emigrants who landed at Southampton from the Royal Mail Company's steamer *Minho*. John had been a passenger on the same voyage, returning from Brazil. The name of the steamer may have irked him because, after building part of the Minho District Railway in Portugal in 1877, he was still fighting the authorities there for payment.

Although some sources suggest that John was involved with the Rio water supply system, this does not appear to be the case. At the end of 1870 the Brazilian government received a report from Andre and Antonio Rebonças proposing to transport water to Rio de Janeiro from the River Ouro, a distance of thirty seven miles. In 1876 Antonio Gabrielli, an Italian engineer based in London, was awarded the contract to construct the water supply over 2½ years. Gabrielli had built the Vienna water supply system, using 14,000 Italian workmen whose good behaviour and work-rate 'formed a striking contrast to the national characteristics of the Austrian labourers', and had also built docks at Chatham and Malta. He placed orders for 80,000 tons of cast iron water pipes with three firms in Glasgow, total value £1.7 million. *Engineering* magazine thought that the size of the combined orders was unparalleled in the history of pipe manufacture. The magazine went on to say that most of the order was for twin conduits to transport water to Rio because 'the area of distribution within the city being already completely and efficiently laid with mains.' It is not clear whether Gabrielli had installed these mains, or whether it could have been Dixon. Gabrielli's contract included the building of fountains in Rio, but it appears that few were built.

Campos water supply and drainage

Campos dos Goytacazes, some 150 miles north east of Rio de Janeiro and on the River Parahyba, had a population of about 18,000 and was surrounded by sugar and coffee plantations. Water was taken unfiltered from the river and distributed by cart. There were no proper drains. The provincial government had granted a concession, for supplying water and drainage to the 2,500 dwellings of Campos over a fifty year period, to the Brazilian businessmen Alberto da Rocha Miranda and Joao van Erven. In London the City of Campos Waterworks and Drainage Corporation Limited was established with a capital of £240,000 and issued its share prospectus in November 1875. It intended to purchase the concession, and offered 4,500 shares of £5 each, accompanied with an optimistic forecast of 10% annual profit. Since the concession made it compulsory for every house to be connected to the drainage system, and water was to be supplied at half the cost as from the existing water carts, it seemed a good investment.

The City of Campos Waterworks and Drainage Corporation appointed Gotto and Beesley as their engineers and also Charles Neate, a civil engineer from Westminster. In October 1875 Neate had visited Campos to report on proposed works. The corporation's prospectus stated that the concession was purchased from Antonio Gabrielli, who had recently installed the Rio water supply, implying that he had acquired the concession from the two Brazilians and was now passing it over to the corporation.

Rather mysteriously, virtually no trace of this venture can be found following the closure of the share offer on 20 November 1875. A few days later a writ for £100,000 damages was issued by the Leeds Mercantile Bank over comments made in the *The Hour* newspaper about the City of Campos Waterworks and Drainage Corporation. *The Hour* newspaper attracted a good many writs for libel and went out of business at the end of 1875. It certainly seems that there was something suspicious about the City of Campos Waterworks and Drainage Corporation leading to its early demise. After this, plans for a water supply and drainage scheme at Campos did not reappear until six years later.

In December 1881 the prospectus was published for the Campos (Brazil) Improvements Company Limited, with a capital of £200,000 to be raised through 20,000 shares of £10 each. This prospectus estimated that the payments from the provincial government for the drainage scheme, which would serve an estimated 2,850 houses on completion, and the revenue from the water supply, would yield 8% revenue on the capital. Only three names in the prospectus had been involved with the City of Campos Waterworks and Drainage Corporation. Charles Neate was now a director and the engineers were, once again, Gotto and Beesley. The chairman was Sir John Swinburne, who inherited the family estate in Northumberland in 1860 and was a Liberal MP from 1885 to 1892. One of the other directors was James Rennie of the London and Glasgow Engineering Company, who had been on the board of the Rio Malagón Mines in Spain when John Dixon was the chairman.

This time the concession was purchased directly from Alberto da Rocha Miranda and Joao van Erven by none other than John Dixon himself, acting on behalf of the company. It seems that it was the engineers (Gotto and Beesley, Neate and Dixon) who were virtually in control of the new enterprise, probably out of frustration with the collapse of the previous company.

Either through nepotism or the security of a known contractor, the contract for construction and one year's maintenance after completion, valued at £151,500, was awarded to John Dixon and Alfred Thorne. Cast iron pipes, valves and fittings were supplied by Charles I'Anson and Son at the Whessoe Foundry in Darlington. Dixon and Thorne placed eight orders with the foundry during the period 1882 to 1888, totalling almost £18,800. Their £1,037 order of 1882 was the largest single order received by the foundry that year. It cannot be assumed that all eight orders were for Campos since Dixon and Thorne were engaged in two other projects requiring cast iron columns at this time. In 1882-83 they were rebuilding the Solway Viaduct, which required some replacement cast iron columns ordered from the Whessoe Foundry but which would have been a relatively small cost. They also ordered the cast iron columns for the pier at Pará, built in 1883-84, but again these would have been comparatively low cost. The last of their orders in the Whessoe records was in 1887. Presumably the Campos work was completed in this year, although John's failing health may have left Alfred Thorne to complete the project. There were small orders from Thorne over the next three years after 1887, but these could have been for a different project.

No references have been found concerning the progress of the works or their completion.

Port facilities on the River Pará

It is difficult to find references to the early development of the port facilities on the River Pará, or indeed anything about John Dixon's contract for building a pier there. In 1852 the Amazon Steam Navigation Company was inaugurated and, by 1870, was operating services with a fleet of eight steam ships. The pier was almost certainly at Belém, the state capital of Pará, on the entrance to the Amazon some sixty miles up the River Pará from the Atlantic Ocean. In 1866 the Amazon, Tocantins, and other rivers were opened up to navigation and, with the rubber trade expanding rapidly, there would have been a need for improved port facilities at Belém at the mouth of the River Pará. Later there were hopes that a steam ship route might be opened up from Pará to the interior of Ecuador. William Scully had described the port of Belém as large and safe, but only frequented by smaller vessels. This was probably due to the absence of harbour facilities. In 1882 the engineer Jerome Burns was commissioned by the Amazon Steam Navigation Company to examine the practicality of building a loading pier on the River Pará. He concluded that it would be impossible, but John Dixon would prove him wrong.

Nothing is known about how John Dixon, almost certainly working with Alfred Thorne, came by the contract to construct a loading pier on the

River Pará. A small stone pier existed at Belém earlier in the nineteenth century, but the surrounding waters were often silted up. Plans were drawn up for a pier in 1840 but not implemented; it seems that later the old fort of São Pedro Nolasco was demolished and a new square and pier were constructed. This was probably the pier built by Dixon. Both the square and the pier were swept away at the start of the twentieth century by the large-scale development of the port by the American businessman Percival Farquhar (1864-1953) and the English engineering contractor Weetman Pearson (1856-1927).

At the end of 1883, John Dixon appointed Edward Hutchinson from Darlington as his resident engineer in Brazil. The area around Belém was notorious for yellow fever, malaria, polio and beri-beri. Some six months after his arrival in Brazil he died, leaving a widow and six young children back in Darlington.

Little is known about the pier, but it can be assumed that it was a conventional pier structure with a timber decking carried on wrought iron girders supported on screwed cast iron columns. Charles I'Anson and Son of the Whessoe Foundry in Darlington supplied iron work for the pier at Pará.

It is not known how the work proceeded after Hutchinson's death. Perhaps John had to rely on the local people engaged on the project. After six months into the work, they would have become conversant with driving piles into the river, building the pier and, most importantly, dealing with the local workforce and local elites.

Who's who?
Edward Hutchinson

The Skerne Iron Works in Darlington was established by a Quaker partnership known as Pease, Hutchinson and Ledward; there were four members of the Pease family involved. In 1872 it became the Skerne Iron Company Limited with Edward Hutchinson as managing director. Hutchinson was a highly competent engineer with a concern for the well-being of his workforce. He designed an efficient overall plan for the Skerne Ironworks with overhead gantries to supply coal to the numerous furnaces, and underground tunnels for ash clearance. Motivated by a desire to improve the working conditions associated with puddling furnaces, he designed and tested a mechanically revolving raddle (the iron rod used to stir and manhandle the iron within the furnace) but perversely the puddlers themselves rejected the development, fearing it would adversely affect their job security.

Edward Hutchinson was well known to John Dixon as the Skerne Iron Works had supplied the wrought iron fabrications for at least three of John's projects: the viaducts on the Whitby to Loftus railway, the Rio Tinto ore-loading facility at Huelva, and the Llandudno pier. He was a member of the Institution of Mechanical Engineers and published a book on girder making and wrought iron bridge construction. In May 1879 the Skerne Iron Company Limited failed, along with two other famous iron companies in Middlesbrough: Lloyd and Company and Hopkins, Gilkes and Company Limited. Hutchinson had to find new employment. In 1880, with a group of Darlington businessmen, he acquired the Bishop Auckland Iron Works, which had been closed for over two years due to the depressed demand for iron. This depression was a consequence of the rapid adoption of steel in place of iron. On 18 August 1881 Hutchinson filed a petition for bankruptcy at the Durham County Court, with liabilities of £30,000. People owed money by a failed business usually have no good feelings towards the cause of their plight, but at the first meeting of his creditors a vote of sympathy was passed for Hutchinson. Subsequently the leading creditors formed a company to take over the works, but this failed again within two years. After unsuccessful attempts to restart the business, the entire works was dismantled at the end of 1888.

Meanwhile Hutchinson valiantly tried to resurrect his career by submitting plans for a bridge at Barnard Castle, but this came to nothing. He was not in the best of health, probably due to the noxious fumes from the iron works which had greatly troubled local residents. John must have known of his plight and, whether through sympathy or self-interest, at the end of 1883 he offered Hutchinson the position of resident engineer for the port works on the River Pará. Edward Hutchinson could not afford to turn the offer down, even although he must have worried about the effect on his health.

Edward Hutchinson should not be confused with the Darlington solicitor, Edward Hutchinson (1846-1918) who acted for some of the Pease businesses.

References

Empire of Brazil
http://en.wikipedia.org/wiki/Empire_of_Brazil
Overview of the development of nineteenth century Brazil.

Health, Hygiene and Sanitation in Latin America c.1870 to c.1950
Christopher Abel
Research Paper 42
University of London, Institute of Latin American Studies
Pages 29 to 34 cover the development of water supplies and sanitation in cities and the countryside, especially in Brazil.

Drainage of the City of Rio de Janeiro
The Morning Post, London, 24 June 1860, page 1
Share prospectus for the company.

Sir Edwin Pearson v The Rio de Janeiro City Improvements Company (Limited), Vianna de Lima and John Frederick Russell (out of the jurisdiction), Thomas Brassey, Alexander Ogilvie and John Charretie
The London Evening Standard, 18 July 1866, page 7
The dispute over payment.

Brazil; its provinces and chief cities, the manners and customs of its people, agricultural, commercial and other statistics
William Scully
Murray and Company, London, 1866
The standard reference to Brazil at that time. At the time of writing, the sewage system in Rio was installed but not the water system.

Drainage of the Lower Thames Valley
The Surrey Comet, Kingston, 24 February 1883, page 4
Letter from Gotto and Beesley with some details of the Rio sewerage scheme.

Foreign and Colonial Notes - Water Supply of Rio de Janeiro
Engineering, London, 2 December 1870, page 412
Report from Andre and Antonio Rebonças on bringing water from the River Ouro to the city.

The Vienna Water Works
Engineering, London, 30 May 1873, pages 387-8
Information on Antonio Gabrielli and his Italian workmen in Vienna.

Money Market and City News
The Morning Post, London, 15 September 1875, page 7
Mr Neate, of Gotto and Beasley, engineers to the Rio de Janeiro City Improvements Company, was to report on the proposed works at Campos.

Empire of Brazil - The City of Campos Waterworks and Drainage Corporation Limited
The Morning Post, London, 13 November 1875, page 1
Company prospectus and offer of shares.

This Day's Money Market
The Pall Mall Gazette, London, 16 November 1875, page 9
Offer of shares in the City of Campos Waterworks and Drainage Corporation Limited.

£100,000 Damages against "The Hour"
The York Herald, 29 November 1875, page 6
Brief report on the writ for damages, but no details given.

Notes from the North
Engineering, London, 7 July 1876, page 16
Three Glasgow firms given contract for water pipes for Rio de Janeiro. Describes the extent of Gabrielli's contract.

Returned Emigrants from Brazil (Special Telegram) Southampton, Tuesday
The Western Morning News, Plymouth, 10 December 1879, page 2
John Dixon raising the case of emigrants with the Borough Bench at Southampton on his return from Brazil.

Prospectus for the Campos (Brazil) Improvements Company Limited
The Times, London, 23 December 1881, page 13
Sets out the objectives of the company, offer of £200,000 share capital in £10 shares, directors, engineers and contractors John Dixon and Alfred Thorne. Refers to John Dixon's previous successful work in Rio de Janeiro. The government guarantees £12,500 pa for the drainage service and the company will have exclusive privilege of supplying water to the town.

Mr Dixon CE on the Drainage of the Lower Thames Valley - To the Editor
The Surrey Comet, 17 February 1883, page 3
Letter suggesting there should be proper treatment of sewage, comparing the situation in England with that in Rio de Janeiro.

Analysis of orders received 1831-1862 and 1882-1891
Whessoe Records, reference D/Whes 6/60
Durham County Record Office, Durham
Lists value of orders with the Whessoe Foundry. Under Dixon and Thorne are £1037 in 1882, £2540 in 1883, £296 and £3,134 in 1884, £7,055 in 1885, £3,417 and £603 in 1886 and £709 in 1887. There are no more orders from Dixon and Thorne after 1887.

Civilising Rio: Reform and Resistance in a Brazilian City 1889-1930
Teresa A Meade
Pennsylvania State University Press, 1948
Chapter 3 Sanitation and Renovation outlines the installation of sewers.

A Historical Perspective of Early Water Policy and Water and Sanitation Policy in Brazil
Ney Albert Murtha, José Esteban Castro, Léo Heller
University of Newcastle upon Tyne, 2015
Covers the introduction of sewers and piped water supplies in Brazil, including mention of Rio de Janeiro but not Campos.

Foreign and Colonial Notes - Steam Navigation on the Amazon
Engineering, London, 4 November 1870, page 339
Amazon Steam Navigation Company has eight steamers.

Gossip
The Western Times, Exeter, 3 September 1877, page 4
Hopes for a steam ship route to the interior of Ecuador.

The Navigation of the Amazon and its tributaries
The Star, Guernsey, 2 July 1874, page 4
Amazon Steam Navigation Company Ltd acquired two Brazilian shipping companies and added two new ships from Laird of Birkenhead. Liverpool has already established two direct lines of fortnightly steamers to Pará.

Obituary - Jerome Burns (1827-1894)
Proceedings of Institution of Civil Engineers, volume 117, 1894
In 1882 he had concluded that a pier on the River Pará was impossible to construct.

The Port of Pará: Oporto da História Amazônia
Luciana Guimarães Teixeira
XI Encontro Nacional da Associação Nacional de Pós-graduação e Pesquisa em Plane Jamento Urbano e Regional-Anpur, 23-26 May 2005
Development of the port facilities at Belém.

Typed notes for early Whessoe history, September 1890, page 4
Whessoe Records reference D/Whes 15/18
Durham County Record Office, Durham
The iron work for the following piers 'among others' was by Whessoe: Rio Tinto, Huelva, Bournemouth, Plymouth, Para (S America), Lisbon, Aldborough, Hornsea and Shanklin.

The Construction and Arrangement of Works for the Manufacture of Iron
Edward Hutchinson
Proceedings of the Cleveland Institution of Engineers, February 8 1872
Proceedings of the Cleveland Institution of Engineers, 14 March 1872 (discussion on above paper)
Office of the Cleveland Institution of Engineers, Zetland Street, Middlesbrough
A good description of the efficient layout of the Skerne Ironworks.

Important Economy in the Manufacture of Wrought Iron
The Engineer, London, 28 February 1873, page 125
Edward Hutchinson's revolving raddle for the puddling furnace.

Girder Making and the Practice of Bridge Building in Wrought Iron
Edward Hutchinson
E and F N Spon, London, 1879
Comprehensive explanation of the processes involved in the manufacture of wrought iron with numerous examples of bridges with iron supplied by the Skerne Iron Works, including some of John Dixon's bridges.

Failures in the Iron Trade - Suspensions of Messrs Lloyd & Co., Messrs Hopkins, Gilkes, & Co. Limited, and of the Skerne Iron Co. Limited
The Northern Echo, Darlington, 15 May 1879, page 3
Failure of the Skerne Iron Works.

Failure in the Iron Trade
The North-Eastern Daily Gazette, Middlesbrough,
19 August 1881, page 3
Failure of Mr Edward Hutchinson of the Bishop Auckland Ironworks. Liabilities of £30,000.

Death of a Cleveland Ironmaster
The North-Eastern Daily Gazette, Middlesbrough,
12 May 1884, page 2
Obituary of Edward Hutchinson.

10 Gibraltar water supply

During the course of some unknown contracting work on the Rock of Gibraltar, probably around 1870, John Dixon found a new fresh water supply. It proved unable to deliver much water before turning saline but became part of the long and sorry history of searching for fresh water in the territory.

Gibraltar's water supply

One of the associated agreements of the complex Treaty of Utrecht in 1713, which settled the War of Spanish Succession, was the ceding of Gibraltar and Minorca to Britain. Over the next ninety years Britain twice lost and then regained control of Minorca, finally returning the island to Spain in 1802. In contrast the government was more dogged in its ownership of Gibraltar, considered of great strategic importance. The Rock was a crucial coaling point on the sea route to Alexandria, and controlled entry into the Mediterranean.

When the British took over Gibraltar, water was supplied by an ancient Spanish aqueduct, various cisterns collecting rainwater, and a well in the governor's garden. Over the following years increased demand and seasonal droughts combined to make water supply critical. More wells were sunk, although water drawn from them was frequently brackish, and householders were encouraged to collect rainwater. Even so, about a third of Gibraltar's inhabitants had to purchase their water from street vendors. In addition to the problems with water supply, drainage was poor and a government report in 1863 revealed that sanitation was 'most offensive and dangerous to health.' This was condemnation indeed given the foetid state of London at that time. As is the usual reaction to such reports, there was no immediate response from the authorities.

It was two years later that a cholera epidemic, resulting in over four hundred deaths, finally provoked the authorities into action. The Gibraltar Sanitary Commission was established, charged with improving water supply and establishing a separate system for flushing. A large new well was sunk, which initially provided a good flow of water, and distribution pipes laid for public and private supplies. Unfortunately, the quality of the water from the new well soon deteriorated, and the piped system was restricted for sanitary use only. This system continues in use today but delivering salt water for non-potable uses.

John Dixon's idea for a water supply in Gibraltar

According to his obituary published by the Institution of Civil Engineers:

> 'Mr. Dixon's discovery of an unexpected supply of fresh water in the rock of Gibraltar was due to his geological knowledge and brought him into high repute with the military authorities and the War Department, who purchased his concession.'

Around the early 1870s John was working as an engineering contractor in the colony. The nature of his contracts is not known, but he became interested in the problems of Gibraltar's potable water supply. He was convinced that there must be fresh water stored in the limestone, either as aquifers or in subterranean caverns. He suggested that an adit (horizontal tunnel) be driven eastwards into the Rock until the limestone was reached.

A shaft was excavated in the area of the Trafalgar Cemetery down to a level about 2 feet above sea level and a gallery opened up to the east until limestone was reached, after a distance of only 8 feet. Then two boreholes were sunk, to depths of 4 feet 6 inches and 19 feet respectively and pumping started. At first fresh water was delivered, but when the pumping rate was increased the water soon turned salty. So, although John was right in believing that a new source of fresh water would be found, it was not capable of sustaining a worth while flow.

Major Tulloch

Disposal of sewage was another problem. Major Hector Tulloch (1835-1898) of the Royal Engineers was Britain's foremost authority on sewerage systems, having advised local authorities the length and breadth of the country and having investigated the source of evil smells in the House of Commons. Major Tulloch was sent to look into both the disposal of sewage and the supply of fresh water in Gibraltar. In 1890 he published two reports in which he was extremely critical of the Gibraltar Sanitary Board, accusing them of maladministration and making the War Office pay more than their fair share of costs. He recommended a tunnel eastward through the Rock to take away piped sewage, with the expectation that fresh water might be found in the course of driving this tunnel. Firmly of the opinion that Dixon had been on the right lines, he thought that his tunnel should have penetrated much further into the limestone, into the very heart of the mountain.

After much acrimonious debate, Tulloch's plan for a tunnel was abandoned on grounds of cost and the uncertainty of finding water. Some boreholes were sunk but proved useless. Eventually all hope of finding fresh water, uncontaminated by sea water, was abandoned. Rainwater collection was improved, and today's water supplies come mainly from desalination plants.

Meanwhile the problems of sewage disposal continued. Work commissioned on sewers in 1882 had been badly carried out. In 1892 a delegation from Gibraltar petitioned Parliament, resulting in the Board being reconstituted and the matter reaching the House of Lords. Lord Knutsford defended the government's actions and said that Major Tulloch had examined and carefully noted several previous reports, including that of John Dixon. It seems that Major Tulloch's plans were then given the go-ahead, with the British Government offering to pay two-ninths of the cost.

'Shipping off Gibraltar' 1880 oil painting by Vilhelm Melbye.
Vilhelm Melbye (1824-1882) was a Danish marine artist who later worked in London where he changed his name to Wilhelm. Of the sixteen vessels in the image, only one is a steamship.
© Christie's Images/Bridgeman Images, reference CH3575591.

Other possible evidence for John Dixon's presence on Gibraltar

The obituary from the Institution of Civil Engineers stated that the War Department had purchased the water supply concession from John Dixon. The only possible reference to this has been found in *The Times* newspaper of 1872. During a Parliamentary debate over the Navy Estimates, it was said that there was £1,500 on account of the water supply at Gibraltar, a matter on which the present government had very little control because it resulted from a previously made agreement. This might refer to the purchase of John Dixon's concession. If so, this would imply that the contract with Dixon had been made by the previous government, and would place this as before the General Election of 1868. Furthermore, it would place the Gibraltar work as one of John's first contracts after he set up his business in London in 1866.

It is known that John Dixon spent some time in Gibraltar in late 1879. In *The Graphic* of 2 August 1879 there is an article about the smuggling of goods from Gibraltar into Spain at the border town of Lineas. An accompanying engraving shows several women secreting tobacco and tea under their clothes, and is taken from a drawing by John Dixon, who is also credited with providing the details for the article. Since the article includes a description of an incident 'a few days ago' when cigars were being smuggled in concealed underneath turkeys' wings, the implication is that it was written in the summer of 1879. There was widespread smuggling from Gibraltar to Spain at this time, particularly of tobacco.

'Smuggling at Gibraltar, contrabandistas preparing to pass the Spanish Custom House after leaving Gibraltar' an engraving by H Woods from an original drawing by John Dixon. Women are evading taxes by various ploys: one hides tea in her bodice, one wraps calico around her waist, one hangs tobacco leaves under her skirt and one conceals packages beneath her pantaloons.
The Graphic, 2 August 1879, pages 112 and 113 © Illustrated London News Limited/Mary Evans.

Acknowledgements

Edward Rose, Royal Holloway, University of London, for background information on Gibraltar water supplies.

Manual Perez, previously of the Aquagib company, for access to the Tulloch report and general assistance.

Anthony Pitalunga, Gibraltar Archives, for searching in vain for relevant material in the Gibraltar Archives.

References

British Attempts to develop groundwater and water supply on Gibraltar 1800-1985
Edward P F Rose, John D Mather and Manuel Perez
200 Years of British Hydrogeology, Geological Society, London, 2004
Special Publications, 225, pages 239-262
Comprehensive history of water supplies on Gibraltar, with a single reference to John Dixon.

Report on the Water Supply and Sewerage of Gibraltar
Major Hector Tulloch, Royal Engineers
Waterlow & Sons, London, 1890
This report recommended driving a tunnel through the rock to carry piped sewerage, with the expectation that a supply of fresh water might be found along the route. Major Tulloch acknowledged that this was based on the original ideas of John Dixon. He described Dixon's shaft and gallery and commented that the plan probably failed because pumping had started before getting into the very heart of the mountain.

House of Commons, Navy Estimates
The Times, 22 March 1872, page 6
Report of £1,500 paid for water supply at Gibraltar, a matter on which the present government had little control as it was the subject of a previous agreement.

Contrabandistas preparing to pass the Spanish Custom House at Lineas
The Graphic, 2 August 1879, page 114 with engraving on pages 112/113
Article and engraving from a drawing by John Dixon of a Spanish woman smuggling goods at Gibraltar.

The Smugglers' Rock (from our special correspondent) Gibraltar, April 10
The Times, London, 26 April 1879, page 5
Lengthy article about smuggling from Gibraltar to Spain.

Record of War Department fresh water tanks and wells on Gibraltar 1886
Reference WO 376/7
National Archives, Kew
Unfortunately sheds no further light on John Dixon's work on Gibraltar or on his water supply.

Imperial Parliament - House of Lords - Gibraltar Sanitary Board
The Standard, London, 17 June 1892, page 2
The problems of Gibraltar's sewers reach the House of Lords.

Gibraltar Sanitary Board
Hansard, House of Lords debate 16 June 1892, volume 5, cc1228-55
Lengthy debate between Lord Knutsford (Secretary of State for the Colonies) and the Earl of Kimberley. Kimberley opposed spending money on the sewers as the death rate in Gibraltar compared favourably with death rates in Britain.

11 Eau Brink Cut Bridge, Norfolk

The Eau Brink Cut of 1821 straightened out the final reaches of the River Ouse at King's Lynn. The original timber bridge at its northern end was replaced in 1873 by an iron bridge designed by Brunlees and McKerrow and constructed by John Dixon. Dixon employed a novel means of construction, building up the entire span on the western bank and hauling it across the piers to the opposite side.

The Eau Brink Cut

The final meanders of the River Ouse, draining the Norfolk Fens into the Wash, were straightened out by the 2½ mile Eau Brink Cut. This channel was designed by the celebrated canal engineers John Rennie and Thomas Telford and excavated by the contractors Edwards Banks and William Jolliffe in 1819-21. It was widened at the suggestion of Thomas Telford in 1829 after problems with silting of the channel. The straight channel was ideal for boat races and an annual regatta was instituted, later becoming the King's Lynn Royal Regatta under the patronage of the Prince of Wales.

John Dixon, coming from Tyneside, would have been interested in the race held on 25 August 1865 when Robert Chambers from Newcastle, Robert Cooper from Redheugh on the Tyne and Henry Kelley from Putney were competing for £250. The week before Kelley had beaten Chambers to become the Champion of the Thames, but Chambers remained the Champion of the Tyne. Many Tynesiders intended to come down for the event, but their vessel was delayed by bad weather in the German Ocean (now the North Sea). Unfortunately for Tyneside, Cooper disgraced himself with several false starts and, although he was first across the finishing line, he was disqualified for impeding Kelley who was declared the winner.

'Old Cut Bridge, Summer 1873' postcard. The wooden 'Free Bridge' built by Edward Banks in the 1820s.
Reproduced by courtesy of EWW via the King's Lynn Forum website at www.kingslynn-forums.co.uk

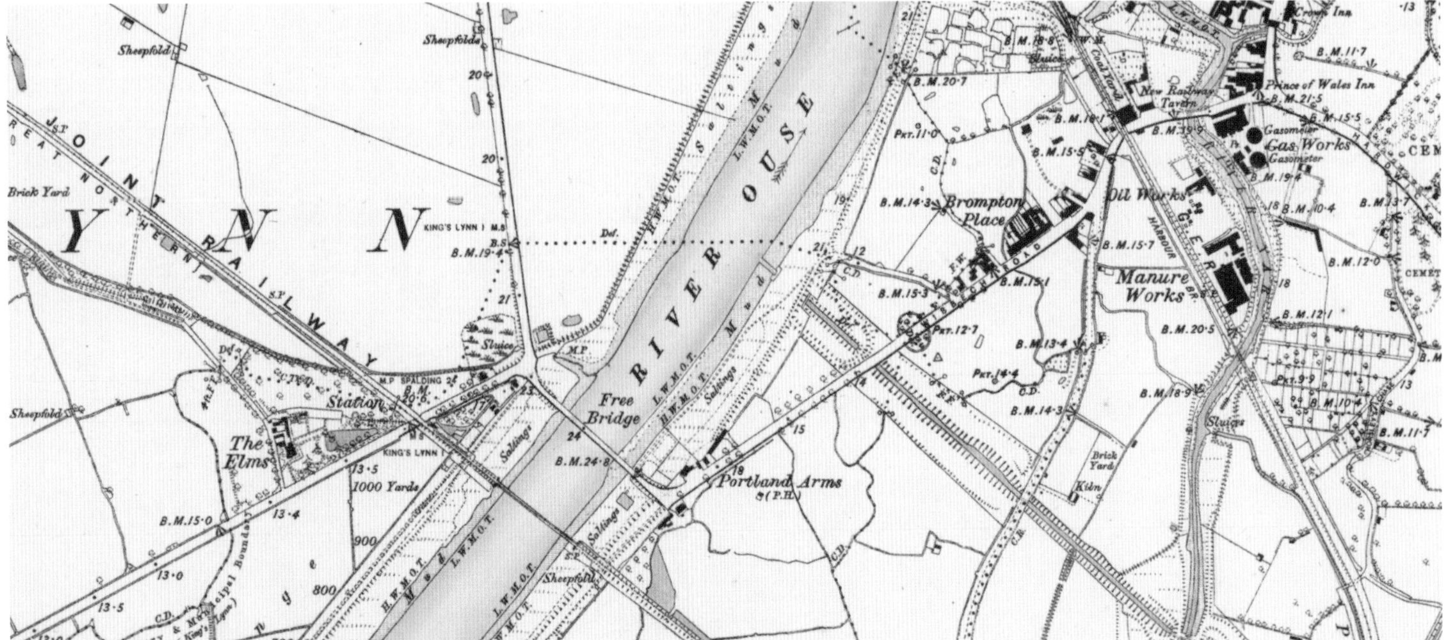

The Eau Brink Cut Bridge (Free Bridge) to the south west of King's Lynn. Ordnance Survey Six Inch Series Surveyed 1884, published 1886, Norfolk XXXIII.SW. Reproduced by permission of the National Library of Scotland.

The Eau Brink Cut was crossed by the wooden 'Free Bridge' about half a mile above Lynn harbour at the extreme northern end of the Eau Brink Cut, connecting Lynn with West Lynn. It was said that Edward Banks constructed the 'Free Bridge' using hard woods from the West Indies, brought in a specially chartered ship, and oak from a Welsh forest which he had purchased. Given the quality of materials, the timber structure was still sound after fifty years but could not carry the increased weight of traffic such as traction engines.

Who's who?
Edward Banks (1770-1835)

Edward Banks was born in North Yorkshire and spent some years at sea before building embankments on the East Yorkshire coast. He then moved south to construct a tramway terminus near Croydon where he met William Jolliffe. They became lifelong business partners, Banks had the practical skills, Jolliffe had access to finance and contacts in high places. After several more building contracts, they increasingly specialised in canal and river work. In 1819-21 Banks and Jolliffe excavated the Eau Brink Cut south of King's Lynn to improve the outflow of the River Ouse from the Norfolk Fens. They completed a £1.5 million contract with the Royal Navy for the Sheerness Dockyard and went on to build the Waterloo, Southwark and London Bridges across the River Thames in London. Banks was knighted in 1822, the first engineering contractor to be so honored.

In addition to his civil engineering contracts, Edward Banks had business interests in iron works, and quarrying, and owned a fleet of thirty narrow boats for transporting coal on the canals. He later ran a steamer service on the Thames and was involved with the General Steam Navigation Company with its fleet of twenty-six steam ships. After the death of his first wife in 1815, he married William Jolliffe's sister-in-law.

The Ouse Outfall Commissioners were responsible for repairs to the bridge and sought, unsuccessfully, either to pass this responsibility on to the county of Norfolk or to charge tolls to cover the costs. In 1862 the entire floor of the bridge had to be replaced and it became increasingly apparent that a new bridge would have to be built. The Commissioners sanctioned the building of a replacement iron bridge immediately south of the wooden bridge. James Brunlees and Alexander McKerrow were engaged to carry out the design.

The new bridge

Brunlees and McKerrow designed an entirely conventional wrought iron girder bridge, supported on cast iron piers, for the 500 feet wide crossing. The cost was to be £20,000, John Paton was their resident engineer and the contract for construction was awarded to John Dixon. The Ouse Outfall Commissioners engaged Charles Driver of Westminster, an architect noted for his artistic taste and skill, to design ornate abutments and other embellishments. Beneath the roadway the abutments were of Staffordshire blue brick, surmounted by an open arch of red and white brick and carved stone on either side with a stone seat under each arch. Elaborate cast iron finials were fitted to the tops of the cast iron columns supporting the main span, and the ironwork painted in black, chocolate, bronze and gold.

The eight piers supporting the wrought iron girders were arranged in four pairs. Each pier was built up from 6 feet lengths of 6 inch diameter cast iron cylinders, flanged at each end. They were sunk 20 to 30 feet down through the river bed simply by excavating the alluvial material from inside the cylinders and allowing them to drop through the silt under their own weight until the underlying solid Kimmeridge clay was reached. They were then filled with concrete. In March 1873 Mr Batterham presented the Lynn Museum with a piece of Kimmeridge clay from the foundations of the new bridge. The brick abutments were constructed by local builder William Harding.

John devised an ingenious method for the construction of the 505 feet long span of the bridge, built from wrought iron girders on either side of the roadway and joined by cross girders which carried the iron plates of the roadway. The complete span was assembled section by section on the western side of the cut and then gradually hauled over to the eastern abutment as a section was completed. Temporary rollers were fitted to the abutment and piers for this operation, which was accomplished by twenty men operating ratchet levers. By this means the rivetters and erectors, with their cranes, fires and other equipment did not need to move, and temporary timber staging across the cut was not required. The technique predated Henry Ford's Detroit assembly line where the workers remained in a fixed place while the partly-built cars were hauled past them.

The idea of rolling the partially completed bridge out across the river must have caught the imagination of George Barclay Bruce, who was soon to work on the Muelle de Rio Tinto in Spain with his friend and colleague John Dixon. At that time there was much debate in London over the question of a new bridge, just below London Bridge, which would not interfere with navigation. In 1876 Bruce proposed a 'rolling bridge' whereby a platform some 300 feet long would be moved back and forth over the 790 feet wide Thames, carried on six piers and two abutments all fitted with rollers. In principle the concept was similar to that of the transporter bridge, which had first been suggested by Charles Smith of Hartlepool some three years earlier with his 'bridge ferry'.

Above) 'Bridge over the Ouse at Lynn' engraving by J H Rimbault of the completed bridge after removal of the old timber Free Bridge, looking downstream. The buildings of King's Lynn can be seen in the distance. Engineering, 5 December 1873, page 463.

Left) 'Cut Bridge Lynn' postcard. John Dixon's completed bridge. Reproduced by courtesy of EWW via the King's Lynn Forum website at www.kingslynn-forums.co.uk

Below Left) 'Free Bridge King's Lynn 763' postcard. Another view of the bridge. Reproduced by courtesy of EWW via the King's Lynn Forum website at www.kingslynn-forums.co.uk

Opening (almost)

The bridge was to be declared open on Wednesday 30 July 1873 by the chairman of the Ouse Outfall Commission, Edward Fellowes MP. John Dixon paid for a sumptuous lunch, prepared by Mr Marshall of the Globe Hotel, under an awning placed over the middle of the bridge. The forty or so guests included James Brunlees and Charles Driver, members of the Commission and 'the Mayor and other principal inhabitants of Lynn and the vicinity'. After raising their glasses to the Queen, there was a toast to the engineer, architect and the contractor.

No doubt to the embarrassment of all present, Fellowes had to explain that he could not officially open the bridge as the contract was not yet completed. John Dixon offered the vague explanation that the non-completion was due to 'variations introduced in matters of detail' but he expected completion within a week or two. Then, ignoring any bureaucratic obstacles, three ponderous traction engines were taken back and forth over the bridge, their total weight causing a deflection of a mere ¼ inch at the centre of one of the spans.

What happened to the bridge?

Gales and floods in November 1875 caused some damage to the bridge. One of the ornate castings which Driver had placed on the top of the arches of the abutments was carried off by the force of the wind.

Into the 20th century, increased traffic flow began taking its toll on the bridge. After talk of closing it for extensive repairs, which would have taken twelve months, it was decided to build a replacement structure. Work began in 1924 on a concrete bridge alongside. Contractors were Holst and Company, and the cost was £29,000. The new Free Bridge, as the crossing is generally known, was opened on 3 November 1925. Dixon's bridge was dismantled, but the four sets of cast iron piers and traces of the abutments still remain in the river.

The dual-carriageway King's Lynn by-pass of 1975 required a new crossing to carry the A47 over the River Ouse, upstream of the Free Bridge, which continued in use.

The replacement concrete bridge under construction in 1924 alongside John Dixon's bridge. Reproduced by courtesy of Apollonine via the King's Lynn Forum website at www.kingslynn-forums.co.uk

References

History, Gazetteer and Directory of Norfolk and the City and County of Norwich
William White, London, 1836
The history of the Eau Brink Cut on pages 401-2.

Lynn - Toll on the Eau Brink Bridge
The Norfolk Chronicle and Norwich Gazette, 24 March 1860, page 6
House of Lords rejected Bill to charge tolls on the bridge.

Great Sculling Match at King's Lynn
Illustrated London News, 26 August 1865, page 198
Aquatic sweepstake between rowers from the Tyne and the Thames.

Lynn - The Museum
The Norfolk News, Norwich, 15 March 1873, page 8
Piece of Kimmeridge clay taken from 70 feet below the surface presented to the museum.

Lynn - Opening of the New Bridge
The Norfolk Chronicle and Norwich Gazette, 2 August 1873, page 7
Account of the construction and opening of the bridge.

Bridge over the River Ouse at Lynn
Engineering, London, 28 November 1873, page 444 with accompanying two-page engraving
Description of the new iron Eau Brink Bridge over the Ouse, designed by Brunlees and McKerrow, constructed by John Dixon of London, with architectural features by C H Driver of Westminster.

Bridge over the River Ouse at Lynn
Engineering, London, 5 December 1873, pages 463-4
Description of bridge with engravings. States that the earlier timber bridge was built by Sir Joseph Banks instead of Sir Edward Banks. Sir Joseph Banks was the naturalist on Captain Cook's voyages and certainly not an engineering contractor!

Lynn - The Gales and Floods
The Norfolk Chronicle and Norwich Gazette, 20 November 1875, page 6
Loss of a cast iron ornament from one of the arches in the gales.

Proposed Rolling Bridge over the Thames
Engineering, London, 10 March 1876, page 188
George Barclay Bruce's idea for a section of roadway that would move across the river while supported on piers fitted with rollers.

Kelly's Directory for Cambridgeshire, Norfolk and Suffolk, 1883, page 373
Brief description of the Marshland bridge.

The Contractors
Hugh Ferguson and Mike Chrimes
Thomas Telford Limited, ICE Publishing, London, 2014
Biography of William Banks.

Lynn Free Bridge
Yarmouth Independent, Gorleston Times and Flegg Journal, Yarmouth, 1 March 1924, page 6
After talk of closing the bridge for extensive repairs, a new bridge was to be built.

Lynn's New Bridge - £29,000 structure opened by Sir Thos Hare
Independent and the Journal, Yarmouth, 7 November 1925, page 11
Opening of the replacement bridge at the Eau Brink Cut.

12 Port Talbot and CwmAvon

John Dixon constructed improved harbour facilities at Port Talbot in South Wales from 1874 to 1876. Port Talbot was greatly used by the sprawling CwmAvon Works, situated some three miles inland, producing iron, copper, tinplate and chemicals. As he was completing the work on the harbour, the CwmAvon Works was in serious financial difficulties. It was purchased by James Shaw and two partners, one being John Dixon, at a bargain price. They proceeded to sell off the copper smelter and the blast furnaces, making a handsome profit, leaving James Shaw to run the remaining part of the business. John left the partnership after two years, having rarely if ever been to the works, with a profit of nearly £40,000.

The development of Port Talbot

John Dixon's obituary in the Transactions of the Institution of Civil Engineers includes the phrase:

> 'Bridges at Waterford in Ireland, and docks and harbour extensions at Port Talbot in Wales, occupied him for some time …'

Industrial development in the Afan, Llynfi and Garw valleys of South Wales began in the 18th century, exploiting local coal and iron ore deposits. A network of tramways soon spread across the landscape and down to the sea, where there were harbours at Briton Ferry on the mouth of the River Neath, and at Aberafan on the mouth of the River Afan. Industrialisation increased with the arrival of railways in the 19th century, and some seventeen railway enterprises appeared across the region. One of these was a proposal in 1864 by the Neath and Pelenna Colliery Company to connect its workings at Blaen Pelenna and Rhondda to the Vale of Neath Railway. The contractor from Swansea was John Dickson (1819-1892), often confused with John Dixon. However not only was the price of coal insufficient to justify the railway, but the Neath and Pelenna Colliery Company itself went into liquidation the following year. Around the same time, John Dickson also surveyed a route for a railway down the Afan valley to Aberafan. When the Afon Valley Railway Act of 1865 authorised construction of the line, Dickson was awarded the contract for £173,000 to be paid in shares and debentures. Due to difficulties over finance and landowner objections, nothing appeared on the ground, and the project was finally abandoned after Dickson's bankruptcy of 1867.

The harbour at Aberafan (usually referred to by the anglicised 'Aberavon' in the 19th century) was an obstacle to industrial growth. Largely through the enterprise of the Talbot family, owners of the Penrice and Margam estates, the harbour was progressively enlarged and improved. The forceful Christopher Rice Mansel Talbot (1803-1890) established the Port Talbot Company and on his death was succeeded by his equally forceful daughter, Emily Charlotte Talbot (1840-1918). Around 1830 Christopher Talbot, along with three local industrialists (John Vigurs, Robert Smith and John Reynolds) and the English Copper Company, instigated a report on possible improvements to the harbour. They balked at the estimated cost of £34,000 but, three years later, joined with one of the partners in the Neath Abbey Ironworks to set up the Aberavon Harbour Company, its major investors being the English Copper Company and Talbot himself. The original plans were for construction of quays and deepening the approach but were soon superseded by a more ambitious scheme. A new river channel was cut to provide a more direct route to the sea, with lock gates to maintain deep water in the harbour, where a new floating dock was constructed. From the harbour a canal was cut to serve the English Copper Company's works. Henceforth the harbour was to be known as Port Talbot. Perhaps by now realising the cost of large engineering works, Christopher Talbot and his partners now approved the estimate of £30,000, although the actual cost later rose to nearly £40,000.

Unfortunately, income from the new Port Talbot was lower than expected and the Aberavon Harbour Company found itself unable to pay dividends or interest on mortgages. Legal action by the English Copper Company precipitated the harbour company into the hands of a receiver in 1868. Christopher Talbot and the English Copper Company then settled their disagreements and the harbour company emerged from its financial difficulties. A period of relative prosperity ensued, with the harbour facilities being enhanced by new railway lines and coal drops, but was short-lived. In 1866 the harbour company again went into receivership, this time initiated by Talbot's claim for unpaid interest. Once again differences were settled, but now all partners agreed that the facilities at Port Talbot needed significant expenditure if they were to become profitable.

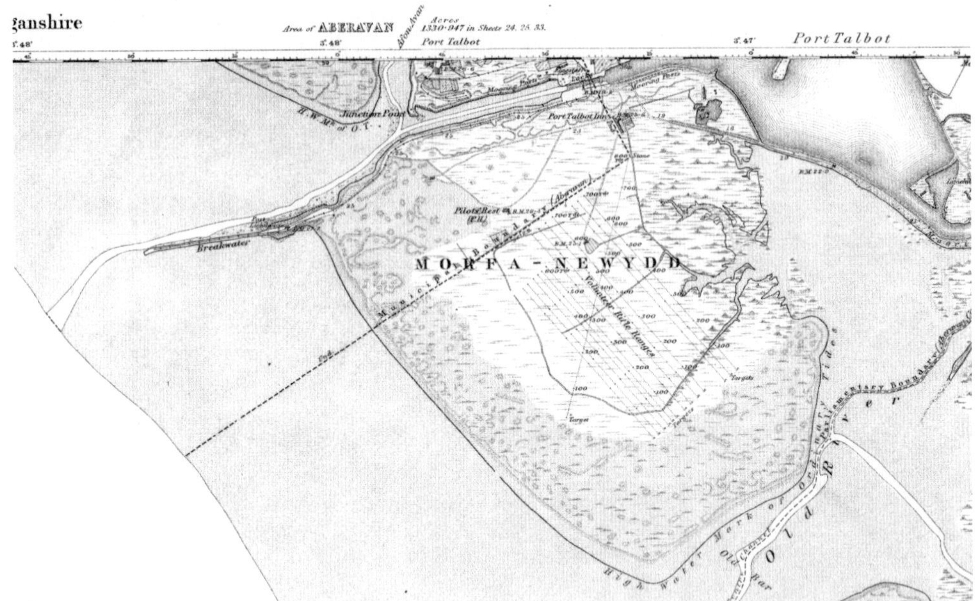

New locks at Port Talbot. The locks appear at the extreme upper edge of the map. Ordnance Survey Six Inch Series Surveyed 1876, published 1883, Glamorgan XXXIII (Inset XXXIIIA). Reproduced by permission of the National Library of Scotland.

In 1872 the Port Talbot partners agreed to build new railways to connect the Rhondda coalfields to Port Talbot, where they would improve the harbour facilities. Although they initially intended to obtain a new Act of Parliament for this work, it never proceeded beyond the Bill stage and the work was paid for using capital authorised by the 1865 Act. In June 1873 they advertised for tenders to carry out the following work:

- Extend the existing breakwater by 377 yards
- Build an additional lock 15 yards wide and 50 yards long
- Extend the wharfage to a total of four wharves
- Dredge and deepen the enclosed harbour.

On 19 March 1874 the contract was let for £33,600 to John Dixon. Given the dubious state of the harbour company finances, the cost was carried personally by Christopher Talbot although some of this was offset by giving him guaranteed preference shares. Talbot assumed overall supervision, with the harbour master becoming clerk of works and a Mr Brady the resident engineer. By April 1874 it was reported that Dixon was 'prosecuting the works with vigour and, subject to favourable weather and freedom from accident, he anticipates completion of both these works about the month of June 1875.' The following month he purchased a five-ton hand crane for use at Port Talbot. The breakwater was constructed using stones quarried at Craig Avon, north of Aberavon. John received his final payment in April 1876.

By the time of his death in 1890 Christopher Talbot owned the entire Port Talbot Company, which was then inherited by his eldest daughter, Emily Charlotte. By then the Rio Tinto company had taken over the CwmAvon copper works and was importing copper ore from Spain, via John Dixon's ore-leading facility at Huelva.

After John's death, a syndicate called the Port Talbot Dock and Railway Company Limited was formed in 1892 with the ambitious plans to take over Port Talbot, extend the facilities, open previously-closed collieries and sink new pits. Discussion took place between Emily Talbot's agent and the syndicate, who then prepared a share prospectus, but nothing came of the initiative. Their engineers were John and Howard Brunlees, sons of John's long-standing engineering colleague Sir James Brunlees.

In a bizarre incident at Winchester in 1902, Howard Brunlees was charged with maliciously wounding a constable when his wife, fearing her husband's violent behaviour, called the police. Constable Muldowney found Brunlees in the house with a gun; Brunlees went out into the street, followed by Muldowney, who attempted to take the weapon. In the ensuing struggle it went off, shattering the constable's hand. Brunlees claimed that Muldowney was trespassing when he entered the house, and that the gunshot was an accident.

Meanwhile, new docks had been built in 1894, and the twentieth century saw continued development, with the construction of the Port Talbot Steel Works, and later the BP chemical plant at Baglan Bay.

CwmAvon Iron Works

John Dixon's contract for the harbour facilities at Port Talbot led to a highly profitable speculation in the CwmAvon Iron Works with James Shaw. John was well-acquainted with Shaw, who had given him the contract for the construction of the Pont des Anglais bridge over the River Nile in 1871.

The CwmAvon works had started in 1757 when two entrepreneurs acquired land up the Avon valley with the intention of opening collieries and smelting copper. After building a horse tramway down to the Avon

Top) View of the lock gates built by John Dixon at Port Talbot, probably taken just before the dock extensions of 1894.

Above) Photograph from 1897 of the extensive redevelopment of the Port Talbot docks, which swept away John Dixon's works.

Both images reproduced by courtesy of Robin Simmonds, author of the two-volume history of Port Talbot.

estuary they sold their embryonic business to the oddly-named Governor and Company of Copper Miners of England (generally referred to as the English Copper Company). The English Copper Company completed the copper works, starting production in 1774 using ore from Cornwall, Anglesey, Scotland and Ireland.

In a separate venture, Samuel Lettsom built a blast furnace at CwmAvon in 1819, to use local deposits of iron ore, limestone and coal. This was soon taken over by John Vigurs and Robert Smith who added a second blast furnace, a tinplate works and a chemical and acid works. Vigurs and Smith inevitably became involved with collieries and tramways to service their works. Then on 29 May 1841 the English Copper Company took over the entire CwmAvon Works, increasing iron-making with three more blast furnaces and adding a rolling mill, an engineering foundry and fitting shops. CwmAvon grew into a mighty business operation, eventually extending to 4,000 acres with about 8,000 people dependent on the works for their livelihood. The copper smelting operation was the largest in the world, with additional mining, colliery and brick-making interests. The company also maintained an office at No.27 Martin's Lane, off Cannon Street in London, and quite close to Dixon's office on Laurence Pountney Hill.

In spite of its spread of businesses, the English Copper Company was unable to pay interest on mortgages with the result that the Bank of England took possession of the works from 1848 to 1852 and reorganised the company. A period of relative prosperity followed, but poor management, a three-month strike, and finally the catastrophic drop in demand for iron rails after the introduction of steel rails, led to the liquidation of the entire business in July 1876. The scene was set for James Shaw's take-over and asset-stripping.

John Dixon's investment in CwmAvon

In April 1877 James Shaw, with partners James Spence of Liverpool and John Dixon, purchased the CwmAvon Works, which had been valued at £1¼ million, for only £55,000. James Spence (1829-1894) was a prominent Liverpool merchant engaged in the trade with America. He was born in Ireland but emigrated to Philadelphia to live with an uncle who was a partner in the Quaker shipping firm of Richardson, Watson and Company. In 1854 he returned to Britain where he set up the shipping merchants of Richardson, Spence and Company in Liverpool. It is not known whether these Quaker Richardsons were related to the Quaker Richardsons of the north-east of England; James Richardson of the leather manufacturers E and J Richardson in Newcastle was John Dixon's brother-in-law. Incidentally, the Liverpool merchant James Spence is not to be confused with the James Spence who owned the Bedlington Iron Works before it was acquired by Jaspar Capper Mounsey and John Dixon in 1861.

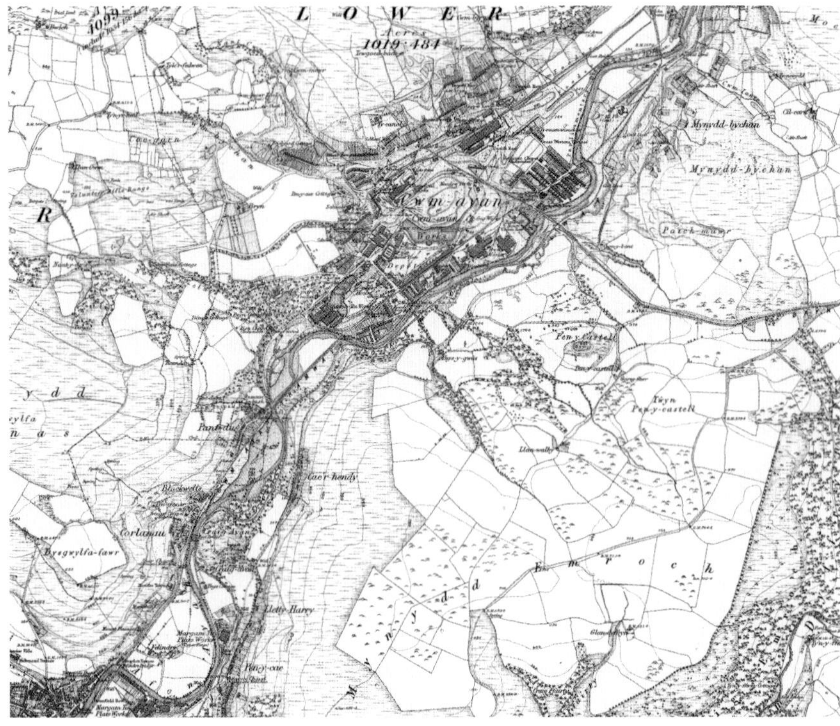

CwmAvon Works. Ordnance Survey Six Inch Series Surveyed 1875-77, published 1884, Glamorgan XXV.
Reproduced by permission of the National Library of Scotland.

Both Shaw and Spence held right-wing views. Shaw was strongly anti-union, blaming the Welsh working man for the demise of the CwmAvon Works, and Spence was a strong advocate to the Southern (pro-slavery) States in America, in spite of his Quaker business associates. John Dixon, with a liberal Quaker upbringing, perhaps had mixed feelings about his new partners, but his appetite for a good business opportunity no doubt outweighed any unease he may have felt.

Right from the time of the acquisition, the intention had been to split the sprawling business up into two or three separate establishments. Within six months the tinplate works had been sold to the Copper Miners' Tinplate Company Limited for £51,000 and a £25,000 sale had been agreed for the blast furnaces. By now the blast furnaces were processing ore from the Rio Tinto mines in Spain, exported via John's Muelle del Tinto at Huelva which had been completed in 1876.

The previous owner's poor management was evidenced by the ready sale of £15,000 of copper furnace bottoms, £15,000 of pig iron, and £12,500 of scrap iron, all of which were lying around on the site. A further £10,000 was realised by the sale of some of the houses to private buyers. So, remarkably, some £128,500 was realised within a year of the partners acquiring the business for just £55,000. The CwmAvon Estates and Works Company Limited continued to operate the remaining collieries, wharves, foundries, engineering and fitting shops, brickworks, chemical and acid works until 1882, with James Shaw as Managing Director. Shaw had dissolved the partnership in 1879, paying Spence and Dixon each £38,500 over and above their initial capital. It was commented at the time that Spence and Dixon never had occasion to spend ten days at the works. Obviously, this had been a very profitable venture for John who, with hindsight, had left the business at just the right time.

Rio Tinto at CwmAvon

By 1881 the health of James Shaw was seriously impaired and he left the CwmAvon works; he died within two years. CwmAvon was then taken over by Samuel Danks (1840-1913), a man with iron industry experience in the Midlands and in Spain. He should not be confused with the Samuel Danks of the Cincinnati Railway Iron Works who devised a mechanical puddling furnace in the 1870s and which was introduced into the Middlesbrough iron industry. The Rio Tinto company in Spain was interested in opening a works in Britain and purchased the CwmAvon copper smelting business from Danks, who continued to run the rest of the works. Rio Tinto imported ore from their Spanish mines, via John's ore-loading pier at Huelva to the CwmAvon wharf at Port Talbot and thence by rail to the smelter.

The quantities of noxious fumes produced by the smelting process resulted in damage to agricultural land within a radius of several miles, adversely affecting some of Emily Talbot's tenant farmers. At first, she reduced their rents but in 1893 she obtained an injunction restraining the smelting. Fear of the consequences for the 500 men employed at the works made her refrain from pressing the injunction, hoping that the company would leave CwmAvon. It was not until 1906 that Rio Tinto ceased operations at CwmAvon and built a new plant at Port Talbot.

CwmAvon Works in 1880, the year after John Dixon left the business, showing employees' houses in close proximity to the works and the pollution caused by the smelting operations. By then, ore from the Rio Tinto mines in Spain was being processed.
Reproduced by courtesy of Robin Simmonds.

Acknowledgements

Robin Simmonds, an invaluable source of information on the development of Port Talbot.

Damian Owen, Port Talbot Historical Society, and Harriet Eaton, Heritage Education Officer at Neath Port Talbot libraries, for assistance with locating images.

References

Milford Haven and its New Pier Works
Henry Davey
Transactions of the Society of Engineers, London, November 1872, pages 89-111
Full description of the iron pier and harbour facilities completed by 1872, not involving John Dixon.

History of the Steel Industry in the Port Talbot Area 1900-1988
Stephen Parry
PhD thesis, University of Leeds, 2011
First chapter covers the early history of the CwmAvon Works and the development of Port Talbot harbour.

Michaelston-Super-Avon, with the Hamlet of Cwm-Avon
Post Office Directory, 1871
Good description of the works, properties and residents at Cwm Avon.

A History of the Port Talbot Railway & Docks Company and the South Wales Mineral Railway Company, Volume 1: 1853-1907
Robin G Simmonds
Lightmore Press, Lydney, Gloucestershire, 2012
Well researched history including the Port Talbot company and the CwmAvon company.

In Parliament - Session 1872 Port Talbot Harbour and Rhondda Valley Railway
The Standard, London, 18 November 1871, page 7
Details of a Parliamentary Bill to authorise construction of railway and port facilities.

Port Talbot Harbour
Engineering, London, 7 November 1873, page 374
Great improvements about to be commenced by John Dixon.

The Governor and Company of Copper Miners in England
The Effect of the Late Strike
Western Mail, Cardiff, 6 April 1874, page 6
Report of the AGM. 'The contract for lengthening the lock and extending the breakwater a length of 377 yards has been let to Mr John Dixon, who has been prosecuting the works with vigour; and, subject to favourable weather and freedom from accident, he anticipates completion of both these works about the month of June 1875.'

Money Market and City News
The Morning Post, London, 8 April 1874, page 7
Contract let for work at Port Talbot to extend lock and build breakwater, cost £33,600.

Advertisements and notices
Western Mail, 16 May 1874
John Dixon's advertisement for a five-ton hand crane at Port Talbot.

Railway and Other Companies
The Times, London, 16 May 1877, page 7
The Cwm Avon Iron Works has been disposed of by the liquidator to Mr James Shaw of 150 Leadenhall Street. It is intended to divide the huge concern into two or three separate establishments.

Railway and Other Companies
The Times, London, 20 October 1877, page 7
Cwm Avon Iron Works. Tinplate works sold for £51,000. Also sold have been £15,000 copper furnace bottoms, £15,000 of pig iron, £12,500 scrap iron, £10,000 private houses. The blast furnaces are about to be sold for £25,000. The collieries, wharfs, foundries, engineering and fitting shops, brickworks, chemical and acid works all remain.

A Successful Speculation
The Cheltenham Looker On, 20 September 1879, page 605
James Shaw of 105 Leadenhall Street bought the works at Cwm Avon in April 1877 with partners James Spence and John Dixon. Partnership just dissolved paying Spence and Dixon each £38,500 over and above their initial capital. 'The business has been entirely managed by Mr Shaw, his two partners never having occasion to spend ten days at the works.'

Notes from the South-West
Engineering, London, 7 January 1881, page 9
Due to the illness of Mr Shaw, the CwmAvon Works will be taken over by a new company.

Struggle for a gun
Pateley Bridge and Nidderdale Herald, 8 November 1902, page 6
The best account of the incident when Howard Brunlees shot a police constable in Winchester.

The Rio Tinto Works at CwmAvon - Generous conduct of Miss Talbot - Important correspondence
South Wales Daily News, Cardiff, 26 June 1893, page 6
The dispute with the CwmAvon Works over pollution of agricultural fields and Miss Talbot's injunction.

13 Viaducts on the Whitby to Loftus Railway

John Dixon designed five viaducts for the railway line between Whitby and Loftus in the early 1870s. These carried the railway across valleys on wrought iron girders supported by wrought iron columns filled with concrete. It was unusual for John to work as a design engineer rather than a contractor, and his design drew praise from the engineering profession for its grace and economy. Unfortunately, shortcomings in the construction resulted in serious problems, initially brought to light by the scathing report of the North Eastern Railway company engineer. The extent of John's responsibility for the shortcomings in the viaducts is open to debate, more blame lying with the contractor, John Dickson. Not surprisingly some material on the viaducts confuses John Dixon with John Dickson.

Sorry beginnings of the railway from Whitby to Loftus

In 1866 the Whitby, Redcar and Middlesbrough Union Railway was granted an Act of Parliament to construct a 16-mile long railway between Whitby and Loftus, where it would join up with the existing North Eastern Railway line to Middlesbrough. In contrast to the over-optimistic prospectus, which predicted high volumes of traffic in ironstone and other minerals, passengers and fish, the line turned out to be a commercial failure. It has been described as 'a more spectacular example of a loss-making branch would be hard to find' and a 'profitless appendage'.

Site work did not begin until May 1871, when the first sod was cut at Sandsend by the Marchioness of Normanby, using a silver spade and an oak wheelbarrow. In spite of a call for divine blessing on the project by the vicar of Lythe, as soon as the Marchioness lifted the spade it started to pour with rain, an omen of the troubles that would afflict the line. Probably in order to facilitate land purchase, the route followed the coastline, in places very close to the cliff edge. This would require many bridges and tunnels, although funds were extremely limited. Economy of construction was a priority but, even so, the final cost of the line would be nearly three times the original estimate. Julian Horn Tolmé (1836-1878) of Westminster was engaged as the consulting engineer, assisted by Arthur Samuel Hamand (1847-1888). The contractor for construction of the line was John Dickson (1819-1892), who agreed to complete the line by midsummer 1873 for a fixed sum. Dickson was assisted by his younger brother James and his son John. In the mid-1880s John Dickson junior moved to Glaisdale Hall on the North York Moors and purchased the Glaisdale Ironworks, which had ceased operation in 1875.

The Directors' Meeting in September 1873 was a sorry affair. They reported that more progress could have been made if John Dickson had exhibited more vigour. Work on the Staithes Viaduct had been suspended pending slight modifications, and there had been great difficulty in recruiting labour. John Dickson, who seconded the vote of thanks to the chairman, was none the less dismissed at the end of 1873 and Tolmé followed him a few months later. Hamand, trained by Brunel and the best of the bunch, was caught in the cross-fire between the board, Tolmé and Dickson. He left in 1874. The directors then asked the North Eastern Railway Chief Engineer, Thomas Elliot Harrison (1808-1888), to make a detailed survey of the line. His report was critical of John Dixon's design for the viaducts, but more critical of Dickson's construction. Harrison's judgement on John Dixon's engineering competence may well have been instrumental in his tender for the Forth Bridge being rejected, as explained in Chapter 22.

North Eastern Railway to the rescue

Towards the end of 1874 the Whitby, Redcar and Middlesbrough Union Railway Company was virtually bankrupt and construction work halted, although the line was still not complete. The North Eastern Railway Company agreed to take the line over but only if much of the cliff-edge route was abandoned in favour of an inland route, which would need another tunnel. The new route was passed by Parliament in July 1876. Construction of the line was completed by John Waddell (1828-1888) of Edinburgh, known in North Yorkshire as 'Paddy Waddell' for his work on the never-completed link line (Paddy Waddell's Railway) from the North Eastern Railway at Skelton to the Esk Valley line at Glaisdale. Further delays meant that the Whitby to Loftus line did not open for traffic until December 1883, more than twelve years after work had started. It survived however until 1958, five years before Dr Beeching's rationalisation plan.

John Dixon's viaducts

Five substantial viaducts were needed to cross ravines; in line order from Whitby these were at Upgang, Newholme, East Row, Sandsend and Staithes. John Dickson gave the contracts for the design and supply of these five viaducts to John Dixon, at a cost of £23,452. Additional smaller timber bridges were not part of John's work on the railway. John Dickson would have been responsible for the erection of the five viaducts working

Who's who?
John Dickson (1819-1892)

John Dickson was born at Berwick on Tweed, but spent much of his early life in Ireland, where he married and had four children. Dickson worked on railway construction until he left Ireland, in his late twenties, to set up as a railway contractor and builder in Wellington, Shropshire. One of his first contracts was for the Shrewsbury and Birmingham railway in 1847-49, and in 1852 he went into partnership with Colin McKenzie and George Knox. They established a large engineering works adjacent to the Shrewsbury and Birmingham Railway, building carriages, wagons and all manner of railway equipment. Dickson then fell out with his two partners who left in 1854, leaving him to struggle on alone. Fortunately, he was awarded the contract for the South Wales Mineral Railway, where Isambard Kingdom Brunel was the company engineer. Unsurprisingly, Brunel specified his beloved broad-gauge track for the line. There was a separate contract for the Gyfylchi tunnel, which Brunel estimated would cost £27,500 whereas Dickson's tender was £25,500. Dickson's tenders were usually low and seem to have been based more on optimism rather than business acumen. He started work on the tunnel in 1856 but within a few months the railway directors instructed Brunel to dismiss him and find an alternative contractor.

Dickson still had work on the Wellington and Severn Junction Railway, but he woefully underestimated the costs when preparing his tender and by January 1857 he was bankrupt. At that time he was also working on five contracts at Swansea harbour. After the acceptance of one of these contracts he admitted 'a clerical error' and increased the price. On another contract, a wall began to give way soon after it was completed.

Discharged from his first bankruptcy in June 1857, Dickson left Wellington for Swansea, where he started up a new business concentrating on railway construction. He surveyed a route for the Afon Valley Railway and was awarded the contract for £173,000. However, due to difficulties over company finance and landowner objections, nothing appeared on the ground. The project was finally abandoned with Dickson's second bankruptcy in September 1867, not altogether Dickson's fault as he had been caught up in the 1866 collapse of the Overend and Gurney Bank.

Discharged from his second bankruptcy in March 1868, Dickson moved to Liverpool. He was awarded the construction contract for the Whitby to Loftus Railway in 1871, which included viaducts designed by John Dixon. Due to a lack of progress and poor workmanship his contract was terminated in December 1873. Dickson's younger brother James and his son John also worked on the Whitby to Loftus line.

Meanwhile John Dickson senior had been awarded a contract for the proposed Mersey railway tunnel at Liverpool. With his chequered history, it might have been thought that company directors would have been wary of accepting a tender from him. He started work on a shaft on the Birkenhead side but, once again, his disregard for the financial aspects of the business overtook him and he was bankrupt for a third time in December 1874.

Emerging from his third bankruptcy undaunted, Dickson proceeded to develop his long-standing interest in a railway between Swansea and Mumbles. His last scheme was for a wide promenade along the shore from Swansea, with hotels and boarding houses. All that was achieved was an artist's impression. John Dickson died in June 1892 and was buried in Wellington. A Swansea newspaper, *The Cambrian*, noted that 'his great forte was as a contractor of railways and in this line of business he attained to a high level of success for many years' and 'in Mr Dickson we lose a man of a kind heart and a great keenness and capacity.' Less reverentially but more accurately a Swansea historian, Paul Reynolds, has written that 'his schemes were often wildly optimistic, his finances were never on a sound footing, and it has to be said that his standards of workmanship were not always the highest.'

John Dickson. The unfortunate contractor in an unfortunate pose, with dividers and ruler. It would not be practicable to take measurments from a drawing on one's lap. Reproduced by courtesy of the City and County of Swansea, Swansea Museums Collection. Reference SM 1896.125.134.

Clockwise from top left)

1) 'Plate 20 Staithes Viaduct' engraving from Girder Making and the Practice of Bridge Building in Wrought Iron by Edward Hutchinson. The viaduct is under construction. It is not clear how workmen gained access to rivet each new wrought iron section as the columns were built up, but it must have been a hazardous operation.

2) Fig 56 from Girder Making and the Practice of Bridge Building in Wrought Iron by Edward Hutchinson, showing how the vertical columns were joined to the bridge spans.

3) 'Upgang Viaduct, Whitby and Middlesbrough Railway' a dramatic engraving of one of John Dixon's viaducts by J Swain, looking inland.
The Engineer, London, 14 March 1873, page 158.

to John Dixon's drawings and specification. It is not known whether Dixon or Tolmé exercised any oversight of John Dickson's work. The responsibilities of the design engineer and the consulting engineer would not include detailed supervision of the contractor but, given the widespread interest in the viaducts, particularly over Staithes Beck, Dixon may have been expected to witness some of the construction. Tolmé did make regular visits in order to deliver progress reports to the directors, but these may have been fairly superficial.

The design of the viaducts was challenging, particularly across the deep ravine at Staithes Beck. Using his experience with pier construction, John provided an elegant and cost-effective solution. Staithes Viaduct was a particularly impressive structure, its 700 feet length divided into seventeen lattice girder spans, and a maximum height of 160 feet over the Staithes Beck, 2 feet higher than the High Level Bridge at Newcastle upon Tyne. Supporting columns were fabricated from 5/16 inch thick wrought iron plate, rolled into tubes which were mounted on cast iron bed-plates embedded in concrete foundations. The shorter tubes were 2 feet 6 inches in diameter, while the longer tubes tapered from 4 feet 6 inches at the base to 2 feet 6 inches at the top. The columns were filled with a concrete mix of 1:4 Portland cement and gravel. Although not obvious at first sight, the viaduct spans were carried by the concrete infill, the wrought iron tubes just serving to contain the concrete. This was achieved by sliding into the top of each column a circular casting, topped with a wide bedplate which projected beyond the outer diameter of the column. As the concrete set, a small clearance was maintained between the lower face of the bedplate and the top of the wrought iron tube, ensuring that the weight of the span was taken by the concrete infill.

John's design for the viaducts followed the pioneering work of James Brunlees on bridges and piers, but with even lighter-weight construction using tubular supports of wrought iron rather than cast iron. He claimed that his invention had the merit of being the cheapest form of pier yet introduced, where the height was great and other conditions favourable. Edward Hutchinson of the Skerne Ironworks commented that the cost was lower than for piers of solid masonry or hollow columns of cast or wrought iron. Hutchinson wisely observed that the stability of the piers would, to a great measure, depend on the quality of the concrete infill. At the time *The Engineer* magazine commented favourably on the design of the viaducts. British practice had been to over-design, ensuring safety by 'reckless extravagance rather than by a well-considered scientific disposition of material'. While not advocating the 'extremes of Continental refinement' or the 'adoption of American recklessness' it was felt that there was room for improvement in British bridge design.

The wrought iron columns and iron work were produced at the Skerne Ironworks in Darlington and may have been taken to the site by sea. Early completion of the viaducts was important to give access to other parts of the line, and by February 1873 four of the five were complete. The Upgang Viaduct had been tested with double the maximum working load and had 'stood the test in the most satisfactory manner, there being no signs of defect or failure in the slightest degree'. The Staithes Viaduct had required some slight modifications in the design of the larger spans but was now in the course of erection and would be completed during 1874, by which time all other work on the line had ceased due to lack of finance. The construction of all the viaducts was noteworthy in that there were no serious accidents during the two years of engineering works.

While the erection of the viaducts was carried out by John Dickson, there was a representative from the Skerne Iron Works managing on site assembly of the wrought iron components. He is believed to have been Henry Kinloch from Darlington, recorded in census returns as a fitter in his late thirties. He may not have appreciated the critical importance of column alignment, and there were never any questions about the quality of the wrought iron work, so there are no grounds for implicating him in the problems with the viaducts.

John Dixon's patent

John Dixon clearly thought highly of his design for the viaducts and attempted to patent the concept.

> 222. J. DIXON, *London, "Piers of bridges and viaducts." – Dated 18th January, 1873*
> This provisional specification describes forming piers of tubes made from plates of iron bent into a cylindrical form and riveted together. The tubes are then filled with concrete which maintains them in form and also aids in supporting the load placed upon them.

This patent number (222) is exactly the same as for his 1868 patent for the floating swimming pool. Certainly 19th century engineers were obsessed with patents; in a typical year *The Patent Journal* might include over 4,000 patents granted.

It is difficult to understand exactly what innovation John had in mind when applying for the patent. The practice of using concrete-filled columns was well established, as made clear in an editorial in *The Engineer* of 4 October 1873. The practice of supporting the superstructure of a bridge on hollow cylinders had been in use for thirty years. Cylinders might be cast or wrought iron, and the function of the iron cylinder was to retain the concrete, and not to carry any of the weight of the bridge. Indeed, the editorial went on to suggest, somewhat mischievously, that once the bridge was completed the iron cylinders might be removed.

'Sandsend Viaduct c1890' by Elijah Yeoman. Elijah Yeoman (1849-1930) was the son of a Coverdale farmer. A highly accomplished photographer, by the end of the 19th century he had studios in Barnard Castle, Hartlepool and Kirkby Stephen. The Bowes Museum at Barnard Castle holds a large collection of his images, and many have been digitised by Keith Orange of Vintage Graphics, Barnard Castle. This view is towards the sea, with the alum works gable end walls clearly visible beyond the viaduct.
The locomotive is North Eastern Railway Class 398 No.1376 built in 1875-76 at Robert Stephenson's Works in Newcastle.
The identity of the gentleman standing by Sandsend Beck is unknown.

SANDSEND, NR. WHITBY, YORKSHIRE

From a Water Colour by JACK MERRIOTT, R.I.

Above) 'Sandsend, Nr Whitby, Yorkshire' British Railways (North East Region) carriage print from a watercolour by Jack Merriott. Jack Merriott (1901-1968) from Greenwich was an artist and poster designer who also taught and wrote books on art. He died from injuries received in a car accident. The scene shows a train on the Sandsend Viaduct as it leaves the station. In the foreground are the gable ends of the alum works and, on the shore, the remains of the sea wall, devastated by a sea mine which broke from its moorings on 26 January 1940. Reproduced by permission of the National Railway Museum (NRM Pictorial Collection / Science and Society Picture Library). NRM reference 1976-9452.

Right) 'Yorkshire Coast near Whitby' London and North Eastern Railway 1937 poster by Frank Mason. Frank Henry Algernon Mason (1875-1965) from Hartlepool was a maritime and poster artist and a founder member of the Staithes Art Club (now known as the Staithes group of artists). Unusually for railway posters, this scene is entirely imaginary. The location does not exist and the train is clearly an LNER east coast mainline express, with nine coaches headed by an A3 Pacific locomotive. Even on holiday weekends the Middlesbrough to Whitby trains would not exceed five coaches, and their engines would be far less glamorous. Reproduced by permission of the National Railway Museum (NRM Pictorial Collection / Science and Society Picture Library). NRM reference 1986-9208.

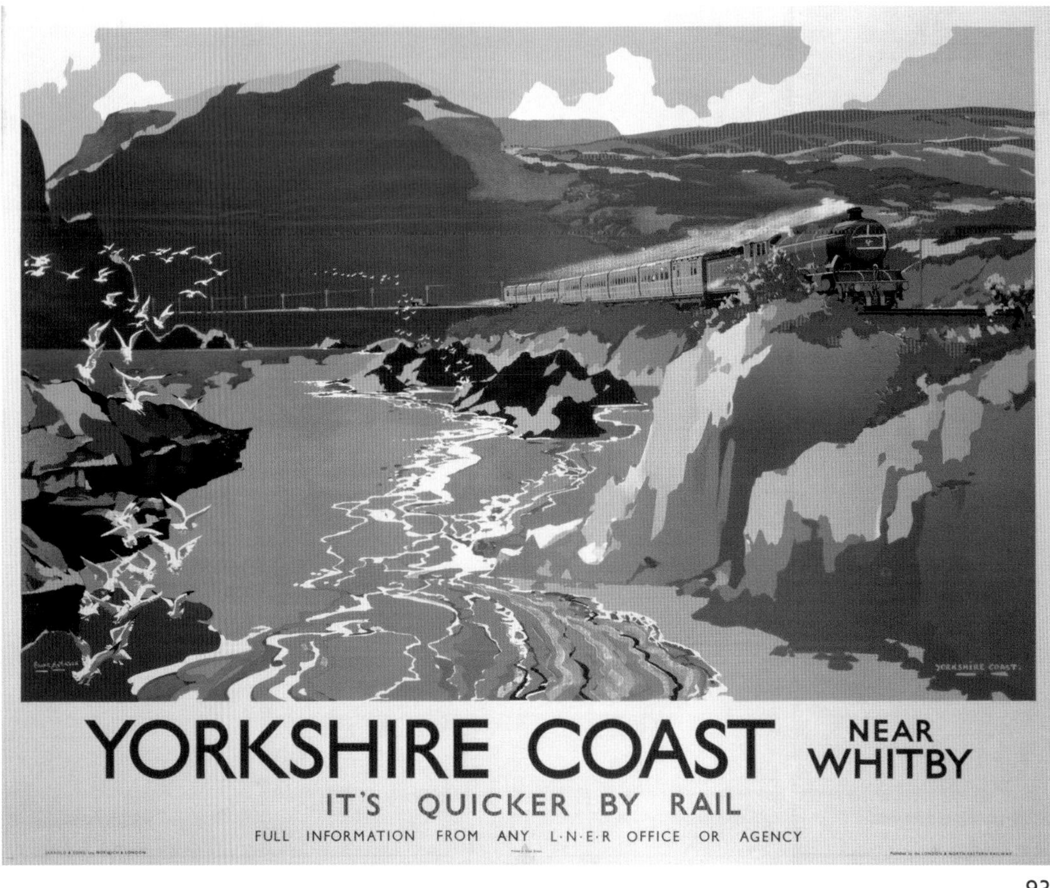

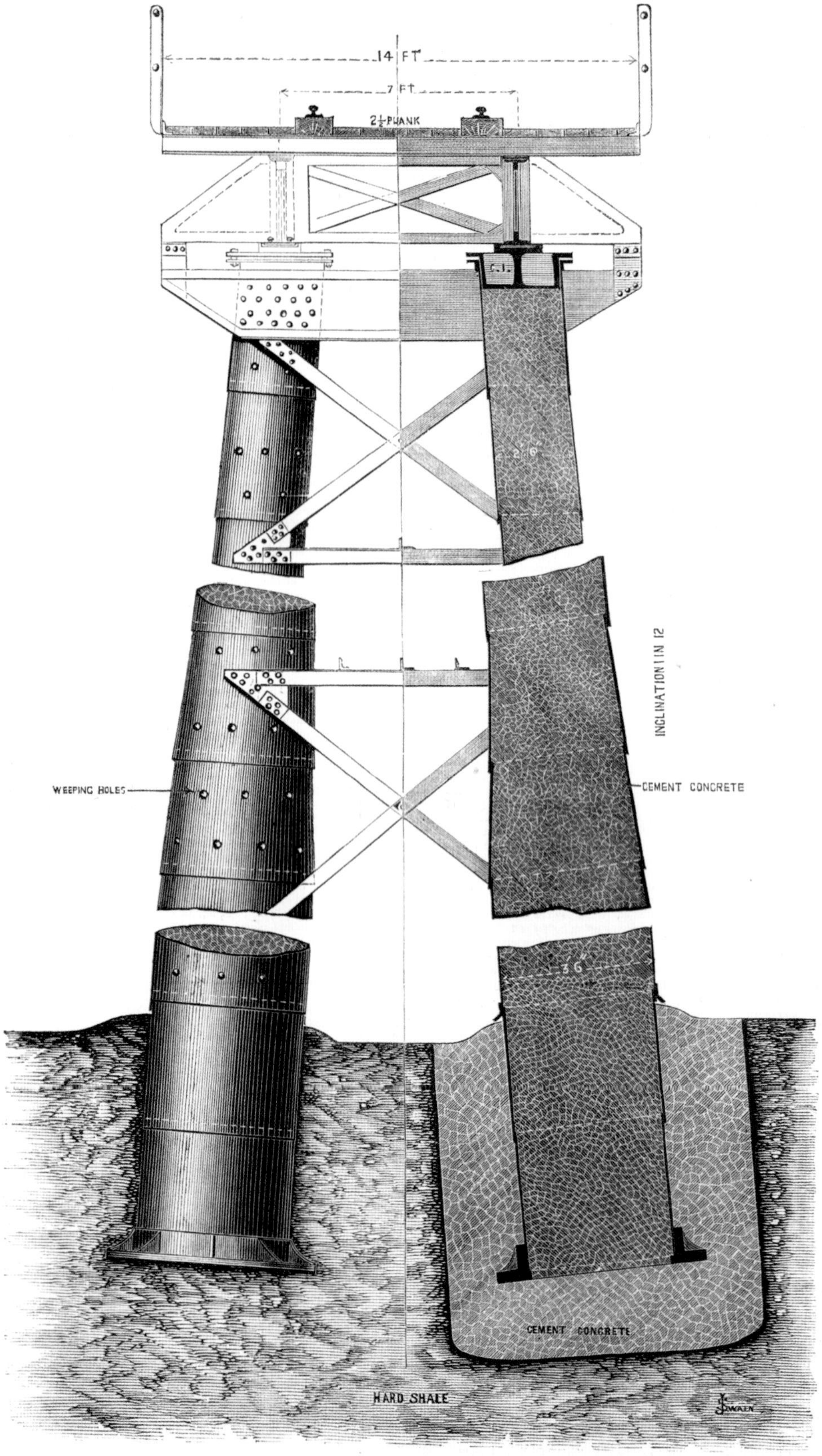

14 FT
7 FT
2½ PLANK
C.I.
INCLINATION 1 IN 12
WEEPING HOLES
CEMENT CONCRETE
CEMENT CONCRETE
HARD SHALE

SECTION OF DIXON'S PATENT PIERS, WHITBY AND MIDDLESBROUGH RAILWAY.

Left) Section of Dixon's Patent Piers, Whitby and Middlesbrough Railway. Engraving by J Swain. John Swain (1829-1898) initially worked as a wood engraver for Punch magazine but later took up technical engravings on metal and was regularly employed by The Engineer. The cross section upper right clearly shows the viaduct supported on the concrete infill rather than on the wrought iron columns. It is some of these castings (marked as 'C.I.' in the engraving) that lie discarded at Sandsend.
The Engineer, 14 March 1873, page 151

Above) The castings from the top of the columns from the Sandsend Viaduct lying alongside the old railway track just west of the site of Sandsend Station.
Discovered by Colin Keighley and photographed by the author.

North Eastern Railway criticism of the line

Thomas Elliot Harrison was the chief engineer of the North Eastern Railway from its formation in 1854 until his death in 1888 (see Who's Who in Chapter 14). In this position, and with his recent survey of the viaducts, he was a key figure in the acquisition of the Whitby to Loftus railway by the North Eastern Railway. Without wishing to be critical of Harrison's qualities, he was probably more of a railway man than a civil engineer, and his civil engineering experience at this time was mainly with masonry, rather than iron, structure. With his knowledge based on practical experience rather than technical training, he tended to be conservative in his judgements. When Harrison made his report to the North Eastern Railway, the many shortcomings of Tolmé and the Dicksons came to light. In fact, his report is so scathing that it is difficult to understand why the North Eastern Railway Company agreed to take the line over. Harrison's report of 14 November 1883 included some specific comments on the viaducts:

> 'The roadway for the permanent way over the viaducts was of the flimsiest character and as such no Govt. Inspector would have under any circumstances have passed, and an entire new roadway was provided for all the viaducts as soon as it could be done without stopping the other work.'
>
> 'It was considered necessary also to provide for the Staithes and Upgang viaducts two rows of longitudinal bracing to prevent buckling of the high piers, and this was done without delay.'
>
> 'It would be difficult to find anywhere a work so thoroughly scamped from end to end as this was when taken over by the company. Viaducts and ordinary bridges badly designed and as badly executed, and in a dangerous state.'

Harrison's criticism of the 'flimsiest character' of the roadway can be challenged. Scaling up from John Dixon's engineering drawing reproduced in *The Engineer* of 14 March 1873, the rails were mounted on longitudinal timbers of section 7 inches x 14 inches. Robert Stephenson used identically sized timbers on the Britannia Tubular Bridge. It would therefore be unfair to condemn John's design, it is possible that Dickson had substituted less substantial timbers in order to economise.

Other defects on the viaducts came to light at this time. Several of the columns were not perpendicular, in one case to the extent of 7 inches, in others between 3 inches and 4 inches. There was evidence of some buckling of columns on the two highest viaducts, at Staithes and at Upgang. The wrought iron girders forming the bridge spans had been prefabricated with the fastening brackets for the piers at fixed positions along their length. This meant that the foundations for the columns had to be in exactly the correct position, a difficult task given the nature of the valley sides. When the girders were being installed, if the top of a pier was not in quite the right lateral position, it would have to be moved to fit, compromising the verticality and possibly initiating some of the buckling.

Photograph of the Staithes Viaduct by Elijah Yeoman. This was taken after the North Eastern Railway demanded two rows of longitudinal girders be installed between the vertical columns. Reproduced by courtesy of Keith Orange of Vintage Graphics, Barnard Castle.

Inspection holes were cut in some of the columns of the Staithes Viaduct, revealing what should have been concrete to be just gravel without any cement. Immediate rectification work was started, installing two rows of longitudinal bracing at Staithes, and one row at Upgang. Liquid cement was pumped into the columns filled with gravel. Misalignment of columns and poor quality of concrete filling, which led to the buckling, would be due to careless erection rather than design faults. It has been suggested however that the problem with the concrete filling may not be 'scamping' but a failure to appreciate that, over the considerable height of a column, the heavier aggregate might migrate down to the base before the concrete had hardened.

Delays in payments to John Dixon

For John to receive monthly payments, as specified in the contract, Tolmé had to issue certificates authorising such payments. Probably because of the company's precarious finances, but much to John's annoyance, Tolmé stopped issuing the certificates in July 1873, in spite of work on the viaducts continuing. The situation was aggravated when John Dickson was dismissed in December 1873, since John's contract had been with him. On 8 May 1874 John wrote a characteristically curt letter to the directors demanding the issuing of certificates and hence payment. By now the final viaduct, at Staithes, was nearing completion. Some payments were made, but John had to pursue the company for several years and, in reality, never received the full amount since some of the payment was in company shares, which were almost worthless.

The aftermath of the Tay Bridge disaster

After the North Eastern Railway had taken over the railway, and while they were working to complete the line, the Tay Railway Bridge collapsed during the night of 28 December 1879. This disaster had far-reaching consequences. It was catastrophic to the career of its designer, Sir Thomas Bouch, and to the supplier of the cast iron columns, Hopkins, Gilkes and Company of Middlesbrough. But it also significantly affected bridges being constructed or planned. With the Court of Enquiry concluding that the Tay Bridge had been blown down, the Board of Trade issued requirements for bridge design to withstand a wind loading of 56 lb/ft^2 (Bouch had admitted to using a value of only 10 lb/ft^2, John Dixon used 28 lb/ft^2 for the Whitby-Loftus viaducts).

With the collapse of the Tay Bridge, suspicion fell on the use of slender iron columns to support bridges, resulting in the over-design of later bridges, notably the Forth Railway Bridge. Although John Dixon's design used concrete-filled wrought iron columns rather than hollow cast iron columns, the North Eastern Railway and the Government Inspectors subjected the viaducts to critical examination.

Inspections reveal serious deficiencies in the viaducts

In his report on the Whitby to Loftus line, Harrison reported that he had seen 'viaducts and ordinary bridges so badly designed and as badly executed as to be in a dangerous condition'. There seems to be no direct evidence to suggest any deficiencies in John Dixon's design. As has been seen, there certainly were serious shortcomings in the construction; gravel rather than concrete in some of the columns, columns not perpendicular and signs of buckling. Longitudinal bracing was added to the viaducts at Staithes and Upgang, and liquid cement was pumped into the columns with defective concrete. In addition, substantial wrought iron wheel guards had to be fitted on either side of the track, and the transverse girders carrying the rails had to be reinforced by riveting channel bars to their undersides. As a result of the new regulations following the Tay Bridge collapse, additional railings were installed to provide a parapet of the specified strength.

The final inspection of the viaducts was by the Government Inspector Major General Hutchinson, who had the dubious honour of having previously inspected the Tay Bridge and declared it safe for operation prior to its collapse. This experience undoubtedly made him apply stringent criteria to the Whitby to Loftus viaducts. His first inspection in July 1883 set down twelve requirements which had to be met before the line could be opened; these included new longitudinal bracing on the Staithes Viaduct and examination of the concrete in all the columns. The Staithes Viaduct, the highest on the line, caused particular concern. Nevertheless, after the additional bracing had been fitted at Staithes, Hutchinson reported that 'as regards vibration and oscillation, the viaducts now behave well with heavy engines passing over them at speed'. A month later a second inspection was carried out, this time by Major Francis Arthur Marindin (see Who's Who in Chapter 21). Marindin paid particular attention to the concrete filling, judging those where cement had been injected to be sound, but this had not yet been done to all the columns so the line could not be opened.

The final inspection report was by Major General Hutchinson in November 1883. The line could be opened on condition that a maximum speed limit of 20 miles per hour was observed on all the viaducts, the bracings should be regularly checked for tightness, and all exposed ironwork must be painted. At Staithes a wind gauge was installed, and rules laid down prohibiting the passage of trains at wind pressures above 28 lb/ft^2. The rectification work on the viaducts had exceeded £30,000 and delayed the opening of the line by eighteen months.

Work in 1893-95

By 1893 some of the bars forming the lattice-work of the girders on the Upgang Viaduct were found to be buckled and two were broken through. This could have been due to excess loading, inadequate design or poor quality wrought iron. Since the Upgang Viaduct had been successfully

East Row Viaduct drawn by Waynman Dixon in 1903. Waynman, now retired from Sir Raylton Dixon's shipyard, had time for leisure activities. It is not known if he drew other scenes from the railway. Original drawing property of the author.

tested with double the maximum working load early in 1873, it would seem that the cause of the failures was deterioration of the wrought iron. Rather than attempt to replace the damaged bars, new ones were fitted alongside. Then the entire length of the bridge was reinforced by riveting on additional ironwork. This was completed by mid-1894, when work began on the East Row Viaduct.

The East Row Viaduct was deemed to be beyond repair due to sea-water corrosion from sea spray in its exposed situation. The original wrought iron girders were replaced by steel ones. To avoid disruption to traffic, the removal of the old spans and installation of the new spans was carried out on Sundays. The East Row work was completed by autumn 1895, from which time it was regularly painted. There were no other problems with the viaducts over the life of the line, which closed in 1958.

The contractor for the repair work on the Upgang and East Row Viaducts was the Cleveland Bridge and Engineering Company of Darlington. This was established in 1877 with its main shareholders being Henry Isaac Dixon and Henry Ernest Dixon, both cutlers in Sheffield. It was said that the impetus to set up the company came from employees of the Skerne Iron Works, which was already in difficulties leading up to its collapse in 1879. In 1885 the Cleveland Bridge and Engineering Company was taken over by Henry Isaac Dixon's son, Charles Frederick Dixon (1859-1898). These Dixons were not related to John.

Demolition of the viaducts in 1960

By the 1950s the Whitby to Loftus line, always in a precarious financial state, was clearly uneconomic. This was mainly due to the greater convenience of the new motor bus services but must have been aggravated by the forecast of £57,000 required for maintenance of the viaducts and tunnels over the next five years. Following closure of the line on 5 May 1958, the viaducts were finally demolished in 1960.

Vestiges of the viaducts remain; at Sandsend one of the bases for the concrete-filled columns still stands in Sandsend Beck and several of the castings from the top of the columns were tipped down the embankment on the east side of the track, north of the station site, where they lie to this day.

Were John Dixon's viaducts adequately designed?

The local historian Michael Aufrere Williams has written the most comprehensive history of the Whitby to Loftus Line. Considering the question of the viaducts, his conclusion was that 'it was not the design that was at fault, but the casual and slack nature of the erection of the viaducts which was to cause so much trouble before the final opening of the line on 3 December 1883.'

It is debatable whether the additional longitudinal bracing at Staithes and Upgang would have been necessary if care had been taken to ensure that the columns were truly perpendicular and correctly filled with concrete in the first place.

While the fundamental design was probably only just adequate, the real faults were due to the 'scamping' during erection. Given the endorsements of John Dixon's work on his previous contracts, it might be supposed that the 'scamping' was by the Dicksons.

Since John was the design engineer rather than the contractor, he would not have been expected to spend much time on site. In any case, he was now taken up with major contracts in Spain and Brazil. A successful engineer achieves the required standard at minimum cost; and it can be argued that the design of the Whitby to Loftus Railway viaducts was marginally inadequate. This was the only occasion when John may have failed to achieve the highest standards of engineering construction.

As the main contractor, Dickson came in for a lot of criticism over his poor standards of workmanship, but some of this criticism has been directed to John Dixon. While it is impossible to be certain, it would appear that John's designs, at least in the case of the two highest viaducts, met the specification but allowed little margin for faults in construction. Unfortunately, supervision during construction was poor, and some faults had to be rectified before the line opened to traffic. These are believed to be the responsibility of Dickson as the contractor, abetted by poor on site inspection by the railway company's engineers. While his design may be exonerated, John should perhaps have spent more time personally on site, particularly as he must have suspected shortcoming in the contractors.

Acknowledgements

Michael Williams, author of several publications about the railway, for discussion of John Dixon's responsibility for the short-comings in the viaducts.

Ken Mell for information sources and images for the Whitby to Loftus railway.

Charles Morris of the Cleveland Industrial Archaeology Society for suggesting a possible reason for deficient concrete filling of the viaduct columns.

Colin Keighley for locating the iron castings from the viaduct column tops at Sandsend.

References

The Whitby-Loftus line: 'a more spectacular example of a loss-making branch would be hard to find'. Is this really the case?
Michael Aufrere Williams
Journal of the Railway and Canal Historical Society, No.216, March 2013
A comprehensive history of the line.

A Difficult Year in the History of the Whitby, Redcar & Middlesbrough Union Railway
Michael Aufrere Williams
Journal of the Railway and Canal Historical Society, No.219, March 2014
The year in question is 1873. This article documents the quarrels between the directors, engineers and contractor, and reproduces in full the scathing report by the NER.

The Viaducts and Tunnels of the Whitby-Loftus Line
Michael Aufrere Williams
Journal of the Railway and Canal Historical Society, No.218, November 2013
Detailed and accurate history of the Whitby, Redcar and Middlesbrough Union Railway and its viaducts by John Dixon. Correctly distinguishes between John Dixon and John Dickson.

Whitby, Redcar, and Middlesbro' Railway, turning of the first sod
The York Herald, 27 May 1871, page 10
Description of the opening ceremony.

Cast-iron and India Rubber: an outline of the life of John Dickson, railway contractor
Paul Reynolds
Bulletin 89, February 2004
South West Wales Industrial Archaeology Society
A comprehensive and accurate description of John Dixon's life and career, although Dickson is credited with the design of the Whitby to Loftus Railway viaducts instead of John Dixon.

The Teign Valley Line
Peter Kay
Wild Swan Publications, 1996
Contains information on the career of John and James Dickson and John Dickson junior on page 61.

Anglesey Central Railway - Opening of the line from Gaerwen to Llangefni
The North Wales Chronicle, Bangor, 17 December 1864, page 8
States that the 'eminent contractors' were Dickson and Russell of Neath and the engineering director was Colin McKenzie CE.

Railway Matters
The Engineer, London, 3 November 1871, page 311
The Mersey Railway Company has a contract with John Dixon of London for a Mersey Railway tunnel. This should have read 'with John Dickson of Swansea'.

Bulmers Directory 1890
J Dickson of Glaisdale Hall bought the Glaisdale iron Works (operational from 1869 to 1875) and 115 acres of land.

Death of Mr John Dickson, the well known railway contractor - A Life of Energetic Work and Considerable Achievement
The Cambrian, Swansea, 17 June 1892, page 8
Lengthy obituary, little mention of his difficulties, no mention of his three bankruptcies.

Whitby, Redcar, and Middlesbrough Union Railway - Half Yearly Meeting
The Northern Echo, Darlington, 19 September 1873, page 3
Troubles reported by the directors.

The Teign Valley Line
Peter Kay
Wild Swan Publications, Didcot, 1996
Contains information on the career of John and James Dickson and John Dickson junior on page 61.

Tomlinson's North Eastern Railway, its rise and development
William Tomlinson, revised by K Hoole
David and Charles, Newton Abbot, 1967
The standard history of the NER. The Whitby to Loftus line had 'light iron viaducts of novel construction' with that at Staithes being 'the most remarkable of the viaducts'. John Dixon is credited with the design of the viaducts, but there is no mention of John Dickson.

Girder Making and the Practice of Bridge Building in Wrought Iron
Edward Hutchinson
E and F N Spon, London, 1879
Includes John Dixon's viaducts in his examples, with some good illustrations of the ironwork. States that the weight of the spans was carried by the concrete and not by the wrought iron tubes.

Viaducts on the Whitby, Redcar and Middlesbrough Railway
The Engineer, 14 March 1873, page 151
Detailed description of the viaducts, with favourable comment on their design.

The Patent Journal - Abstracts of Specifications - Class 5 - Building
The Engineer, London, 1 August 1873, page 78
J Dixon's provisional specification for concrete-filled columns for bridges.

Editorial - Bridge Cylinders
The Engineer, London, 4 October 1872, pages 233-34
Editorial stating that iron cylinders filled with concrete were an established method of supporting bridges.

Completion of the Staithes Iron Railway Bridge
Whitby Times and North Yorkshire Advertiser, 19 February 1875, page 1
Bridges built by contractors Skerne Iron Works Limited of Darlington 'under management of Mr H Kenlock'. All bridges completed without any accident of consequence. From the local census records, the only man fitting this description would have been Henry Kinlock, born 1835, who was a fitter living in Darlington.

Strengthening the East Row and Upgang Viaducts on the Whitby and Loftus Railway
William Robertson Lidderdale Forrest
Proceedings of the Institution of Civil Engineers, London, Volume 130, 1897, (Paper 2995)
Describes repair work carried out on the two viaducts for the North Eastern Railway in 1893-95.

Whitby, Redcar and Middlesbrough Union Railway
Ken Hoole
Hendon Publishing Company, Nelson, 1981
Photographic record of the line with brief historical introduction.

The Tay Rail Bridge disaster revisited
T Martin and I A MacLeod
Proceedings of the Institution of Civil Engineers, Bridge Engineering 157
December 2004, Issue BE4, pages 187-192, paper 13596
Considers alternative failure modes of the bridge including cast iron fatigue, dynamic instability due to trains passing over misaligned track, and insufficient strength of tie bars, but agrees with the official enquiry at the time that it was excessive wind pressure which caused the collapse.

The Whitby Loftus Line
Michael A Williams
Jet Coast Development Trust Ltd, Staithes Gateway Centre, 2012
Another version of Williams's complete history of the line.

14 Muelle del Tinto, Huelva, Spain

In 1873 the Spanish government sold the Rio Tinto mines in Andalucia to the Rio Tinto Company Limited, based in London. A contract was agreed for the railway to carry ore from Rio Tinto to the port of Huelva, with an ore-loading facility. The original contractors completed the railway but withdrew from the rest of the project. This resulted in John Dixon being given a contract in 1874 to construct the ore-loading facility, a pier 1,900 feet long with railway tracks at three levels, known as 'El Muelle de Rio Tinto' or 'Muelle del Tinto'. It was a wrought iron structure supported on cast iron columns, similar in design to a seaside promenade pier but much larger and more elaborate. Shipping stopped using the Muelle del Tinto in 1975, and in 2003 the rail tracks were removed when the structure was opened as a leisure facility.

Privatisation of the Rio Tinto mine

Spain had been largely unaffected by the rapid industrialisation of 19th century Europe. Ruled by a conservative monarchy, impoverished by the loss of New World colonies, and with a rugged landscape hostile to the construction of railways, Spain remained rural with its economy based on agriculture. The overthrow of Queen Isabella in 1868 provided an opportunity for the country to catch up with the rest of Europe, but this would require foreign investment and foreign technology.

In the south west of the Iberian Peninsula lies a vast deposit of iron pyrite (iron sulphide FeS_2) with other minerals. Known as the Andevallo, it extends over an area some 90 miles long and 20 miles wide. As early as 2,500 BC, copper was being extracted from copper carbonates which, in some places, contained up to 10% copper, although the general level of copper in the Andevallo is below 3%. In one of the years just before the Rio Tinto Company Limited acquired the mines, the 61,000 tons of ore mined only yielded 850 tons of copper (1.4% by weight of ore). Silver was also extracted. Roman mining for copper and silver had been on a grand scale; a series of large water wheels for removing water from workings thirty metres below the surface has come to light. After the Romans, copper and silver production continued intermittently and at a much-reduced scale, sometimes by private individuals, sometimes by government agencies. But the huge potential of the mineral deposits was never quite grasped by the authorities in Seville.

In May 1871 the Spanish government offered the mines for sale through an auction, with a reserve of £4,086,000. The enormous capital outlay required and an uncertain political situation in Spain deterred potential investors, and all bids were well below the reserve. However, Heinrich Doetsch, a partner in the trading business Sundheim y Doetsch based in Huelva, believed that Rio Tinto could become a successful venture. He travelled to London in search of the capital needed and found Hugh Matheson.

Hugh Matheson, a devout Christian, had turned down an offer to join the family business in China (Jardine, Matheson) because of its trade in opium, and instead joined their London office, concentrating on the import of tea and silk. The London office then experienced financial difficulties and was re-formed in 1848, with Hugh Matheson at its head. Matheson had a high reputation as an entrepreneur and was trusted by the banks. When Heinrich Doetsch persuaded him of the potential of the Rio Tinto mines, Matheson was able to assemble a syndicate to purchase and develop the mines. Capital came from Deutsche Bank (56%), Matheson and Company (24%) and the railway engineering contractors Edwin Clark, Punchard and Company (20%).

The Rio Tinto photographed by the author.
The derivation of the name Rio Tinto is obvious!

Edwin Clark and William Punchard

Edwin Clark and William Punchard had formed a partnership to build railways. There is no doubt that their interest in the new Rio Tinto Company was with an eye to securing the contract for constructing the railway from the mine to the coast at Huelva.

Who's who?
Edwin Clark and William Henry Punchard

Edwin Clark (1814-1894) had a remarkably varied career. His father was a lace manufacturer in Buckinghamshire. After education in France, Edwin began training as a solicitor but gave this up to work as a science teacher. He studied classics at Cambridge but had to abandon university when his father's money ran out. Turning to engineering, he presented himself unannounced at Robert Stephenson's London office and so impressed Stephenson that he was offered a position analysing the forces on the Britannia tubular bridge. This led to his appointment as resident engineer at the bridge site, after which he published an important book on the Conwy and Britannia tubular bridges and his reputation was made. Many bridge designs followed and he worked on electrical telegraphs, developing the block system on the railways for controlling traffic. Another of his inventions was the hydraulic lift dock, as used in his 1870 design for the Anderton Boat Lift in Cheshire which opened five years later. His brother, Josiah Latimer Clark (1822-1898), was a key figure in the development of the electric telegraph and submarine cables.

William Henry Punchard (1835-1891), the son of a Devon farmer, became an international railway contractor. His partnership with Clark, formed around 1870, constructed railways and tramways in South America, Tasmania, and England. By 1873 they had contracts running worth over £5 million. Living at Poulett Lodge from 1870 to 1880, Punchard was a near neighbour of John Dixon at Kingston on Thames. John's son George married Punchard's daughter, Elsie Kitty, in 1914. Three of Punchard's sons became civil engineers.

Financial problems beset the partners after the Rio Tinto railway venture, and in April 1879 Edwin Clark submitted a petition for liquidation with liabilities of £760,000. This was soon followed by a similar petition from William Punchard with liabilities of £900,000. Although not significantly adding to their liabilities, their involvement with the Lisbon Steam Tramway Company had certainly added to their troubles. Clark and Punchard had joined with Albert Grant in 1871 to construct fifty-one miles of tramway from Lisbon to Sintra, but became enmeshed in accusations of a fraudulent prospectus, incompetent directors and collusion between the company and the contractors. Court cases ensued. Needless to say, Clark's ten-page obituary by the Institution of Civil Engineers tactfully omits any reference to his financial problems or to the Lisbon Steam Tramway Company.

The Rio Tinto Company acquires the mine

Undeterred by the failure of the first auction, the Spanish government arranged a second auction for the Rio Tinto mines in the summer of 1872. Matheson's syndicate made an offer of £3,680,000, providing that Spain relinquished any future claim on the mine in perpetuity. Their offer was formally accepted by the Spanish government in February 1873. Matheson appointed David Forbes, an experienced mining engineer, to visit Rio Tinto and report on the potential for the mines. Forbes estimated that an annual profit of £960,000 could be achieved. In 1873 the Rio Tinto Company Limited was floated, with a share capital of £2,250,000. It was to extract copper and, later, sulphur (to supply the rapidly increasing demand for sulphuric acid), from the ores which were optimistically said by geologists to be 'practically inexhaustible and of extreme richness'. There was a rush for the shares, enabling the original investors (Deutsche Bank, Matheson and Company and Edwin Clark, Punchard and Company) to reduce their investments by two-thirds.

Constructing the railway along the Rio Tinto

Before the purchase of the mine by Rio Tinto, ore had been mined by hand and carried away by donkeys, apart from an unsuccessful experiment using camels. The Rio Tinto Company planned a railway from the mine to Huelva, where a loading pier would be built on the estuary of the River Odiel, to export the expected 2,000 tons of ore daily. At the same time, imported Welsh coal would be carried from Huelva up to the mine site for the various boilers and locomotives. George Barclay Bruce was appointed as the consulting engineer for the railway and ore-loading pier.

George Bruce appointed John Robinson (1833-1909) to carry out the detailed design work in London, and William Ridley (1841-1916) as his site engineer. Robinson was a civil engineer who had worked for Bruce before, from 1864 to 1872, on railways in Prussia, India and Honduras. He had left to work in Argentina but returned in 1874 to prepare the working drawings for the Rio Tinto railway and the ore-loading pier. William Ridley, from Bedlington in Northumberland, worked as a railway engineer in Mauritius followed by irrigation and canal work in India. After the Rio Tinto railway he went on to be chief engineer for the Natal Government Railway before working with Edwin Punchard on railways in South America.

A photograph in the Rio Tinto mine archives shows the staff working on the railway in 1873, many of them young engineers who would build on this valuable experience to establish themselves as civil engineers in their own right. Mark William Carr (1856-1886) from Gateshead was just seventeen. Bruce's son, George Barclay Bruce (1853-1899), was from Newcastle and twenty years old. George Shortrede (born 1848) was twenty-five. William Langdon (1846-1933) was twenty-seven and went on to be chief engineer for the Rio Tinto mine until he was fifty.

THE ILLUSTRATED LONDON NEWS, AUG. 7, 1875.— 132

PORT OF HUELVA WITH THE RIO TINTO PIER.

VIEW ON THE RIO TINTO RAILWAY

VILLAGE & MINES OF RIO TINTO.

THE RIO TINTO MINES, IN SOUTHERN SPAIN.

Above) 'Staff on the construction of the Rio Tinto line' photograph from 1873. Alfred Thorne, James Pring, George Barclay Bruce junior, Miguel Villaplana, Thomas Gibson, William Ridley, Mark William Carr, Robert Wilfrid Graham, Dr J Law, George Shortrede, William Langdon and Rev Rose.
Photograph reproduced by courtesy of El Archivo Fundación Río Tinto, Minas de Riotinto, Spain.

Right) 'The Rio Tinto Mines in Southern Spain' by an unknown engraver. The Illustrated London News commented that the railway had just been opened and the pier was nearing completion. Not surprisingly, the engraving of the pier is not entirely accurate, for example the locomotive should be pushing the wagons from the rear. Railway track was laid to a narrow gauge of 3 feet 6 inches, in the view of the railway it seems to be a very broad gauge!
The Illustrated London News, 7 August 1875, page 132
© Illustrated London News Limited/Mary Evans. The engravings later appeared in 'La Illustracion Española y Americana'.

Needless to say, as members of the original syndicate, Edwin Clark and William Punchard expected to get the contract for the railway (occasionally they are referred to as Clarke, Punchard and Curry). They submitted preliminary estimates of £500,000 for a 3 feet 6 inch gauge railway and a further £50,000 for the ore-loading pier. When the route, following the course of the Rio Tinto, was studied in detail it was realised the work would be far more extensive. To maintain the specified maximum gradient of 1 in 75, a large number of cuttings, embankments, tunnels and more bridges would be required, and a stronger track with additional ballast and heavier rails was now specified. Estimates were revised and a contract agreed for the railway, ore-loading pier, locomotives and rolling stock at a price of £775,000. The ore-loading pier was to project a distance into the harbour of 350 metres from high-water line and be capable of shipping 2,000 tons of ore per twelve-hour day. There were incentive payments for early completion, tapering down from a maximum of £50,000, and clauses covering failure of the contractor to complete the work.

Clark and Punchard started construction work in July 1873. Considering the magnitude of the work, they made excellent progress. Their workforce of some 3,600 men, working seven days a week, managed to complete the railway three months ahead of schedule, thus earning Clark and Punchard a £22,500 bonus. The railway opened in July 1875 at a final cost of £767,190, leaving precious little for the ore-loading pier.

By now the estimates for the pier had increased from the original £50,000 to £93,675. Perhaps not surprisingly Clark and Punchard declined to construct the pier. Sections 31 and 32 of the printed contract covered defaults by the contractor: the Rio Tinto Company could take over remaining work after giving the contractor fourteen days' notice and was entitled to seek payment from the contractor to cover any costs in excess of the original contract price. However, Clark and Punchard seem to have got off lightly, since they only had £50,000 deducted from their payment, while the current estimates for the pier had risen from the original £50,000 to £93,675. Why they were not pressed for the additional £43,675 is not clear, but the reasons for their lenient treatment may be because they were significant shareholders in the Rio Tinto company and because they had overcome all difficulties to complete the railway to Huelva early.

Ingenious design of the loading pier

George Bruce designed the ore-loading facility. The structure was similar to a sea-side promenade pier, but on a much larger scale. The first 600 feet went straight out from the shore, the next 775 feet curved along a radius of 600 feet, with the final straight length of 525 feet. It terminated in a shipping dock capable of accommodating four vessels at a time. Cast iron columns screwed down into the river bed supported a wrought iron superstructure carrying railway tracks at three levels. Bruce had considered several options, including a low-level pier with a hydraulic lift at the end to take ore-laden wagons up to ship deck level, but settled on the ingenious three-level pier. At a time when convention would have dictated a masonry pier, this was a most innovative design, and it took the conservative Spanish authorities several months to be convinced.

At South Shields, George Bruce had seen wagons running out to shipping and back under gravity on the Tyne Dock, designed by Thomas Harrison, and he used this concept at Huelva. The upper level of the pier carried two central tracks, sloping up a 1 in 75 gradient to the mid-point of the pier then falling at 1 in 200 towards the end, where there was a final upturn of 1 in 30 and sets of points. A line of loaded wagons could be pushed by a locomotive up to the mid-point, from where one wagon at a time would be allowed to roll under gravity to the end of the pier, where the final upturn brought it to a halt. Immediately the points were switched to direct it back down one of the mid-level tracks on each side

Who's who?
George Barclay Bruce (1821-1908)

George Barclay Bruce was a celebrated railway engineer and a great friend of John Dixon. Born in Newcastle upon Tyne, he was the son of Dr John Bruce, who had taught John in Newcastle. He was Robert Stephenson's second apprentice and had protested at Stephenson's insistence that he spend five years in the engine shops so that he should become a mechanic before becoming an engineer. John Dixon was later to be an apprentice with Robert Stephenson. Stephenson had been a pupil of Dr Bruce and sought to repay his old teacher by giving his son a start in life, and the two men remained friends.

At the age of twenty-four George Bruce was appointed resident engineer on the Royal Border Bridge at Berwick, working for Robert Stephenson and Thomas Harrison (this was the Thomas Harrison who was later the chief engineer of the North Eastern Railway). Bruce then worked on railways in England and India. In India he rejected the common practice of using forced labour, instead devoting much time and patience to recruit free labourers. On his return from India in 1856 he established a consulting practice in Westminster, from where he continued his work on railways in England, Germany, South America and South Africa. Between 1873 and 1876 he was the engineer on the Muelle del Tinto, where he was joined by his son, also George Barclay Bruce and also a civil engineer.

George Barclay Bruce was president of the Institution of Civil Engineers for 1887 and again for the following year and was also a member of the Institution of Mechanical Engineers. In 1888 he received a knighthood. Bruce was a strong advocate of the Presbyterian Church in England, to which he made generous donations and built a church at Wark-on-Tyne.

of the pier. When over a loading chute, the hopper doors were opened and the ore discharged. A conveyor belt, which could be raised or lowered to accommodate the state of the tide, dropped the ore into the waiting ship's hold. There were two loading stations on each side, so four ships could be loaded at once. Empty wagons rolled under gravity down the outer tracks, which sloped down at a gradient of 1 in 100, soon reducing to 1 in 200, with a final braking upturn of 1 in 75 at the shore end. A third level, some 5 feet above high-water level and well below the two ore-wagon levels, was for use as a conventional dock by other vessels. This carried a single line which branched out into three about halfway down the length of the pier.

Who's who?
Thomas Elliot Harrison (1808-1888)

Thomas Elliot Harrison (1808-1888) spent most of his life in the north east, where for many years he worked with Robert Stephenson on railways and on the High Level Bridge at Newcastle, and he designed the railway station at York. While he was working with Robert Stephenson on the York, Newcastle and Berwick Railway, George Barclay Bruce acted as their resident engineer for the bridge at Berwick. Thomas Harrison was the chief engineer of the North Eastern Railway from its formation in 1854 until his death in 1888. He was president of the Institution of Civil Engineers 1873-75.

Harrison would certainly have been well known to both George Bruce and John Dixon, and was no doubt flattered when his Tyne Dock design was adopted for the much larger installation in Spain.

In 1883, when the North Eastern Railway took over the Whitby, Redcar and Middlesbrough Union Railway, Harrison was very critical of the viaducts, which had been designed by John Dixon. However, the problems may have been more to do with poor workmanship by the contractor rather than John's design.

Around the end of the pier a timber shipping deck was constructed, supported on cast iron piles but separate from the ore-loading pier so that any collision from a ship would not cause damage to the main structure. A 10-ton capacity crane from Cowans Sheldon was installed on this timber shipping deck for off-loading heavy goods or machinery.

Substituting for Clark and Punchard

The unexpected withdrawal of Clark and Punchard faced George Bruce with a serious challenge: how might he to find a reliable and competent engineering contractor, at short notice, capable of constructing the ore-loading pier? Bruce knew most of the practising civil engineers, through the Institution of Civil Engineers (by now he was a member of their council) and through the usual business contacts. This was particularly true of the civil engineers from his native north east England, and it was two men from Newcastle upon Tyne who ensured that the ore-loading pier would be built without delay. The pier was to be constructed using piles, built up from flanged cast iron column sections, bolted together, and screwed into the river bed. This design was by then well-developed for bridges and seaside piers, and both men had proven experience in this technique. The two men appointed were Thomas Gibson as resident site engineer and John Dixon as the contractor.

Who's who?
Thomas Gibson (1843-1899)

Thomas Gibson (1843-1899) was born just outside Newcastle but started his engineering career in London with the engineering contractors George Saunders and T W Mitchell. Mitchell's grandfather, Alexander Mitchell (1780-1868), had been the inventor of the screwed pile. Whilst in their employ, Gibson worked on the Madras Railway Pier, a large screwed pile structure, and later worked with his father on screwed pile structures in the docks at London and elsewhere.

In 1869 Gibson was appointed resident engineer on the Redheugh Bridge at Newcastle upon Tyne under Thomas Bouch of Tay Bridge notoriety. After the Muelle de Rio Tinto, Gibson built twelve bridges for the Seville and Huelva railway. Returning to England, he set up his own engineering business. One of his later contracts was a bridge at Salamón for the Rio Tinto railway. Thomas Gibson died of complications following diabetes at the age of fifty-six.

Given John Dixon's commitments, most on site management was left in the capable hands of Gibson, whose detailed knowledge of all stages of construction is apparent in his paper to the Institution of Civil Engineers in 1878. John did visit Huelva as evidenced by his letters in connection with the Guimarães Railway in Portugal when he travelled via Lisbon, staying at the Central Hotel.

Sub-contractors, all from the north east of England

John Dixon was under pressure to order the components for the pier as quickly as possible following the unexpected withdrawal of Clark and Punchard. All the components for the pier would have to be prefabricated in England and shipped out to Spain. John needed suppliers he could trust, and it is probable that he relied on Jasper Capper Mounsey, his close friend and iron merchant, and possibly sought the opinion of his brother Raylton, in Middlesbrough, for the two suppliers of the cast iron columns. Raylton Dixon had started his own iron ship-building yard in 1862 on

'Plate 28 - The Huelva Pier' engraving from Girder Making and the Practice of Bridge Building in Wrought Iron by Edward Hutchinson. This engraving was originally commissioned by The Engineer and appeared four months after completion of the structure, yet bears little resemblance to the actual pier with, for example, no sign of the three different levels and the ore loading stations.

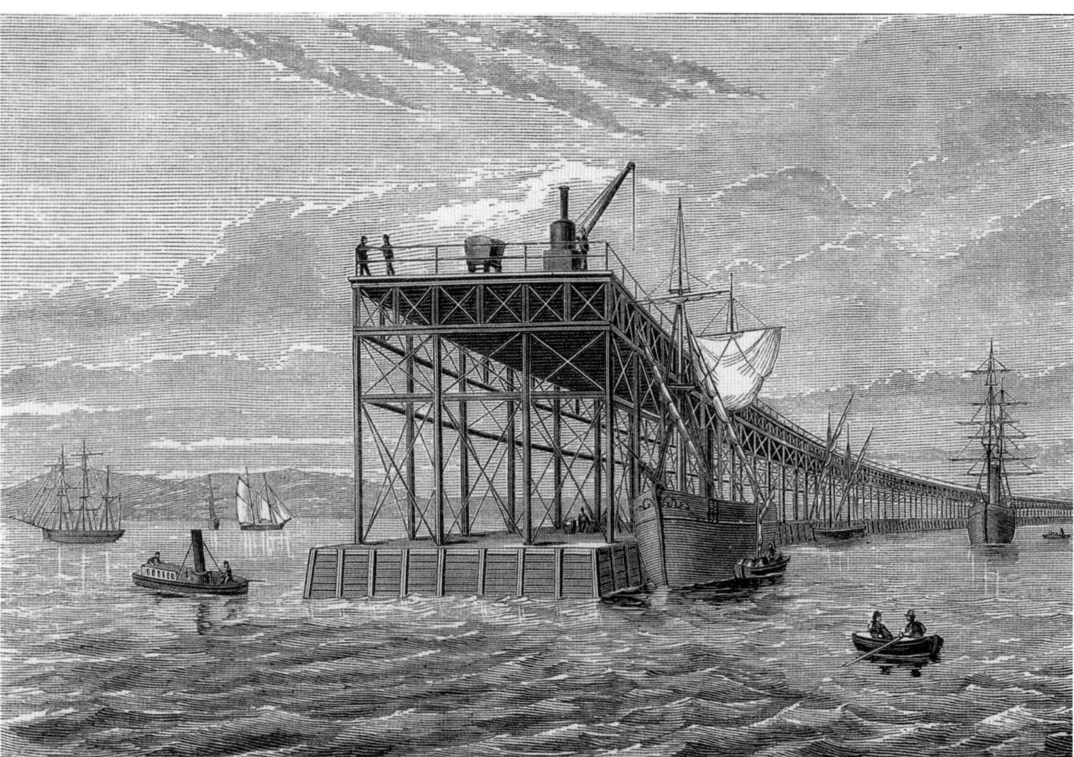

Below) One of the column sections cast by the Stockton Forge Company. Each column had an identification number, in this case CR25.
Author's photograph.

the River Tees in Middlesbrough. With his engaging personality and entrepreneurial skills, he was soon a prominent member of the Teesside business community and was a personal friend of many owners of iron making and engineering companies. He would have been in an excellent position to advise his brother on trusted suppliers of iron castings and wrought iron work. Thus the iron column sections were cast by Charles I'Anson and Son of Darlington and the Stockton Forge Company, with wrought iron from the Skerne Ironworks Company. It is likely that two foundries were used in order to have the great quantity of cast iron columns completed at short notice.

Charles I'Anson (1809-1884) was a Quaker who had taken over the Hope Town Foundry in Darlington from his cousins William and Alfred Kitching. Two of I'Anson's sons, Charles I'Anson (1838-1884) and Joseph I'Anson (1842-1915) were good friends of Raylton Dixon and Joseph worked alongside his father at the foundry. Quaker family and business networks were an important factor in many dealings, and Raylton Dixon and his two brothers had been brought up as members of the Society of Friends by their mother, although by now John and Raylton had moved into the established church. Names from the Darlington I'Anson family appear in the 'Balla Wray' visitors' books. The property 'Balla Wray' on the west shore of Lake Windermere was the home of Jeremiah and Mary Dixon, the parents of John and Raylton, suggesting a close relationship between the two families. It would be personal friendship rather than lingering Quaker allegiances that would have led Raylton to suggest the I'Anson foundry.

The Stockton Forge Company was owned by Joseph Dodds (1819-1891). Dodds was a Stockton solicitor with a remarkably wide range of interests. He had financial interests in at least six Teesside iron works, was clerk to the Tees Conservancy Commissioners from 1858 to 1889, and MP for Stockton from 1868 to 1888. Although Raylton Dixon did not join the Tees Conservancy Commission until 1884 he, along with everyone in the Teesside business community, would have known Joseph Dodds. Raylton's relationship with Dodds deteriorated in later life; they crossed swords on the Tees Conservancy Commission and, with Dodds a Liberal and Raylton a Conservative, they were political opponents. Dodds' career as a solicitor came to an abrupt end; he was struck off for fraud in 1889.

Apart from any recommendation from Raylton, the Skerne Ironworks Company at Darlington was well known to John Dixon, having supplied the wrought iron for his viaducts on the Whitby to Loftus railway. He would again use them for the Llandudno pier iron work in 1876. The Skerne ironworks had been established in 1864 by six partners, including no fewer than four members of the Quaker Pease family.

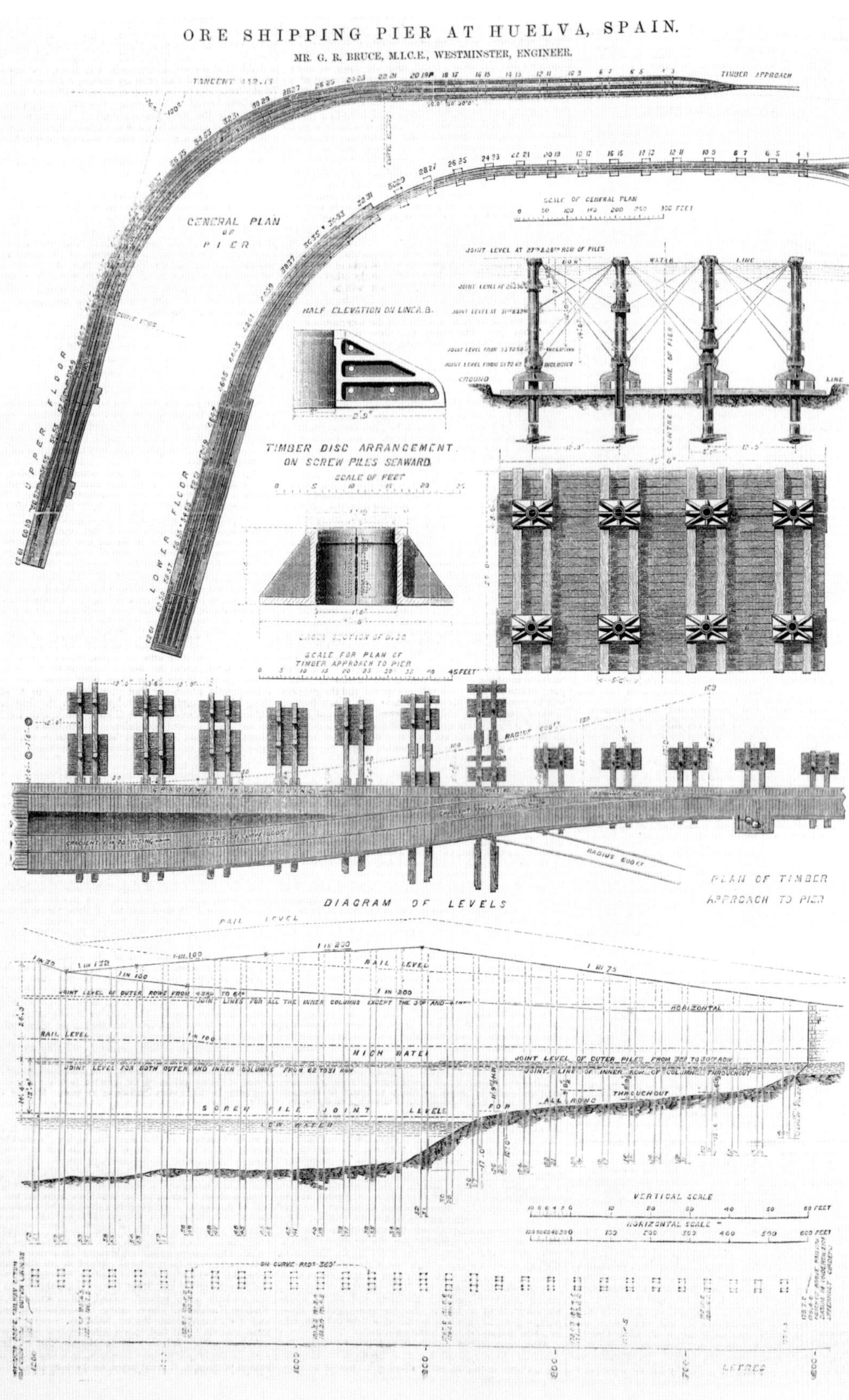

Cowans Sheldon and Company was set up by John Cowans and Edward Sheldon, both from Newcastle upon Tyne, in partnership with William and Thomas Bouch, the designer of the ill-fated Tay Bridge. Like John Dixon, Cowans and Sheldon had been apprentices at Robert Stephenson's Forth Street Works, although nearly twenty years earlier. Cowans Sheldon specialised in railway and dock cranes and would have been the obvious choice for the ore-handling equipment and cranes on the Muelle del Tinto.

Constructing the loading pier

The narrow-gauge railway from the mines terminated at Huelva, where an embankment and an elevated section of line on timber supports carried the track to the start of the pier. The pier was supported by 16 inch diameter cast-iron piles, made up from sections 17 feet long, and arranged in thirty groups of eight. The lower end of each pile carried a 4 feet diameter screw. John Dixon's test borings in August 1874 showed that the river bed was soft blue clay, extending to a depth of at least 80 feet. Bruce, Gibson and Dixon were worried that this would not provide a secure foundation for the weight of the three-level pier, with out-going laden wagons and returning empty wagons, and it was decided to increase the diameter of the pile screws from 4 feet to 5 feet and sink them to a greater depth. These changes meant that the steam-driven machine intended for pile-sinking was rendered inadequate, and John fell back on the old-fashioned method using hand-operated capstans. The first six rows, each of eight piles, were driven during August and September 1874. At the shore end sixteen men were sufficient to work the capstan. In the deep water 110 men were employed.

Ore-shipping Pier at Huelva, Spain. Details of the Muelle del Tinto. In the top right can be seen the arrangement of the screwed cast iron piles and the timber platforms clamped onto them to prevent sinking into the river bed.
The diagram of the levels can be seen in the lower part of the picture.
The Engineer, London, 12 May 1876, page 360

This view is dominated by the large water tank installed to supply water to the fire-fighting main running the length of the pier. Railway tracks in the foreground serve the lower level and are for general commercial traffic, quite separate from the ore-loading facility. Posts for later telegraph communication with the pier end can be seen. Photograph reproduced by courtesy of Rio Tinto and the London Metropolitan Archives, reference LMA/4543/12/01/047

'Copies of the Royal Album: Rail Bridge Pier and River' photograph. This view shows the rail track carried on wooden supports leading up to the pier, and the pier itself. The vast quantity of timber in the foreground is probably destined for the Rio Tinto mines. Photograph reproduced by courtesy of Rio Tinto and the London Metropolitan Archives, reference LMA/4543/12/01/319

An early photograph of the pier before steam power had totally taken over from sail. The telegraph wires and lighting standards were later additions.
Photograph reproduced by courtesy of El Archivo Fundación Río Tinto, Minas de Riotinto, Spain, reference RioTintoCompanyPierDetail.

'Muelle de Riotinto en Huelva (Rio Tinto Pier)' photograph from the Rio Tinto archives. The steam powered ore carriers contrast with the traditional local boats in the foreground.
Photograph reproduced by courtesy of Rio Tinto and the London Metropolitan Archives, reference LMA/4543/12/01/084

'El Muelle de la Ca de Minas de Rio Tinto' photograph by Hauser y Menet, Madrid. Swiss photographers Oscar Hauser Muller and Adolfo Menet Kurstiner established their graphic arts printing company in 1890. Specialising in postcards, the firm amazingly continued until 1996 when it succumbed to financial pressures. This view, taken from the far end of the pier, shows the switching points to direct wagons to the ore-loading stations. The delightful shelter is reminiscent of English seaside piers. Photograph reproduced by courtesy of El Archivo Fundación Río Tinto, Minas de Riotinto, Spain.

Photograph by Baldoniero Santamaria fotógrapho – Huelva. Shows the outer end of the lower deck, looking back towards Huelva, with another of the 'seaside pier' shelters. The lower deck extended beyond the end of the upper levels, providing docking facilities for other vessels. Running along the edge of the deck on the right is the fire-fighting water main.
Photograph reproduced by courtesy of El Archivo Fundación Río Tinto, Minas de Riotinto, Spain, reference LOF_8231.

'Rio Tinto (Huelva) – Detalles del Muelle'. The end of the upper level showing the points to switch wagons onto the outer, ore-loading, levels. Although the deck sloped up here to provide some natural slowing of incoming wagons, sturdy wooden buffers are fitted at the end of the tracks.
Photograph reproduced by courtesy of El Archivo Fundación Río Tinto, Minas de Riotinto, Spain, reference Muelle RT2.

'Rio Tinto (Huelva) – Detalles del Muelle'. Wagons are unloaded onto a conveyor belt which discharges ore into the ship's hold. Note the three men with long scrapers making sure ore is not left adhering to the sides of the wagon. The wagons on the upper level have been uncoupled from the locomotive and will be slowly running under gravity to the end of the pier.
Photograph reproduced by courtesy of El Archivo Fundación Río Tinto, Minas de Riotinto, Spain, reference Muelle RT4.

Above) 'Rio Tinto (Huelva) – Detalles del Muelle'. Two tugs and a dredger moored on the lower level.
The locomotive on the upper level is pushing the laden wagons towards the mid-point, from where they will run under gravity to the end.
Photograph reproduced by courtesy of El Archivo Fundación Río Tinto, Minas de Riotinto, Spain, reference Muelle RT3.

Top left) 'Rio Tinto (Huelva) – Detalles del Muelle'. The end of the extended lower deck with Cowans Sheldon cranes for handling cargoes from non-ore shipping.
Note the lighthouse on the upper deck.
Photograph reproduced by courtesy of El Archivo Fundación Río Tinto, Minas de Riotinto, Spain, reference Muelle RT1.

Left) The pier today after conversion to a leisure facility.
Photograph by the author.

In October and November tests were carried out by placing weights on the piles and measuring any settlement. In the worst case, it was found that piles were sinking 24 inches over a four-day period, clearly an unacceptable situation. The solution was to build timber platforms from Baltic pine around each group of eight piles, then adding rails and pig iron to sink them down to the river bed. Once settled on the river bed, cast iron plates were fitted to the upper surface of the pine platforms and secured to the piles with collars. In an example of the thoroughness with which Bruce, Gibson and Dixon went about the project, they had commissioned special tests on Baltic pine to establish its load bearing capacity. With the submerged platforms in place, settlement was reduced to an acceptable level, and pile-sinking began again in December 1874.

It was with great relief that Bruce and Dixon returned to London in January 1875 after several weeks in Spain. The railway was making rapid progress with completion expected in July and the problems in anchoring the pier supports in the river bed had been solved. Impressed, *Engineering* magazine commented:

> 'All the difficulties experienced in securing foundations for the pier on a bed of mud of unknown depth have been ingeniously overcome and bearing in mind the proverbially slow progress of works in Spain, the directors, engineers, and contractors are to be congratulated on these probable and unexpected results. All the concessions, contracts, and arrangements with the Spanish Government have been finally confirmed and gazetted, so that nothing now stands in the way of the successful realisation of the vast schemes of this colossal enterprise.'

Piles were sunk to depths from 15 feet at the shore end to 32 feet in deep water. In the deeper water each pile required over a hundred men, working twin capstans each with eight arms 15 feet long. In some places there was a layer of sand and gravel above the clay, and progress was facilitated by pumping high pressure water down the inside of the pile, fluidising the material around the base. John had previously used this technique on the pier extension at Southport. George Bruce had thoughtfully included a simple ball joint at the top of the submerged columns. This meant that, even if a submerged column had deviated from the perpendicular as it was driven into the river bed, the upper sections could still be set vertical.

With all the piles in position by July 1875, work could begin assembling the superstructure. Wrought iron girders and bracings had been manufactured at the Skerne Ironworks in Darlington, shipped to Spain and taken out to the pier by raft. The pier was completed in January 1876, and timber decking laid to carry the rail tracks. Had the pier been constructed in England the rails would have been carried on additional ironwork, and this would have been preferred by John. However, George Bruce knew this ironwork would increase the cost and extend the construction time, and so timber was used. Concerns about fire risk with the dry climate and steam locomotives were allayed by laying a water main the entire length, fed from an 11,000 gallon cistern.

The mine and the pier come into operation

Pyrite was mined at Rio Tinto for the extraction of copper; the presence of sulphur rendered it unsuitable for the manufacture of iron. Rio Tinto ores were classified into three types depending on copper content. The lowest quality ores were processed on site. Pyrite was roasted in open heaps, smouldering for up to a year while continuously emitting sulphurous gases which blighted the lives of local inhabitants and vegetation, followed by a cementation process which precipitated copper from solution in the presence of iron. The medium grade ores were exported to Britain, France, Germany and the United States. The richest ores were calcined before being processed on site in twenty blast furnaces. The resulting material, now about 40% copper, was sent away for smelting. After 1884 this was carried out at CwmAvon in South Wales.

In the years immediately prior to Rio Tinto company operation, around 60,000 tons of ore were mined annually. Over its first few years the company increased output by a factor of at least ten, and by the end of the 19th century nearly two million tons were being extracted each year by the workforce of around 10,000 men. In spite of the investment in the railway and ore loading pier, most of the ore was processed on site, only 25% to 33% being exported for processing abroad, suggesting that the pier was operating at less than one third its capacity.

The pier came into use on 23 March 1876. Total weight of the ironwork was 3,408 tons, believed to exceed any similar structure in the world. As with the railway, additional work proved necessary and the eventual cost was £145,166 (one source quoted £163,000), but the facility worked perfectly. One wagon could discharge seven tons of ore into a ship's hold in under one minute. John Dixon commented that 'anyone who stood on the pier could not but witness the pleasure of the working of the trucks on the reverse gradient.' In the four hours of working up until midday, 1000 tons of ore could be shipped through each of the four loading spouts.

In contrast to the highly-mechanised operation of the loading operation, the mining was primitive. Excavation was part open-cast, part underground, mainly carried out manually. Amid clouds of smoke from calcining minerals and streams of hot slag running down the hillsides from blast furnaces, thousands of children, both boys and girls, carried small wooden trays of ore to fill the railway wagons.

There was later criticism in Spain that the Rio Tinto mine had been sold far too cheaply, and that British companies were draining funds from Spain. The dividends paid by the company partially support this claim. Rio Tinto dividends in the three years after operations began in earnest were 5% in 1879, 8% in 1880 and 14% in 1881. Over the period 1873 to 1913 the average annual dividend was almost 14%. However, it remains a fact that Hugh Matheson's syndicate were the only people willing to take the initial risk. Rio Tinto soon became the world's leading producer of copper.

The CwmAvon connection

One of the major smelters of Rio Tinto ore was the CwmAvon Copper Works near Port Talbot. John Dixon had been the contractor for improved harbour facilities at Port Talbot in 1874-75, and in 1877 he took a financial stake in the CwmAvon works, which he relinquished two years later, making a handsome profit of £38,500. His decision to invest in CwmAvon must have been based on his first-hand experience of the potential Rio Tinto ore exports and the increased import capacity at Port Talbot and also his earlier personal experience of ore mining in Wales.

A few years later, after John's interest in CwmAvon had ended, there were more formal connections between Rio Tinto and Cwm Avon. In 1882 William Edmonds from the Cwm Avon works went to Rio Tinto to take charge of their on site smelting operations. Rio Tinto then leased one of the copper smelters at Cwm Avon in 1884, and two years later Edmonds returned to Wales to manage the Rio Tinto smelter at Cwm Avon.

Working conditions at Rio Tinto

Working conditions and living conditions, since most of the workers lived on site, were very poor. There were many accidents, mainly due to falls. Respiratory problems arose due to the burning of iron pyrite. Rio Tinto pyrite contained more sulphur than any other pyrite, with 53% sulphur. The initial roasting of the pyrite, in the open air, produced clouds of sulphur dioxide. Workers had to endure this sulphurous atmosphere at work and at home, since many lived virtually on top of the mines. In 1888 there was a demonstration against the polluted atmosphere. The governor of Huelva called out the militia, who opened fire, killing an unknown number of protestors. For many years this incident was covered up, but more recently received much publicity by the publication of the novel *El Corazon de la Tierra* (The Heart of the Earth) published in 2001 and made into a film in 2007.

Following the 1888 demonstration and the outcry over the deaths of some demonstrators, the government immediately banned the practice of open-air roasting, but was forced to rescind this ban under pressure from the Rio Tinto company. Eventually improved methods of extracting the copper, combined with an increasing sulphur demand to manufacture sulphuric acid, made open-air roasting obsolete in 1907.

Nationalisation, closure and rehabilitation

In the twentieth century the Rio Tinto Company diversified, through new investments and mergers, into Rhodesia, Australia, and America, and the Rio Tinto mine became less important. The original Rio Tinto mine was returned to Spain, notwithstanding the agreement for Rio Tinto Company ownership in perpetuity, with the nationalisation of the mines in the 1950s. Mining ceased in 2001. Since then copper prices have risen five-fold, and currently there are plans to reopen the mine, which is claimed to have reserves of over 600,000 tonnes of copper.

Muelle del Tinto ceased to be used by shipping in 1975, with the opening of a new dock at Huelva. It was estimated that over its lifetime the facility had handled 150 million tons of ore. A section of the pier was dismantled to make way for a new road along the shore-line, involving the removal of three rows of cast iron columns (rows 19, 20 and 21). In 1980 a survey showed the above-water structure to be in good condition and, two years later, an under-water survey revealed that the timber platforms were also sound; although the wood had lost some of its original density there was no sign of mollusc attack. Since there had been no dredging of the river bed in the vicinity of the piles, a layer of silt up to four metres thick had been deposited over the platforms, providing additional stability. With this assurance that the pier was fundamentally safe, the structure was restored by the Huelva Town Hall (Ayuntamiento de Huelva) in conjunction with the Ministry of Development (Ministerio de Fomento) and the Ministry of Education, Culture and Sport (Ministerio de Educación, Cultura y Deporte) in 2003. Loading chutes and associated equipment, the cranes, and the rails were all removed, with new pedestrian walkways at all three levels. So the main structure of Muelle del Tinto has been preserved, with a new life as a promenade pier. It is frequented by tourists and local anglers and provides a unique location for wedding photographs and fashion shoots.

Acknowledgements

Carol Morgan, archivist at the Institution of Civil Engineers, London, for access to ICE archives.

Juan Manuel Pérez López, Director of the Archivo Histórico at Minas de Riotinto, and staff at the mine.

Alan Betteney for information on the sub-contractors from Darlington and Stockton.

References

The Rio Tinto Company, an economic history of a leading international mining concern 1873-1954
Charles E Harvey
Alison Hodge, Penzance, Cornwall, 1981
Detailed account of the establishment of the Rio Tinto Company, and of the building of the railway and the pier.

Railway Contract
Indenture made 7 July 1873 between the Rio Tinto Company and Edwin Clark and William Henry Punchard
Archivo Histórico Minero Rio Tinto
Plaza del Museo, 21660 Minas de Riotinto, Huelva
Printed and bound contract in English. The contract clearly included the loading pier at Huelva. The price is £775,000 to include the railway, the pier and all engines and rolling stock. There were clauses covering failure to deliver by the contractors.

Money Market
The Standard, London, 9 July 1873, page 4
Announcement of issue of 200,000 shares of £10 each in the Rio Tinto Company Ltd.

Muelle embarcadero para el Ferro-carril de Rio Tinto al Puerto de Huelva, Memoria
Archivo Histórico Minero Rio Tinto, reference 60/6/Z
Plaza del Museo, 21660 Minas de Riotinto, Huelva
Hand written copy of the contract for the pier between the company and John Dixon, in Spanish.

Photograph of Staff on the construction of the Rio Tinto Railway in 1873
Archivo Histórico Minero Rio Tinto
Plaza del Museo, 21660 Minas de Riotinto, Huelva
Mr Thorne, Mr (James) Pring, Mr G B Bruce junior, Dr Miguel Villaplana, Mr (Thomas) Gibson, Mr (William) Ridley, Mr (Mark William) Carr, Mr (Robert Wilfrid) Graham, Dr J Law, Mr (George) Shortrede, Mr William Langdon, Rev Rose.

Rio Tinto Mining Company
Engineering, London, 29 January 1875, page 86
G B Bruce and John Dixon just returned from Spain. Difficulties in securing foundations for the pier have been ingeniously overcome.

The Rio Tinto Mines
Illustrated London News, 7 August 1875, page 138, illustrations page 132
Short article with the comment that the railway had just opened and the pier was almost finished. Incorrectly stated that three, rather than four, steamers could be accommodated at the pier head. Engravings of the Rio Tinto pier at Huelva, a view of the railway, village and mines at Rio Tinto.

The Huelva Pier
The Engineer, London, 12 May 1876 pages 360 (illustrations) and 363 (article)
This is based on information from John Robinson, who carried out the detail design work in London. It is generally similar to Thomas Gibson's later paper but has additional information on sub-contractors.

Huelva Pier
The Engineer, London, 19 May 1876, page 372 (article) and 374 (illustrations)
Concluding description from the previous week's issue.

Girder Making and the Practice of Bridge Building in Wrought Iron
Edward Hutchinson
E and F N Spon, London, 1879
The Huelva pier is one of the examples described in this excellent book. Hutchinson quotes the final cost as £163,000 and comments that iron at that time was at an extremely high price. The two engravings illustrating the pier have many inaccuracies!

Public Companies
The Standard, London, 28 April 1876, page 7
Report on 3rd Annual Meeting of Rio Tinto Company Shareholders. The railway was in excellent order, the pier was opened on 23 March but the works were not entirely complete.

The Huelva Pier
The Engineer, London, 12 May 1876, page 363 with illustrations on page 360
Description of the railway, William Ridley resident engineer, contractors Clarke Punchard and Curry. Description of pier and its operation.

Huelva Pier
The Engineer, London, 19 May 1876, page 372 with detailed illustrations on pages 374-5
Further details of the pier.

The Huelva Pier and Rio Tinto Railway
Thomas Gibson
Minutes of Proceedings of the Institution of Civil Engineers, 2 April 1878, volume 53, pages 130-158
Full description of the work, including tables of the tests on the settlement of the piers. John Dixon was present at the reading of the paper and made comments about aspects of the design and construction.

The Huelva Pier and the Rio Tinto Railway
Minutes of Proceedings of the Institution of Civil Engineers, 2 April 1878, volume 53, pages 159-163
G B Bruce, A C Pain, J Robinson, Sir J Ramsden and T Gibson
Further details of design and construction of the pier.

Obituary, Edwin Clark
Minutes of Proceedings of the Institution of Civil Engineers, volume 120, part II, 1895, pages 344-354

Obituary, Thomas Gibson
Minutes of Proceedings of the Institution of Civil Engineers, volume 140, part II, 1900, page 282

Obituary, Sir George Barclay Bruce
Minutes of Proceedings of the Institution of Civil Engineers, volume 174, part IV, 1908, pages 369-372

George Barclay Bruce knighted
The Engineer, London, 8 June 1888, page 469
Describes how Bruce protested at Stephenson's insistence that he became a mechanic before becoming an engineer.

Obituary, John Robinson
Minutes of Proceedings of the Institution of Civil Engineers, volume 176, part II, 1909, pages 331-333

Obituary, William Ridley
Minutes of Proceedings of the Institution of Civil Engineers, volume 204, part II, 1917, pages 430-431.

The Rio Tinto Mines
The Engineer, London, 16 September 1887, page 225
Describes the operations at Rio Tinto, how the different grades of ore are processed and the working conditions.

The Role of Britain and France in the Finance of Portuguese Railways 1850-1890, a comparative study in speculation, corruption and inefficiency
Antonio Lopes Viera
PhD Thesis, University of Leicester, October 1983
Includes a good account of the Lisbon Steam Tramways Company in pages 226-241.

The Rio Tinto Mine, its history and romance
William Giles Nash
Simpkin, Marshall, Hamilton, Kent and Company, London, 1904
History of the mines up to the time of the sale by the Spanish government to the Rio Tinto Company.

Not on Queen Victoria's Birthday, the story of the Rio Tinto Mines
David Avery
Collins, London, 1974
Sponsored by the Rio Tinto Company on the occasion of its centenary, covering the history of the mines.

The Rio Tinto Company, an economic history of a leading international mining concern
Charles E Harvey
Alison Hodge, Penzance, 1981
Good history of the company with details of original shareholding and costs of the railway and pier.

A technical history of the Rio Tinto mines: some notes on exploitation from pre-Phoenician times to the 1950s
Leonard Unthank Salkield, edited by Maurice J Cahalan
The Institution of Mining and Metallurgy, London, 1987
Detailed description of the mine workings, metal processing and other aspects of Rio Tinto.

Mineral wealth and economic development: foreign investment in Spain 1851-1913
Charles Harvey and Peter Taylor
Economic History Review, 2nd series XL, 2(1987), pages 185-207
Comprehensive analysis of British investment and returns in Spanish mining, including Rio Tinto's dividends.

Dos ejemplos britanicos de cimentaciones de estructuras maritimas sobre plataformas de madera en el siglo XIX
González García de Velasco and Miguel González Vílchez
Proceedings of Seventh National Congress on Construction History, Santiago, 26-29 October 2011
Editors: S Huerta, Gil I Crespo, S Garcia, M Tain
Instituto Juan de Herrera, Madrid, 2011
Two examples of British 19th century piers on screw piles: Maplin Sands lighthouse and the Huelva pier. Description of the Huelva pier is from Thomas Gibson's 1878 paper, with additional information on the surveys of the structure in 1980 and 1992, and the restoration in 2001 by the Spanish company Freyssinet SA.

El Muelle Cargadero de Mineral de la Rio Tinto Company Limited
Jaoquín Barba Quintero
Clásicos de la Arqueología de Huelva 8
Excma. Diputación Provincial de Huelva, 2002
Covers the Spanish government's difficulties with the initial auction and eventual sale of the Rio Tinto mine. Describes the alternative loading methods considered and the construction of the pier.

The Rio Tinto Railway
Alan Sewell
Plateway Press, Brighton, 1991
Comprehensive illustrated history of the railway but with little mention of John Dixon's ore loading pier. Details of the pier are incorrect (layout of tracks and materials of construction).

Letter from John Dixon to Hintze Ribeiro, dated 8 March 1882 written from the Hotel Central, Lisbon on his headed notepaper with the address as Laurence Pountney Hill.
Fundo Particular Hintze Ribeiro 5.1.4045
PT/BPARPD/PSS/HRHR/1775
11 July 1881 to 27 September 1883
Direção Regional da Cultura
Biblioteca Publica e Arquivo Regional de Ponta Delgada, Azores
John Dixon wrote that he was proceeding to the Rio Tinto Mines where he would be staying for a week before returning to Lisbon.

15 Customs House piers, Lisbon

In 1874 John Dixon proposed building four jetties at the Lisbon Customs House to facilitate the off-loading of vessels. His plans impressed the Portuguese Government but, after much debate, only two of the piers were built in 1876. They were soon extended and incorporated into later dock developments along the northern bank of the River Tagus. Today there is no trace of them since the site is buried under concrete extensions to the river frontage.

Difficulties unloading shipping at the Lisbon Customs House

Maritime cargoes arriving at Lisbon on the River Tagus had to be transferred onto lighters to be unloaded at the graceful steps on the waterfront of the Praça do Comércio and the Grande Alfandega (Customs House). This operation was recognised as slow, hazardous, and costly. Over the years there had been proposals to construct jetties stretching out into deep water to enable direct off-loading from vessels. One of these was for two jetties in the form of bridge spans carried on masonry pillars, the so-called 'architraves mechanicas', which had been designed as early as 1857. Although the profile of the river bed was well known from several hydrographic surveys, it was uncertain whether it was stable enough to support masonry pillars, and there were concerns over the costs of construction.

John Dixon's proposal

John Dixon must have become aware of the talks about jetties at the Lisbon Customs House when he started work on the ore-loading terminal at Huelva in Spain in 1874. He travelled to Huelva via the steamer to Lisbon, where he stayed at the Grand Hotel Central, on the waterfront barely half a mile west of the Customs House. Always sensitive to new business opportunities, he would have soon heard about the 'architraves mechanicas' and it would have been obvious to him that his experience in pier construction could be applied at Lisbon. On 21 September 1874 John addressed a proposal to the Portuguese government that four landing piers could be built in front of the Customs House quayside so that even the largest vessels could unload directly. The piers were to be of conventional design, with cast iron columns and a timber decking which would be a minimum of five feet above high-water level. In all probability John would have been given access to the detailed hydrographic surveys of the river bed carried out for the 'architraves mechanicas'. The following year the government decided to adopt Dixon's proposal, and were so impressed by his plans that they awarded him a Knighthood of the Royal Military Order of Christ (Ordem Militar dos Cavaleiros de Nosso Senhor Jesus Christo) by Dom Luís 1, King of Portugal. This honour was a relic of the days of the crusades and restricted to Catholics until 1834, when it became a secular award, not often conferred on foreigners.

John submitted a formal tender; the first pier would cost £16,400 with the other three pro rata based on floor area. If all four piers were to be on the same contract, there would be a discount of £5,900 (costs were quoted in Portuguese réis, here converted at 1.0 million réis to £220). The authorities stipulated that Dixon would be responsible for the maintenance of the piers for an unspecified period, but helpfully excluded damage caused by passing shipping or earthquakes. Materials imported from England for the construction would be landed free of duty. The cast iron columns, of 15 inch diameter and 1 inch thickness, were to be driven into the river bed to a depth of between 6 feet and 12 feet. Clearly his experience at Huelva, where he had great difficulty sinking the pier supports sufficiently deep to ensure stability, caused him to insert a clause into the tender that if the columns had to be sunk deeper than 12 feet he would be reimbursed for additional materials and work.

Arguments delay starting the work

Various disagreements between the government and local authorities in Lisbon delayed the start of work. The wondrously named Bento Fortunato de Moura Countinho de Almeida d'Eça was the Director General of Public Works. He had surveyed the existing dock facilities in Lisbon and was in favour of accepting John Dixon's plans with some minor modifications. However, there was much debate over the best material to use for the columns. John had assured them that cast iron was more resistant to corrosion in sea water than wrought iron, but others took the opposite view. The matter was decided in Dixon's favour but, just as it seemed that construction might commence, the entire justification for the landing piers was questioned by two men of great standing. João Crisóstomo de Abreu e Sousa (1811-1892) had been an army general and was now a government minister destined for high office; he would become Prime Minister in 1890. Carlos Ribeiro (1813-1882) had a distinguished military and engineering career and had worked closely with the Ministry of Public Works over many years. They both considered the landing piers would be an unnecessary duplication of facilities after completion of the new docks being planned for the port of Lisbon.

In fact, the early improvements to dock facilities were developed without any overall plan. A scheme for docks immediately to the east of the Torre de Belém was ratified and a contract awarded to a Franco-Portuguese company by the Minister for Public Works in March 1876. Following this there was much talk about ambitious ideas for dock facilities right along the northern shore of the River Tagus, from the Torre de Belém at the river mouth to Beato some eight miles upriver. Many schemes would be put forward, including those of Sir John Coode and James Abernethy from Britain. A Government Commission deliberated over the matter from 1883 to 1886, before charging the Portuguese engineers João Joaquim de Matos and Adolpho Loureiro to draw up definitive plans. The absence of any clear definition of these large-scale docks in the 1870s only added to the delays in the Customs House piers project.

As if all of this wasn't enough, questions were then raised about the appearance of the landing piers, which it was felt would detract from the beauty of the Praça do Comércio, the centre-piece of the rebuilding of Lisbon by the Marquês de Pombal after the 1755 earthquake. The last straw was when José Victorino Damásio Ribeiro, an engineer and son of Carlos Ribeiro, questioned the use of cast iron where there might be tensile stresses and high levels of vibration. He was in favour of wrought iron screwed piles, as invented by Alexander Mitchell (1780-1868). Screwed piles would also be cheaper to install, only needing a crane and winch and no pile-driver.

Faced with these conflicting opinions, on 30 April 1875, the government made the bold decision to approve John's contract. But there were further delays and three months later, with no sign of progress, *The Times* correspondent in Lisbon was still able to complain about the arrangements for off-loading cargoes at Lisbon via lighters, making no mention of the piers.

By now John's plans for four piers had been reduced to two along the frontage of the Customs House. After further changes to the dimensions of these two piers, the final contract cost was agreed at £48,400.

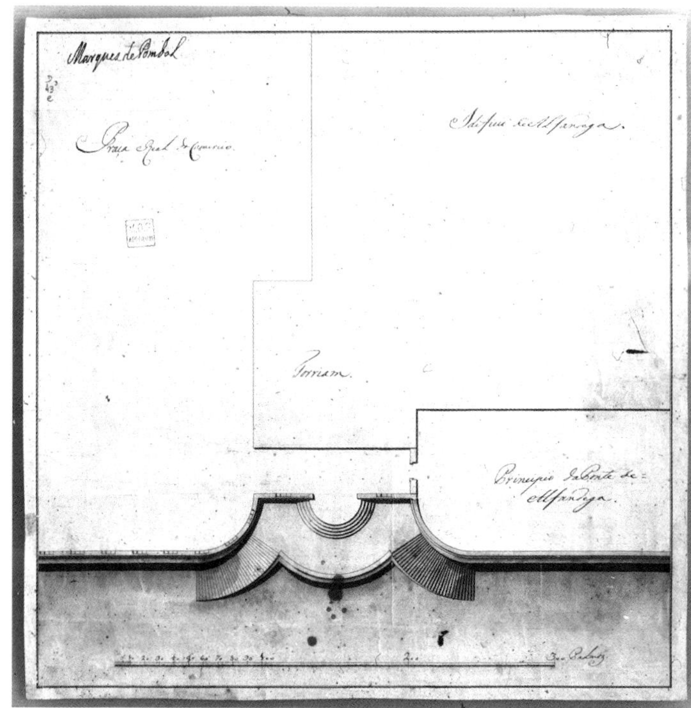

Top) Plan of the Customs House with the curved steps leading down to the water, before construction of John Dixon's piers. Núcleo de Documentação e Arquivo, Direção de Serviços de Documentação, Comunicação e Relaçãoes Públicas, Rue Vale do Pereiro 4, Lisbon.
Above) 'Cais da Alfandega em 1877 (BAPL)' an early view of the landing pier outside the Customs House (Alfandega) which can be seen on the right. The rail-mounted steam cranes are evident.

From page 78 of '100 Anos do Porto de Lisboa' by Nabais, António José Castanheira Maia Nabais and Paulo Oliveira Ramos, Administração do Porto de Lisboa, 1987. Núcleo de Documentação e Arquivo, Direção de Serviços de Documentação, Comunicação e Relaçãoes Públicas, Rue Vale do Pereiro 4, Lisbon, reference 002747C/a BAHOP

'Lisboa, Estação de caminhos de ferro de Sul e Sueste' 1910 painting by Alberto Sousa. Alberto Sousa (1880-1961) was a noted Portuguese watercolourist. The title translates as 'Lisbon Railway Station South and Southeast' but is clearly shows the western end of the Alfandega and the curved steps leading down to the water. The jetty is substantially as built by John Dixon and enlarged by Frederick William Reeves, with the later metal sheds. The large, concrete-filled, columns at the end of the pier were installed to protect the structure from collisions with shipping and to increase the stability of the jetty. A steam-operated derrick crane can be seen in the centre distance.
Collection of Museu de Chiado.
© MNAC-Museu de Chiado, Direção-Geral do Património Cultural / Arquivo e Documentação Fotográfica (DGPC/ADF) Rua Serpa Pinto 4, Lisbon.

Two piers are built

It seems that construction of two piers in front of the façade of the Alfandega started in 1876. It is difficult to determine the exact shape and size of the piers because different sets of plans show slightly different designs, and it is not easy to distinguish actual constructions from proposals which may never have been implemented. The best authority is undoubtedly Adolpho Ferreira Loureiro (1836-1911), distinguished as a military man, an engineer, a writer, poet and politician. He produced detailed histories and plans of every Portuguese dock and harbour. His drawings show two piers of substantially the same configuration as the 'architraves mechanicas', with the western jetty 'T' shaped area and the eastern jetty 'L' shaped area. During construction the area of both piers was increased, with the eastern pier becoming a trapezoidal shape. It was found that the river bed was less stable than assumed, so John Dixon recommended driving two 75 inch diameter wrought iron columns filled with concrete at the outer ends of the piers and stabilising the river bed by tipping stone around the bases of these columns. Construction then continued. Timber strakes were added to protect the structure from contact with ships' hulls. Two steam-driven tugs were ordered to assist with manoeuvring vessels alongside the piers. John Dixon's final contribution was to draw up a proposal for steam-driven cranes on rails running along the piers with an estimated cost of £4,520.

Lighting was added a few years after opening the piers, and in 1881 the timber decking was replaced by galvanised iron plating.

Major changes were made in 1885 when General José Joaquim de Paiva Cabral Couceiro (1830-1916) proposed extending and repairing the two landing piers, adding corrugated iron sheds with glazed roofs. The contract was entrusted to Frederick William Reeves, an English engineer resident in Lisbon. Reeves had constructed water supply systems and railway bridges in Portugal, and had also worked on the ill-fated Tay Bridge, causing him to be called back from Portugal to appear before the Board of Trade Enquiry in 1880. For the pier extensions Reeves used screwed piles taken down to a depth of 60 feet.

Large-scale harbour works

Throughout the 1880s there was much debate about an overall development scheme for the Lisbon river frontage from Belém in the west to Beato in the east, along some eight miles of foreshore. Among the engineers who put forward plans were the British engineers Sir John Coode and James Abernethy. The government then charged João Joaquim de Matos and Adolpho Loureiro to draw up a definitive plan, which they did by February 1886. A

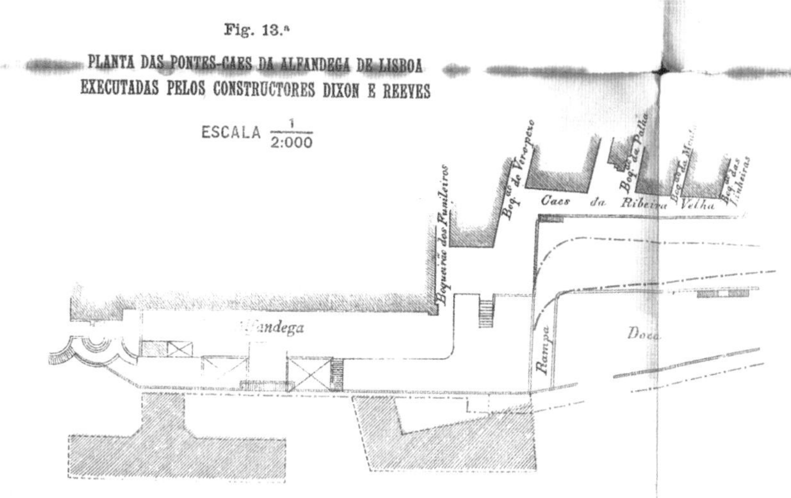

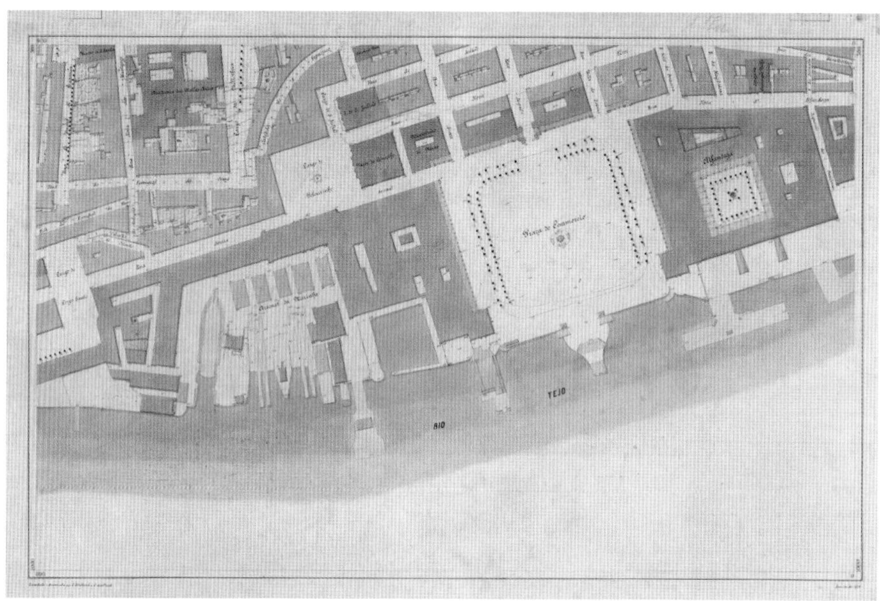

Top) 'Fig 13.a Planta das Pontes-Caes da Alfandega de Lisboa executes pelos Constructors Dixon e Reeves' This rather schematic drawing shows two piers, one in 'T' plan and one in 'L' plan with the trapezoidal extension. It does not correspond exactly to the 1877 photograph or the 1910 painting by Alberto Sousa.
Os Portos Maritimos de Portugal e Ilhas Adjacentes by Adolpho Loureiro (Inspector geral de obras publicas), Atlas III, Est III, Imprensa Nacional, Lisbon, 1907. Núcleo de Documentaçáo e Arquivo, Direção de Serviços de Documentaçáo, Comunicação e Relaçáoes Públicas, Rue Vale do Pereiro 4, Lisbon, reference 554 D11.

Above) Another plan which agrees with the Adolpho Loureiro plan but apparently not with the photographic evidence.
Plan No.51 from Terreiro do Paço 1879, Levantamento topográfico de Francisco e César Goullard.
Núcleo de Documentaçáo e Arquivo, Direção de Serviços de Documentaçáo, Comunicação e Relaçáoes Públicas, Rue Vale do Pereiro 4, Lisbon, reference PRAÇA DO COMÉRCIO.

river wall was to be built parallel to the foreshore, and far enough out into the river to allow large vessels to moor alongside it. Various docks and basins would then be built in the area between the wall and the foreshore. In front of the Customs House there was to be a basin for barges and small craft, with a water surface area of 3.7 acres (the plans imply that this basin was actually to the east of the Customs House). A paper presented to the Institution of Civil Engineers in 1888 mentions that a rubble and stone wall, some 33 feet wide, might be built in front of the Customs House. The accompanying plans show a long wall from the Arsenal Basin, stretching across the frontage of the Praça do Comércio and the Customs House, and extending further to the east. The area between this wall and the old river bank, which is where the Dixon and Reeves piers were situated, would be filled in and concreted over.

The harbour works were put out to tender, but by the closing date of 26 March 1887 only two engineers responded, Pierre Hildebert Hersent (1827-1903), a French civil engineer who had recently built the docks at Antwerp, and Frederick William Reeves. Reeves unwisely suggested some changes to the Matos and Loureiro plans with the result that his tender was not considered. In the event Hersent made changes to the plans, but only after he had secured the contract. Construction started in 1887 and dragged on for many years. Works concentrated on the larger docks to the west of the Praça do Comércio, leaving the Dixon and Reeves piers intact. The intention to construct a wall in front of the Customs House seems to have been abandoned, at least for the time being, since the 1910 painting by Alberto Sousa clearly shows the piers as built by John and extended by Reeves.

'Antiga Estação dos Caminhos-de-Ferro e Vapores do Sul e Sueste (ant 1908)' photograph showing the Dixon and Reeves jetties. The concrete-filled columns protecting the structure are clearly visible. Official visitors to Lisbon traditionally landed at the steps in the centre of the Praça do Comércio, the destination of the boat in the foreground.
The website states that the jetties continued in use until 1932.
Website Lisboa de Antigamente at http://lisboadeantigamente.blogspot.co.uk/2017/01/

The piers disappear

It is difficult to follow the development history of the area in front of the Customs House, not least trying to differentiate between proposals and actual construction. At some time early in the 20th century it seems that the 1886 plans for the area along the Customs House frontage were implemented, with the construction of a large concrete apron projecting out into the river. This would have destroyed the Dixon and Reeves piers, but at least retained the marble walls and steps along the frontage of the Praça do Comércio.

Later this apron was extended westwards right up to the side of the marble steps at the centre of the Praça do Comércio, the historic landing place for royalty and ambassadors visiting Lisbon. This action completely destroyed half of the graceful marble frontage of the Praça do Comércio, which the earlier city fathers had feared would merely be obscured by two of John's piers. The final obliteration of any trace of John's work took place in the early 2000s when the Terreiro do Paço Metro station was built directly underneath the site.

Acknowledgements

José M Pages Sanchez of Hamburg University for suggesting contacts in Lisbon.

Irene Catarino, Arquivo Municipal, Câmara Municipal de Lisboa, for searching for records of the Lisbon Customs House piers in the municipal archives.

João Nuno Reis, Sistema de Informação para o Património Arquitetónico, for searching the records of the collection previously known as Direção Geral dos Edifícios e Monumentos Nacionais for any material on the Lisbon Customs House piers.

Centro de Documentação e Informação, Porto de Lisboa, for finding the book on port development by Adolpho Loureiro.

Especially to archivists Paula Ucha and Alda Vicente, Núcleo de Documentação e Arquivo, 4 Rua Vale do Pereiro in Lisbon, for hours spent guiding me through references in Portuguese.

Maria de Aires, Museu Nacional de Arte Contemporânea do Chiado, Lisbon and Tânia Olim, Arquivo de Documentação Fotográfica/DDCI, Lisbon, for tracking down the painting by Alberto Sousa of the pier.

References

Projecto de uma nova ponte cais para serviço do armazém da Alfândega Municipal de Lisboa, 1857.
Lisbon Municipal Archives: Núcleo de Documentação e Arquivo
Direção de Serviços de Documentação, Comunicação e Relações Públicas
Rua Vale do Pereiro, 4, 1250-141 Lisbon
Reference CSOPM, DC 18571002, C 0598
Two-sided hand-written report (in Portuguese) on the proposed bridge jetties supported on six pillars of stonework, with estimated costs. This is the earliest reference (1857) to the proposal for off-loading jetties at the Customs House.

Planta hydrográfica do Caes d'Alfandega grande de Lisboa (Sistema de arquitraves mecânicas para elevação do desembarcadouro na Alfândega Grande de Lisboa)
António Joaquim Pereira De Carvalho
Administração do Porto de Lisboa (APL), Lisbon, 1861
Lisbon Municipal Archives: Núcleo de Documentação e Arquivo
Direção de Serviços de Documentação, Comunicação e Relações Públicas
Rua Vale do Pereiro, 4, 1250-141 Lisbon
Reference: D 30-1 C BAHOP
Details (in Portuguese) of river depths for the proposed bridge-like piers. These surveys would probably have been made available to John Dixon.

Estudo Cais da Alfandega Grande, Lisboa
Plano horizontal & projecto de um desembarcadouro na Alfandega grande de Lisboa pelo systema de "architraves mechanicas" apresentado ao Governo Portuguez
António Joaquim Pereira De Carvalho, 1861
Lisbon Municipal Archives: Núcleo de Documentação e Arquivo
Direção de Serviços de Documentação, Comunicação e Relações Públicas
Rua Vale do Pereiro, 4, 1250-141 Lisbon
Reference: D30-2 C BAHOP
Plans (in Portuguese) for two bridge-like structures on masonry supports, the south-west 'T' in plan, the south-east 'L' in plan, the 'architraves mechanicas'. John Dixon's piers are to much the same layout.

Proposta para estabelecer caes de serviço da Alfândega Grande de Lisboa em frente dos actuaes, e a distancia a que fique altura d'água suficiente para poderem atracar os navios e descarregar ou carregar sem as baldeações para as fragatas como actualmente se pratica.
José Victorino Damazio, 26 July 1867
Lisbon Municipal Archives: Núcleo de Documentação e Arquivo
Direção de Serviços de Documentação, Comunicação e Relações Públicas
Rua Vale do Pereiro, 4, 1250-141 Lisboa
Reference CSOPM, DC 18610726, C 1392
Hand-written notes (in Portuguese) about the proposal to establish off-loading piers for the Grand Customs House at Lisbon, with sufficient depth of water to allow ships to be moored and load or unload without transfer to lighters as was current practice.

Lisbon Harbour Improvements
The Times, London, 7 April 1875, page 13
Description of the pier works at the Custom House in Lisbon, Portugal.

Miscellanea - Improvements at Lisbon
The Engineer, London, 9 April 1875, page 245
John Dixon is to construct landing piers.

Lisbon Harbour Improvements
Engineering, London, 16 April 1875, page 332
Work to be carried out by Mr John Dixon.

Portuguese Finance - from our special correspondent
The Times, London, 23 July 1875, page 4
Laments the antediluvian procedures for unloading vessels via lighters at Lisbon, which was disgracefully deficient on port facilities. This article, over three months after the announcement of the new piers, makes no mention of them.

Money Market - Thursday evening
The Standard, London, 5 May 1876, page 6
Report of the Portuguese Minister of Finance for the preceding financial year included expenses for quays and piers of the Lisbon Customs House.

On the projected Lisbon Harbour Works
Engineering, London, 4 March 1887, page 201-2
Final agreement on definition of the harbour works, with a long river wall built parallel to the foreshore, with enclosed docks between the river wall and the foreshore in front of the Customs House.

Os Portos Maritimos de Portugal e Ilhas Adjacentes
Adolpho Loureiro (Inspector geral de obras publicas)
Volume III, Parte I
Imprensa Nacional, Lisbon, 1906
Lisbon Municipal Archives: Núcleo de Documentação e Arquivo
Direção de Serviços de Documentação, Comunicação e Relações Públicas
Rua Vale do Pereiro, 4, 1250-141 Lisbon
Reference: 544 D-3
Several volumes (in Portuguese) describing all the port installations in Portugal and the Portuguese islands. John Dixon's piers are described in pages 191-197.

Os Portos Maritimos de Portugal e Ilhas Adjacentes
Adolpho Loureiro (Inspector geral de obras publicas)
Atlas III, Est III
Imprensa Nacional, Lisbon, 1907
Lisbon Municipal Archives: Núcleo de Documentação e Arquivo
Direção de Serviços de Documentação, Comunicação e Relações Públicas
Rua Vale do Pereiro, 4, 1250-141 Lisbon
Reference: 554 D11
This is one of the atlases, with large fold-out drawings, accompanying the volumes describing the port installations. There is a plan for 'Dixon and Reeve' in Est III.

100 Anos do Porto de Lisboa
Investigação histórica de António José Castanheira Maia Nabais and Paulo Oliveira Ramos Administração do Porto de Lisboa (APL), Lisbon, 1987
Lisbon Municipal Archives: Núcleo de Documentação e Arquivo
Direção de Serviços de Documentação, Comunicação e Relações Públicas
Rua Vale do Pereiro, 4, 1250-141 Lisbon
Reference: 002747C/a|BAHOP
Includes a photograph of the pier constructed by John Dixon and photographs of the construction of the masonry wall in the frontage of the Customs House.

Melhoramentos do Porto de Lisoa: Atlas
Ministério das Obras Públicas Comércio e Indústria, Lisboa
Lisbon Municipal Archives: Núcleo de Documentação e Arquivus
Direção de Serviços de Documentação, Comunicação e Relações Públicas
Rua Vale do Pereiro, 4, 1250-141 Lisbon
Reference: 000007FF BAHOP
Plans of the harbour and jetties all along the northern shore of the River Tagus from Belém to Beato.

On the Projected Lisbon Harbour Works
Joaquim Ben-Saúde
Tracts 8vo, volume 451, bound together February 1888
Reprinted from *Engineering*, London, 1887
Presented to the Institution by the author, 29 September 1887
Comprehensive description of the proposed harbour works, with the suggestion of a 33 feet wide wall outside the Customs House and a basin to the east.

16 Woosung to Shanghai Railway, China

A great many sources credit John Dixon and Richard Rapier with the construction of the first railway in China, from Woosung to Shanghai, in 1876. It was Dixon's men who laid the 2 feet gauge track and his friend Richard Rapier who built the locomotives and rolling stock. From the start the railway was opposed by the traditionalist Chinese government, but was pushed through by Jardine, Matheson and Company. It was hoped that the authorities, when they saw the completed railway and its potential for developing China, would be more enthusiastic. Although the railway was a commercial success, popular with local people, the mandarins remained implacable. It was agreed that they would purchase the railway, but three weeks after paying the final instalment they started to dismantle the track and tear down the buildings. Ostensibly the railway was being transferred for rebuilding on Formosa. Track, locomotives and carriages were taken to the island but left to rot away on the foreshore. The Dixon and Rapier railway had only survived for seventeen months.

John Dixon's involvement

John does not seem to have taken an active role in the work in China, probably never visiting the country and delegating virtually everything to his capable site engineer Gabriel Morrison. One reason for this would have been the time taken to travel to China from England. Although the opening of the Suez Canal and the introduction of steam ships had more than halved the journey time from England to China, it still required some forty days to reach Shanghai. Since any significant site visit would therefore take three months, it would not be surprising if John decided he could not afford this time away from his other business.

Proposal for the Woosung Road

The nineteenth century was the closing period of the Ching dynasty in China. Their administration was seen as extremely conservative and insular, and they were greatly suspicious of the new western technologies which, while they might operate successfully in Europe, were not considered suitable for China. The mandarins were also suspicious of the motives of the Western diplomats and businessmen, who were concentrated in Shanghai, rightly sensing that they were mainly interested in the profits that might be made by exploiting Chinese resources. Foremost in the Western businesses in China at that time was Jardine, Matheson and Company.

William Jardine and James Matheson, two young Scotsmen, set up a Far Eastern trading company in 1832. Dealing in silks, spices and tea, they also smuggled opium from India into China. Their venture was spectacularly successful, but a source of concern to the Chinese authorities who had banned the use of opium. Chinese attempts to close down the trade led to the 1839 Opium War, after which the victorious British gained control of Hong Kong and acquired extensive trade concessions. Jardine, Matheson and Company judiciously then moved on from opium into more respectable trading businesses.

In 1864 a retired partner in Jardine Matheson asked Sir Macdonald Stephenson, an engineer who had built many railways in India, to give an opinion as to the scope for railways in China. He presented his ideas for a network of railways, and how to raise the necessary finance, to Viceroy Li Hung Chang, the governor of the province which included Peking. Viceroy Li saw the impetus behind the proposed railways as the desire of foreign merchants to exploit Chinese resources, and politely turned the plans down.

Jardine, Matheson and their associates were unwilling to abandon the thought of building a railway in China. They knew of the success of railways in opening up trade in Asia and America but appreciated that the Chinese ruling elite were strongly opposed to the idea. The only chance of success was to start in a small way, and with a certain degree of subterfuge. They commissioned an English engineer, Harry Robinson, to map out a route. In November 1872, a group of Shanghai-based traders wrote to Shen Ping Cheng, the local official or Taotai, proposing the 'Shanghai to Woosung Road'. The use of the term 'road' rather than the more explicit 'railway' was deliberate and resulted in a favourable response but would later result in much acrimony. The Woosung Road Company was launched, with a board of eight local merchants and a capital of about £14,000, to build a 'road' between Woosung and Shanghai. Land was purchased for the roadway, much was over existing gardens and some was on the site of burial grounds. Robinson had envisaged respecting the dead by elevating the track above the burial grounds on stilts, but the Woosung Road Company found that suitable financial compensation was a more practicable alternative. John Dixon later recalled that land had been purchased from 237 different proprietors and, when it was seen that there was compensation for going over burial sites, one man had claimed that he had five mothers-in-law buried on a strip of land wanted for the railway. Rights over the land purchased were agreed by the Taotai, although the authorities were still under the impression that this was for a road rather than a railway. It was not clear whether the Taotai kept his local governor, Viceroy Shen Pao Chen, or Viceroy Li Hung Chang in Peking, fully informed of these developments.

At this point two of the original members of the Woosung Road Company withdrew and Francis Bulkeley Johnson (1828-1887) of Jardine Matheson joined the board. From now on Jardine Matheson took a more active role in the project. It was decided to register the Woosung Road Company Limited in London, and additional capital was raised. The company looked for a suitable contractor, and engaged Antonio Gabrielli (1814-1891), an Italian contractor based in Westminster, who had worked on docks at Chatham and Brindisi. He appointed Frederick Augustus Sheppard (1819-1884) from Sussex as his site engineer. Sheppard left England for China on 25 July 1874. Permission was obtained to build jetties and a warehouse at Woosung, but with still no mention of a railway. Gabrielli and Sheppard submitted an estimate of £100,000 for the nine miles of standard gauge (George Stephenson's immortal yet illogical 4 feet 8½ inches) railway, much to the discouragement of the London-based directors. However, the Shanghai shareholders decided to continue work, building embankments on the lands they had purchased to indicate their ownership. There was some local opposition and one of the Shanghai shareholders was attacked on 3 February 1875. On 12 March 1875 Gabrielli and Sheppard withdrew. Incidentally, around the same time Antonio Gabrielli was working on the provision of water supplies to Rio de Janeiro, probably alongside John Dixon.

By now the Chinese railway scheme was close to collapse. The London directors recommended abandoning the railway, but the Shanghai shareholders again kept it going. They persuaded Sir Thomas Wade (1818-1895), the British Minister in China who spoke Mandarin, to claim that the Chinese authorities supported the railway and that it could legally proceed. Perhaps the deciding factor was the involvement of Richard Rapier and John Dixon.

Richard Rapier and John Dixon

Richard Rapier harboured ambitions to build a railway in China. Between 1873 and 1874 he designed and built a small engine at Ipswich which he thought suitable for introducing the Chinese to railways. This was a 2 feet gauge 0-4-0 locomotive. He emphatically denied that it had ever been intended as a present for the Emperor, as stated in Morrison's first-hand account of the project, and in many subsequent histories.

Dixon and Rapier probably remained in touch since their Stephenson apprentice days, although John was not known for his social correspondence. Ransomes and Rapier supplied narrow gauge railway

Who's who?
Richard Christopher Rapier (1836-1897)

Richard Rapier was born at Morpeth, son of the Rev Christopher Rapier. Richard was an apprentice at Robert Stephenson's Forth Street Works at the same time as John Dixon. After his apprenticeship he remained at Stephenson's works for several years until 1862, when he joined the Quaker family business of Ransomes, manufacturers of agricultural machinery in Ipswich. Ransomes had worked with John Fowler (1826-1864) on ploughing engines; John Fowler was a Quaker from Wiltshire and married a daughter of Joseph Pease. He should not be confused with the two other contemporary John Fowlers. John Fowler (1817-1898) was a railway engineer and bridge builder, who later in life designed the Forth Railway Bridge with Benjamin Baker. He advised the Khedive of Egypt and knew John and Waynman Dixon. John Fowler (1824-1888) was engineer to the Tees Conservancy Commissioners and well known to Raylton Dixon, who was a member of the Tees Conservancy Commission for many years.

After John Fowler (1826-1864) left to set up his own business in Leeds in 1860, Ransomes increasingly turned to steam railway work. In 1868 Ransomes separated their agricultural and railway businesses. Richard Rapier was appointed manager of the railway department and in 1869 designed their new Waterside Iron Works. He became a partner in the company in 1869. Rapier was also involved with river navigation and built the sluices on the Manchester Ship Canal. He became managing director when the company became Ransomes and Rapier Limited in 1896.

Rapier took a keen interest in the welfare of his workforce, providing them with allotment gardens, and was actively involved with Friendly Societies. Like John, he was a freemason.

equipment to mineral lines around the world, and so Richard and John may well have had commercial dealings together. When John heard about Richard's ambition to send his small locomotive to China, he was very enthusiastic and offered to provide half a mile of track work to accompany it.

Agreement to construct the railway

About this time Richard Rapier and John Dixon learned of the Woosung Road Company. In the spring of 1875 they invited James MacAndrew and Bulkeley Johnson to view the little locomotive running at Ipswich. MacAndrew and Johnson were Woosung directors, and also senior figures in Jardine, Matheson and Company. They judged the locomotive 'large enough to work well, too small to be objected to', and it was optimistically named *Pioneer*. The locomotive was then taken to Felixstowe where, for several days, it offered rides round a circuit of track. Impressed, Jardine Matheson entered into negotiations with Rapier and Dixon. *Pioneer* was modified for Chinese service, including widening the gauge to 2 feet 6 inches, enlarging the cylinders and water tank, and fitting wrought iron wheels. Rapier's estimated cost of building a narrow-gauge (2 feet 6 inches) railway from Shanghai to Woosung was much lower than the previous £100,000, but still exceeded the £20,000 available. At this point John stepped in with an offer to construct and equip the line for £20,000, putting in £8,000 of his own money in exchange for company shares. This was too good to turn down, and an agreement between Rapier, Dixon and the Woosung Road Company was signed on 18 November 1875 to build nine miles of narrow gauge railway between Woosung and Shanghai. Implacable mandarin opposition was expected, but it was felt that this might be overcome once the mandarins could appreciate the potential of railways through seeing a small section of track in operation. After all, there had been initial opposition to steam-powered shipping, but now such vessels were accepted and there was even Chinese ownership of some Yangtze steamers.

'Locomotives for the first Chinese Railway'. Richard Rapier built Pioneer before the railway had been constructed; it was judged 'large enough to work well, too small to be objected to.' The later Celestial Empire clearly shows design changes brought about by operating experience, notably its increased size and large capacity water tanks. Engineering, 14 July 1876, page 29.

Site engineer Gabriel Morrison

Rapier and Dixon, in the spirit of mutual trust, appointed Gabriel Morrison as a combined site engineer and contractor's agent. Morrison was then thirty-five years old and had worked for James Brunlees from 1863 to 1874. James Brunlees was about to design the pier at Llandudno which was constructed by John in 1876-77.

George Barclay Bruce (1821-1908) agreed to be the Woosung Road Company's honorary engineer in England. He was a great friend of John's and was already working with him on the ore-loading pier at Huelva in Spain for the Rio Tinto Company.

Morrison left England on 1 October 1875 with his wife Jessie, travelling via New York and San Francisco, and arriving in China on 2 January 1876. On 15 October John Dixon despatched a shipload of navvies, rails and other materials to China. At the end of the month five men from Rapier's Works, accompanied by the locomotive *Pioneer* and permanent way materials, sailed aboard the steamer *Glenroy* direct to China, arriving on 20 December. This was seen as an exotic adventure, with an editorial in *The Engineer* speculating on how many miles of railway might be built in 'the Flowery Land' over the next fifty years. 1875 was the fiftieth anniversary of the Stockton and Darlington Railway

Who's who?
Gabriel James Morrison (1840-1905)

Gabriel James Morrison was born in London and served an apprenticeship with Robson, Forman and McCall, civil engineers in Glasgow, including study at Glasgow University. He briefly worked on Scottish railways before joining James Brunlees in London, where he remained for eleven years. With Brunlees he was engaged in work on railways and docks, including the Solway Junction railway (John Dixon later rebuilt the Solway viaduct after it was damaged by ice). In 1874 he started his own consultancy in Westminster but was soon offered the position in China by Dixon and Rapier. The appointment would prove to be a significant turning point in Morrison's career. On completion of the railway he remained in Shanghai, where he established himself as one of their leading engineers. In 1885 he went into partnership with the engineer and architect Frederick Montague Gratton (1859-1918) and together they undertook many major projects in Shanghai and other parts of China.

In 1902 he returned to London and was working with Sir John Wolfe Barry and partners. They were the consulting engineers for the Shanghai-Nanking Railway. Morrison had the pleasure of seeing the rebuilding of the Woosung to Shanghai railway, which became part of the Shanghai-Nanking Railway. The railway's first locomotive was named *Gabriel James Morrison* in his honour.

ARRIVAL OF STAFF AND MATERIALS AT WOOSUNG.

'Arrival of staff and materials at Woosung'
Photograph between pages 98 and 99, Remunerative Railways for New Countries by Richard Rapier, E and F N Spon, London, 1878.

and, looking ahead a further fifty years, the editorial commented 'John Chinaman of that day may chance to imitate the people who are now furnishing them with this their first line, and themselves celebrate a railway jubilee!'

The first work was to build bridges over fifteen small creeks along the route. Sleepers and rails were taken by boat to various points along the way, and track-laying began. It had been put about that the land was being purchased for a road, but when the first spike was driven by Mrs Morrison on 20 January 1876 the purpose was apparent, although there was still no mention of steam locomotives.

ARRIVAL OF THE FIRST LOCOMOTIVE IN CHINA.

'Arrival of the first locomotive in China'
Photograph between pages 98 and 99, Remunerative Railways for New Countries by Richard Rapier, E and F N Spon, London, 1878
© British Library Board. All rights reserved / Bridgeman Images.

The railway opens amid growing official hostility

Events now took a severe turn for the worse. Early in 1876 Feng Chun Kuang had replaced Shen Ping Chen as Taotai, and immediately recognised his uncomfortable situation, with unofficial railway construction proceeding in his region which he knew would be opposed by the Shanghai governor, Viceroy Shen Pao Chen. He announced that foreigners were building a railway without permission. The partially-completed sale of a piece of land intended for the railway at Woosung was halted, and early in February the lower district officials, Tipans, who had arranged the land sales were imprisoned and beaten up, as a result of which one died. Now the matter of the unofficial railway had reached the Peking governor, Viceroy Li Hung Chang, who had rejected earlier plans for railways. Viceroy Li, described in the English press as 'one of the most enlightened and energetic men among the high governing class of China', decided that the railway would have to be acquired by the Chinese, and that this would have to be achieved by Viceroy Shen not only arranging the purchase but also finding the money. Whether Viceroy Li was personally in favour of the railway is not clear but, not surprisingly, his decision greatly annoyed Viceroy Shen, who nevertheless had to accept his superior's decision. From this moment Viceroy Shen was determined to remove all trace of the railway although, greatly to his credit, he paid the Woosung Road Company a handsome price.

Undeterred, and still believing that the first-hand experience of an operational railway would convince the authorities, the Woosung Company pressed ahead with construction. On 14 February 1876 sixteen coolies carried *Pioneer* to a completed section of track where it was steamed. There could now be little doubt as to the true intentions of the Woosung Road Company, although in an attempt to ameliorate any concern *Pioneer* was dismissed as a Valentine gift for the scheme's promoters.

Ignoring the growing condemnation of the railway by Taotai Feng Chun Kuang and the two Viceroys, Morrison completed the full length of track. *Pioneer* ran an unofficial and impromptu service, offering seats in empty ballast wagons to the large numbers of curious Chinese who came to see the 'fire-breathing cart'. Provoked, Taotai Feng despatched a lengthy letter to the British Consul, detailing seventeen statements against the railway and claiming that, if China wanted railways, they would have no difficulty in making them for themselves. The Consul delayed any reply, optimistically still hoping that when the railway was complete the Taotai would see the potential benefits and withdraw his objections.

By the end of May the line was indeed completed as far as Kangwan and at 5:00pm on 27 May 1876 *Pioneer* hauled a special excursion train along the route. Three days later the first permanent engine, the 0-6-0 *Celestial Empire*, with six carriages and twelve wagons, arrived from England. The official opening took place at 5:35pm on Friday 30 June, when *Celestial Empire* hauled six carriages and one wagon with 150 invited guests, out of the Shanghai station and over 4½ miles to Kangwan. Crowds lined the route, with people stopping work in the fields and running towards the line. The timetabled rail service began on 3 July with six trains a day in each direction between Shanghai and Kangwan.

Right) 'Opening of the first railway in China; the first train starting from Shanghai' an engraving taken from a photograph.
The Illustrated London News, 2 September 1876, page 220
© Illustrated London News Limited/Mary Evans.

Below) 'The Pioneer and the permanent train on the opening day' Photograph between pages 102 and 103, Remunerative Railways for New Countries by Richard Rapier, E and F N Spon, London, 1878.
© British Library Board. All rights reserved / Bridgeman Images.

'Chinese crowd at the opening of the railway'
Photograph between pages 102 and 103, Remunerative Railways for New Countries by Richard Rapier, E and F N Spon, London, 1878.

On 9 July 1876 John sent the following letter to *The Times* of London:

> 'My agent in charge of the works of the Shanghai and Woosung Railway sends me the following telegram:
> "Shanghai, July 5, 150 foreigners to Kangwan Friday evening. Chinese travelled free all Saturday. Six trains each way daily. Crowded. Receipts in proportion. Gabriel Morrison."
> In these times of depression it will interest many a commercial circle to see the first railway in China open with such fair prospects of success.
> John Dixon.'

Others were equally optimistic, as shown by the following comment in *Engineering* magazine. It is interesting to note the Victorian view that railways would be good for the military and the businessmen, without mentioning society at large.

> 'So far, then, the line appears to be a success, and as the anticipated interference on the part of the authorities has not been manifested, it is to be hoped that the Shanghai line will prove to be the first instalment of a vast system of Chinese railways. Whether regarded from a military or commercial point of view, there can be no question that railways would prove of immense benefit to that vast and densely populated country.'

John Dixon was so pleased with events in China that he arranged a grand dinner at the Langham Hotel in London on Thursday 20 July 1876. Among the thirty-six guests were William Cotton (MP and Lord Mayor), Sir Rutherford Alcock (Consul and later Minister in China from 1844 to 1871), several partners of Jardine, Matheson and Company including Robert Jardine, Alexander Matheson and Hugh Matheson, Captain Tyler (the Board of Trade Inspector of Railways) and Robert James Ransome (Richard Rapier's partner in the Ipswich business). During the course of the meal Alexander Matheson announced that the railway company had ordered six more carriages and at the end of the evening glasses were raised to John Dixon and Richard Rapier.

Living in China was not healthy

Conditions in China for ex-patriots were not good. John Sadler, Rapier's foreman, caught dysentery and died in September 1876. Two more men had to return to England through illness. Morrison's wife Jessie, who had driven the first spike of the railway, died in Shanghai on 22 September 1881 after a short illness. A few years later Gabriel remarried in Shanghai.

A fatality on the line

It was hoped to complete the remainder of the railway within a month, as twelve of the thirteen bridges were complete and seven of the nine miles of track had been laid. In spite of an enthusiastic reception by all who saw and used the 'fire-dragon carriages', the expected opposition of the mandarins soon became apparent. The first signs of trouble were in July when two men inspecting the telegraph lines alongside the track were set upon. Then a mob tore down some fencing near Kangwan. When the Kangwan station master tried to intervene, he was attacked and his station was wrecked. It was suspected that these incidents had been initiated by Chinese officials. Worse was to follow. On 3 August 1876 there was a fatal accident, which again some believed was deliberately staged, others thought it suicide. John Dixon was in no doubt, later referring to it as 'the suicide of a stupid maniac.' Engine driver David Banks, of Ransomes and Rapier, saw a man walking along the track towards the oncoming train. Banks sounded the whistle and the man stepped off the track, but as the train approached he deliberately stepped back onto the track. Banks applied the brakes but could not avoid running over the man, who was instantly killed. The authorities demanded that Chinese employees who had been on the train at the time of the accident be handed over and, more ominously, that Banks be punished for killing an innocent man going about his normal business. Banks was put on trial with demands for his death. Fortunately, he was acquitted, but then word went around that an angry mob was about to destroy the line.

Quite separately at this time, the British diplomat, Sir Thomas Wade was pressing a compensation case against the Chinese for Augustus Margery, a British official who had been murdered while exploring possible trade routes between China and Burma. The Chinese government could now counter with the murder of a man from China by the British. It took all Wade's skills in diplomacy and the Chinese language to reach a settlement. Initially he calmed emotions by ordering the suspension of railway operations from 24 August 1876, pending discussions. Agreement was reached on 24 October whereby the Ching government would purchase the railway through payments to be made in three instalments over the following year. Trains would continue to run over the completed section of the line, and construction of the remainder of the track would be completed.

The line was valued at £78,375, paid in instalments which the Chinese later said were exorbitant. This claim was no doubt true, since the first instalment on 29 December 1876 was sufficient to settle all the Woosung Road Company's debts, including the payments to John Dixon.

The controversy over the railway even reached the letters page of *The Times* in London. In October one of the regular reports from China in the newspaper related how the railway, popular with local people, was viewed with hostility and jealousy by the mandarins. *The Times* correspondent had a low opinion of the mandarins, seeing them as completely incompetent to manage the government of China, as evidenced by his report that their response to a famine at the time was to pray for rain rather than to purchase grain and build roads to distribute it. This prompted 'Justum' of London to write a long letter about how the Chinese had been duped by the railway company and that now the line was operational 'nearly every mail brings news of riots and disturbances in connection with the railway.' A week later a spirited defence of the railway came from Ransomes and Rapier, which must have been written by Richard, stating that it was too ridiculous to suppose that the railway promoters would have been as careless as 'Justum' claimed. In reply 'Justum' repeated his charge that the railway had been built surreptitiously by referring to a road rather than a railway, before suggesting that the railway could precipitate open conflict between the British and the Chinese. He blustered that the newspapers were 'full of statements about the Chinese troops surrounding Shanghai.'

John Dixon's eventual reply was, for him, unusually temperate. Nine-tenths of the objections had not been raised by the Chinese government or people. The objectors were 'talkative politicians' and those who were 'vexed and disappointed that the work had been begun and is likely to lead to good results without their being participators.' Since this letter appeared three weeks after the letter from 'Justum' it is probable that John had consulted with Morrison in Shanghai, who had advised diplomacy.

Reopening of services and completion of the line

The railway reopened on 1 December 1876, by which time the track-work into Woosung had been completed. There were seven services in each direction daily. Two more locomotives were delivered from England, the 0-6-0 *Flowery Land* and the 0-6-0 *Viceroy*. Although their boilers were designed for pressures up to 200 lb/in^2, normal operation was to be at 120 lb/in^2 in order to meet 'any contingencies that may arise at the hands of the Chinese firemen.'

Prospects seemed good for the railway by the start of 1877, although construction had been difficult and the Chinese, as has been seen, were not always cooperative. A fourth locomotive was ordered from Ransomes and Rapier. After four months of operation, an editorial in *The Engineer* commented:

> 'The fact of the introduction and now unmolested working of a Western innovation of such wide-spreading sequence, into a country so opposed to anything not originating in itself, is a matter of much interest.'

The line was popular and there was often a large crowd at the stations, with up to 210 people crowding into the carriages designed to carry 150 passengers. Railways seemed to have secured a sound footing in China, and western observers at least anticipated the rapid expansion of railways across the thickly populated country. But this optimism was short-lived.

In February 1877 some Chinese merchants set up a bus service along the route, with a fare only half the third-class ticket on the railway. Much more seriously, October was approaching when the Chinese would assume ownership of the railway. Given the great uncertainties over the future of the line, it was unfortunate that the fourth locomotive, named *Viceroy* in an attempt to appeal to Viceroy Shen Pao Chen, did not run until September.

Brief Chinese ownership

Some entertained hopes that the Chinese would continue to operate the service, which had proved popular and profitable. But fears that the British and others would use the line to extend their trade concessions from Shanghai into the hinterland and that freight trains would compete with the Chinese Yangtze steamers, together with the old mistrust of western technology, all conspired to bring about the end of the railway. Conveniently for the authorities opposed to the railway, the governor of Formosa had expressed a desire for a railway to develop the island's coal mines, so it was decided to take the railway to Formosa. At the time many believed that this was little more than a convenient reason to take up the railway, and indeed on 2 August 1877 a letter had been sent by Woosung Road Company to the British Foreign Secretary with the suspicion that the Chinese had no intention of re-erecting the line on Formosa. This turned out to be the case.

In London *The Times* was kept informed of events by their correspondent in Shanghai. Two weeks before the final instalment a long editorial contrasted the implacably opposing views of the railway by the Europeans and the Chinese Mandarins. In the editor's opinion there was 'little use trying to make a stream flow upwards, or to force even the most conspicuous benefits of civilisation upon barbarism'. It would be a long time before the official class in China would 'tolerate any of the beauties of European civilisation.' Two days later John replied, urging more optimism. He had built a railway which had run successfully for over a year and produced a 10% to 15% dividend. The trains had been so crammed full that they constantly had to start long before the appointed time. Some setbacks were to be expected, but he believed that the funeral dirge of the Woosung and Shanghai Railway was not yet to be sung. The next few weeks would justify the editor's view.

The final train, hauled by *Viceroy*, left Shanghai just after noon on Saturday 20 October 1877 with 400 passengers on board and crowds lining the route. That afternoon the Chinese handed over the final instalment of the payment for the railway. Shareholders in the Woosung Road Company had made a five-fold profit on their initial investment. John would have seen a good return on his investment. On Monday morning two Mandarins and twelve assistants turned up at the Shanghai depot to take possession of the railway. After a cursory look at the plant and equipment in the depot they embarked on an inspection of the route, refusing the offer of a special train, preferring to travel the length of the line by sedan chairs. They told Gabriel Morrison that the Viceroy would decide what was to be done with the railway. Three weeks later this became apparent when work started to lift up the track and demolish the buildings.

The engines were partly dismantled and dropped into the packing cases which had brought them to China. These cases, along with some track and other ironwork were loaded onto barges. Carriages were thrown into the sea and floated across. On reaching the island of Formosa everything was dumped on the muddy shore and left to rust, washed over by successive tides.

The Engineer magazine commented that railways would have eased China's famine, and it was not the people who objected to the innovation but a few of the wealthy, who were not affected by famine.

Some final comments

Most of the histories of the line are written from a British standpoint, suggesting that the Chinese were deceitful in their dealings with the company and incapable of any form of organisation. In contrast some Chinese histories portray the British as deceitful, contemptuous of the Chinese way of life and only interested in making unreasonable profits. The truth was probably that the British, with their total confidence in technology and capitalism, simply could not understand the Chinese, with their traditional and spiritualist mentality. In the early days of the railway the Chinese, in order to placate fears that steam locomotives would disturb the spirits of the dead, had insisted that the railway company only used oxen and horses to pull the trains. And at the end of the railway's short life the Shanghai station was pulled down and replaced by a 'Temple of Heaven'. This complete antipathy towards the Chinese was evident in a letter written to *Engineering* magazine in 1885:

> 'There is a magnificent field for engineering enterprise in that region if only we could get the "Heathen Chinese" to see those things as we do. I am afraid, however, that it will be rather difficult to accomplish this.'

John Dixon himself, in a letter to *The Times*, showed that his view of the potential for railways in China was more about increased trade for Britain rather than benefit to the Chinese:

> 'To remove the antiquated objections of the Chinese Government is the sole difficulty in the way to opening to the world a magnificent market, in the trade of which England has energy and vitality enough to secure the lion's share.'

Gabriel Morrison, who remained in China and developed an understanding of how China was governed, insisted that the fate of the Woosung to Shanghai railway would not befall any other proposed railway in China. At the highest levels of government there was a conflict between traditionalists and modernisers, and he was optimistic that eventually China, which was 'centuries behind England', would accept Western technology and finance. The Ching government in Peking continued to oppose railway development and it was not until 1881 that the next railway began to appear. Claude Kinder (1852-1936), a British railway engineer who had worked on Japanese railways, was engaged by a colliery company to build a track to transport coal in Northern China. Against implacable official opposition Kinder had to construct a canal along most of the route but did manage to introduce a short length of track on the condition that mules were used for haulage. Kinder, not to be defeated, secretly built a steam locomotive and the over-riding economic advantage of transport by railway became obvious. The line was extended in 1886 but Krupp from Germany won the tender to supply rails, seen as a bad omen for British companies since it was thought that the Chinese, once a relationship was established with a company, would continue to use the same supplier. Kinder had warned English manufacturers about their complacency towards the potential Chinese market. Whilst he believed that English products were second to none, American, German and Belgian suppliers were carefully listening to Chinese requirements and then supplying goods more quickly and more cheaply. Kinder wrote that in future England must show 'a spirit of adventure and true trade sagacity' or her engineers would lose out to foreign competition. In spite of their initial mistrust of Kinder, he was eventually awarded the *Imperial Order of the Double Dragon* by the Chinese government.

As late as 1889 there was still opposition to the expansion of railways in China, exemplified by the belief that the fire in the Imperial Palace was a sign of celestial displeasure at a proposed extension of the railway to Peking. But by then those in power generally turning their thoughts toward the future rather than the past.

Significant development of Chinese railways only began at the start of the twentieth century when, as predicted, Britain had to share the huge market with America, Belgium, France, Germany, Japan and Russia.

Acknowledgements

Carol Morgan, archivist at the Institution of Civil Engineers, London, for access to James Morrison's report on the railway and Richard Rapier's book.

References

Remunerative Railways for new countries: with some account of the first railway in China
Richard C Rapier
E and F N Spon, London, 1878
First-hand account of the concept and construction of the railway, its operation, difficulties with the authorities and destruction. It is clear that John Dixon was Rapier's partner in the venture, despite Peter Crush virtually ignoring him in his 1999 book (see below).

The History of the Shanghai and Woosung Railway, compiled from the official records of the Woosung Road Company Ltd
Gabriel James Morrison
Engineer and General Manager, Shanghai, 1879
Hand written 82-page manuscript in the Archives of the Institution of Civil Engineers, London
Detailed description of the railway, with additional note inserted by Richard Rapier firmly stating that the locomotive *Pioneer* had never been intended as a present for the Emperor.

The Woosung Road, the Story of the First Railway in China 1875-77
Alan Reid
Published by Alan Reid, printed by Hadden Best and Co Ltd, Ipswich 1977
Good history with copies of accounts for 1876 (John Dixon was paid £17,266 in that year) and 1879.

Woosung Road, the story of China's First Railway
Peter Crush
The Railway Tavern, Shatin, Hong Kong, 1999
Detailed history of the railway written in China. Strangely the author only mentions John Dixon once, in connection with him putting £8,000 into the venture for his friend Richard Rapier. There is quite a lot about Gabriel Morrison but nothing to suggest that John Dixon, as the contractor, was his employer.

An Unsung Horsham Hero
Susan C Djabri
The Horsham Society Newsletter
January 2002
On pages 3 and 4 a biography of Frederick Augustus Sheppard (1819-1884).

Editorial - Navvies for China
The Engineer, London, 15 October 1875, page 270
Comment on John Dixon sending a shipload of navvies and rails to China.

Railway Engines from Ipswich to China
The Ipswich Journal, 4 March 1876
Background to the railway project and description of the locomotives supplied by Ransomes and Rapier.

Ransomes, Sims & Jefferies and Ransomes & Rapier
Ipswich Transport Museum website at
http://www.ipswichtransportmuseum.co.uk/Ransomes.htm
History of Ransomes and Rapier's involvement with the Shanghai to Woosung line, especially Richard Rapier and the other Ransomes and Rapier employees.

The English in China, from our own correspondent
The Times, London, 30 March 1876, page 4
Report on progress of the line and the problems with Chinese authorities.

China (from our own correspondent) Shanghai, March 31
The Times, London, 22 May 1876, page 6
Optimistic report on the progress of the railway and its reception by the ordinary Chinese.

The First Railway in China
Engineering, London, 2 June 1876, page 455
John Dixon's Chinese railway enterprise had overcome all difficulties due to 'Prince Li Hung Chang'.

Money Market and City Intelligence
The Times, London, 10 July 1876, page 9
John Dixon's letter about the opening of the railway.

The Railway in China
The Ipswich Journal, Ipswich, 25 July 1876
Account of the celebration dinner at the Langham Hotel.

A Railway in China - Locomotives for the first Chinese Railway
Engineering, London, 14 July 1876, page 29
Descriptions of *Pioneer*, *Flowery Land* and *Celestial Empire*, with illustrations of *Pioneer* and *Celestial Empire*.

The English in China, from our own correspondent
The Times, London, 17 August 1876, page 6
Opening of the railway amid great Chinese curiosity.

China - from our own correspondent
The Times, London, 2 October 1876, page 10
Relates the fatal accident on the railway and the mandarins' jealousy of the line.

The Woosung Railway, To the Editor of The Times
The Times, London, 5 October 1876, page 5
Lengthy letter from 'Justum' in support of the Chinese position over the railway.

The Woosung Railway, To the Editor of The Times
The Times, London, 12 October 1876, page 7
Response from Ransomes and Rapier, presumably written by Richard Rapier.

The Woosung Railway, To the Editor of The Times
The Times, London, 18 October 1876, page 6
Reply to Richard Rapier from 'Justum' with wild claims about hostilities between the British and the Chinese.

The Woosung Railway, To the Editor of The Times
The Times, London, 26 October 1876, page 3
Letter from John Dixon, writing as the contractor for the building and equipment of the railway, in answer to previous letters from 'Justum' who opposed the railway as it did not have official permission.

The English in China, from our own correspondent
The Times, London, 6 December 1876, page 4
Mandarins' opposition surfaces, staged suicide and trial of engine driver. Threat to destroy track, averted by temporary closure of the railway pending negotiations.

The English in China, from our own correspondent
The Times, London, 2 January 1877, page 6
Continued closure of the railway but a promise of a future twelve months' operation.

Editorial - Railways in China
The Engineer, 9 February 1877, page 100
Optimism at the secure footing of railways in China and the goodwill of the Chinese authorities in payment for the line.

Editorial
The Times, London, 13 October 1877, page 9
Evenly balanced article contrasting European and Chinese (at least the ruling classes) views of the railway, believing that to change the Chinese view would be akin to pushing water uphill.

The Woosung Railway - To the Editor of The Times
The Times, London, 15 October 1877, page 6
John Dixon urged more optimism over the future of railways in China, signing himself 'John Dixon, Constructor of the Line.'

Railway Matters
The Engineer, London, 7 June 1878, page 403
The Shanghai-Woosung railway dismantled and intended for a coal mine in Formosa. It was only a few of the wealthy who objected to the railway.

Engineering in China - To the Editor of Engineering
Engineering, London, 22 November 1878, page 425
Claude Kinder's plea to English manufacturers to treat the Chinese market with more respect.

Editorial - Railways in China
The Engineer, London, 10 January 1879, page 30
Review of the circumstances leading to the transfer of the railway to Formosa.

China as a field for future railway enterprises
Engineering, London, 18 July 1879, pages 59-61
James Morrison explains the background to the mandarins' opposition to the Woosung railway, and suggests that this shouldn't be taken as opposition to all other railways in China.

Engineering in China - To the Editor of Engineering
Engineering, London, 14 August 1885, page 164
Letter from J W C Haldane criticising the attitude of the Chinese towards modern technology.

Chinese Railway Enterprise - To the Editor of The Times
The Times, London, 1 September 1885, page 7
John Dixon summarises the history of the railway, with land brought from 237 proprietors and over fifteen months the line carried ¾ million passengers.

Chinese Progress- To the Editor of Engineering
Engineering, London, 11 December 1885, page 576
Claude Kinder's riposte to the above letter with a warning to English engineering complacency.

Railways in China
The Engineer, London, 24 September 1886, page 246
Review of the state of railway development in China some ten years after the Woosung to Shanghai railway.

Editorial - Chinese Railways
The Engineer, London, 3 May 1889, page 377
Rumours of powerful opposition to development of Chinese railways.

Gabriel James Morrison (1840-1905)
Obituary
Institution of Civil Engineers, volume 161, 1897

Richard Christopher Rapier (1836-1897)
Obituary
Institution of Civil Engineers, volume 129, 1905

The Chinese Railways, a historical survey
Cheng Lin
China United Press, Shanghai, 1935
Pages 2-8 cover the Woosung Road from a Chinese perspective. This publication claims that the Woosung Company promised to use horses and oxen rather than steam locomotives to haul the trains, and states that the attitude of the British Government greatly incensed the Chinese people.

17 Guimarães Railway, Portugal

The Minho District Railway Company Limited, registered in London, was set up to build a railway from the main line north of Porto, inland to Guimarães. When their first engineering contractor failed, the work was taken over by John Dixon in 1877, who completed the first part of the route. Meanwhile, the railway passed into Portuguese ownership, and the new owners refused payment. John vigorously pursued his claim for payment, first with the new railway company and then with the Portuguese government. The dispute was eventually conducted at the highest levels between the Foreign Ministers of Britain and Portugal. After seven years, and quite unexpectedly, John received the full amount due to him. Given the sorry history of English financiers and contractors in Portuguese railway schemes, John Dixon should perhaps have avoided involvement in the Guimarães Railway. His efforts to secure payment provide good evidence of his tenacity; he never gave up in spite of much despondency along the way.

A mysterious sixty-mile long railway

Some authors state that, following the construction of the Lisbon custom house piers, John Dixon went on to construct some sixty miles of railway track in the vicinity. For example, his obituary in *The Times* of 4 February 1891 described his Portuguese works thus:

> 'His next enterprises were in Portugal, where he constructed the Custom-house piers at Lisbon, and a 60-mile line of railway, and where the confiscation and tardy payment by the Government required the intervention of our own Foreign Office and the suspension of a Government loan on the Stock Exchange before honest payment could be enforced.'

This is clearly a description of the problems encountered with the Guimarães railway, even although it was only twenty miles long when completed and John only built a small section. Since the distance from the old Porto terminus at Boa Vista to Guimarães was 59.3 kilometres, there may have been confusion between kilometres and miles.

The dismal record of English railway promoters in Portugal

Given the success of the Lisbon piers, John must have looked around for other contracting opportunities in Portugal, and so became involved with the Guimarães railway. This was an unfortunate involvement which would lead to much anguish. He surely must have been aware that English financiers and engineers who worked on Portuguese railways had found dealings with the Portuguese very taxing. All the previous railway schemes in Portugal had become mired in financial, legal and political problems, yet he went ahead.

Portugal had neither the capital nor the expertise to construct railways yet had a pressing need to connect Lisbon with Porto in the north and with Spain to the east. The country turned to England, and later France, to develop a railway network. The first scheme was to connect Lisbon with Spain, with the Central Peninsular Railway Company formed in 1852 and led by Charles Waring, an established railway entrepreneur. Initial construction was by the contractors Shaw, Waring and Company, its directors being William Shaw, Charles Waring and his brothers William and Henry Waring. The Central Peninsular Railway Company collapsed in 1857 before the line could be completed, amid accusations of financial mismanagement and dishonest practices. Much of the odium fell on Charles Waring, but the Portuguese were by no means innocent. The second scheme was a line north from Lisbon to Porto, promoted by the celebrated English railway developer Sir Morton Peto. This also collapsed in 1860 due to an inability to raise sufficient capital, generating legal and inter-governmental disputes, with some criticism directed to Morton Peto himself. The third scheme was the South Eastern Portugal Railway Company, building seventy-eight miles of railway south of Lisbon. This had English financiers, including the Waring brothers, and a Spanish contractor. Although the line was completed, it was caught up in the 1866 financial crisis, and teetered on the verge of collapse for the next four years. Finally came the absolute disaster of the Lisbon Steam Tramways Company in the 1870s, which must have been well known to John, who had spent time in Lisbon when he was working on the Customs House piers and passed through the city on his way to Huelva.

The Lisbon Steam Tramways Company of 1871 sought to build light railways between Lisbon and Sintra and Lisbon and Torres Vedras. It seems to have been a fraudulent scheme from the outset, devised to benefit its promoters, the Duke of Saldanha, who was Portuguese Ambassador in London, and an unscrupulous English speculator, Albert Grant. An unusual French system was used, with a central wheel running on a single rail, and two outer wheels running on the ordinary road surface. Saldanha and Grant engaged Edwin Clark, Punchard and Company as contractors who, at the same time, were building the Rio Tinto railway in Spain. The tramway branch from Lisbon to Sintra opened in 1873, but problems due to poor construction, frequent breakdowns, and low passenger numbers resulted in it running at a loss. The other branch, to Torres Vedras, faced similar difficulties. Following some turmoil, the company was wound up in 1877. Grant, Clark and Punchard were taken to court by one of the shareholders, a Mr Twycross, who won his case for reimbursement of his investment. Twycross v Grant and others became an important case in civil law precedent. The affair even reached Parliament in 1876 when one of the directors of the Lisbon Steam Tramways Company, Lord Henry Lennox, resigned as First Commissioner of Works following the company being publicly revealed as a swindle through the legal action of Twycross v Grant and others. Lennox made a statement to the House in front of the Prime Minister, Benjamin Disraeli who, as a personal friend, expressed some sympathy for him.

The Guimarães railway

Guimarães is a city in northern Portugal. In earlier times it was the capital of Portugal but by the 19th century was seen as relatively remote. It lies about 230 miles from Lisbon and 30 miles from Porto (Oporto in English), the regional capital on the estuary of the River Douro and Portugal's second city. Guimarães was in the old province of Minho, the provincial administrative centre being at Braga. It was in the middle of an area of agricultural production and light industry, with most of its output destined for Porto. The only means of transport was by road, using horse, mule and bullock carts.

In 1871 Simão Gattai obtained a concession from the Portuguese Government to construct a one-metre gauge railway from the small town of São Martinho de Bougado, via Santo Thyrso and Vizella, to Guimarães (Santo Thyrso is now written as 'Santo Tirso' but the earlier spelling will be used here). São Martinho de Bougado was strategically situated about halfway along the route of the railway from Porto to Braga. Gattai's first thoughts of using animal haulage were soon dropped in favour of steam traction. A specification for a one-metre gauge passenger and goods railway was drawn up, with contracts for its construction to be let in five kilometre sections, but no further progress was made.

Minho District Railway Company Limited

By 1875 the single track, broad gauge railway of the Caminhos de Ferro do Minho e Douro, going north from Porto, had crossed the River Ave between Trofa and Lousado and reached Nine, eight miles south of Braga. Lousado was an obvious location for a line from Guimarães to meet up with the Porto-Braga line. In June 1874 the Minho District Railway Company Limited was registered in England, with a share capital of £260,000 and the objective of constructing and operating a narrow-gauge railway over the twenty miles from São Martinho de Bougado to Guimarães (although São Martinho de Bougado is often quoted as the western end of the terminus of the Guimarães railway, in fact it was Lousado). In a shrewd move, Gattai had sold his concession to the new company for £9,500. An attractive prospectus offered £10 shares, to be paid in four instalments, to investors in England and Portugal. If the share capital was not fully subscribed, individual deposits would be returned in full, and interest at the rate of 6% would be paid during the construction phase. A meeting of civic leaders and businessmen at Guimarães in August enthusiastically endorsed the new line, although uncertain of how much new business it would create. This enthusiasm, underpinned by the promises of the prospectus and confidence in the trustworthiness of English companies, led to Portuguese investors forming 230 out of the 260 shareholders, subscribing some £65,370, and later claiming that no shares had been taken up in England. In spite of the company's commitment to return deposits if not all the shares were taken up, construction went ahead financed entirely with Portuguese capital. There was no tendering procedure before a contract was given for the construction of the line.

No. 68

ANNO 1874 PAGO

THE MINHO DISTRICT RAILWAY COMPANY, LIMITED.

CAPITAL, £260,000.

IN 26,000 SHARES OF £10 EACH.

INCORPORATED UNDER THE COMPANIES ACT, 1862 & 1867.

THE MINHO DISTRICT RAILWAY COMPANY, LIMITED.

This is to Certify that Henrique da Costa Correa Leite of Porto is the Proprietor of Ten Shares of £10 each Numbered 1279 to 1288 inclusive of the MINHO DISTRICT RAILWAY COMPANY, LIMITED, subject to the Articles of Association and regulations of the said Company, and that to this day there has been paid up in respect of each of such Shares the sum of £4. Given under the Common Seal of the said Company this 6th day of November 1874.

Wilfrid Brett — DIRECTORS.

A. Marshall Fay — SECRETARY.

NO TRANSFER OF THE ABOVE SHARES WILL BE REGISTERED UNLESS ACCOMPANIED BY THIS CERTIFICATE.

Minho District Railway Share Certificate.
Reproduced by courtesy of Mario Boone at the Scriptophily Center, Antwerp, Belgium, an international auction house for historic share and bond certificates. Website at www.booneshares.com

Later, with the company in financial ruin, the Portuguese shareholders felt they had been swindled. Scathing criticism was directed at the Minho Board, so it is appropriate to consider the standing of the Board members. There were five English directors and two Portuguese directors:

- Admiral Sir William Hall, director of the P&O Steam Navigation Company
- Edward Pakenham Alderson, director of the Great Eastern Railway
- Arthur Pratt Barlow, director of the Royal Mail Steam Navigation Company
- Charles Balfour of Balfour and Company
- Sir Wilford Brett, director of the Chelsea waterworks
- Eduardo da Costa Correa Leite, Porto banker
- Agostinho Francisco Velho, Managing Director, Porto branch of Banco Lusitano of Lisbon.

Eduardo Moser was closely involved in Portugal with Leite and Velho but was not listed as a director. Although the directors appear to be men of good reputation, the apparent absence of any English investors and the lack of any tendering process for the construction suggest at the very least a lack of attention to the company's affairs. This is in spite of the fact that each director received an annual salary of £500. The presence of two shipping companies is significant since English shipping, which held a virtual monopoly of Portuguese trade with the outside world, stood to lose out with the development of railway links into Spain and the rest of Europe.

The company's engineer was James Blair of Westminster. James Fairlie Blair (1831-1876) was born at Irvine in 1831. Educated at Edinburgh University, he joined the staff of John Fowler in London but in 1863 he set up his own practice in Glasgow. He continued to collaborate with John Fowler, particularly on the City of Glasgow Union railway and the St Enoch Station in Glasgow from 1870 to 1879. After his early death at the age of only forty-five, the Minho directors engaged George Barclay Bruce, the long-standing colleague of John Dixon since their shared apprentice days in Newcastle. Bruce had just finished working with Dixon on the iron-ore loading jetty, the Muelle del Tinto, at Huelva in Spain.

Construction starts but soon stops

Construction of the line was to be carried out by Sandiforth Featherstone Griffin, a London-based contractor who had undertaken the initial survey of the route and claimed impressive prospects for the line. He estimated that the large quantity of passenger and agricultural traffic that could be carried by the railway might result in an annual profit of £38,000 (Portuguese currency in this chapter is generally converted into sterling using exchange rates prevailing at that time). There would even be the opportunity of bringing fresh fish to the dinner tables of Guimarães.

The Minho directors planned to spend £230,000 on land acquisition, earthworks, bridges, stations, and laying track, leaving £30,000 for the purchase of rolling stock. No competitive tenders were sought for the construction of the line. In June 1874 the contract was handed to Sandiforth Griffin along with an initial payment of £38,580 in cash and £55,000 in paid-up shares, to construct, maintain and work the railway. This was a very generous contract for the 32 kilometres of railway, more than 30% above the norm for Portuguese railways. Taking advantage of the excitement caused by the start of construction, the English directors called in a further £43,000 from the Portuguese investors, who had already put in £65,000.

Whereas the western end of the line was referred to as São Martinho de Bougado, in reality it was at Lousado. São Martinho de Bougado is situated south of the River Ave, while Lousado is on the opposite, northern, side. There was no point building a bridge to carry the Guimarães line over the river since it could meet with the Minho line at Lousado. The original proposal for a one-metre gauge track was abandoned in favour of Portuguese broad gauge (1.664 metres) so as to be compatible with the Minho line. At noon on 24 November 1874, in the presence of Walter and Charles Balfour, work commenced. With supreme optimism, it was hoped that the entire line to Guimarães would be complete by the end of 1875.

Initial optimism soon evaporated and, after working on less than four kilometres of track, Sandiforth Griffin returned to London, bankrupt. The actual extent of Griffin's work is unclear, but it was estimated that he had spent less than £7,000 on the railway, and the rest of his initial payment had vanished. It was beginning to look as if this railway would follow its predecessors in dubious dealings or even outright fraud.

John Dixon steps in

The Minho Railway venture would be known of in London's engineering circles, and no doubt John sensed a potentially profitable opportunity. Of course, he had recent experience of engineering projects on the Iberian Peninsula with his ore-loading jetty at Huelva and his work at Lisbon. He carefully went through the company's books, acquired some of the Minho shares and probably had a quiet discussion with James Blair, the company engineer. In echoes of the occasions when he had stepped in to save projects abandoned by their original contractors (ore-loading jetty at Huelva and the Woosung Railway in China) John approached the Minho District Railway directors. He would invest a substantial amount of his own money to complete the first section of the railway in return for a debenture stake in the railway, with the entire assets of the company as security against his investment. This proposal was put to a meeting of shareholders on 9 February 1877 when it was accepted, despite some concerns that the securities demanded were such that 'Mr Dixon might sweep the whole company into his pocket'. The fact that the shareholders'

Who's who?
Sandiforth Featherstone Griffin (1819-1902)

Although Sandiforth Featherstone Griffin pursued many interests during his life, and styled himself as a civil engineer, he does not appear to have been either formally qualified or particularly competent. He was the son of George Griffin who, with his brother Charles, owned Beale's Wharf, Tooley Street in Southwark, although their partnership ended in 1850.

At the height of the railway speculation fever, in 1845, Sandiforth Griffin was listed as engineer in share prospectus notices for no fewer than eight proposed railway enterprises, none of which came to fruition:

- Birmingham and Boston Direct Railway
- Direct Macclesfield and Chester Railway
- Direct Sheffield and Macclesfield Railway
- Great Eastern and Western Railway from Great Yarmouth to Swansea
- Isle of Man Railway
- London, Hounslow and Western Railway
- Manchester to Rugby Direct Railway, built on the atmospheric principle
- Reading to Reigate Atmospheric Railway, also on the atmospheric principle.

There was incredible speculation in railways at the time. By the end of 1845, 1,263 railway companies provisionally registered, but by the end of the year 879 of these had failed to deposit plans with the authorities and therefore would not proceed. No fewer than 718 lines had been proposed during 1845 alone, 549 had disappeared. *The Times* of London denounced the unhealthy extent of railway speculation, but Griffin had fewer scruples, and clearly put potential personal gain above any proper consideration of engineering works.

Sandiforth's father, George Griffin, was the principal promoter of the Irish Channel Submarine Telegraph Company of Ireland, registered in temporary offices in 1851 with Sandiforth as company secretary. In spite of having nine apparently distinguished directors, there was an absence of any electrical expertise. Little was achieved and the following year the company was re-launched as the Electric Telegraph Company of Ireland, again with Sandiforth Griffin as secretary and also now as the engineer for the undersea cable. A cable was laid between Scotland and Ireland but was unsuccessful and the company was wound up in 1854, followed by the collapse of its bankers in 1856. Much litigation ensued.

By 1862 the Griffins had set themselves up as civil engineering contractors, with a contract to carry out work at the Wheal Abraham mine. Within three years this had become mired in financial difficulties. Both father and son took out patents on a range of bizarre inventions, George's included the corking of bottles and improvements to railway tracks, while Sandiforth's included improvements to naval vessels and the distillation of petroleum. Sandiforth also published a book of piano forte music.

Perhaps not surprisingly both father and son ended up bankrupt. In 1859 George Griffin, then described as a paint manufacturer, was declared an insolvent debtor. His son Sandiforth became insolvent six years later.

One of the few surviving relics of the Minho District Railway. This crest mounted on a gate is at the Museo Ferroviario de Lousado, Largo da Estação de Lousado, Lousado, Portugal. Photograph by author.

meeting was held in London would mean that there were very few shareholders, other than the directors, present.

The work thus passed to John, who finished the six-kilometre section of the line between Lousado and Santo Thyrso. John later said that he had purchased the land, laid the track to Portuguese broad gauge, built several stations and installed a telegraph system, implying that Griffin had done very little. Following the usual contracting arrangements, he obtained signed certificates for parcels of completed work from the company engineer, who was by now John's old friend George Bruce. He then presented certificates for £23,392 to the company and agreed to be paid by bills of exchange. By his own account John had only spent around £10,000 of his own money into completion of this section of the line, and later the Portuguese would accuse him of grossly inflating his costs to the £23,392 total. This latter sum was confirmed by John's appeal to the King of Portugal in 1883, in which he stated that he was owed £24,000.

The first section of the new railway was straightforward to construct, running on level ground along the northern bank of the River Ave with only a few small streams to cross. Six kilometres beyond Santo Thyrso, heading towards Guimarães, a substantial bridge would be required. This would carry the line over the Rio Ave at the junction of the Ave and Vizella, from where the route followed the Rio Vizella to Vizella, finally turning north to Guimarães.

On 1 March 1877 Mr Galway, John's resident engineer, began work. By the end of the year the section of the line to Santo Thyrso was completed. A handsome dressed granite station, with nine rooms, was built at the end of this section on the north-eastern edge of Santo Thyrso.

Collapse of the Minho District Railway Company

The following year, 1878, the parlous financial state of the Minho District Railway Company was becoming apparent to John Dixon and to the Portuguese shareholders. John was none too perturbed since he had an agreement with the Portuguese Minister for Public Works at the time, Lourenço António de Carvalho (1837-1890), that, in the event of the Minho District Railway Company becoming bankrupt, he would be able to apply for the concession to operate the line himself. Whether deliberately or not, this agreement was never formally written down and would later prove of little value, especially after de Carvalho left office on 1 June 1879. Confusingly, Lourenço António de Carvalho was replaced by Augusto Saraiva de Carvalho (1839-1882). The Portuguese shareholders were increasingly anxious and, at the end of the year, resolved to have ownership of the railway transferred to Portugal.

In 1878 Dixon, still unpaid and by now concerned that he might never be paid, successfully petitioned the Court of Chancery in London to have the Minho District Railway Company liquidated. The Court appointed Henry Chatteris, an accountant, as official liquidator in September 1878. The Court of Chancery actions were repeated in Portugal where, at Porto, the Minho District Railway Company was declared bankrupt at the start of 1879.

Now was the time for John to fall back on his agreement with Lourenço António de Carvalho. He requested the concession to operate the line but de Carvalho, whom John considered to be an honourable man, suggested that, as the original Portuguese shareholders wished to take on the line, why not let them have it on the express condition that the line

The old Santo Tirso Railway Station. This photograph was originally published in the 'Gazeta dos Caminhos de Ferro No. 1094' of the 16th July 1933, and scanned by the Hemeroteca Municipal de Lisboa. Dated 16 July 1933.
The present broad-gauge railway track runs behind (south of) the old station at Santo Tirso. The old one-metre gauge track has been taken up and replaced by a road 'Rua do Alberto Pimentel'. This is the dressed granite station building with twelve rooms mentioned by John Dixon in his correspondence. At present the station building is used as a headquarters by the local fishing association Clube Pesca Desportiva Além-Rio. The roof has been rebuilt to a different design and some of the original internal walls have been taken down to make larger rooms.
The image on the right shows the same building in 2017, photograph by author.

The present day broad-gauge line past Santo Tirso follows the north bank of the River Ave, with some deviations from the route of John Dixon's original narrow-gauge line. On the right side of this map, the K34 street was laid down over the narrow-gauge line, leaving his station sandwiched between the street and the broad-gauge line. The present Santo Tirso station is on the extreme top left of the map, at Quinta. There is a new road linking the station with the 508 road, not shown on this map.
Extract from Carta Militar de Portugal Santo Tirso Folha 98, Instituto Geográfico do Exército, Lisbon.

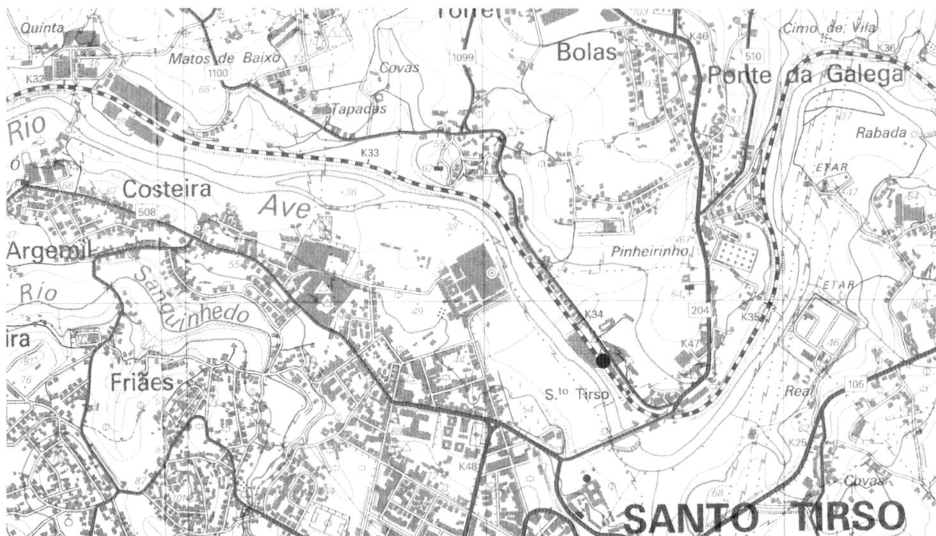

Reproduced courtesy of Carta Militar do Centro de Informação Geoespacial do Exército, Av. Dr. Alfredo Bensaúde, 1849-014 Lisbon. EXÉRCITO

would be valued by the Portuguese authorities and John would be paid this valuation within six months. It would be an express condition of the transfer that the new company would take responsibility for the debts of the old company. John agreed.

Companhia Caminho de Ferro de Guimarães acquire the line

The new company, Companhia do Caminho de Ferro de Guimarães, was set up by a partnership between Visconde da Ermida of Porto and António Soares de Moura Velloso, two of the leading Portuguese shareholders in the old Minho District Railway Company. In March 1879 they officially acquired the concession for the railway from the Porto Tribunal, on the clear understanding that they also took over the responsibilities of the previous company. The concession was to operate the railway, but they did not yet own the actual track between Lousado and Santo Thyrso. It was their intention to acquire this section of track, join it to the main line and then complete the line on to Guimarães. They applied and obtained from the authorities agreements that imported materials for the railway would be free of duty.

After the liquidation of the original Minho company the Lousado to Santo Thyrso section was valued by the Portuguese Government's Commission of Engineers. In spite of this being done at a time of commercial depression (Dixon claimed that rails for which he had paid £9 per ton were now selling at £4 per ton) the six-kilometre section of railway was valued at £18,666. This implies that it was nowhere near the woefully deficient state as surveyed by the new company only two years later, even although it was significantly less than the £24,000 sought by John.

Trusting the new Minister for Public Works, Augusto Saraiva de Carvalho, John expected to be paid within six months of the new company acquiring the concession.

What then followed must be judged as duplicitous, if not illegal. The new company, which boasted that it had control over the Porto courts, had already managed to have the Porto Tribunal seize the railway in spite of its ownership technically being with the British liquidator, Henry Chatteris. John successfully appealed to a local judge but the new company, demonstrating its influence over the Porto courts, had this overturned. There was then a series of auctions through which the Porto Tribunal attempted to sell the six-kilometre section of railway, including the rights to the land involved.

The first auction was held on 16 October 1879, with a reserve equivalent to the full valuation of 81 contos (one conto = one million réis) equivalent at that time to about £19,000. John's attorney in Porto, William Gruis, was present at this first auction and asked that the proceeds of the sale be used to pay his client, but there were no successful bidders. A second auction on 9 January 1880, with a reserve now half the earlier valuation again found no takers. A third auction, on 20 April 1880, was also unsuccessful in spite of the absence of any reserve price. It was only on the 27 April 1880, at a fourth auction, that the Companhia do Caminho de Ferro de Guimarães bought the line for 31 contos. Not only was this a remarkably low price, but they did not pay any money into the court, rather presenting a bond for future payment (which was apparently never made). Not surprisingly John believed that there was collusion between the Portuguese authorities and the new company.

The absence of bidders at the first three auctions led to questions about how effectively they had been advertised. At the fourth auction Senhor Vianna, William Gruis's partner, took part in the bidding. This must have been John's last chance to acquire the assets of the railway; with it under his ownership he would have retained the operating income and hence recoup his construction claim and the cost of purchasing the railway at the auction. Obviously, there would have been a limit to the price it would have been sensible to offer, and Senhor Vianna withdrew from the bidding before the hammer fell at 31 contos.

John Dixon seeks payment

John believed that, as the principal creditor of the failed Minho District Railway Company whose only asset was the partly completed line, he would at least receive the proceeds of the auction. Accordingly, he again pressed for payment receipt of the £7,000 auction price plus a further £3,000 from the Portuguese partners (he had expended about £10,000 of his own money on the line). Nothing was forthcoming.

Then, in March 1881, the existing government fell with the result that Augusto Saraiva de Carvalho left office and was replaced by a new Minister for Public Works, Ernesto Rodolfo Hintze Ribeiro. John reckoned that the officials in the Ministry were in the pocket of the railway company.

Who's who?
Ernesto Rodolfo Hintze Ribeiro (1849-1907)

Ernesto Ribeiro was born at Ponta Delgada on the island of São Miguel in the Azores and rose to be a prominent Portuguese politician and statesman. He studied law at Coimbra, the leading university in Portugal, marrying Joana Rebelo de Chaves in Ponta Delgada in 1873; there were no children. Ribeiro's dealings with John Dixon took place when his political career was on the rise. He joined the conservative Regeneration Party and was elected to the Cortes in 1878. Close to the then leader of the Regeneration Party, António Maria de Fontes Pereira de Melo, Ribeiro was appointed Minister of Public Works when Fontes became Prime Minister (for the third time) in 1881. One of Ribeiro's achievements at this time was the inauguration an undersea telegraph cable between Portugal and the Azores. Ribeiro was made acting Foreign Minister in 1883, a position which maintained his involvement with John Dixon as the matter of payment had by then escalated to inter-governmental levels.

Subsequently Ribeiro served three periods as Prime Minister between 1893 and 1906, longer than any other politician of his time. Given his home on the Azores, it is not surprising that he introduced some autonomy for the Azores and Madeira. He died in Lisbon but his archive of letters, documents, and other papers are preserved in the Azores Archives at Ponta Delgada.

In 2001 the bridge across the River Douro at Castelo de Paiva, completed in 1886 and named Ponte Hintze Ribeiro, collapsed killing fifty-nine people. Its integrity had been undermined by the unofficial extraction of sand by local men who put personal gain above wider issues.

Ominously the deadline for payment was now unilaterally extended. John applied to the English Court of Chancery, to the liquidator Henry Chatteris and to the Porto Tribunal, but there was no response.

The state of the partly completed railway

When the Portuguese investors set up their partnership they instigated a survey of the state of the partly completed railway, in 1881. The survey revealed a catalogue of deficiencies and deterioration. There was inadequate drainage along the line with considerable quantities of timber being completely rotten, including sleepers, fences, gates, telegraph posts and the station at Santo Thyrso. Even given problems with drainage and the fact that Minho is the wettest part of Portugal, it is still surprising that so much rot was in evidence in under six years. In addition to the extensive wood rot, basic equipment was missing: there was no turntable, no water reservoir, no goods facilities, etc. The survey made no apportionment of blame between the two contractors, Griffin and Dixon, and it was in the Portuguese interest to attach the maximum blame to the English contractors. An indication of the surveyors' intent to give the worst report possible is that included in their long list of missing equipment were the kilometre marking posts, surely a relatively unimportant detail.

Given the quite handsome £18,666 valuation by the Portuguese government only two years previously, it is hard to believe that this new survey was entirely accurate.

Incidentally, two years later when the North Eastern Railway took over the partly completed Whitby to Loftus line in Yorkshire, there was a similar scathing report on the poor condition of the line, blamed on the previous contractor. Recently it has been suggested that the deficiencies were exaggerated to alleviate criticism of the time it would take North Eastern Railway to complete the railway and start operating trains. It is possible that a similar motivation was at play in Portugal.

John Dixon continues to seek payment

In May 1882 John wrote a detailed and carefully reasoned letter to Portuguese authorities. By accepting the debts of the old company, the new company would have been bankrupt. It should present itself to the courts and the legal ownership of the completed section of line should have transferred to the authorities or to himself. Instead, it had arranged a farcical series of public auctions through which one of the new company's partners, ostensibly acting as a private individual, had acquired the completed section of line at the very low price of £7,000 compared to a valuation of over £18,000. In fact, the railway was acquired without any transfer of money; all that was needed was a bond and the appointment as president, on a good salary, of the son-in-law of the Minister for Foreign Affairs.

The courts then reversed their previous position and agreed that the new partnership was now the rightful owner of the line, although this was apparently subject to appeal. None of the above changed the official position; the Companhia do Caminho de Ferro de Guimarães was still liable for the debts of the Minho District Railway Company because its partners were all the shareholders of the old company, and because it had been an express condition when the new partnership was granted the concession.

In response the Companhia do Caminho de Ferro de Guimarães, in the name of its manager, Antonio de Moura Soares Velloso, denied any liability for settling with John. He was adamant that Dixon's contract had been with the old company, and now the Companhia do Caminho de Ferro de Guimarães had rightful ownership of the completed section of line, as acquired at the last auction. He questioned the amount sought; George Bruce had originally claimed £8,300 in England for this work but in Portugal John Dixon had inflated this to £24,000. John was accused of making malicious insinuations, and false assertions. This foreigner had accused the commercial court in Porto of concocting an auction, the tribunal in Porto of authorising a swindle, the Portuguese judiciary of bending to personal influence, and the House of Deputies and the Ministry of Public Works of making precipitous decisions.

Diplomatic pressure

When the new company acquired the railway through the final auction, they set about completing the track to Guimarães and pressed for permission to operate trains over the section completed by John from Lousado to Santo Thyrso. With no realistic prospect of payment, John appealed directly to the Foreign Secretary Lord Granville (Granville Leveson-Gower). It may be thought surprising that the Foreign Secretary would become involved with a routine matter such as a dispute over payment between a contractor and his client, but John had achieved national fame when erecting Cleopatra's Needle on the Thames Embankment in 1878. At that time there was much favourable press comment and some (unanswered) calls for him to be honoured. Possibly the government felt it was in some debt to Dixon and here was an opportunity to compensate for what many had seen as shabby treatment by the establishment.

Lord Granville instructed the British Ambassador in Lisbon, Sir Charles Lennox Wyke, to take up the matter. During the next five years an extensive series of letters was exchanged between the British and Portuguese authorities, with numerous internal memos passing between and within the British Foreign Office in London and Lisbon. Over 150 items from this correspondence are held in two leather-bound volumes at the National Archives. Seventy-six of these items were reproduced in print form to support a presentation to Parliament by the Foreign Office, although these transcriptions contain quite a few mistakes in the spelling of names. In the dramatis personae of this long-running saga John Dixon rubs shoulders with the following senior government ministers and diplomats.

British Foreign Secretaries:
- Lord Granville (Granville Leveson-Gower), 1880-1885
- Marquis of Salisbury (Robert Gascoyne-Cecil), 1885-86
- Lord Roseberry (fifth Earl of Rosebery), 1886
- Earl of Iddesleigh (Stafford Northcote), 1886-87

British Ambassadors in Lisbon:
- Sir Charles Lennox Wyke, 1881-1884
- George Glynn Petre, Ambassador to Portugal, 1884-93

Parliamentary Under-Secretaries for Foreign Affairs:
- Sir Charles W Dilke, 1880-1882
- Lord Fitzmaurice (Edmond Fitzmaurice), 1883-1885

Permanent Under-Secretary for Foreign Affairs:
- Sir Julian Pauncefote, 1882-1889

Portuguese Foreign Ministers (Ministros dos Negócios Estrangeiros):
- António de Serpa Pimental, 1881-1883
- Ernesto Rudolpho Hintze Ribeiro, 1883 (acting)
- José Vicente Barbosa du Bocage, 1883-1886
- Henrique de Barros Gomes, 1886-90

Much of the credit for the eventual resolution of the matter must go to Walter Baring, the long-serving British Chargé d'Affaires in Lisbon from 1882-85. He showed a remarkable persistence, in spite of his accurate assessment of the situation in a letter to the Foreign Secretary (Lord Granville) dated 30 August 1882 in which he observed 'a satisfactory solution of the question is beset with many difficulties, created chiefly by the influential position of the persons opposing Mr Dixon.' On the same day as Walter Baring wrote this letter, *The Times* published a lengthy article on John Dixon's case. The newspaper thought Dixon's chances of success in the courts was small, and that 'any foreigner who has the misfortune to be a creditor in Portugal will do well to avoid litigation, as he will probably only throw good money after bad.'

The British Government repeatedly pressed the Portuguese authorities not to declare the new company duly constituted unless it accepted full responsibility for the debts of the old company. The Portuguese Foreign Minister, António de Serpa Pimentel, refused to act. He said that, while committing nothing in writing, John Dixon must instigate legal action in the proper Portuguese Tribunals and inform the Portuguese Government of this, whereupon the government would state that the new company would have to accept the debts of the old company. John claimed that de Serpa's son-in-law was president of the Companhia do Caminho de Ferro de Guimarães, that the company was claiming that they had the power over the Oporto Tribunal, and that even if judgement went against them they would ignore it. Given this background, he was worried about starting any legal action in Portugal, writing in a letter to Sir Julian Pauncefote on 12 October 1882 that a legal action would drag on, and in the meantime the new railway would start operation and he would be left high and dry. He concluded his letter with the phrase 'they are so slippery a lot that it is as well to be cautious.'

Walter Baring continued to demand written confirmation that, once John Dixon's legal action had been initiated, the government would issue a 'Portaria' requiring the new company to be responsible for the debts of the old company. Eventually, in a letter to Lord Granville on 20 October 1882, de Serpa conceded the point. However, the new company now came up with a new reason for evasion; it was only bound to answer for debts according to the Portuguese law, and a purchase at auction carried no responsibility for real or personal obligations of the former owner. And de Serpa delivered another blow; even if Dixon started legal proceedings, the government would not stop the railway from going ahead.

The Portuguese newspaper *Correspondencia de Portugal*, which was in reality an organ of the Foreign Minister de Serpa, printed a reply to the criticisms printed in *The Times* at the end of August. Under a cloak of anonymity de Serpa wrote that the Portuguese Government had no responsibility in the matter, and privately he told Walter Baring that *The Times* article had annoyed the Portuguese government and had been counter-productive.

While the government's pressure was applied through diplomatic correspondence, an impatient John Dixon wanted more direct action. He learned that the Portuguese Government was seeking a loan from the London Stock Exchange, so he wrote to the Stock Exchange Committee in October 1882 asking them to refuse a loan to Portugal and making sure that this was reported in *The Times*. The Committee expressed their sympathy but said it was outside the scope of their rules.

A mysterious anecdote

George Longstaff recalled a mysterious anecdote, apparently relating to this time. Around 1881 John Dixon had told him a story of calling on the Portuguese ambassador to demand payment of a five-figure sum. The ambassador, described as a man of small stature, protested that he had no instructions to pay John, but begged him be seated. But John, who was tall and with considerable presence, stood with his back against the door. After his insistent demands met with no response, he addressed the ambassador.

> 'Your Excellency, your Government intend early next week to bring out a new Loan in London for further railway construction. I have influential friends on the London Stock Exchange and I have the *entrée* to the 'Times.' This is Friday: if I am not paid a substantial sum on account before I leave this room, a letter will appear in Monday's 'Times' setting forth plainly how your Government has treated a well known English engineer, and the chance of your Loan being successfully floated will be gone.'

Longstaff concluded the tale with the words 'the little man was fairly cowed, and John Dixon left the room with a large cheque in his pocket.'

The matters of the Stock Exchange loan and the letter to *The Times* surely place this anecdote at this stage in the dispute, but John did not receive payment for another five years. And it seems unlikely that the ambassador would have been able to immediately sign a cheque for such a large amount. The accuracy of Longstaff's memory, twenty-five years after John Dixon related this anecdote to him, can perhaps be questioned.

The Portuguese complete the railway

When the Companhia do Caminho de Ferro de Guimarães acquired the six kilometres of broad gauge line from Lousado to Santo Thyrso in 1880, they decided that it would be better to complete the line to the originally intended one-metre gauge. This involved replacing the short section of broad gauge track laid by Griffin and Dixon, laying two kilometres of narrow gauge track inside the Minho Railway broad gauge from Lousado to Trofa, and completing the 25 kilometres from Santo Thyrso to Guimarães. Construction was entrusted to Domingo Busquets of Barcelona, who would also supply three 0-6-0 tank locomotives, twenty coaches and four luggage vans, and twenty-six goods wagons. The locomotives were manufactured by Hudswell Clarke of Leeds: Works Nos.242 *Santo Thyrso*, 243 *Negrellos* and 244 *Vizella* (these are the old form of place names, now Santo Tirso, Negrelos and Vizela).

The new narrow-gauge track connecting Lousado with Trofa, the replacement narrow-gauge track from Lousado to Santo Thyrso and new track to Vizella were completed at the end of 1883 at a cost of £250,000. On 22 May 1882 John wrote to Hintze Ribeiro with an estimate for completing the entire line in narrow-gauge of £166,000, in addition to the £78,500 already paid or committed, giving a total of £244,500. It is difficult to understand why John should have written this letter since he was certainly not going to carry out any more work on the railway himself. Perhaps he was responding to a request from Hintze Ribeiro for a second opinion on the cost of conversion to narrow-gauge, and perhaps he hoped that his reply might generate some goodwill with Ribeiro.

Naturally, once the line was completed, there was local agitation to start running trains, something de Serpa had already said would not be opposed. John was surprised to learn of the disregard for Hintze Ribeiro's solemn promise not to allow completion of the line until he had been paid, but by then would be used to broken Portuguese assurances. On 31 December 1883 the line was officially opened when a train had left Porto at 7:30am with the official party. They alighted at Trofa and boarded a narrow-gauge train for Lousado, Santo Thyrso and Vizella, hauled by the locomotive *Negrellos*. They arrived at Vizella at 10:14am, to an enthusiastic crowd. Four months later there was a civic reception, with lunch accompanied by music from a band.

The line to Guimarães was completed the following year.

Little hope for payment

With the Portuguese now running trains and generating income, the outlook for John was looking increasingly bleak and, in a desperate effort to salvage at least some of his money, he offered to accept £10,000. This was about half of the £18,666 valuation or the signed construction certificates for £23,392. His offer, which had been conditional on early acceptance otherwise there would be reversion to the full claim. The company refused, and also refused an alternative of negotiating an agreement for a share in the operating profits of the line.

Bearing in mind that John believed that the new railway company and the local officials had virtual control of the Porto law courts, the new company may have been worried at the possibility of being over-ridden by Lisbon. In this context, Conde de Margaride, attorney to the Companhia do Caminho de Ferro de Guimarães, wrote to the King of Portugal on 22 August 1883. Considering the recipient, the letter was remarkable for its defamatory language and its accusations. From the start British dealers had opened the share subscription in Portugal without the necessary authority. There had been no English investors. Construction had started but now the company was bankrupt, having failed to deliver the railway. The Portuguese government had not stood up to the English robbers; it had all been done by the dealers and their friends. The concession was now with the Portuguese. The Portuguese should not pay the little English rascal (John Dixon) after they had been tricked. Portugal wasn't an English colony and it wasn't cowering under the shadow of the English flag. The English were hated all over the world but they did have one good point; they would accept the result of a legal tribunal. The Earl did not believe that the Portuguese government should meddle and should leave the outcome to Portuguese legislation. The reputation of the royal family as at stake, and he was counting on the monarch's goodwill.

In September 1883 Lord Granville suggested arbitration. John agreed but the railway company refused.

In mid-1883 de Serpa moved on; he would be Prime Minister by 1890. His successor was none other than Ernesto Rudolpho Hintze Ribeiro, so the change of minister had little effect on John's prospects, as Hintze Ribeiro was seen to be hand in glove with the railway company. John wrote:

> 'Senhor Hintze Ribeiro is now the acting Foreign Minister. He will shrug his shoulders and say "very sorry".'

These concerns were entirely justified. On 10 September 1883 Hintze Rebeiro sent a long letter to London. He wrote that John Dixon's court case had not been recognised by Portuguese Courts and the railway should be opened for traffic. The British Ambassador in Lisbon, Sir Charles Wyke, had confided to the Foreign Secretary, Lord Granville, that there was not much point in pursuing the Portuguese government.

The last straw

At this point John had taken the first steps in recourse to the courts. The newspaper *Correspondencia de Portugal* of 20 August 1883 carried a letter from its editor, Senhor Felipe de Carvallo, who was sympathetic to John Dixon. It said that the Porto action was in the hands of Dr Pinto Coelho for Dixon and Dr Jozé Maria da Fonseca for the Companhia do Caminho de Ferro de Guimarães, both described as 'celebrities of the Portuguese Bar'. Celebrities do not come without cost, and John must have gone no further than briefing Dr Coelho for fear in incurring additional losses.

The railway company acted on Hintze Ribeiro's assertion that there was no reason why the railway should not start operating. The Porto press reported that the first trains would run on 31 December, accompanied by repetition of the official view that Dixon's case must be pursued in the courts and that the government held no responsibility in the matter. In a letter of 5 September 1883, Walter Baring gave his opinion of the Portuguese government:

> 'They are particularly afraid of offending their supporters in Oporto and in the neighbourhood, and prefer committing an act of injustice to a British subject than incurring a small amount of transient unpopularity and possibly losing a few votes in these districts.'

Hintze Ribeiro was only at the Ministério dos Negócios Estrangeiros for a matter of months on his way to higher office. He was Prime Minister in 1893-97, again in 1900-04 and finally, for two months only, in 1906. The climate did not improve with the arrival of his successor, José Vicente Barbosa du Bocage, an academic zoologist turned politician. Barbosa du Bocage eliminated any last hopes of John receiving payment by rejecting de Serpa's view that the new company might be bound to accept the debts of the old, and by reiterating that the Portuguese government had nothing to do with the matter.

Up until now the Portuguese Foreign Office had at least appeared to acknowledge some of John's claim, although their actions were always to deny him any chance of success. Perhaps they were mindful of the need for British capital and expertise in the development of the country's economy. Earlier de Serpa had specifically pointed out the bad effect that the denial of justice to the British subject, who had spent his capital in Portugal, would have in England. For many years the official position had been that John Dixon should begin legal proceedings in the Portuguese courts for the full value of his work on the railway, whereupon the government would decree that the new company would have to honour the debts of the old company. Although there was every reason to suppose that this was merely talk, Barbosa du Bocage now denied any government involvement.

At this point, given that the Portuguese government had publicly washed its hands of the affair, and the British Foreign Office had done much the same privately, the only way ahead was through the Portuguese courts.

A direct appeal to the King of Portugal

In September 1883 John took the extraordinary action of writing directly to the King of Portugal, Dom Luís I. This four-page letter, which must rank among the longest letters ever written by him, exhorted the monarch to grant redress since, by the action of the Minister of Public Works, he appeared:

> '... likely to be deprived of every penny, notwithstanding the most urgent and strong representations of the British Minister by direction of Her Majesty's Principal Secretary of State for Foreign Affairs, after a most minute investigation of all the facts, a proof in itself the case must be just and honourable.'

John did little to hide his anger and frustration, going on to write:

> 'To this day neither I nor anyone else has ever received one penny but we have been put to endless expense in the futile endeavour to obtain justice, having been again and again thwarted by overt acts of the Minister of Obras Publicas.'

For a man whose letters were usually brief and to the point, he continued at great length:

> 'What I do crave is your Majesty's consideration to the personal injustice thus being done to an innocent individual whose only mistake is having believed in the good faith of some of your Majesty's Ministers. In that belief I have spent my money, in that belief I commenced an expensive action and I crave in return the honourable fulfilment of the promise which I feel confident your Majesty will not knowingly permit to be violated to the serious prejudice of your petitioner and damage to the fair name of Portugal in the English Parliament and in financial circles thus checking the flow of capital for the development of Public Works and creating an ill feeling that can benefit no one. All for the sake of benefiting a few local people who have certainly done nothing to deserve it.'

The 6½ kilometres of railway had cost him 'with one thing and another' nearly £30,000.

Surprisingly John Dixon's letter did not mention that the King of Portugal had been elected an honorary member of the Institution of Civil Engineers in 1877. Since this would surely have added weight to his appeal perhaps he was unaware of this fact.

John Dixon's legal action in Portugal

No doubt many would have accepted the previous advice of *The Times* and rejected the prospect of pursuing the Portuguese partnership through the slow and contorted Portuguese courts, obstructed by differences in interpretation between the king and government in Lisbon and the provincial authorities in Porto. But John Dixon was not a man to give up easily. Over the course of his career he had resorted to other legal actions, although these did not have successful outcomes (against the Curwen estate over the Windermere ferry and against the Burrells over their salvage claim for Cleopatra's Needle).

The Portuguese legal system was unduly ponderous and opaque. Matters improved early in 1883 when the government promised to withhold 'all privileges and facilities' from the Companhia do Caminho de Ferro de Guimarães and reminded them that their concession to operate the line depended on their agreement to accept the debts of the old Minho District Railway Company.

In February 1884 John informed Lord Fitzmaurice that his lawyer in Lisbon was taking steps to proceed with the case in the Tribunal of First Instance and thought that it may be heard about the end of the year. It would then go to the Tribunal of Second Instance and then to the Supreme Tribunal in Lisbon, all of which would take many years.

A lengthy editorial in *The Times* of 4 June 1884 outlined the tortured history of the railway and commented that a gross hardship had been inflicted upon Mr Dixon. His experience would serve as a warning to English investors and contractors about any assurances given by the Portuguese. The following day John had a letter published in *The Times* thanking them for their support and contrasting the past assurances from Senhor Carvalho with the subterfuges of the new company and Senhor Foules at the Ministry of Public Works.

John's despondency grew as the months of 1884 went by with no sign of the legal action reaching a hearing. In August he wrote to Lord Granville:

> 'The whole proceeding seems to me a hopeless farce. I see the action cannot be pushed and can only have one result, loss and expense.'

In the same letter he again asked the British Government to hold the Portuguese Government responsible. Although, as has been seen, the Foreign Office opinion was that there was not much point taking on the Portuguese government, to their credit they sought expert legal opinion. On 27 November 1884 the Foreign Office was advised that the British government should take no further diplomatic action, and John was given this bad news six days later.

New Ministers in London and Lisbon and final satisfaction

Beyond the end of 1884 there is little correspondence or other record. It is possible that John withdrew his legal action for fear of escalating cost. But his fortunes would change quite unexpectedly with rapid changes of ministers in London and Lisbon. The career of Lord Granville, now aged seventy, was coming to an end. For eight months from June 1885 the

Prime Minister, the Marquis of Salisbury, also headed the Foreign Office. Lord Rosebery was then Foreign Secretary for six months until August 1886 when Earl of Iddesleigh occupied the position for five months, after which the Prime Minister again took charge. It would seem likely that, with four changes of Foreign Secretary in under two years, there would have been an absence of strong leadership. This would leave George Petre, now the ambassador in Lisbon and sympathetic to John's cause, some freedom to press his case.

At the same time there were changes in Lisbon with the Progressive Party's electoral success, which swept away the Regeneration Party, who had been in power since 1881, throughout the time John had been pursuing payment. Henrique de Barros Gomes replaced Barbosa du Bocage in 1886. Barros Gomes had trained as a civil engineer before entering politics and may have felt for his fellow civil engineer. Exactly what transpired following the arrival of Barros Gomes is unknown, but it resulted in a memo from the Foreign Office In London dated 29 July 1887 stating that John Dixon's case had been settled satisfactorily. On the same day John wrote to Julian Pauncefote, the Permanent Secretary at the Foreign Office. After seven years of constant pressure he had settled for the full amount, but with no interest, and had already received the first instalment, representing two-thirds of the total. No indication of the actual amount was in either communication, but as John described it as 'the full amount' it was presumably in the region of £20,000.

It is not known if the settlement came from the Portuguese government or from the railway company. Certainly by 1887, with over two years' income from the railway, the company would have been in a position to settle. Dixon's claim of £20,000 was relatively small compared with the £250,000 they had spent completing the line to Guimarães. It seems likely that Dixon's money came from Portuguese government sources since the railway company had never shown any inclination to settle the matter. The government must have been taken aback by the involvement of the British Foreign Office in the matter, and mindful of the effect of a continuing dispute on future British investment in Portugal.

An extraordinary publication

In the spring of 1883 an account of their dispute with John Dixon was published by the new company. It was written in the most defamatory language with unsubstantiated opinions and gratuitous insults, and peppered with exclamation marks, double exclamation marks, block capitals, etc. The affair demonstrated the 'pertinacious cunning, incarnate in Mr John Dixon' and the new company could not possibly be liable for the fraudulent claims of a 'voracious and unconscientious speculator'.

The Minho District Railway Company had entered into 'a monstrous contract' with Sandiforth Griffin. The company directors were guilty of 'an illusion, a falsehood and a criminal fraud' in implying that there were English subscribers whereas the loss of the company was carried solely by the Portuguese shareholders. The directors themselves did not own a single share.

In signing off his certificates for completed work, George Bruce was 'a creature of Mr Dixon's'. The enormous sum of money expended on the initial section of line was for barely six kilometres of railway, 'without a single bridge, tunnel, high level passage, remarkable cutting or viaduct'. Why had Mr Dixon become involved with the railway when he knew that the Minho company 'did not possess a farthing'. It was all 'a disgusting swindle'. Mr Dixon 'only indulges in violent means to suit his purposes and in pompous and indecorous pressures'.

The publication even denigrated John Dixon's work at Lisbon, for which he had been honoured by the King of Portugal. The piers at the Lisbon Custom House were 'of little use and obstruct the Tagus'.

Later operations on the Guimarães railway

Largely fulfilling the promises of the original London prospectus, the Companhia do Caminho de Ferro de Guimarães prospered. A large workshop was built at Lousado (now an engaging railway museum), improvements were made to the existing track and, in 1907, the line was extended by twenty-two kilometres to Fafe.

It became part of the Companhia dos Caminho de Ferro do Norte de Portugal in 1927, which was in turn absorbed into the state-owned railway operator Comboios de Portugal in 1947. In 1986 the Fafe extension was closed and converted into a cycleway. At the end of the 19th century the entire Guimarães line was replaced in broad gauge, taking a new route to the east of Trofa. New stations were built, including one at the north-western end of Santo Tirso. The re-routed broad-gauge track now runs between John Dixon's station and the River Ave, the old track bed has become a road and the station building has been taken over by the local angling association, Clube Pesca Desportiva Além Rio, as its headquarters.

What was the truth?

It is impossible to ascertain the truth from the available English sources and Portuguese sources, given national prejudice and translation problems.

John had undoubtedly become involved in the railway sensing a good profit from relatively straightforward work, while accepting some element of risk. The apparently poor state of the completed section of line was probably due to shortcomings in local supervision; it is unlikely that John personally supervised the construction. However, the shortcomings may well have been exaggerated by the Portuguese in order to discredit him. He accepted what he believed to be guarantees against non-payment. When it became clear that these would not be honoured, he was greatly aggrieved, believing that there had been collusion between the new company, the local officials and the Portuguese government. John must have thought long and hard about whether to launch legal action on the Portuguese courts, balancing his desire to obtain satisfaction against the reality that court action would be costly and lengthy. Even after he abandoned the court action he did not give up. His persistence eventually paid off when, probably to his great surprise, his claim was settled in 1887.

The British Foreign Office view was that, under Portuguese law, the new company was liable to pay John Dixon, but that it was wilfully ignoring this responsibility with the connivance of the government. What seems remarkable is the amount of time the Foreign Office spent on the case, although they all but gave up by the end of 1884.

In Portugal the new railway company appear to be more culpable than the government. They believed that the British Minho company had acted immorally and swindled its Portuguese investors, and they were then faced with an exorbitant demand from a 'cunning and pertinacious' contractor who resorted to 'low and ungentlemanly tricks' for a short length of sub-standard railway track. They clearly evaded their responsibilities to Dixon by completely ignoring Britain and Lisbon, and by manipulating local officials.

At first the Portuguese government ostensibly supported Dixon's case, but this support steadily drained away. The government did not wish to become actively involved, leaving it up to John to pursue the matter through the Portuguese courts, knowing he would abandon this before it could ever reach a verdict. The Guimarães railway case was not the only example of troubles faced by British investors in Portugal at that time. It would take a change of government, with the consequent change in ministers, to settle the matter.

By the time of the eventual settlement in 1887 John Dixon's health was already failing. He died just over three years later at the age of fifty-six.

Other evidence of John Dixon in Portugal

In *The Graphic* of 14 Apri1883 there is a short article and an engraving made from a sketch made by John Dixon of the Glasgow steamer *Arlandhu* which had been in collision some forty miles south of the River Tagus with the *Kron Prinz*, striking her broadside and sending her to the bottom in a few minutes. The engraving shows the damage to the bows of the *Arlandhu* with the vessel beached on the foreshore. In this article, John Dixon was reported to have been in Lisbon on 18 March 1883.

Acknowledgements

Diego Bezerra da Silva for assistance with translation from Portuguese.

Luis Fernandes and Lucinda Simoes, Arquivo Municipal Alfredo Pimenta, Câmera Municipal de Guimarães for assistance with Guimarães railway records.

Ana Cristina Moscatel, Glória Silva, Válter Rebelo and staff at the Regional Archives of the Azores, Biblioteca Publica e Arquivo Regional de Ponta Delgada for locating and copying John Dixon's letters to Hintze Ribeiro.

Rui Vilaça, Fundação Museu Nacional Ferroviário Nucleo de Lousado, Largo da Estaçâo de Lousado, Lousado for explanation of route of John Dixon's track.

Clube Pesca Desportiva, Alé-Rio, Santo Tirso for access to the interior of John Dixon's station at Santo Tirso.

Staff at the Tourist Information Office, Santo Tirso, for information about the locations of railway stations at Santo Tirso.

References

Journal do Porto, 21 June 1874
Enthusiastic commentary on the prospects for the railway in exporting agricultural products to Porto and Lisbon, as well as bringing bathers to the mineral springs at Vizella and fresh fish to Guimarães.

Money Market & City Intelligence
The Times, London, 15 July 1874, page 10
Prospectus issued for the Minho District Railway Company Limited.

Advertisements and Notices
The Morning Post, London, 17 July 1874, page 1
Details of offer of shares in the Minho District Railway Company Limited.

The Late Mr. Dixon, C.E.
The Times, London, 4 February 1891, page 3
Obituary mentioning a 60-mile railway in Portugal which must be the Guimarães railway of which John Dixon only built 6½ kilometres.

Biographical Dictionary of Civil Engineers in Great Britain and Ireland, Volume 2, 1830-1890
M R Bailey, M M Chrimes, R C Cox, P S M Cross-Rudkin, B Lawrance Hurst, R C McWilliam, R W Rennison, E C Ruddock, R J M Sutherland and T Swailes
Thomas Telford Publishing (Institution of Civil Engineers), London, 2008
Incorrectly states that John Dixon built a 60-mile railway in Portugal, the location of which had not been identified, prior to the Guimarães railway.

The London Gazette, 2 July 1878, pages 3922-23
Court of Justice, Chancery Division, granted the petition by John Dixon dated 18 March 1878 for the Minho Railway Company to be wound up.

The London Gazette, 3 September 1878, page 4991
Court of Chancery appoints Henry Chatteris, accountant, to be official liquidator of the Minho District Railway Company in response to John Dixon's petition to the Court.

The Guimarães Railway Company and John Dixon, late contractor of the Minho District Railway Company Limited
Typographia de Antonio José da Silva Teixeira
Rua da Cancella Velha, 62, Porto, Portugal, 1883
The vitriolic attack on the original Minho District Railway Company, John Dixon and George Bruce.

A Construção da Rede Ferroviária do Minho (1845-1892)
Hugo Silveira Pereira
Cultura, Espaço & Memória, No.2 , 2011
University of Porto, Portugal
History of the Minho District Railway Company from 1850 in Portuguese. Page 18 has details of John Dixon's involvement, claiming that he completed the line but with very poor quality and excessive costs. Pages 23-27 cover John Dixon's legal case.

Letter from John Dixon to Hintze Ribeiro, dated 8 March 1882 written from the Hotel Centrale, Lisbon on his headed notepaper with the address as Laurence Pountney Hill.
Fundo Particular Hintze Ribeiro 5.1.4045
PT/BPARPD/PSS/HRHR/1775 11 July 1881 to 27 September 1883
Direção Regional da Cultura
Biblioteca Publica e Arquivo Regional de Ponta Delgada, Azores
Joh Dixon was en-route to the Rio Tinto Mines and requested an audience with Hintze Ribeiro on his return to Lisbon in a week's time. He wished Ribeiro to enforce the condition of payment of Minho District Railway Company debts on the new company.

Despatch from Sir R Moriers, March 1882
Parliamentary Papers Reference No.2587
National Archives, Kew, London
John Dixon's agreement that, in event of Minho District Railway Company going into liquidation, he would be able to obtain the concession to operate the line.

Letter from John Dixon to Hintze Ribeiro, dated 10 April 1882 and written on notepaper headed *Grand Hôtel Central, Lisbonne*.
Fundo Particular Hintze Ribeiro 5.1.4048
PT/BPARPD/PSS/HRHR/1775
11 July 1881 to 27 September 1883
Direção Regional da Cultura
Biblioteca Publica e Arquivo Regional de Ponta Delgada, Azores
John Dixon has heard that important privileges are to be granted to the new company. He reminds Ribiero that he had been offered the concession, but declined on the basis that he would be paid by the new company. He pressed Ribeiro to secure this payment.

Letter from John Dixon to Hintze Ribeiro, dated 20 April 1882 and written on notepaper headed *Grand Hôtel Central, Lisbonne.*
Fundo Particular Hintze Ribeiro 5.1.4042
PT/BPARPD/PSS/HRHR/1775
11 July 1881 to 27 September 1883
Direção Regional da Cultura
Biblioteca Publica e Arquivo Regional de Ponta Delgada, Azores
Hintze Ribeiro had emphatically assured him that the new company would be bound by the Tribunal and laws being hurried through the Cortes. Dixon doubts if this will be the case in practice. In a post-script he acknowledges that he was part paid in bills but these were subsequently dishonoured, and it could not be right that this resulted in his being downgraded from a privileged creditor to an unprivileged one.

Letter from John Dixon to Hintze Ribeiro, dated 22 May 1883 and written on Minho District Railway headed notepaper with the address as Laurence Pountney Hill.
Fundo Particular Hintze Ribeiro 5.1.4050
PT/BPARPD/PSS/HRHR/1775
11 July 1881 to 27 September 1883
Direção Regional da Cultura
Biblioteca Publica e Arquivo Regional de Ponta Delgada, Azores
Quotes the original prospectus cost of £230,000 for the acquisition of land and construction of the line. Also lists the £78,500 already paid or committed, and £166,000 to convert from broad gauge to narrow gauge, giving a total of £244,500.

Money Market and City Intelligence
The Times, 30 August 1882
Lengthy article, critical of the Portuguese Government's handling of John Dixon's case.

Money Market and City Intelligence
The Times, 27 October 1882, page 9
John Dixon's petition to the Stock Exchange Committee asking them to refuse a loan to Portugal for the conversion of Minho Railway bonds. The Committee expressed their sympathy but said it was outside the scope of their rules.

The Langstaffs of Teesdale and Weardale: materials for a history of a yeoman family gathered together by George Blundell Longstaff
Mitchell Hughes and Clarke, Wardour Press, London, 1923
Anecdote about John Dixon confronting the Portuguese Ambassador, Appendix IX, page 401.

Mr John Dixon's claim against the Guimarães Railway Company
Foreign Office Correspondence reference FO 63/1201
National Archives, Kew, London
Bound volume of the original correspondence from March 1881 to December 1883.

Mr John Dixon's claim against the Guimarães Railway Company
Foreign Office Correspondence reference FO 63/1202
National Archives, Kew, London
Bound volume of the original correspondence from April 1884 to July 1887.

Further correspondence relating to Mr John Dixon's claim against the Guimarães Railway Company 1882-1884
Foreign Office Correspondence FO 425/157 and FO 881/4957
National Archives, Kew, London
These are two identical folders containing printed transcriptions of the letters from 30 August 1882 to 23 April 1884. Names are often incorrectly spelt in these transcriptions.

Portuguese Government, its action in the case of the Guimarães railway, from evidence of facts contained in correspondence, presented to the English Parliament by command of Her Majesty, in 1882 and 1884.
Printed address by John Dixon to the Committee of the Stock Exchange, London, 17 September 1884
In Foreign Office Correspondence reference FO 63/1202, National Archives, Kew, London
Summary of John Dixon's case against the Guimarães Railway from the demise of the original company to the issuing of the decree by the King of Portugal authorising the opening of the railway.

Letter from John Dixon to Dom Luís, King of Portugal and the Algarve, dated 27 September 1883
Fundo Particular Hintze Ribeiro
Fundo Particular Hintze Ribeiro 5.1.4090
PT/BPARPD/PSS/HRHR/1775
11 July 1881 to 27 September 1883
Direção Regional da Cultura
Biblioteca Publica e Arquivo Regional de Ponta Delgada, Azores
Four page letter setting out the history of the matter and appealing to the king to favour his case for payment. The letter includes:
- The original verbal agreement with Lourenço António de Carvalho
- The claim that he was owed £24,000
- His request for the concession withdrawn on understanding that the new company would honour the debts of the original company.
- His attempts to pursue the case through the Portuguese courts and the intervention of the British government.
- Surprise that the new company had been given permission to complete the railway and commence running trains.

The Institution of Civil Engineers
The Engineer, London, 2 March 1877, page 142
King of Portugal elected honorary member at the meeting of 6 February.

Leading article, Mr. John Dixon and the Guimarães Railway
The Times, 4 June 1884, page 9
Lengthy comment on the risks of English capital going abroad, as evidenced by John Dixon's experience. This article clearly states that the new Guimarães Railway Company was obliged under Portuguese law to accept acts of the old Minho District Railway Company.

Mr. John Dixon and the Portuguese Government
The Times, 5 June 1884, page 12
Letter from John Dixon explaining the background to the railway dispute, his assurance from Senhor Carvalho, the actions of his successor in having the railway seized and put up for auction and the various subterfuges of the new company and the Ministry of Senhor Foules.

Short History of the Firm of Crouch & Hogg
Inaugural Address, Session 1952-53, 10 October 1952
Liston Carnie
Institution of Civil Engineers, Glasgow and West of Scotland Association
Includes biographical details of James Blair.

The Electric Telegraph Company of Ireland
Steven Roberts
Article in the website *History of the Atlantic Cable & Undersea Communications*
http://atlantic-cable.com//
Biography of Sandiforth Griffin.

Projected Railways
The Times, London, 7 January 1846, page 3
List of 718 railway plans deposited by the end of 1845, 549 having disappeared. "A more sufficient proof of the unhealthy extent of the railway speculation, for denouncing of which we were honoured with so much scurrilous abuse a few months since, could not be desired."

Railways - The Defunct Schemes
The Times, London, 14 January 1846, page 6
Of 1,263 railway companies provisionally registered, 879 had failed to deposit plans by the year end.

Improvements in the construction of vessels of war and batteries on land
Patent Number 1156, 21 April 1862
Sandiforth Featherstone Griffin
Eyre and Spottiswood, Great Seal Patent Office, London

Apparatus to be used in the distillation of petroleum, or any oleaginous, resinous, or alcoholic bodies
Patent Number 2341, 22 August 1862
Eyre and Spottiswood, Great Seal Patent Office, London

The London Gazette, 2 August 1861, page 3250
1843. George Featherstone Griffin, of New Adelphi Chambers, Civil Engineer, for the invention of improvements in the permanent way of railways.

The London Gazette, 19 May 1871, page 2444
1517. George Featherstone Griffin, of 19 Great George Street-street, Westminster, Civil Engineer, for an invention of a certain novel application to the corking of bottles, enabling the cork to be withdrawn without injury thereto.

The London Gazette, 30 December 1862, page 6592
Sandiforth Featherstone Griffin of New Adelphi Chambers Civil Engineer, has given notice in respect of the invention of 'improvements in apparatus to be used in the distillation of petroleum, or any oleaginous, resinous, or alcoholic bodies.'

The London Gazette, 30 June 1865
Sandiforth Featherstone Griffin bankrupt.

The Role of Britain and France in the Finance of Portuguese Railways 1850-1890, a comparative study in speculation, corruption and inefficiency
António Lopes Vieira
PhD Thesis, University of Leicester, October 1983
An excellent analysis of the early development of railways in Portugal, which are described as speculative, inefficient, uneconomic, costly and foreign-orientated. There are histories of all the four railway schemes promoted by English financiers prior to the Minho Railway, and a comprehensive account of the Minho railway itself in pages 242-252.

Lisbon Tramways Company - Twycross v Grant - Personal Explanation.
Hansard Commons Sitting on 17 July 1876
Reference HC Deb 17 July 1876 volume 230, cc 1481-6
Statement by Lord Henry Lennox on his involvement with the Lisbon Steam Tramways Company.

Narrow Gauge Railways of Portugal
W J K Davies
Plateway Press, East Harling, Norfolk, 1998
Pages 17-22 have a history of the Guimarães railway with details of the original locomotives and rolling stock. Drawing of the Hudswell Clarke locomotives for the Guimarães railway on page 33.

Lá vem o comboio novo!
Manuel Alves de Oliveira
Guimaraes, 1982
Portuguese publication on the early railways. The chapter 'A Ligação Trofa- Guimarães' on pages 54 to 75, covers the early history of the railway, and includes the text of the letter from Conde de Margarida to the monarch.

A Steamer's Bows after Collision
The Graphic, London, 14 April 1883, page 384
States that John Dixon was in Lisbon on 18 March 1883.

18 Llandudno Pier

After several false starts, the present Llandudno Pier was conceived in 1875. John Dixon was awarded the contract for its construction, the design being by James Brunlees who had worked with John on several previous projects. The pier opened in 1877. Five years later John submitted the lowest tender for an angled extension from the shore, a pavilion and swimming bath, but was not given the work. Llandudno's magnificent pier is today acknowledged as probably the finest of all the British piers.

The first Llandudno Pier Company

For many years the old wooden jetty of the St George's Harbour Company, opened in 1858, was the only means of transferring passengers and goods between shipping and the shore. In October 1859 it was badly damaged in a gale, but was repaired and remained in service, albeit in a poor condition. There were calls for a new pier at Llandudno, initially for landing passengers from boats rather than for promenading. By September 1862 the town commissioners, always keen to develop Llandudno as a holiday resort, had plans drawn up by Eugenius Birch for a pier of 1,350 feet in length in the middle of the bay. Eugenius Birch (1818-1884) had designed the country's first iron pier, at Margate, and was then engaged on the North Pier at Blackpool. The commissioners set about obtaining Parliamentary approval, but public approval was a different matter, and there was an outcry that this 'unsightly mass of iron' would desecrate Llandudno's natural beauty. This resulted in revised plans repositioning the proposed pier to the end of the bay, at an estimated cost of £25,000. Board of Trade approval was given in April 1863, but nothing happened on the ground. By the end of the summer questions were being asked, but it was not until the beginning of 1864 that the Llandudno Pier Company Limited published their prospectus, offering 4,000 shares each of £5. Once again, there were many months of inactivity, until the company was quietly wound up in 1871.

The second Llandudno Pier Company

At the end of 1872 it was reported that a new company had been set up to provide Llandudno with a pier, but once again there was little discernible action. Letters appeared in the newspapers in the summer of 1873, generally in support of the venture and wondering why it was that that Llandudno still did not have a pier.

The third Llandudno Pier Company

The third attempt to give Llandudno a pier was initiated by the most influential men in the town, and not surprisingly made rapid progress. The Llandudno Improvement Commissioners and Lord Mostyn, the local land owner, had ambitions to develop Llandudno into a prestigious sea-side resort following reclamation of the marshy ground between the two bays and installation of a sewerage scheme. Part of their vision was a new pier, and they successfully obtained the necessary Parliamentary approval, registering the Llandudno Pier Company in November 1875. Within a fortnight of going on sale, over 1,800 of the £10 shares had been taken up. Unusually, 60 of the 160 shareholders were ladies. The formal order for the pier was issued by the Board of Trade, which was much more concerned with ferry passengers and goods than with promenaders merely there for the views and sea air, although the pier company could erect shops, saloons, bazaars, reading, waiting and refreshment rooms. The London and North Western Railway Company agreed to sell the old wooden jetty, which lay in the path of the new pier, and the right to tolls to the new company for £1,250. The same tolls were to be applied to the new pier, the detailed list included charges for blubber and bones, cheese and chimney pots, guano and gunpowder, turbot and turtles. The Board of Trade reserved the right to review the tolls if the company's annual income exceeded its costs by 10%.

The pier designed

James Brunlees, who had designed the piers at Southport and Rhyl, and his partner Alexander McKerrow, designed a 1,234 feet long pier, the far end standing in about a foot of water at the lowest tides. By this time, after the opening of more than forty piers around the coast, basic pier design had evolved into a fairly standard form. The Llandudno pier

'Holiday makers on Llandudno beach with the second pier behind them, c1880' photograph.
It is described as 'the second pier' becuase it came after the old wooden jetty ('the first pier').
This shows the pier as built by John Dixon, before the addition in 1884 of the angled extension to the promenade with a swimming pool and pavilion. Victorian dress codes made few concessions for life at the seaside.
Reproduced by courtesy of the Conwy Record Office, The Old Board School, Lloyd Street, Llandudno. Reference CP 458/2/5.

Photograph of the pier from the Great Orme, again before the 1884 additions. Reproduced by courtesy of the Conwy Record Office, The Old Board School, Lloyd Street, Llandudno. Reference XS 2224/19/5/1.

conformed to this standard, with wrought iron lattice girders supported on piles built up from cast iron columns, each of 12 inch diameter and 11 feet in height, with flanges at either end. While the basic structure was conventional, Brunlees and McKerrow consulted the eminent architect, Charles Henry Driver, an indication of their desire to create a distinctive and harmonious design which would make it something of an aristocrat among the other piers of the realm. Driver had worked with Brunlees on the Eau Brink Cut Bridge at King's Lynn a few years earlier. There were recesses along the pier for seats and shelters, and at the far end the deck widened out to form a pier-head on which it was planned to build a concert room and hexagonal pavilions for refreshments and cloakrooms. Below the pier-head were landing stages for shipping, accessed by staircases from the promenade deck. The landing stages would be used by passengers for the Isle of Man ferry. Optimistically, hopes were expressed that Llandudno might replace even Holyhead as the embarkation point for the ferry to Ireland.

'The Pier, Llandudno' engraving of the original entrance to the pier. Reproduced by courtesy of Martin Easdown from his Marlinova Collection.

John Dixon's tender accepted

John Dixon successfully tendered £24,000 for the construction of the pier and started work as soon as the contract was signed. Iron castings were supplied by Walter Macfarlane of Glasgow and John's site manager was a Mr Double. The first pile was driven on 10 July 1876. By August the shore abutments had been built and piles driven for a quarter of its length. John's men moved at a faster pace than the civic leaders, who had organised a formal ceremony of driving the 'first pile' on 15 September, by which time 110 feet of the structure had been completed. The weather remained fair, despite some threatening clouds, and Llandudno was decked out in flags with decorated boats in the bay. At one o'clock, after several speeches extolling the charms of town, Lord Hill Trevor pulled a rope to set off a detonator to drive in a pile, after begging the ladies not to be too much alarmed and amid loud and prolonged cheers from the many thousands present. This was a deliberately staged event since the piles were never driven by explosive charges. John was thanked for his spirit and energy, and for ensuring the comfort and safety of all at the ceremony. Luncheon, in the billiard room of the Imperial Hotel, was accompanied by more speeches in praise of Llandudno, several toasts, including one to the prosperity of the Llandudno Pier Company, and music from Mr Hatton's Band.

'Plate 27 - Pier at Llandudno' engraving from Girder Making and the Practice of Bridge Building in Wrought Iron by Edward Hutchinson.
There is an interesting comparison in the way in which the engraver has depicted the sea in each of these illustrations. In the first it is shown as a smooth surface of water by horizontal lines, obviously simpler to engrave. In the second the engraver has attempted to be more realistic in the lower left part of the picture.

At the first General Meeting of the Pier Company in November, it was reported that the contractor was evidently using every exertion to push forward the work. The ironwork was of good quality and was being erected to the Company's satisfaction. The quality of construction was tested in the violent storms of February 1877, when there had been considerable damage to property and shipping in the area. Some minor damage was done to the unfinished end of the structure, where some unsecured columns were broken, but the length of completed pier was perfectly intact. Some items from the smithy and the joiners' stores on the old jetty, beneath the new pier and being used for storage of equipment and materials, were washed away.

The materials used in the construction of the pier were 600 tons of wrought iron, 450 tons of cast iron piles, 50 tons of cast iron parapets, 5000 ft^3 greenheart timber and 4500 ft^3 pitch pine flooring. The cast iron piles were driven between 5 feet and 7 feet into the ground; it seems that conventional screw piling was used. All the iron work was painted with Griffith's patent enamel paint. Four kiosks were erected (one was in use as an office, the other three were shops: bookseller, fancy goods and draper). Two more kiosks were added later for another shop and a refreshment room. Not far from the far end of the pier steps led down to the landing stage.

With the completion of the new pier, the old jetty was dismantled and the timbers and metalwork auctioned as scrap.

Official opening

As if to compensate for holding the ceremony of 'driving the first pile' well after construction had started, the official opening took place before the pier was completed. On Wednesday 1 August 1877 the pier was formally transferred from the contractor to the directors, with press reports that 'the manager, foreman and workmen have been exerting themselves to the utmost to bring matters to a proper style, and as a result the pier looked wonderfully trim, considering that the works were actually in progress.' This was the day of the official opening, although the far end of the pier was still to be completed (in fact the last pile was not driven in until half-past eight in the evening of 6 August to hurrahs from the workmen). At midday, and before the public were admitted, there was a short ceremony at the far end of the pier. Dr and Mrs Nichol, Major Thursby, Mr Thomas Williams, Mr Herbert Neal (resident engineer for Brunlees and McKerrow), Captain Cheeseman (the newly appointed pier-master) and Mr Double (John's site manager) all gathered at the end of the pier. Dr Nichol, a leading figure in Llandudno society, addressed the assembled workmen, expressing his belief that the pier would be of incalculable benefit to visitors and inhabitants alike. In return, they gave three cheers for the success of the pier, further cheers for John Dixon and his site manager, Mr Double, for Mr Neal and lusty hurrahs for the Queen. The gates were then thrown open to the public.

The conduct of the workmen had impressed the Llandudno residents, with a local paper commenting 'Upon the whole, a more steady and civil body of men never worked for almost a year in the excellent manner the pier workmen have done, and their cheerfulness and willingness to work have been generally admired.' John Dixon also must have impressed the Llandudno Improvement Commissioners in contrast to their contractor installing the new sewerage scheme in the town; he went bankrupt bringing work came to a standstill. The only criticism of the work came from some local boatman who claimed their boats had been damaged by a raft used in the pier construction and took out an action in the Conway County Court for £40 compensation.

Enthusiasm at the opening of the pier was tempered by a serious accident three weeks later. The new pier passed diagonally over the old wooden one, which had been used as a storage area during the construction, with a sloping plank providing access between the two structures. A workman, William Tooth, slipped off this plank while carrying a heavy iron bar and fell to the foreshore below, breaking an arm and a thigh, and dislocating his shoulder. Captain Cheeseman, the pier master, and Mr Double administered brandy and took him to his lodgings, where he was attended by Dr Nichol (who had led the cheers on the opening of the pier). The local paper reported that Tooth was 'lying in a rather precarious condition' in his lodgings, but he seems to have survived since there were no deaths of a William Tooth registered in Wales or England during the last five months of 1877.

John Dixon's tender rejected

Five years later the Llandudno architect Benjamin Nelson drew up plans for additions at the shore-end of the pier. There was to be an angled extension from the promenade, passing the Grand Hotel, with a pavilion and swimming bath. The work was put out to tender and attracted eighteen bids, some only for specific parts of the project. John submitted the lowest tender, covering the entire work save for some stone abutments, of £14,000. For unknown reasons this was rejected and the work put out to a revised second tender. Not surprisingly, John did not respond this time but twenty-three companies did submit bids from which six were selected. The work was completed in 1884. The pavilion was designed as an Egyptian Hall complete with hieroglyphics. Bearing in mind the Cleopatra's Needle project of 1877-78, John would have been in his element, but it was not to be. Rather sadly, a different contractor, the capable Andrew Handyside of Derby, was used.

The unheated indoor swimming pool was never popular and in 1900 was filled in and the space used as a cinema and later as an amusement arcade. During the 1880s plans were drawn up for a floating swimming bath alongside the pier. This project would have interested John, with his early work on floating swimming baths, but nothing came of it.

The finest of British piers

Llandudno's pier proved extremely popular with almost half a million visitors in 1888. The directors of the pier company wisely preferred to invest in the pier rather than pay out large dividends. A proper landing stage was built and electric lighting installed. James Brunlees was called back to advise on widening the entrance area, which was carried out, but plans to widen the entire length of the pier were abandoned on cost grounds.

Llandudno's magnificent pier is today acknowledged as probably the finest of all the British piers. Its pavilion has also been host to many famous names including Malcolm Sargent, who conducted the Pier Orchestra 1926-27, George Formby, the Beverley Sisters and Cliff Richard. Llandudno was a place for political party conferences, and the pavilion has been the venue for speeches by Lloyd George, Winston Churchill and Margaret Thatcher, not to mention Oswald Moseley.

In 1969 a ghost train ride was being installed under the pavilion, in the space originally occupied by the swimming bath. A plaque came to light reading:

Engineers:
James Brunlees, C.E.,
Alexander MacKerrow C.E.,
Resident: H. Neal, C.E.
1878
John Dixon, C.E., London
Contractor

The pier continues to be highly regarded and much used, in spite of a fire which destroyed the pavilion in 1994. Different plans for developing the pavilion site have been rejected, and its future is uncertain.

'Llandudno on the sunny North Wales Coast' London Midland and Scottish Railway 1930 poster by Charles Pears. Charles Pears (1873-1958) from Pontefract was a marine artist and an official naval artist in both World Wars. The angled extension at the start of the pier, added in 1884, can be seen. The pleasure steamer St Tudno, a turbine-powered vessel built in 1926, was the third ship of the Liverpool and North Wales Steamship Company with that name.
Reproduced by permission of the National Railway Museum (NRM Pictorial Collection / Science and Society Picture Library). NRM reference 1978-8902.

Llandudno Pier photographed by Joe Cornish. Joe Cornish, born in Exeter in 1958, is probably Britain's most successful landscape photographer. For many years he has lived in Great Ayton, where he is a friend of the author. He kindly donated this image from 2001 for this book. Typical of his dedication was shown by the hour he spent adjusting the colour balance in the sky and foreshore, sharpening the image of the pier and removing slight imperfections in this image. © Joe Cornish.

Acknowledgements

Staff at the Denbighshire Record Office,
The Old Gaol, Rythin.

Staff at the Caernarfon Record Office,
Victoria Dock, Caernarfon.

Staff at the Conwy Record Office,
Old Board School, Lloyd Street, Llandudno.

References

Piers of Wales
Martin Easdown and Darlah Thomas
Amberley Publishing Plc, Stroud, 2010
Comprehensive history of the Llandudno Pier.

Llandudno - The Pier
North Wales Chronicle and Advertiser for the Principality, Bangor, 23 August 1862, page 3
It was universally admitted that the town needed a pier for landing from boats.

Llandudno - Town Commissioners' Meetings
North Wales Chronicle and Advertiser for the Principality, Bangor, 11 October 1862, page 8
Plan of a pier by E Birch.

Llandudno Pier
The Liverpool Mercury, 5 January 1863, page 7
Lengthy article describing the pier as an act of robbery by the commissioners by taking away the beauty of the bay.

Llandudno Pier
North Wales Chronicle and Advertiser for the Principality, Bangor, 24 January 1863, page 8
Revised plans for E Birch's pier, re-sited so as not to interfere with the bay.

Local Piers and Harbours
The Manchester Courier and Lancashire General Advertiser, 24 March 1866, page 5
Board of Trade approval for the Llandudno pier.

The Pier
North Wales Chronicle and Advertiser for the Principality, Bangor, 24 January 1863, page 8
It was rumoured that the delay to starting the pier was waiting to see if the new pier at Rhyl would be a success.

Public Notices - Llandudno Pier Company Limited
North Wales Chronicle and Advertiser for the Principality, Bangor, 23 January 1869, page 8
Share offer by the Llandudno Pier Company Limited.

Money Market and City News
The Morning Post, London, 2 February 1871, page 2
Creditors to lodge claims against the Llandudno Pier Company by 15 February.

Llandudno - A New Pier for Llandudno
North Wales Chronicle and Advertiser for the Principality, Bangor, 30 November 1872, page 4
A new pier company reported to have been set up.

Llandudno Improvements
The Wrexham Advertiser, 25 December 1875, page 6
Messrs Brunlees and McKerrow said the pier would be completed, except for the landing stage, by July 1876. £18,000 of the £30,000 shares had been taken up.

Llandudno Pier Order 1876
Caernarfon Record Office, Victoria Dock,
Caernarfon LL55 1SH
Reference XM/623/228
The Board of Trade Order for the construction of the pier.

New Pier for Llandudno
The Wrexham Advertiser, 1 July, 1876, page 6
Work has started and will be completed by 1 May 1877. Contractor is John Dixon of London, whose tender was £24,000.

Llandudno New Pier Company
The North Wales Chronicle and Advertiser for the Principality, 11 March 1876, page 7
Even at time of depression, £20,000 shares taken up. Bill about to be introduced in Parliament.

Llandudno, the New Pier
The Carnarvon and Denbighshire Herald, 12 August 1876, page 6
'It must be a source of gratification to all taking an interest in Llandudno to notice the steady progress made with the pier. Piles have been driven in for 300 yards out of the 1,200 yards. The abutments are of solid masonry and good workmanship.'

Inauguration of Llandudno Promenade Pier
The Liverpool Mercury, 16 September 1876, page 7
Comprehensive description of the proposed design and the driving of the first pile.

Driving the First Pile of the New Pier at Llandudno
The North Wales Chronicle and Advertiser for the Principality, 23 September 1876, page 7
Long article describing the ceremony of 'first pile' being driven in on 15 September by Lord Arthur Trevor MP. In fact, the first 110 feet had already been completed by that date. There is a full description of the structure, the luncheon and virtually the entire text of the speeches.

Llandudno, the New Pier
The Carnarvon and Denbighshire Herald, 23 September 1876, page 7
Long article describing the imposing ceremony of driving in the 'first pile' on 15 September, before a fashionable and numerous assembly.

The Llandudno Pier Company
The North Wales Chronicle and Advertiser for the Principality, 25 November 1876, page 6
First Ordinary General Meeting of the company. Report by Brunlees & McKerrow : first pile driven 10 July, now 48 in position. 'The contractor is evidently using every exertion to push forward the work. The ironwork throughout is of good quality, and is being erected to our satisfaction.'
Llandudno

The Carnarvon and Denbighshire Herald, 24 February 1877, page 6
Violent storms the preceding week had not damaged the completed part of the pier.

Llandudno Promenade Pier
The Derby Mercury, 30 May 1877, page 8
Report of meeting of the Civil and Mechanical Engineers' Society on 24 May where Charles H Rew read a paper on the pier, with 30 sheets of drawings, and materials used in the pier.

Llandudno Promenade Pier
Engineering, London, 1 June 1877, page 431
Paper on the pier presented to the Civil and Mechanical Engineers' Society by Charles H Rew. Herbert Neal was the resident engineer.

Llandudno, the New Pier
The Carnarvon and Denbighshire Herald, 4 August 1877
Report on the opening of the pier, which was complete with the exception of the T-part at the far end. 'Without doubt it is one of the neatest, airiest-looking, and withal the strongest structures of its class to be found in any of our British watering-places.'

The Opening of the New Llandudno Pier
The North Wales Chronicle and Advertiser for the Principality, 11 August 1877, page 3
On 1 August the pier was formally transferred from the contractor to the directors. The last pile was driven at half-past eight on Monday night to the hurrahs of the workmen.

Llandudno, Serious Accident on the Pier
The Carnarvon and Denbighshire Herald 25 August 1877, page 6
William Tooth, a workman on the new pier, had been seriously injured in a fall.

Conway County Court December 6th
The North Wales Chronicle and Advertiser for the Principality, 8 December 1877, page 3
Conway County Court case brought by Llandudno boatmen for £40 compensation for damages to boats caused by a raft involved in the pier construction. Case adjourned until January.

Tenders - the Llandudno Pier Extension, Pavilion and Swimming Baths
The Engineer, 26 January 1883, page 62
List of contractors submitting bids for first and second round of the tendering. Includes details of work and costs.

19 London tramways

John Dixon was the contractor for two of London's many tramways, the Southwark and Deptford and the South London, in 1880. The Southwark and Deptford was delayed in a maze of bureaucracy, which tested his patience, meaning that he had to work day and night to complete the contract. Both tramways used an advanced type of track, with composite steel and wrought iron rails set on at least six inches of concrete.

Horse-drawn tramways

With the advent of the railways, and their ability to transport large numbers of people into the centre of cities, London expanded rapidly. But the railways did little to facilitate travel within the metropolis, and later this need was met by the new underground railways and by tramways laid along existing streets. The first four tram lines were authorised by an Act of Parliament in 1870, and were very popular, providing smooth and cheap transport. New tram companies were formed, and shares were eagerly taken up now that the liability of shareholders was limited to the value of their investment. A typical tramcar of the period carried up to forty passengers and was hauled by two horses.

Southwark and Deptford Tramways Company

Following the passing of The Tramways Act (1870), numerous private bills were progressed through Parliament for tramways in many towns and cities. Although there had been a suggestion for a specialist Metropolitan Tramway Board in London, the only attempt at coordination was left to the Metropolitan Board of Works to approve individual plans. The tramway bills had to jostle for priority with the multitude of railway bills seeking approval at the same time.

In South London there were rival proposals for tramways from two companies, the Southwark and Deptford Tramways Company and the South London Tramways Company. In spite of their rivalry, John would be the contractor for both companies. The Southwark and Deptford Tramways Company took a lengthy and circuitous route through many administrative bodies before it could start laying down track, a journey which would have been appreciated by Gilbert and Sullivan.

The Southwark and Deptford Tramways Bill wound its way through Parliament, completing its three readings in the Commons and in the Lords in June 1879. But in parallel it needed its plans to be approved by the Metropolitan Board of Works, and the Board was conscious of 'the necessity for having a proper control over one of the most important means of communication in the metropolis.' There were also seven parish church vestries involved; vestries were the units of local administration before today's system of local government came into effect in 1894. Vestries were keen to ensure their parochial views were taken into account. Although the majority of residents supported the introduction of trams, owners of conventional horse-drawn vehicles objected, fearing loss of business, and owners and occupiers of properties along the routes feared loss of amenity.

Conflict between unfettered private enterprise and local authority control, both Victorian ideals, was inevitable.

The Metropolitan Board of Works referred the matter to their Works and General Purposes Committee. This committee approved some of the South London lines, but none of the Southwark and Deptford, apparently because of insufficient distance between the track and the kerb in narrow streets. Bermondsey presented a petition with over 4,000 signatures in favour of both schemes and threatened to appeal directly to the House of Commons, to which the Board responded by passing the matter back to their committee. Finding itself out on a limb after the bill had been passed by Parliament and the seven vestries were pressing for a decision, the Board withdrew its objections but added conditions designed to protect the maintenance of sewers.

In July 1879 the company issued its prospectus with 7,000 shares of £10 each on offer. To dispel any doubts, the prospectus listed four existing tramway companies whose £10 shares were now trading at between £12 and £15. It appears that only 4,500 shares were issued at this time, raising sufficient capital for a tramway from 'The Bricklayers' Arms' on the Old Kent Road, south east through Rotherhithe and on to Deptford High Street, with a branch via the South Eastern Railway Station. John was awarded a contract to construct the tramway by 1 March 1880, not only to lay the lines but supply all the rolling stock and even the horses, which must have been a new experience for him. The Company boasted:

Southwark and Deptford Tram No.25, photographed when new about 1882-83. As far as is known, this is the only existing image of the Southwark and Deptford Tramways Company before it became the London, Deptford and Greenwich Tramways Company in 1893.
Reproduced by courtesy of Bob Appleton
The Tramway and Light Railway Society Archive.

> 'Special care will be taken to construct a first-class Tramway Line, with steel rails and every modern improvement which experience has suggested, and Mr. Dixon's reputation and energy stand guarantee for the prompt execution of the Works, and also that the Lines will, in the solidity of their construction, be second to none in the kingdom.'

By the end of July, it was reported that the contractor, Mr Dixon, was ready to start work immediately. Local bureaucracy was still in control, and deeds of covenant had to be agreed with individual vestries before John's men could begin. Then amazingly the Bermondsey Vestry refused to accept the rails specified by the Board of Trade and 'long and tedious discussions ensued' before Bermondsey agreed to accept them. Quite why this vestry thought itself competent to judge the technical merits of different rails is a mystery. There were also disputes about how much of the road alongside the rails should be paved at the company's expense.

Much to John's frustration it was March 1880, eight months after Parliamentary approval, before he could finally start construction. By working day and night he was able to complete 200 yards of tramway per week. By September real progress had been made, but the shareholders were becoming worried about the delays in tram operations getting underway with consequent effects on their dividend prospects. Not for the first time, John, perhaps unwisely, volunteered a personal commitment to his client's finances. A small balance of share capital remained unsubscribed and, if shareholders put their hands in their pockets to cover this, John offered to pay 5% interest on this sum until he completed the line, which he would do within four months. This was yet another example of Dixon's immense self-confidence. In addition to the work of laying the rails, John had purchased tramcars 'of the two-horse type, to hold 40 passengers, and of the most recent pattern.' The tram company also used five or six, single-deck one-horse trams built by the Metropolitan Carriage and Wagon Company of Saltley, Birmingham.

The first section of the tramway opened to the public in December 1880, giving local residents direct access to the railway lines at Cannon Street and Charing Cross stations in the city. At this time a second share offer was made of 2,500 shares of £10 each, to complete the lines authorised in the Southwark and Deptford's first Act of Parliament. These lines were completed in June 1881 and worked with nine tramcars and ninety-eight horses.

The engineer for the Southwark and Deptford Tramways Company was William Shelford, who was probably on good terms with John Dixon through his Newcastle connections and mining interests.

Who's who?
William Shelford (1834-1905)

The son of a Suffolk clergyman, William Shelford trained as an engineer in Glasgow. From 1856 to 1860 he worked as an assistant engineer for John Fowler (co-designer of the Forth Railway Bridge) on River Nene improvement works and then the Metropolitan District Railway in London. After further work on railways, in 1865 he set up his own consulting engineering business in Westminster, for ten years in partnership with Henry Robinson (1837-1915) and then on his own. Henry Robinson had worked at William Armstrong's in Newcastle. Shelford undertook much work on railways at home, in Europe and the Americas. He was also connected with several mines in Europe and the Americas. After 1875 the partnership was dissolved, and Shelford increasingly worked on tramways. He later worked with his son, Frederick, on railways in Africa. In 1863 he married Anna Sopwith, a daughter of Thomas Sopwith (1803-1879), the Newcastle surveyor and civil engineer. Thomas Sopwith was an associate of William Armstrong and of Robert Stephenson, and he accompanied Stephenson on his visit to Egypt in 1856. William Shelford was called on as an expert engineering witness in many Parliamentary Committees. He was knighted in 1904.

Top) South London Tramways Company No.47, a maker's photograph from 1882-83 taken as the tram left the works.
Reproduced by courtesy of Bob Appleton, the Tramway and Light Railway Society Archive.

Above) Postcard of horse tram No.19 of the South London Tramways Company at Queen's Road, Battersea, while travelling to Chelsea Bridge via Lavender Hill. Card House post card serial number 2895. Reproduced by courtesy of Bob Appleton Collection.

The Southwark and Deptford Tramways Company had further Acts of Parliament for additional lines, but it is not known if John continued to work for the company. From 1893 the company was known as the London, Deptford and Greenwich Tramway Company.

South London Tramways Company Limited

The South London Tramways Company Limited gained Parliamentary approval in 1880 for capital of £70,000. In May 1880 the company issued a prospectus for an initial offer of 5,000 shares of £10 each, covering eight miles of tramway from Battersea, passing Battersea Park, the stations of the London, Brighton and South Coast Railway and the London, Chatham and Dover Railway, and on to a point near the Steamboat Pier at Nine Elms. The company was, as ever, optimistic about its prospects, explaining that 'the population is of a class requiring tramway accommodation, and is increasing at a greater rate than any other Metropolitan district.' The engineer was Augustus John Darling Cameron (1841-1884).

In June 1880 advertisements were placed in the press seeking tenders, and John was successful. The 600 tons of rails were supplied by Brown, Bayley and Dixon of Sheffield. In July 1880 the company advertised in *The Sporting Times* for offers from persons willing to provide horses for the Battersea trams, at first sight perhaps an unusual journal in which to find draught horses but the tramcars used were one-horse, light vehicles. These smaller vehicles soon proved inadequate and larger tramcars, hauled by three horses, were introduced.

It seems that the progress of the South London Tramways Company's line was more straightforward than that of the Southwark and Deptford, at least partly because there was only one vestry, at Wandsworth, to deal with and they were very co-operative. John started work in September 1880 and by March the following year a four-mile section to Nine Elms was completed.

The South London Tramway opened on 1 January 1881, running with no fewer than twenty-eight tramcars. However, the days of horse-drawn trams were numbered, and in 1885 the company had successfully demonstrated a battery driven tramcar.

At the time there were numerous designs of track for tramways. Both of John's tramways were laid using the Meakins' system, pioneered by the engineer Joseph Gurdon Leycester Stephenson (1856-1917) from Somerset. A steel rail was riveted between two angle-irons, this assembly resting on a thick concrete foundation, with granite setts laid between the rails. The composite rail construction was necessary because British rolling mills would not produce these wide-base rails in one piece. Even so, there were delays in obtaining rails. Stephenson was able to obtain these rails in one piece from the Phoenix Works at Ruhrort, Duisburg in Germany.

Acknowledgements

Bob Appleton, Tramway and Light Railway Society, for providing images and information on the tram companies.

Mark Wingham, Picture Postcard Monthly, for help in locating images.

References

Southwark and Deptford Tramways
Robert J Harley
Middleton Press, Midhurst, West Sussex, 1994
John Dixon was the contractor for this tramway in 1879 which used horse-drawn trams.

Tramways, their construction and working with special reference to the tramways of the United Kingdom, Second Edition
D Kinnear Clark
Chapter V Reconstruction of the South London Tramways, pages 135-139
Crosby, Lockwood and Son, London, 1894
The construction of the Southwark and Deptford Tramway and the South London Battersea Tramway using the Meakins' system of track.

Metropolitan Tramways
Engineering, London, 11 February 1870, page 96
Suggestion by William Booth Scott of the St Pancras Vestry for a Metropolitan Tramway Board.

Public Notices - In Parliament Session 1879 - Southwark and Deptford Tramways
The South London Press, 30 November 1878, page 8
Publication of the application to Parliament for thirteen tramways in Southwark and Deptford.

The Metropolitan Board of Works - Tramways in the Metropolis
Pall Mall Gazette, London, 28 February 1879, page 7
Metropolitan Board of Works approved some of the lines proposed by the London Tramways Company but did not give consent to the lines of the Southwark and Deptford Tramways Company.

Metropolitan Board of Works - Yesterday
The South London Press, 8 March 1879, page 5
Bermondsey petition for both companies to be given approval.

The Southwark and Deptford Tramways Company
The Standard, London, 8 July 1879, page 1
Notice of closure of applications for shares, with details of the company and favourable comments on their contractor, John Dixon.

Bermondsey Vestry - The Southwark and Deptford Tramway
The South London Press, 26 July 1879, page 4
Mr Dickson (sic) was ready to start work immediately.

Bermondsey Vestry - The Tramways
The South London Press, 25 October 1879, page 5
Trials of rails from Nicholls, Smith and Haynes rail and also Gowan's rail.

Tramway Permanent Way
Engineering, London, 30 April 1880, pages 347-9
Seven different systems are described, but no mention of Meakins.

The South London Tramways Company
The Times, London, 6 May 1880, page 17
Public notice of issue of shares in the South London Tramways Company.

The Sporting Times, London, 31 July 1880, page 8
Advertisement for horsing the South London Tramways Company.

The Southwark and Deptford Tramways Company
The South London Press, 4 September 1880, page 4
Report of second general meeting on progress with the tramway.

Opening of the Southwark and Deptford Tramways
The South London Press, 4 December 1880, page 10
Opening of the first section of tramway.

The Southwark and Deptford Tramway Company
The South London Press, 3 September 1881, page 5
Report of fourth general meeting, all shares subscribed, lines completed and opened at the beginning of June.

Our Portraits
The Graphic, London, 7 October 1905, page 417
Obituary and portrait of Sir William Shelford.

Directory of British Tramways, Volume One, Southern England and the Channel Islands
Keith Turner
Tempus Publishing Limited, Stroud, 2007
Pages 107-9 briefly describe the Southwark & Deptford Tramways and the South London Tramway, with opening dates.

Notice to Contractors
London Daily News, 11 June 1880, page 1
Notice seeking tenders for lines in Nine Elms, Battersea Park Road and York Road.

Iron, Steel, Tinplate and Coal Trades
London Daily News, 9 August 1880, page 7
Messrs Brown, Bayley and Dixon (Limited) have contract for 600 tons rail and angle iron for the South London Tramway Company.

The South London Tramways Company
The South London Press, 4 September 1880, page 5
Half yearly meeting report. The contract was with Messrs Dixon.

New Tramways Extension
The Morning Post, London, 22 March 1881, page 6
South London Tramways Company line open to Nine Elms.

South London Tramways Company
The Globe, London, 14 April 1881, page 5
First meeting of shareholders. Four miles of track completed.

The South London Tramways Company - Meeting yesterday
The South London Press, 27 August 881, page 7
Shareholders' meeting. Problems obtaining rails.

20 Douro Bridge tender, Porto, Portugal

Following Gustave Eiffel's elegant railway bridge across the River Douro at Porto in northern Portugal, in 1880 a competition was held for designs of a road bridge. John Dixon entered a novel design but was unsuccessful. Detailed calculations for the bridge and his itemised tender were published at the time in the engineering press.

Gustave Eiffel's railway bridge

The river Douro flows across northern Portugal into the Atlantic Ocean at Porto. For much of its course it is in a deep valley with steep sides, challenging the capabilities of nineteenth century bridge designers. A suspension bridge was built at Porto in 1842. In 1875 a competition was announced for the design of a bridge to carry the Lisbon to Porto railway across the Douro valley. In 1877 Gustave Eiffel (1832-1923) designed the bridge known as the 'Ponte Maria Pia' to carry the railway across the Douro just east of Porto. His graceful wrought iron arch was the longest single arch bridge of its time, with a span of 525 feet. Eiffel's winning design was the least costly of the four entries, emphasising his skill as an engineer.

At the time Eiffel credited his partner, Théophile Seyrig, and Henri de Dion with the design calculations. Construction started in January 1876. Because it was impossible to build a temporary timber supporting structure under the arch, the bridge was built out from each bank, with the cantilevered sections of the arch held by steel cables until the two sections of arch were joined above the centre of the river. This technique had been pioneered by Captain James Eads for the St Louis Bridge across the Mississippi in 1872. The bridge was completed in October 1877 and opened on 4 November 1878 by the king, Dom Luis I, and Queen Maria Pia of Savoy.

Competition for the bridge at Porto

With the success of the Ponte Maria Pia, thoughts turned to the replacement of the old suspension bridge at Porto which linked the city with Vila Nova de Gaia on the opposite bank. The bridge commissioners at Porto announced a competition for a new bridge in 1880. There were to be twin-decks and a span of 560 feet, the lower deck about 40 feet above water level to connect the quays on both river banks, the higher level about 200 feet above water level to connect the upper parts of the two communities. The competition rules included specified working stresses for cast iron and wrought iron, which were significantly lower than English practice. This resulted in designs which were probably heavier than necessary but reflected understandable caution when considering such a wide span. The closing date was 12 November 1880.

The competition attracted entries from ten companies, five from France, three from Belgium and two from England. Two entrants offered a choice of designs.

Société Fives-Lille, Lille, France	£48,766
Société J F Cail et Cie, Paris	£61,074
Schneider et Cie, Creusot, France	£67,600
Gustave Eiffel et Cie, Paris	£70,400
Alphonse Lecocq et Cie, Hals, Belgium	£74,000
Rolin et Cie, Braine-le-Comte, Belgium	£75,200
Société de Construction des Batignolles, Paris (alternative design)	£79,902
Andrew Handyside and Company, Derby	£81,200
Société de Construction et des Ateliers, Willebroek, Belgium (preferred design)	£82,000
John Dixon, London	£94,540
Société de Construction des Batignolles, Paris (preferred design)	£95,902
Société de Construction et des Ateliers, Willebroek, Belgium (alternative design)	£99,200

Most designs were based on an arch, the exceptions being those of Fives-Lille, Lecocq and John Dixon. The Fives-Lille design, a simple double-Warren girder, could hardly be more basic. At the opposite end of the range the Lecocq design could hardly be more complex. The Handyside's design was by Max am Ende, a German civil engineer working in London, and based on the design of a railway bridge in Costa Rica built by Handyside. The Schneider design was the only steel bridge, and steel was an untried material for large bridges at this time (the Forth Railway Bridge would be the pioneer of large steel bridges).

John Dixon's design was unconventional, with the upper roadway supported on two inclined struts and the lower roadway suspended below. After the debacle over payment for the Guimarães Railway, it might have been thought that John would avoid further work in Portugal. He had also worked mainly on construction rather than design work, his previous design of the viaducts on the Whitby to Loftus railway had not been wholly successful, but since then he had acquired more experience of structures and was obviously tempted by the challenge of this river crossing. Unusually for him, John's tender was at the upper end of the price range at £94,540. Gustave Eiffel's erstwhile partner, Théophile Seyrig, had two designs submitted by Société Construction et des Ateliers, Willebroek in Belgium.

Competition designs for the new bridge over the River Douro, at Oporto. It is easy to see why two entries were dismissed on account of their appearance; the Fives-Lille bridge (No.6) was considered too ugly and the Lecocq bridge (No.5) was thought to be an incoherent design. John Dixon (No.7) had given ease of construction precedence over visual aspects. The winner was Théophile Seyrig (No.9).
Engineering, London, 24 December 1880, page 594-5.

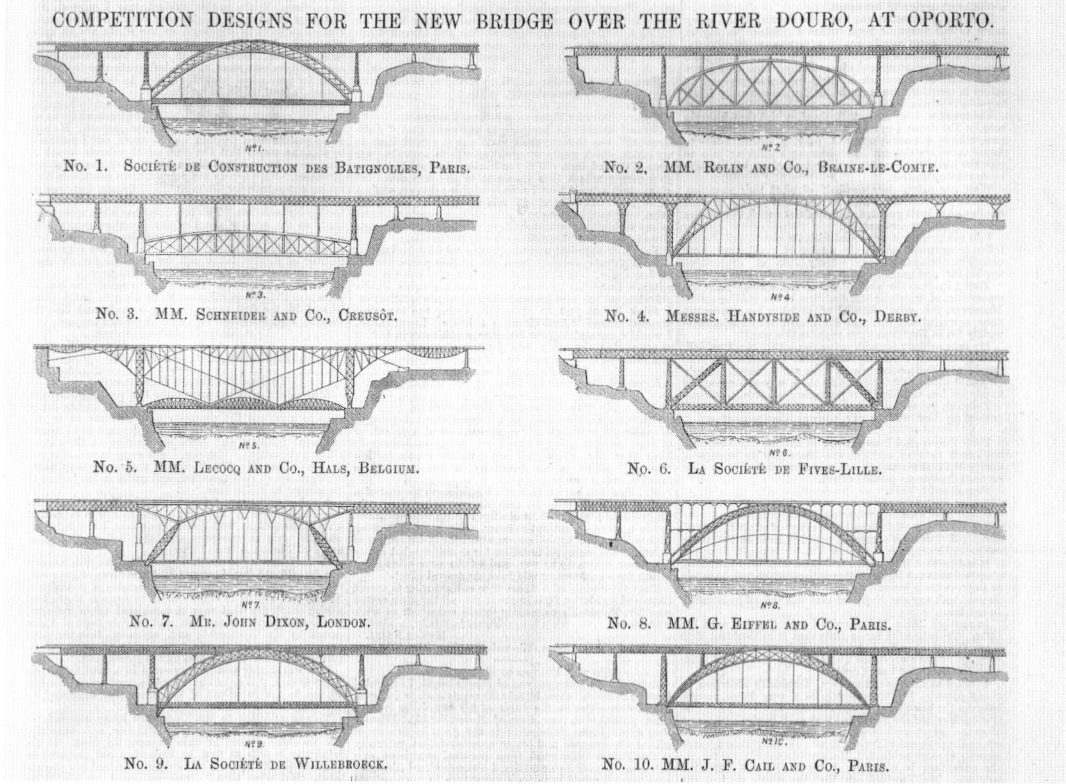

The judges' decision

The judges were faced with a difficult decision. They rejected the Fives-Lille as being too ugly, a noteworthy decision given its low cost, although this was thought to be suspiciously cheap. Lecocq's bridge was rejected due to its incoherent appearance. As a virtual copy of Eiffel's Ponte Maria Pia, the Cail design was probably rejected on the basis that Gustave Eiffel had submitted a new design which was likely to be more suitable. John's design, functional rather than graceful, did not find favour.

The final decision seems to have been between designs of Théophile Seyrig and Max am Ende. Ende's bridge impressed the judges with its interesting and original features, but it was one of the two Seyrig bridges, a graceful arch tapering towards the centre of the bridge, which was selected. An advantage of Seyrig's tapered arch was that it facilitated construction with the larger portions of the arch closer to the river banks.

John Dixon's design

Whereas most of the other designs were based on an arch, similar to Eiffel's railway bridge, John's design was more radical. He proposed two huge cantilevers meeting at the centre of the span, each supported by a strut inclined upwards from the river bank and meeting the cantilever about one-third of its distance from the top of the valley side. In design concept it was similar to the Forth Railway Bridge of John Fowler and Benjamin Baker, but with the mid-points of the cantilevers supported by the inclined struts rather than the masonry piers of the Forth Bridge. Fowler and Baker carried out their design work in 1881 with the bridge going out to tender in September 1882, when John submitting one of the bids. So he cannot have taken the form of his Douro bridge from the Forth Bridge design, it must have been his original work. However, it would be stretching matters too far to suggest that the Forth Bridge was based on John's Douro design!

There were two main reasons for the cantilever design; to provide a large span and to ease construction. With his practical experience as a contractor, it was natural that John would concern himself with how to build the bridge. Construction would begin with the struts held in a vertical position by anchor cables. Most of the iron work would then be assembled from each river bank, with a minimum of scaffoldings. By paying out the anchor cables, each half of the bridge would be lowered into position and the two cantilevers joined in the centre of the span.

The Engineer printed a full analysis of the design with the critical calculations, many of which were carried out for John by Henry Reilly, a twenty-six year old civil engineer, from his office in Lonsdale Chambers, Chancery Lane.

The validity of some of the methods used to calculate forces on the bridge

'Dom Luis Bridge, Porto' photograph by Jack Malipan. The elegant design by Théophile Seyrig was a worthy winner of the competition for the River Tagus crossing. John Dixon's design, although easier to construct, was no match for this graceful structure. The two vessels in the foreground used to bring the casks of Douro valley wine down river to the port producers' lodges at Vila Nova de Gaia, on the opposite side of the river from Porto.
© Alamy Images reference DB08FE.

was questioned in two letters to *The Engineer* by a man from Greenock, hiding behind the pseudonym 'A Common Five-Eight' (a term of uncertain origin for the common man). On both occasions Henry Reilly defended his calculations; if his Greenock critic had known that Henry's father, Calcott Reilly, was a professor of civil engineering perhaps he would not have raised his challenges.

The tender

This is the only one of John's tenders where his detailed breakdown of costs has survived:

Preliminary expenses, agency during construction, maintenance for twelve months, interest of guarantee deposit of 5%, bank and finance charges, local fees, &c.	£4,500
Excavation, masonry and concrete in foundations and approaches, construction of roadways and footpaths, flagging and paving	£8,000
Cost of ironwork, ex ship in Oporto, all of quality equal to English Admiralty tests, 3,500 tons at £13	£45,500
Cost of erection, painting and finishing, including use and waste of plant, 3,500 tons at £4 10s.	£15,750
Margin for profit and contingencies	£20,790
Total tendered price	£94,540

The use of costs per ton for the iron work would have been normal practice. There would have been industry norms for these, but with his wide experience of contracting work, John probably used his own values. The allowance for profit and contingencies is interesting, not least because the implied profit is so obviously shown. It would be more usual to include the profit hidden within each item of expenditure. This margin is 28% of the construction cost. Contingencies might normally be expected to be 10% leaving a relatively high profit margin, and one reason why John's tender was one of the most expensive.

Discussion at the Institution of Civil Engineers

In 1881 Théophile Seyrig presented a paper in London on the methods of erecting iron bridges. He described three of the designs submitted for the Douro Bridge, those of Schneider et Cie, John Dixon, and his own design as submitted by Société de Construction et des Ateliers, Willebroek. Seyrig did not believe that working from the river, using pontoons or staging, was at all practicable given the depth of water, shifting sands and changing tides, and so did not favour the Schneider design. He was obviously impressed by John's design, explaining how the bridge was to be built out from each bank, initially as two cantilevers and finally forming an arch as they were lowered into position. His own design was based on the nearby Eiffel railway bridge, but with the method of construction modified by the experience of its construction. Modestly comparing his bridge with the Eiffel bridge, he said 'the form of the new arch might also perhaps be considered more elegant, and to some extent it might be regarded as an improvement.'

It is significant that Seyrig singled out Dixon's design from the twelve entries as being a viable alternative to his own design. John, who was present for the session, was very complimentary about the Eiffel railway bridge, and 'could not but accord to Mr Seyrig, who had had the chief control and design of the entire work, great praise and credit for the manner in which it was carried out.' He went on to say that 'the Institution was greatly indebted to a member of the French engineering profession (which had carried engineering science to a state of such perfection) for coming to England to read a paper on so interesting a subject.'

Construction of Seyrig's winning design

Société de Construction et des Ateliers of Willebroeck began construction of Seyrig's design in November 1881. As with Eiffel's earlier railway bridge, steel cables were taken across the river valley to support the structure as it was assembled, with components for the span being hauled up from barges. The upper deck of the bridge was opened on 1 November 1886, when fifteen to twenty thousand people flooded onto the structure causing considerable oscillation at the centre of the span. Before the lower deck could be completed the abutments of the old suspension bridge had to be demolished, delaying the opening of the new bridge until the following year. The bridge was named Ponte Dom Luis I, although the king himself was not present at the opening ceremonies.

Tolls were charged for traffic over both decks until 1944, and in 2003 the upper deck converted to carry metro trams and pedestrians only.

References

The St Louis Bridge
Engineering, London, 4 October 1872, page 245-7
Cantilever bridge design by Captain James B Eads with construction from overhead cables taken across the river.

Bridge across the Douro - 525 feet span
The Engineer, London, 7 June 1878, page 409
Description and engraving of Eiffel's railway bridge.

The Douro Viaduct
Engineering, London, 7 June 1878, pages 457-8 and double page engraving
Also 14 June 1878, pages 463-4; 21 June 1878, pages 485 and 493-4; 19 July 1878, pages 39 and 58-60
Comprehensive description of Eiffel's railway bridge with details of construction and calculations.

Proposed Road Bridge over the Douro
Engineering, London, 10 September 1880, pages 218-9
Announcement of competition for design.

The Oporto Bridge Competition
Engineering, London, 19 November 1880, page 466
Tenders received were made public at Oporto on 12 November, details of companies and prices.

Foreign Iron and Steel Contracts
The Sheffield Daily Telegraph, 2 December 1880, page 2
List of tenders received for the bridge from their Paris correspondent.

The Proposed New Bridge over the Douro
Engineering, London, 24 December 1880, page 594-5
Good description of entries with illustrations.

Discussion on the Erection of Iron Bridges
Minutes of the Proceedings of the Institution of Civil Engineers, London, Volume 63, January 1881, pages 183-201
Seyrig evaluates three of the designs for the Douro Bridge, including John Dixon's, and John Dixon is complimentary about Seyrig's ability.

The New Bridge over the Douro at Oporto
Engineering, London, 11 February 1881, page 150
Commissioners have decided on Seyrig's design at a cost of £82,000. Final decision was between this design and that of M am Ende of Handysides whose design had some very interesting and original features.

Proposed New Bridge over the Douro
The Engineer, London, 11 March 1881, page 175, illustration page 182
Description of the entries received for the competition to design the Porto bridge.

Proposed New Bridge over the Douro
The Engineer, London, 20 May 1881, page 364-6
Description and calculations for John Dixon's design.

The Theory of Arches exemplified by a design for the bridge over the River Douro
Engineering, London, 3 June 1881, pages 557-8 and 17 June 1881, pages 609-10
Article by Max am Ende based on his design for the Porto bridge.

Letters to the Editor - Proposed Bridge over the Douro
The Engineer, London, 3 June 1881, page 405
'A Common Five-Eight' from Greenock asks questions about the bridge analysis.

Letters to the Editor - The Proposed Bridge over the Douro
The Engineer, London, 10 June 1881, page 427
H Reilly of Lonsdale Chambers refutes the criticism by 'A Common Five-Eight'.

Letters to the Editor - Proposed Bridge over the Douro
The Engineer, London, 24 June 1881, page 459
'A Common Five-Eight' returns to his criticisms, but states he has nothing against the design of the bridge, but he believes the method chosen to analyse the forces (Clark-Maxwell) was inappropriate in this case and should not go unchallenged.

Letters to the Editor - The Proposed Bridge over the Douro
The Engineer, London, 1 July 1881, page 6
H Reilly of Lonsdale Chambers refutes the further criticism by 'A Common Five-Eight' of the validity of his geometric method for analysing the forces on the bridge.

The Luiz I Bridge at Oporto
The Engineer, London, 30 July 1886, page 87
Summary of article in *Memoires de la Société des Ingénieurs-civils*, Paris, 1886 describing the new bridge by T Seyrig.

New Bridge over the River Douro at Oporto
The Graphic, London, 8 January 1887, pages 27 and 30, with engraving on page 29
Opening of the upper deck.

The New Bridge at Oporto
Illustrated London News, 5 March 1887, page 9
Brief description of the bridge.

21 Rebuilding the Solway Viaduct

The Solway viaduct, designed by James Brunlees, carried the railway across the Solway Firth. Its design was, in effect, a very long seaside pier. In 1881 the viaduct was severely damaged when huge ice floes hammered against the cast iron columns supporting the bridge spans. Following an official inquiry, it was rebuilt by John Dixon and Alfred Thorne and re-opened in 1884.

The Solway Junction Railway

The Solway Junction Railway was built to shorten the route from ironstone mines in Cumberland to iron works in Lanarkshire and Ayrshire. The chosen route crossed the Solway Firth on a viaduct about 1¼ miles long which, when it was opened in 1869, was the longest bridge in Europe. James Brunlees was the consulting engineer for the railway, including the viaduct. Already experienced in bridges using cast iron piles to support wrought iron girders, he adopted this principle for the Solway Firth. There were 193 spans, each supported on five cast iron columns driven into the estuary bed. An initial attempt to use screwed piles was abandoned as the estuary bed proved too intransigent, and a steam pile-driver was brought into service. The construction contract for £100,000 was awarded to the Waring Brothers from York, who were experienced railway contractors.

Disaster befalls the viaduct

During the first five years of operation cracks appeared in over thirty-five columns, caused by the freezing of rainwater which had seeped inside. To alleviate this problem, drain holes were drilled through the columns just above the high-water level, although the cracked columns were not replaced. Worse was to follow.

The end of January 1881 saw the start of a thaw after an exceptionally cold period, and the Solway Firth was full of thick ice. On Saturday 29 January three of the outer columns were broken by ice crashing against the bridge, causing a passenger train to be held up for two hours until it was decided that the crossing was safe. Following this incident, the structure was kept under constant observation by John Welch and three watchmen, who sheltered in the small cabin part-way along the viaduct. Early the next morning there was a very high tide. As it began to ebb, great blocks of ice were brought down the estuary. In the darkness the noise of this ice hitting the hollow cast iron columns could be heard from a mile away. Later witnesses described blocks of ice up to twenty yards square and over six feet thick in the water. At 3:00am Welch decided to evacuate the viaduct, and the four men ran across the spans to Bowness. As dawn broke it was apparent that the bridge had suffered serious damage, with many columns swept away although all the spans and the track still remained, some hanging unsupported above the waters. A brave man might have walked across the entire length of the viaduct, but clearly it was impossible to allow trains to cross.

'Engraving from 1865 showing the original viaduct under construction. Reproduced by courtesy of the Cumbrian Image Bank www.cumbrianimagebank.org.uk, reference ct02169.

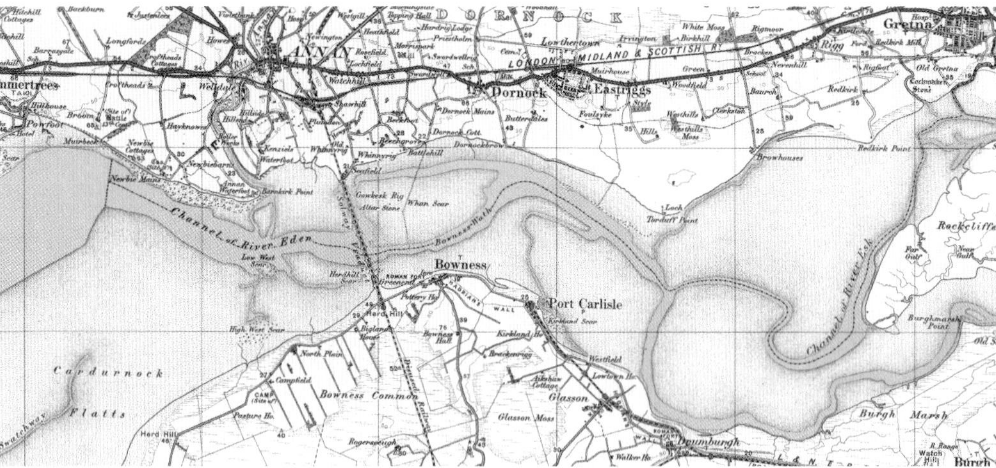

Clockwise from top left:
1) The original columns, all cast iron
Reproduced by courtesy of Peter Burgess, www.cumbria-railways.co.uk

2) Solway Firth Viaduct. Ordnance Survey One Inch Series Revised 1921-22, published 1925, Solway Firth and River Esk, Sheet 89
Reproduced by permission of the National Libraries of Scotland.

3 & 4) Images from 'Book of of Solway Viaduct showing damage in 1881'. One photograph shows the Scotch Gap, with the hanging rail. The other photograph shows the Scotch Gap in the foreground and the wider Cumberland Gap in the distance. The small cabin evacuted by John Welch and the three watchmen is perched on the edge of the Scotch Gap. Reproduced by courtesy of National Records of Scotland, Records of British Railways Board, Solway Junction Railway, Miscellaneous Books and Records, Repository Code 234, reference BR/SJR/4/2. Permission to reproduce given by the Department for Transport under the Open Government Licence.

Extract from 'Plans, elevations and sections showing existing condition of Solway Viaduct and for proposed reconstruction (Solway Junction Railway) 10 December 1881'. Reproduced by courtesy of National Records of Scotland, Records of British Railways Board, Solway Junction Railway, Miscellaneous Books and Records, Repository Code 234, reference RHP49503. Permission to reproduce given by the Department for Transport under the Open Government Licence.

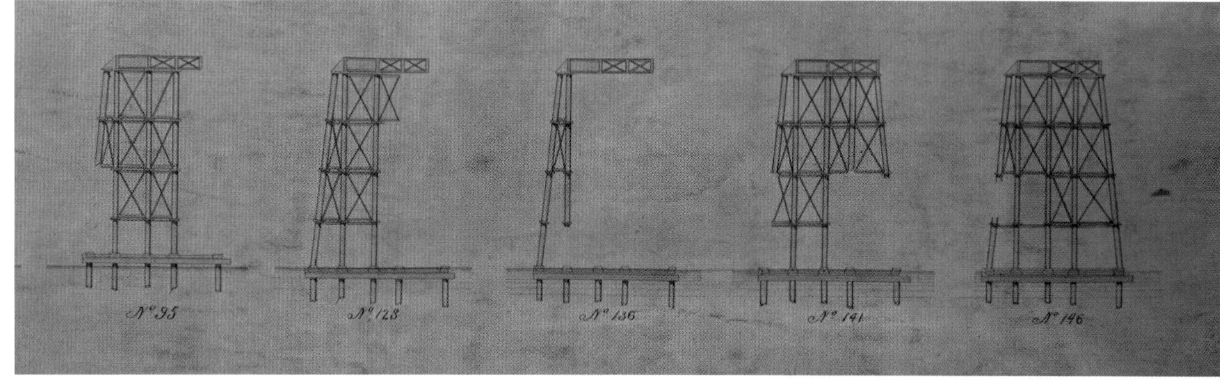

High tides brought more ice to batter the viaduct, which was now hidden in a fog. Just before nightfall on Tuesday the fog lifted to reveal two sections of the structure had been swept away. On the turn of the tide on Thursday it was possible to inspect the viaduct from a boat. Forty-four columns had been lost and in total 340 had been damaged. Immediately adjacent to the watchmen's cabin there was a gap of 150 feet, confirming the wisdom of their decision to run. Referred to as the 'Scotch Gap' all that remained was a length of rail hanging forlornly over the water and the remains of wrecked columns below. Nearer the centre, the 'Cumberland Gap' was 900 feet wide, with no sign of the bridge at all. Alexander McKerrow, James Brunlees son-in-law and business partner at the time, arrived at the scene on Monday 7 February to find that two sections of the viaduct had vanished.

This happened just one year after the failure of the Tay Bridge, and unfortunately Brunlees had described his design as 'exactly that same in construction as the Tay Bridge', the only difference being that the Solway viaduct used cast iron columns, while on the Tay Bridge these were wrought iron. Although there had been no loss of life, the Tay Bridge disaster meant that there was great public disquiet. Questions were asked of Joseph Chamberlain, President of the Board of Trade.

The official inquiry

An official investigation into the failure of the Solway Viaduct was led by the redoubtable Major Marindin. He concluded that the disaster was caused by cumulative shocks inflicted on the columns by pieces of floating ice, at a time when the extreme cold would have made the cast iron very brittle.

Who's who?
Major Marindin (1838-1900)

Francis Arthur Marindin, the son of a clergyman, was born at Weymouth. Following an education at Eton and the Royal Military Academy at Woolwich, he joined the Royal Engineers in 1854. After a distinguished military career, which included service in the Crimean War, Mauritius and Madagascar, in 1860 he married the daughter of his commanding officer in Mauritius. He retired as Major Marindin (by which name he was always known) in 1879 to join the Board of Trade Railway Inspectorate. Later in life he renewed his association with the army and became an honorary colonel. An outstanding footballer, he founded the Royal Engineers' football team, where he was credited with developing the passing game rather than relying on the long-ball or dribbling. He played in the first FA Cup Final in 1872 and was President of the Football Association from 1874 to 1890.

He was renowned for plain-speaking coupled with a complete mastery of his subject. One of his duties in the Railway Inspectorate was to hold inquiries after serious accidents. His strongly-worded report after a guard was crushed to death after being on duty for twenty-two hours led to a House of Commons Select Committee and regulated hours of work for railway employees. On another occasion he instructed the railway companies to install effective signalling equipment to prevent collisions. It was well known that he was not likely to allow irregularities to remain long unnoticed.

Major Marindin acted as one of the inspectors during construction of the Forth Bridge and carried out work for the Egyptian State Railways. He was knighted in 1897.

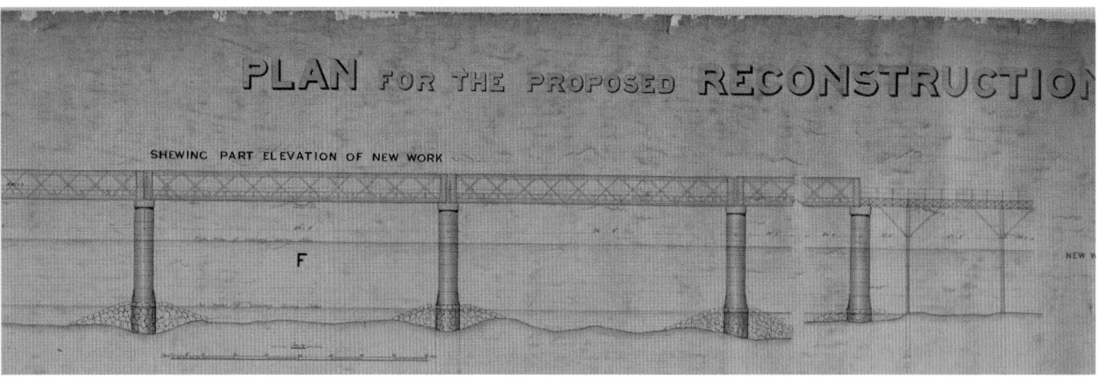

Extract from 'Plans, elevations and sections showing existing condition of Solway Viaduct and for proposed reconstruction (Solway Junction Railway) 10 December 1881' showing the John Strain's proposal for a replacement viaduct. Reproduced by courtesy of National Records of Scotland, Records of British Railways Board, Solway Junction Railway, Miscellaneous Books and Records, Repository Code 234, reference RHP49503. Permission to reproduce given by the Department for Transport under the Open Government Licence.

Marindin wrote that it had been a mistake to position the piers so close together, making the viaduct such an obstacle to ice floes, while acknowledging the unprecedented nature of the ice. It would have been prudent for a designer to assume that the impossible is sure to happen, and should be provided against, although it was easy to be wise after the event. James Brunlees came in for criticism, being compared unfavourably with Robert Stephenson who had taken great care to accommodate floating ice in his design for the St Lawrence Bridge in Canada, although this bridge was supported on masonry piers. But the hostility towards Brunlees was nothing compared to the odium heaped on Thomas Bouch for neglecting to take account of wind pressure in his design for the Tay Bridge. This was understandable as there was no loss of life on the Solway Viaduct, whereas the Tay Bridge claimed up to eighty-five lives (the actual number is still disputed). With their usual cavalier judgements, the public blamed penny-wise pound-foolish policies of engineers and company directors, an attitude which led to the arguable over-engineering of the Forth Railway Bridge.

Major Marindin recognised that cast iron columns were unreliable in situations where they might be exposed to sudden shocks but stopped short of recommending a complete change to wrought iron columns. The inner columns could remain as castings, but the outer columns, known as 'rakers', should be replaced with wrought iron columns filled with concrete. The estimated cost was £30,000.

The Caledonian Railway Company

Financially, the Solway Railway Company was in a sorry state. West Cumberland had started to process its own ironstone, and the Scottish blast furnaces were using imported ore, thus depriving the railway of its primary source of income. And the Caledonian Railway now provided an alternative, inland, route for ironstone up to Scotland via Carlisle. Already unable to pay dividends and interest on its loans, the damage to the viaduct was calamitous for the company. Some shareholders hoped that the company would be taken over by the Caledonian Railway, but not the Solway directors, who appeared incapable of action. The Caledonian directors offered a loan of £30,000 at 4%, but with two conditions which were unacceptable to the Solway directors. Payment of their interest would take precedence over all other Solway shares and debenture, and the North British Railway (a competitor of the Caledonian) was not to be granted running powers over the Solway lines. They then sat back and waited for the Solway board to capitulate. In no mood to give in, the Solway directors obtained authority to raise £30,000 through a share issue, with these shares taking precedence over all existing shares, including £60,000 preference shares held by the Caledonian Railway Company. Naturally, this infuriated the Caledonian directors, who responded with a successful legal challenge. The Solway then won an appeal, the Caledonian took the case to the House of Lords where they ultimately lost in July 1884, two months after the viaduct was re-opened.

National Records of Scotland hold a 'Plan for the Reconstruction of the Solway Viaduct' drawn up by John Strain, a civil engineer based at 154 West George Street, Glasgow, and dated 10 December 1881. This has detailed drawings of the damaged sections of the viaduct and, curiously, a completely different central section with pairs of wrought iron columns, 6 feet in diameter, supporting the spans in place of Brunlees' cast iron piles. Such a design would have cost much more than restoration of the original structure and would have been far beyond the reach of the Solway directors. A possible explanation is that the Caledonian commissioned Strain to survey the damage and suggest a replacement viaduct.

In fact, rebuilding was to be based on restoration of the Brunlees design, but with the outer cast iron columns replaced with wrought iron. No reference to John Strain's alternative design has been found, other than his drawing of 10 December 1881.

Rebuilding the Solway viaduct

John Dixon had been a pioneer of using concrete-filled wrought iron columns in his viaduct designs for the Whitby to Loftus Railway ten years previously. In August 1882 he was given the contract for the rebuilding at a cost of £30,000, and he asked Alfred Thorne to work with him.

Who's who?
Alfred Thorne (1847-1923)

Alfred Thorne was born in Greenock where his father was a wine merchant. He married Fanny Emma Parker in Shropshire in 1874 and moved to London where he started his engineering business. From 1886 to 1912 Alfred and Fanny Thorne lived in a house in Kilburn previously owned by Friedrich Engels, the author with Karl Marx of the Communist Manifesto. Thorne worked with John Dixon on the drainage and water supply schemes in the 1870s in Rio de Janeiro and Campos, and then spent some years working with John at No.1 Laurence Pountney Hill. In late 1877 he was in charge of the fund John had set up for dependents of the six sailors lost at sea when attempting to reach the obelisk vessel *Cleopatra*. Alfred then ran his own civil engineering business in Westminster and was later joined by his son Philip. Alfred and John remained good friends and collaborated on the rebuilding of the Hammersmith Suspension Bridge over the River Thames in 1884-86.

Thorne became a prolific builder of seaside piers, using cast iron columns driven into the sand: Shanklin Pier 1891, Dover Pier 1893, Bangor Pier 1896, Tenby Pier 1899, Cromer Pier 1901 and Cowes Pier in 1902. He also strengthened the cables on Conwy Suspension Bridge in 1903, and built several bridges, including the Newport Transporter Bridge in 1906.

This Thorne family should not be confused with the contractors Peter and Alexander Thorn who built Blackfriars Bridge, opened in 1869.

Top) Recovery of some of the broken castings and dredging operations prior to rebuilding.
Reproduced by courtesy of Peter Burgess www.cumbria-railways.co.uk

Middle) Photograph of a passenger train with three coaches passing over the rebuilt viaduct. Note the new outer columns of wrought iron do not have the flanged joints of the cast iron columns.
Reproduced by courtesy of the Cumbrian Image Bank (www.cumbrianimagebank.org.uk), reference ct00379.

Bottom) Two well-dressed young men waving at a mixed passenger and goods train on the rebuilt viaduct.
Reproduced by courtesy of Peter Burgess www.cumbria-railways.co.uk

It is said that John Dixon arrived at the site at low tide and left some equipment on what he thought would be a safe stretch of shore. When he returned the next morning, everything was buried in wet sand and he had to hire a team of local men to recover it. Having agreed a contract, the men formed a circle round the heap of sand burying the equipment and, to Dixon's amazement, joined hands and began to dance around it. What he perhaps thought was a primitive attempt to engage supernatural assistance was in fact quite logical. By the action of their stamping feet the majority of the moisture was drained away, making the excavation much easier.

Reconstruction began immediately, with the wrought iron girders being salvaged from the estuary for re-use. The outer columns of each set of piers, which would bear the full impact of any ice flows, were formed from a double-skinned tube of wrought iron plate, filled with concrete. These outer columns were each formed by riveting an outer jacket of wrought iron, each side bent outwards to form a vertical flange, around an inner tube. The vertical flanges were orientated so as to present a sharp edge to any ice being carried downstream. Apart from these outer columns, the remainder of the bridge was rebuilt to Brunlees' original design, with the replacement cast iron columns secured onto the stumps of the existing columns with cast iron clips.

Replacement cast iron columns were supplied by Charles I'Anson and Son at the Whessoe Foundry in Darlington. The foundry received orders from Dixon and Thorne in 1882 and 1883, but at the same time Dixon and Thorne were also ordering materials for major works in Brazil so it is not possible to quantify the cost of the columns, which would have been relatively small as only a few of the original columns required replacement.

A large number of workmen were engaged on the work. The contract called for completion by the beginning of September 1883, although there was some initial optimism (it should be said not on the part of Dixon or Thorne) that it might be complete by April. Difficulties with winter weather dashed any hopes of an early completion and it was not until June that the final section of rail track was laid. By August an engine and tender had crossed the rebuilt bridge several times, and Dixon and Thorne met the contract completion date. However, there was an unexpected delay, probably due to the Board of Trade insisting on some modifications, before the viaduct opened for traffic on 1 May 1884 following a final inspection by Major Marindin.

The press complimented John Dixon and Alfred Thorne on their workmanship and timely completion.

What happened to the Solway Viaduct?

Declining traffic, mainly due to foreign imports of iron ore going directly to Scottish ports, caused the closure of the Solway viaduct in 1921. This was much to the annoyance of thirsty residents on the Scottish side who could easily take the train to England on Sundays where public houses were open. In 1934 it was dismantled for scrap. A few remaining piles can be seen at the southern end of the old bridge, now a tourist curiosity.

In 2016 there were proposals to build a new bridge across the Solway Firth, following the route of the viaduct, to carry electricity-generating turbines driven by the tidal flows in the estuary.

'Solway Coast, ruined remains of the Solway Viaduct' photograph by Andrew Finlay. When the viaduct was dismantled in 1934 a few of James Brunlees' cast iron piles were left on the southern shore.
© Alamy Images reference F7R02R

References

Serious damage to the Solway Viaduct
The Scotsman, Edinburgh, 1 February1881, page 3
Description of the damage.

The Solway Firth Viaduct
The Times, London, 1 February 1881, page 10
First reports of damage.

The Solway Firth Viaduct
The Times, London, 2 February 1881, page 10
More damage to the viaduct.

The Solway Firth Viaduct
The Times, London, 4 February 1881, page5
Inspection by boat revealed 44 entire piers gone, over 300 pillars broken, two complete gaps in the viaduct.

The Solway Viaduct
The Engineer, London, 11 February 1881, page 110
Description of the damage to the viaduct with an illustration.

The Solway Firth Viaduct
The Times, London, 1 February 1881, page 10
Opening of the inquiry. Reported that in the winter of 1875 over thirty piles were cracked by frost but were still standing.

Railway Matters
The Engineer, London, 25 February 1881, page 175
Major Marindin opens the inquiry into the failure of the viaduct.

Editorial - The Solway Viaduct
The Engineer, London, 15 April 1881, page 278
The inquiry approves the rebuilding of the viaduct.

Report on the Solway Viaduct Disaster
The Edinburgh Evening News, 18 March 1881, page 3
Major Marindin's report on the cause of the failure of the bridge.

The Accident to Solway Viaduct
Engineering, London, 15 April 1881, page 385
Major Marindin's report issued.

The Solway Viaduct and the Tay Bridge
The Northern Warder and Bi-Weekly Courier and Argus, Dundee, 19 April 1881, page 2
Public hostility towards penny-wise pound-foolish policies of engineers and directors.

The Solway Viaduct
The Carlisle Journal, 25 November 1881, page 4
Solway Railway Company meeting to consider what action to take.

Plan for the Proposed Reconstruction of the Solway Viaduct
John Strain, 154 West George Street, Glasgow,
10 December 1881
National Records of Scotland, Edinburgh, Repository code 234, Reference RHP 49503
Large drawing with detailed drawings of the damage and a replacement central section supported on pairs of wrought iron columns each 6 feet diameter.

Contract for the rebuilding of the Solway Viaduct
The Dundee Advertiser, 4 September 1882, page 6
Mr Dixon, engineering contractor, London, was given the contract for £30,000.

Analysis of orders received 1831-1862 and 1882-1891
Whessoe Records, reference D/Whes 6/50
Durham County Record Office, Durham
Costs of orders received from Dixon and Thorne, but with no identification of individual project.

The Solway Viaduct
The Scotsman, Edinburgh, 5 December 1882, page 3
Progress report on the reconstruction.

The Solway Viaduct
Aberdeen Evening Express, 26 June 1883, page 3
Construction work nearing completion, Board of Trade inspection booked for July.

The Solway Viaduct
The Dundee Advertiser, 29 August 1883, page 6
Completion of the work which 'seems to have been satisfactorily performed.'

Public Companies - Dividends, Reports, and Meetings
The Glasgow Herald, 26 September 1884, page 5
Report on the Solway Railway Company's half-yearly meeting which contains a summary of the legal case brought by the Caledonian Railway Company over the loan for the reconstruction.

Obituary - Sir Francis Marindin
The Times, London, 24 April 1900, page 6

The Solway Junction Railway
John B Howes
Typed manuscript, Jackson Collection,
Carlisle Public Library
Reference Class Number 2B9 SOL 625,
Stock Number 8617
Contains original anecdotes about the damage and how the contractor recovered equipment from the wet sand.

Proposals for the Solway Energy Gateway
http://www.solwayenergygateway.co.uk/
Proposals for a tidal energy generation station along the line of the original viaduct.

22 Forth Railway Bridge tender

The Forth Bridge carrying the London to Inverness railway across the Firth of Forth is one of the most recognisable engineering structures in the world. Its designers, Sir John Fowler and Benjamin Baker, and its principal contractor William Arrol became household names, with Baker and Arrol later receiving knighthoods for their work on the bridge. Fowler had been knighted in 1885, a few years before the bridge was built, for his maps of the Upper Nile. Given different fortunes, John Dixon may well have been part of this illustrious company. In all that has been published on the bridge, there is no mention of John Dixon having submitted the lowest tender for its construction. Possible reasons for his failure to be awarded the contract are considered.

Taking the railway north of Edinburgh

Early railway development north of the border was dominated by two companies, the Caledonian Railway and the North British Railway. The Caledonian started in 1845, laying down a line from Edinburgh, through Glasgow and south to Carlisle where it joined with the London and North Western Railway, now known as the west coast route from London to Scotland. On the east coast, the North British, established in 1844, owned the track from Edinburgh to Berwick-upon-Tweed from where, by 1850, there was a direct line to London. There was a bitter and costly rivalry between the two companies, particularly over routes to the north of Scotland. The Caledonian laid down a track through central Scotland, via Stirling, Perth and Forfar to Aberdeen. A competing route for the North British would have to cross the River Forth and the River Tay. Until this could be done, North British passengers travelling north were at the mercy of the Caledonian directors, who delighted in delaying North British trains using Caledonian lines, or had to take the ferry over the Forth from Granton to Burntisland. The ferry, designed by the young Thomas Bouch when he was still a conscientious engineer, opened in 1850 and was the first roll-on roll-off train ferry. Only goods wagons were transported, with the unfortunate passengers having to leave the train on one shore and board another after the six-mile crossing. Thomas Mackay, in his biography of John Fowler, described the ferry journey as involving 'the most terrible discomfort and inconvenience' and in winter gales it was often impassable.

Proposals for early Forth railway crossings

Histories of the Forth Bridge are sometimes confused about the early bridges. Before the arrival of the railways there had been plans for crossings of the Forth: in 1805 for a tunnel and then, in 1818, for a chain suspension bridge by James Anderson, but both came to nothing. On the latter design Westhofen sarcastically commented that its structure was of 'very light and slender appearance, so light indeed that on a dull day it would have hardly been visible, and after a heavy gale probably no longer to be seen on a clear day either.'

In 1860 the North British Railway Company decided on a bridge between Blackness and Charleston, some six miles west of Queensferry, and obtained the necessary Act of Parliament but then abandoned the idea. The company then considered a train ferry crossing at Queensferry, with floating landing stages rising and falling with the tides, but this was deemed impracticable due to the frequent bad weather.

At the end of 1863, articles appeared in newspapers about two railway bridges across the River Forth, one as part of the proposed Glasgow and North British Railway and one by the newly-formed Forth Bridge Railway Company. Both these enterprises were superficially separate from the North British Railway Company. Each bridge was to be over two miles in length and constructed from lattice girders supported on about fifty piers.

The first was the Stephenson and Tone bridge. In 1862 the chairman of the North British Railway Company had consulted George Robert Stephenson and John Furness Tone, both from Newcastle upon Tyne, as to the practicality of building a bridge across the River Forth. Tone restricted his contribution to soundings taken across the river and setting out the commercial interests of the Scottish railway companies that would benefit from the bridge. Stephenson designed the bridge and prepared estimates of cost. George Robert Stephenson (1819-1905) was the son of George Stephenson's younger brother, Robert. He worked as an assistant engineer for his uncle George and then for his cousin Robert, becoming a managing partner in the Forth Street Works in 1859. John Furness Tone (1822-1881) worked for the North British Railway Company but also had many other business activities in railways, docks and waterworks, as well as owning coal mining, coking, and brick making businesses. He was bankrupt in 1869. The design of the bridge is often credited to 'the engineering firm of Stephenson and Toner' but, quite apart from the almost universal yet incorrect spelling of Tone's name, Stephenson and Tone only worked together on the design of the bridge and were not an established engineering partnership in their own right. Incidentally, Tone had been a pupil at Dr Bruce's Academy in Newcastle at the same time as Bruce's son, George Barclay Bruce, who would later be the consulting engineer on the Rio Tinto railway and John Dixon's ore-loading terminal in the 1870s.

In December 1863 the Stephenson and Tone bridge was incorporated in proposals for a new Glasgow and North British Railway, which was supposedly independent of the North British Railway Company although it must have been created with their full knowledge, possibly on account of the parlous state of the North British Railway and its anxious shareholders.

Quite separately, the Forth Bridge Railway Company was set up at the end of 1863 to build a new railway between the existing lines of the Edinburgh and Glasgow Railway at Pardovan and the North British Railway at Charlestown, on the north banks of the Forth. The company recognised that it would need to reach agreements with the Edinburgh and Glasgow, the North British and the Caledonian. Unlike the rival Stephenson and Tone bridge, there does not appear to have been any detailed design work done for this bridge.

There was the inevitable opposition to both bridges from Scottish railway companies and river navigation interests, while the North British Railway Company was ambivalent. The matter was considered at a special meeting of shareholders on 20 May 1864. It was certain that Parliament would not sanction both bridges and, while there was general enthusiasm for a Forth Railway Bridge, it was decided to wait and see which scheme would be favoured by Parliament. Events took a surprising turn; the Forth Bridge Railway Bill was withdrawn and the Edinburgh and Glasgow Railway and the North British Railway virtually merged, with plans for their own bridge, rendering the plans of the Glasgow and North British Railway obsolete.

North British Railway plans for a crossing at Queensferry and then Alloa

The North British Railway Company engaged Thomas Bouch to design their bridge across the Firth of Forth at Queensferry. Bouch proposed a similar design to that of Stephenson and Tone, with wrought iron girders supported on sixty-one piers of cast iron columns rising from a masonry base. The spans would rise towards the centre of the bridge, where the four longest spans, each 500 feet length, would provide a clearance of 125 feet above water level. While the construction of the bridge above the river level was conventional, apart from its sheer size, designing suitable foundations for the piers was a different matter, particularly for the five central piers that supported the longest spans. Investigation of the river bed had revealed up to 120 feet of silt over the bedrock. Bouch believed that, given sufficient loading area, masonry foundations could be built directly on the silt. His first attempt to settle a caisson in the silt of the river bed, in November 1864, failed. He then decided to construct a huge timber raft which would be floated out into the river where the combined weight of a caisson and 10,000 tons of pig iron would settle the raft on the river bed. Working inside the caisson, a masonry base would then be built on the raft. When it was complete the caisson and pig iron would be removed and used on the next pier. The prototype raft was constructed seven miles downstream, at Burntisland, on the north bank of the estuary, and was launched on 14 June 1866 amid great celebrations.

Celebrations were short-lived, for the raft never left its moorings at Burntisland. The enfeebled finances of the company could no longer support its heavy capital expenditure and, by the end of the year, the chairman and entire board had resigned. There followed two years of near bankruptcy, but by 1869 the new directors were prepared to think again about a Forth crossing. Nervous at the challenges of the Queensferry route, their first thoughts were for a bridge at Alloa, seventeen miles upstream of Queensferry. Optimistically they thought that the townsfolk of Alloa might raise most of the required capital, and the bridge foundations could rest on solid boulder clay. Thomas Bouch designed a bridge 500 yards long, with its two central spans swinging open to allow passage of shipping. It didn't take long for the directors to realise that the Alloa crossing was far from ideal, and in any case Alloa had only been able to raise £35,000 of the required £55,000, so the idea was dropped. Although Bouch's swing bridge was never built, a similar swing bridge was constructed by the Caledonian Railway and opened in 1885.

Back to the Queensferry crossing

By late autumn 1872 the North British Railway Company was widely reported to be seriously considering a railway bridge at Queensferry. Recognising that they would never be able to finance the work on their own, the old Forth Bridge Railway Company was reformed, with the Forth Bridge Railway Act, 5 August 1873, establishing the company as a sometimes-uneasy alliance between four railway companies (North British, Midland, North Eastern and Great Northern) who stood to benefit from the bridge. The North British shareholders, aware that they were already financing the construction of the Tay Bridge, sought assurances from the directors who were disingenuous to say the least, claiming that shareholders would be liable for not one shilling of the expense. In reality, the company had already pledged up to £100,000 for the Forth Bridge and had engaged and been paying Thomas Bouch for design work. A Parliamentary Bill was drawn up and started its progress through the House of Commons, surviving opposition from only the Caledonian Railway Company, and being passed in August 1873.

While the Bill was going through Parliament, Thomas Bouch had been exercised by the problem of achieving secure foundations on the river bed silt. His solution, unveiled just as the Parliamentary Bill passed into law, was little short of a sensation. Two suspension bridges of 1,500 feet span were to be constructed either side of the island of Inchgarvie, with towers 600 feet high carrying the suspension cables, which were to be of steel. By this time steel was replacing wrought iron for structural purposes but had yet to achieve a consistent quality. Thomas Bouch's brave design won general approval, even admiration, from the engineering establishment.

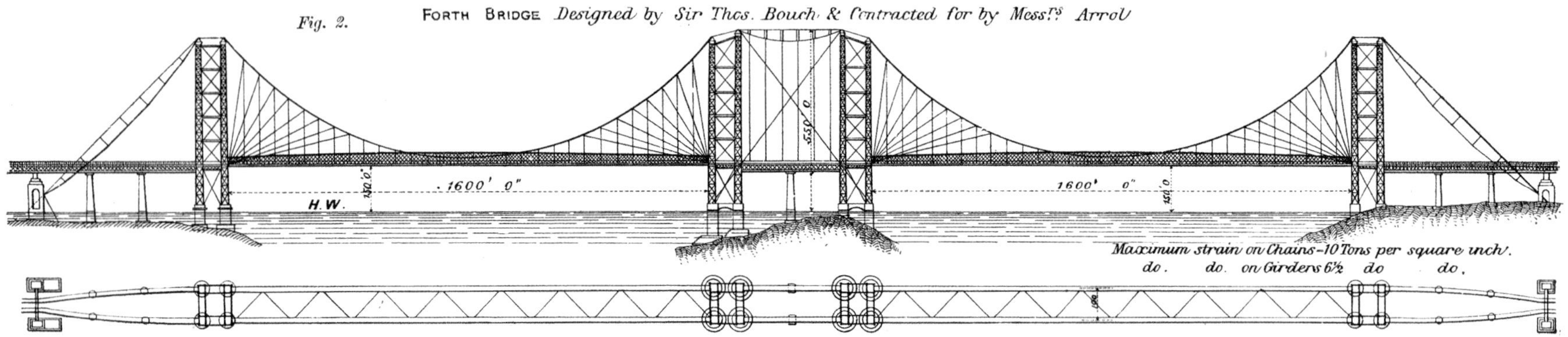

Thomas Bouch's mighty design for double suspension bridge across the Firth of Forth. Hailed as a masterpiece until the Tay Bridge disaster. Engineering, London, 28 February 1890, page 4, figure 2.

With the 1873 Act passed, a second Bill appeared that November, giving the North British a leading role in the work. Once again, the shareholders were wary, and arguments broke out between the board and a substantial number of shareholders, at which point the chairman walked out, followed by the other directors. The Bill was temporarily withdrawn, and was followed by a succession of reworked Bills, but there was no doubt that the North British was directing all aspects of the new bridge apart from the raising of capital. Meanwhile the contractors on the Tay Bridge abandoned the work over rapidly rising costs, leading to Bouch engaging Hopkins Gilkes and Company of Middlesbrough. Edgar Gilkes had previously worked for Bouch on railway viaducts. Hopkins Gilkes would later shoulder much of the blame for the Tay Bridge collapse. With the completion of the Tay Bridge and the final Forth Bridge Railway Bill successfully through Parliament, in the summer of 1878 the North British directors could turn their attention to constructing their bridge.

Laying the foundation stone

Published and internet sources are confused over the laying of the foundation stone for Thomas Bouch's suspension bridge, variously quoting 1873, 1878 or 1879. As can be seen from the many contemporary newspaper accounts, it took place in 1878. Possibly some authors thought that the foundation stone could not have been laid until after the design had been finalised and contractors appointed, which was ten months later in the summer of 1879. The date of 1873 may just be a poorly printed 1878. As it happens, the laying of the foundation stone was purely a technical move to comply with a requirement from the Forth Bridge Railway Act that work had to start by 1 October 1878. Because of this, and perhaps wishing to avoid the premature jubilation which accompanied the launch of Thomas Bouch's last attempt to build a bridge at Queensferry, the laying of the foundation stone was a low-key affair.

In deteriorating weather on the morning of 30 September 1878, boats took sixty or so people from South Queensferry across to the island of Inchgarvie. The proceedings were led by contractor John Waddell who was a director of the Forth Bridge Company. Apart from Waddell there were no directors of either the North British or Forth Bridge Railway companies present. An introduction by Waddell was followed by a touching prayer for the success of the bridge, whereupon Mrs Bouch laid the foundation stone with a silver trowel. After cheers for Mr and Mrs Bouch, the two companies and Waddell himself, the party retreated to the Hawes Inn for lunch. The whole event had taken barely fifteen minutes, lunch took considerably longer.

The year after the laying the foundation stone

In September 1878 the Board of Trade examined the plans for the huge twin suspension bridge. Thomas Bouch's request for a reduction in the clearance for shipping from 150 feet to 135 feet was turned down, but permission was given to increase the length of the suspended spans from 1,500 feet to 1,600 feet. He had wanted these changes to reduce the cost of the bridge by a claimed £30,000 but at the hearing he was vague as to details, even admitting that he had forgotten how he had arrived at cost estimates. For those who cared to listen, this was further evidence of how Thomas Bouch might be good at concepts but had a poor grasp of details, an ominous portent indeed.

Thomas Bouch finalised his design by August 1879 and at the half-yearly meeting of the Forth Bridge Railway Company on 6 August 1879 it was announced that plans and specifications had been completed. The company did not advertise for tenders but invited six contractors of acknowledged standing to submit offers, which the directors opened on 1 September. The Forth Bridge Railway directors then held many meetings behind the closed doors of the North British Railway offices and, a month later, announced that the whole of the work would be undertaken by William Arrol and Company of Glasgow for £880,529, with the exception of the steel chains which would be supplied by Vickers and Son of Sheffield for £205,000. By this time Arrol had built up a high reputation as an effective and innovative contractor.

Following the laying of the foundation stone, John Waddell was instructed to continue masonry work at Inchgarvie up to the high-water mark since all the measurements for the structure would be taken from a datum on Inchgarvie. This work was never put out to tender; remember that John Waddell was a director of the Forth Bridge Railway Company. Waddell went on to construct the approach lines and the whole of the masonry for a cost of £239,381 apparently without having had to submit a competitive tender for the work. By April 1879 he had started work on one of the central towers.

The total cost was to be just over £1.12 million, with an estimated construction time of six or seven years. At last work could start. In February 1880 Arrol started to build his workshops on land next to the Hawes Inn at Queensferry and to recruit his workforce, expected to be about 400 men.

It was one thing to secure the foundation stone for Bouch's Forth Bridge, but quite another to secure the capital required, particularly in light of the continuing suspicions of the North British shareholders. In December 1879 the Forth Bridge Railway Company sent 70,000 letters to the shareholders in its four constituent railway companies, and issued a prospectus to raise £1.25 million, mostly from £10 shares with a guaranteed 5% dividend. There was still great enthusiasm for the bridge except among some disgruntled North British Railway shareholders. On 26 December 1879 *The Times* commented 'vast as the undertaking seems, there is every reason to have confidence in its practicability' and went on to say:

> 'The engineer is Sir Thomas Bouch, C.E., whose greatest achievement hitherto, the Tay Bridge, has turned out a splendid success, a success recognized and endorsed in the honour of a knighthood awarded to him on its completion.'

Two days later, about 7:20pm on Sunday 28 December while a train was passing through the central section, the Tay Bridge collapsed in high winds. It was the longest bridge in the world, nearly two miles from shore to shore. Its single track was carried on eighty-five lattice girders, supported on vertical cast iron columns. The bridge had been officially opened in May 1878, and the royal train took Queen Victoria across the following year. Victoria expressed her delight with the structure by conferring a knighthood on its designer. Although Sir Thomas Bouch was seen as the foremost bridge designer at that time, John Fowler had never trusted the Tay Bridge and forbade his family from using it. He was very critical of the narrow base of its columns and commented, while visiting a Holbein exhibition including the famous portrait of Henry VIII, that if Bouch had given his bridge the 'Holbein straddle' it would be still standing.

With over seventy people meeting their deaths in the icy waters of the 'Silv'ry Tay' as immortalised by William McGonagall's poem, the apparent

Who's who?
William Arrol (1839-1913)

William Arrol was probably the most respected of the Victorian engineering contractors, and an outstanding example of how it was possible to rise from the lower levels of society to the very top. He left school before he was ten to work as a thread boy in a cotton mill. Four years later he managed to obtain an apprenticeship with a blacksmith and attended night classes in mechanics and hydraulics. In the years immediately after his apprenticeship it was difficult to obtain a steady job, and Arrol spent several years travelling round the south west of Scotland in search of work. Then, in his early twenties, he was taken on as foreman at Laidlaw's engineering works in Glasgow. Here he gained sufficient experience in building iron bridges to allow him to start his own business in 1868. Surviving initial financial difficulties, he built up his reputation and opened his Dalmornock Works in 1872. He always applied his inventive mind to improving working processes, notably designing a hydraulic riveting machine which rapidly gained widespread use. He had started building Thomas Bouch's suspension bridge across the Firth of Forth when Bouch's Tay Bridge fell down, resulting in the abandonment of the Forth Bridge. But by 1882 he had the contract for the two most famous bridges in the world at the time, the replacement Tay Bridge and the cantilever Forth Bridge.

Arrol's commitment to his work is shown by his typical week. He would be up by 5:00am on Monday and at the Dalmornock Works by 6:00am. Then he took the 8:45am train to Edinburgh to check progress on the Forth Bridge. On Tuesday evening he went by train to Dundee to be at the Tay Bridge site by 6:00am on Wednesday morning. Back home to Glasgow on Wednesday evening, he would be at the Forth and Tay sites on Thursday and Friday before travelling by sleeper to London ready for meetings with the engineers of both bridges on Saturday. Another overnight train took him back to Glasgow where he would be at the Presbyterian Church service on Sunday, taking the collection.

In 1890 William Arrol was knighted for the Forth Bridge work and he became MP for South Ayrshire 1895-1906. Sir William Arrol and Company continued in business until 1969 when it was acquired by Clarke Chapman.

invincibility of Victorian engineering was shattered. Sir Thomas Bouch and two of the Middlesbrough suppliers of materials to the bridge were ruined; Bouch himself died ten months after the disaster.

The suspension bridge abandoned

At first the Forth Bridge Railway directors seem to have been oblivious of the impact the Tay Bridge disaster would have on their own structure which, after all, was a different design using different materials of construction. Two weeks after the event they calmly signed the contracts for the construction of Thomas Bouch's giant suspension bridge. Bouch saw this a good time to again raise the possibility of lowering the spans by ten or fifteen feet, a proposal originally rejected by the Board of Trade. William Arrol was in no doubt about the future of the suspension bridge, ordering 10,000 tons of Bessemer steel plates from Krupp at Essen having rejected English suppliers, probably because he could not rely on them to turn out steel of a consistent quality.

Other engineers were more cautious. An *Engineering* editorial, 6 February 1880, accused the directors of being less than honest with potential shareholders. Virtually nothing had been stated about the potential difficulties in building such a huge structure. The risks had never been set out in terms which 'a country parson and the usual run of shareholders could understand' and the directors' apparent guaranteed dividend was based on expected traffic once the bridge had been completed. Of the directors it was said that 'like smart men of business they quietly transfer all the risk and responsibility to the shoulders of the unsuspecting country parson and his companions.' In the next issue, the editor cast serious doubts on the practicalities of building the bridge and its stability on a gale, and also claimed that several eminent bridge-builders had declined to build the bridge. This probably explains why there was no tendering process.

The Board of Trade Inquiry into the Tay Bridge collapse ran from January to June 1880. Once again Thomas Bouch was ill-prepared and vague in his evidence, especially as to whether he had made an adequate allowance for wind pressure. With somewhat diminished confidence, the Forth Bridge Railway Company directors nevertheless decided to continue with the construction of Bouch's suspension bridge, but to place a limit of £25,000 on expenditure.

Early 1880 saw two alternative designs emerge for the Forth crossing; Max am Ende proposed a steel arched bridge, Andrew Barclay a variation on the cantilever principle. Ende had two arches, one on each side of Inchgarvie, each one remarkably similar to the 20th century Newcastle Tyne Bridge or Sydney Harbour Bridge. Andrew Barclay proposed a cantilever design, with much in common with modern cable-stayed bridges, such as the new Forth Road Bridge. Nothing more was heard of either design.

Belatedly, the inevitable happened at the half-yearly meeting of the Forth Bridge Railway Company shareholders on 13 January 1881. In 1873 the directors had been assured by eminent civil engineers that Bouch's design was safe, even in high winds. Now the directors had asked for a revised opinion, but this was declined. It was also feared that it might not be possible to produce a design which would satisfy the new Board of Trade requirements for such bridges. Apparently Bouch had changed his previous specification for the towers from wrought iron to cast iron, the material implicated in the Tay Bridge failure. Work on the mighty suspension bridge would be abandoned and the contractors paid off. John Waddell was re-elected as a director at the same meeting.

In spite of the directors' claim that they had settled with William Arrol, this was not true. He was forced into legal action to secure sufficient funds to save him from bankruptcy, resulting in a payment of £27,500 with release from sub-contractor's claims and compensation for all on site materials. The £27,500 was subject to conditions, 40% was to be treated as on account should he obtain the contract for a replacement Tay Bridge and 35% similarly for a replacement Forth Bridge. This 35% (£9,625) would be critical when the tenders for the new cantilever bridge were considered. The suppliers of the approach girders, P and W McLellen, settled but compensation for Vickers at Sheffield went to arbitration. Sir Thomas Bouch had died in October 1880. His executors optimistically claimed £31,157 from the Forth Bridge Railway Company but settled for £16,144.

The cantilever bridge arrives

Hardly surprisingly, there was talk of winding up the Forth Bridge Railway Company, and a bill was drawn up to obtain the necessary Parliamentary approval for the abandonment. But the railway companies supporting the scheme were more resolute, and asked their respective engineers, William Henry Barlow for the Midland, Thomas Harrison for the North Eastern and John Fowler for the Great Northern, to consider whether it was feasible to build a railway bridge across the Firth of Forth to the new requirements of the Board of Trade, either by modifications to the Bouch plans or by an alternative design.

Thought of modifying the Thomas Bouch design was rejected, not because of the notoriety by then attaching to his name, but because of the additional cost. Alan Stewart, who had done the original calculations, redesigned the structure with an estimated of £700,000 to sufficiently strengthen the bridge. The three engineers then came up with four possibilities: three suspension bridges and a 'continuous girder' bridge (later referred to as a cantilever bridge). William Barlow would have preferred a tunnel, in spite of his 1858 patent for a bridge based on a girder suspended from cantilevers, the basic design of the future Forth Bridge. His tunnel was easily rejected because of the inordinately long approaches necessary to reach the required depth. Although the modified Bouch design had been dismissed, the three suspension bridges all generally followed his concept, with twin spans either side of a central tower on Inchgarvie, but with towers of masonry rather than iron. However, it became clear that the cantilever bridge would be superior in terms of strength and cost. Initial estimates were £1,365,000 compared with the suspension bridges' £1,646,000 to £1,827,000. Barlow suggested modifying Fowler's outline design, replacing angled struts in the towers carrying the cantilevers with vertical columns and lengthening the cantilevers, thus reducing the length of the spans between the ends of the cantilevers. Barlow's modifications produced a more aesthetically pleasing structure, demonstrating the old engineering adage 'if it looks right it probably is right.'

Having reported this to the four railway companies, Harrison, Fowler and Barlow were asked to submit a design of a bridge and take the necessary steps to obtain the approval of the Board of Trade and Admiralty. It was agreed that the detail design should be entrusted to John Fowler and Benjamin Baker. Fowler was said to be 'about the ablest engineer they had in the kingdom' and 'if anyone could build a bridge which would be as permanent and endure as long as the railways endured, it was Mr Fowler'.

At a historic meeting of the Forth Bridge Railway Company, held on 30 September 1881 in Edinburgh, it was unanimously agreed to build a steel cantilever bridge to the design of Fowler and Baker, with double railway tracks. The cost was then expected to be £1,550,000 (the final cost of the Forth Railway Bridge was over £3 million). The bill to abandon the bridge was withdrawn, but by now the Forth Railway Bridge Company had run out of capital.

A new bill was submitted to parliament, approved and in September 1882 notices were posted in the press inviting tenders for the new bridge. John Dixon would have seen this as an irresistible opportunity to end his career with what was clearly destined to become one of the world's greatest bridges. Before deciding to submit a tender he probably discussed the matter with his old friend James Brunlees. Dixon had worked with Brunlees on the piers at Southport and Llandudno and had reconstructed the Solway Viaduct originally designed by Brunlees. James Brunlees had submitted a plan for rebuilding the Tay Bridge using some of the existing piers with the addition of angled columns in much the same way as the Solway Viaduct had been rebuilt. Although this had been rejected it meant that James Brunlees would have current experience of the problems of constructing large bridges across Scottish estuaries for railway companies.

Tenders received

On 19 October 1882 the directors of the Forth Bridge Railway Company met at Westminster, probably in John Fowler's offices, to consider the six replies to their invitation to tender for the bridge. The only surviving evidence of the individual tenders is a small hand-written note buried in the Minute Book of the Forth Bridge Railway Company:

John Dixon	£1,487,000 (including £18,000 for plant)
William Arrol & Co	£1,548,640 (including £10,000 for plant)
Falkiner & Tancred	£1,600,000 (including £3,000 for plant)
Vernon & Ewens	£1,923,000 (including £10,000 for plant)
A Handyside & Co	£2,301,760 (including £8,500 for plant)
Westwood & Baillie	£1,529,800

Presumably the tenders quote plant costs as these would have a resale value at the end of the project. In a paper read to the British Association in the autumn of 1884, Benjamin Baker said that the tenders had ranged from £1,487,000 to £2,301,760, which is in agreement with the above list.

Looking at the list it appears that few of the engineering contractors were brave enough to bid. The task was formidable. In terms of its cantilever design, its use of steel plate and its sheer size, it was unprecedented. In addition to the engineering challenges this project would make or break the reputation of any contractor. It would be the sixth railway bridge planned across the Forth, and the third at Queensferry, with the anxious shareholders, the local and national press and engineers around the world at large taking a close interest in the work. Most of all, it would have to exorcise the ghost of the Tay Bridge.

It is worth considering the relative merits of the six tenderers. Westwood, Baillie and Company were boilermakers, bridge and ship builders with premises at London Yard on the Isle of Dogs. They had successfully built railway bridges and would appear to have been capable of taking on the Forth Bridge, but their tender was on the condition that it was for the supply of materials only and was to be subject to the rise and fall in the iron and steel market. As such it was hardly worthy of serious consideration.

William Arrol's workshops, built next to the Hawes Inn at Queensferry for the Thomas Bouch suspension bridge, were now idle and he was being paid a retainer to keep them available for the new bridge. Not only that, £9,625 of his settlement after the suspension bridge was cancelled was to be payment on account should he get the contract (although this was hardly significant when compared with the overall cost of the bridge). In October 1881 Arrol had signed the contract for the replacement Tay Bridge, and was making an excellent impression on the Forth Bridge Railway directors. Clearly he was a preferred contractor.

Travers Hartley Falkiner had worked on railways in Ireland and Europe before being appointed consulting engineer to the government of New

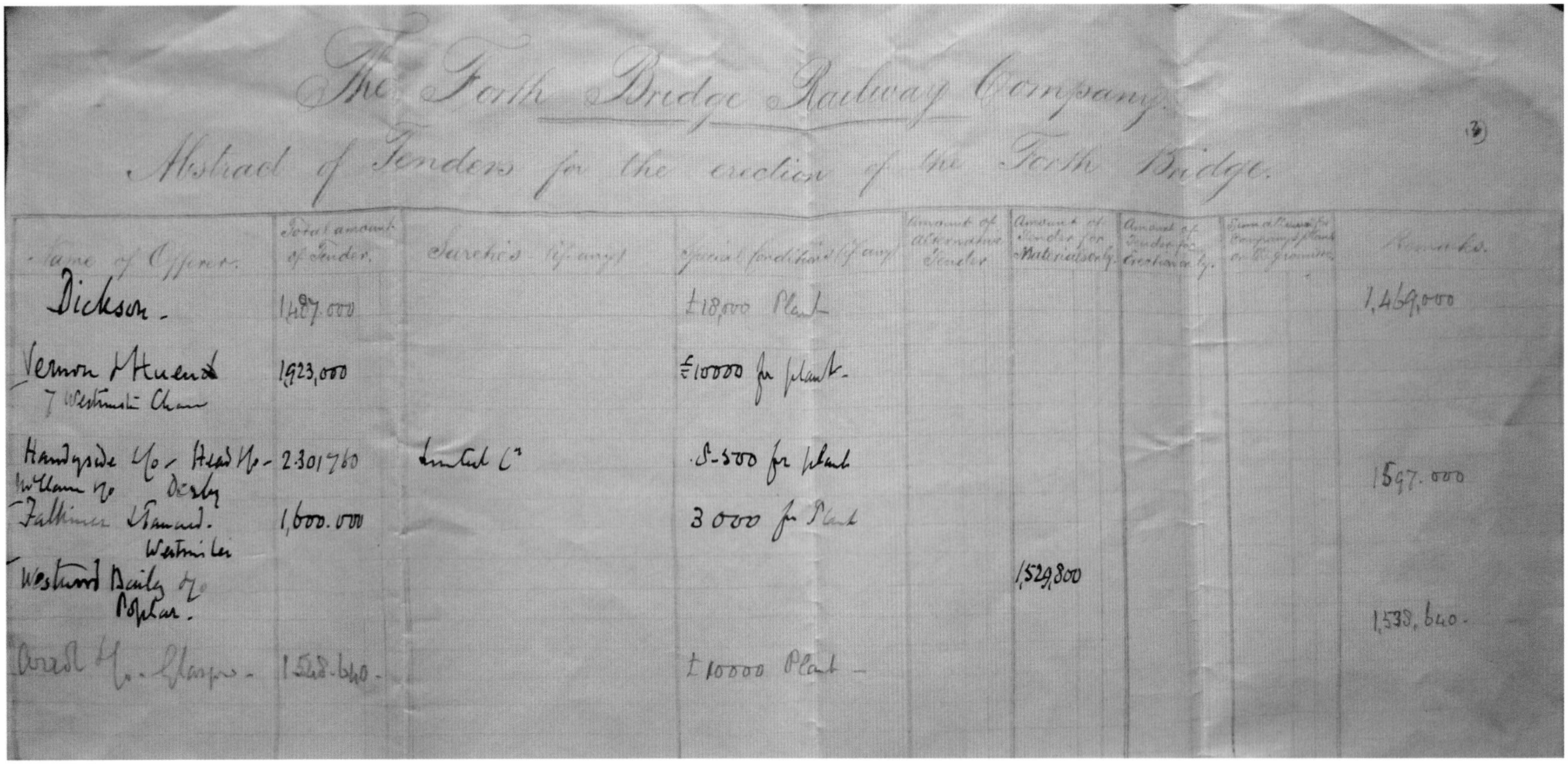

The Forth Bridge Railway Company

Abstract of Tenders for the erection of the Forth Bridge.

(3)

Name of Offerer	Total amount of Tender	Sureties (if any)	Special conditions (if any)	Amount of Alternative Tender	Amount of Tender for Materials only	Amount of Tender for Erection only	Sum allowed for Company's plant on the ground	Remarks
Dickson.	1,487.000		£18,000 Plant					1,469,000
Vernon & Ewens 7 Westminster Cham	1923,000		£10000 for plant.					
Handyside Co. Head Off. Derby William Co	2301760	Limited Co	5-500 for plant					1597.000
Falkiner & Tancred. Westminster	1,600.000		3000 for Plant					
Westwood Baily & Co. Poplar.					1,529,800			1,538,640.
Arrol & Co. Glasgow.	1,528.640.		£10000 Plant					

Tender list clearly showing John Dixon had submitted the lowest tender (unfortunately the spelling of his name is incorrect, it certainly wasn't John Dickson). This was with the Minutes of the Meeting of the Forth Bridge Railway Company held on 19 October 1882 at Westminster. It is significant that this information was written on a loose piece of paper, and not in the official minutes.
Reproduced by courtesy of National Records of Scotland, General Register House, Princes Street, Edinburgh, reference BR/FOR/4/3.
Permission to reproduce given by the Department for Transport under the Open Government Licence.

Zealand, where he worked closely with George Bruce (later to be the engineer for the Rio Tinto mine railway and John Dixon's ore-loading terminal) and Sir Thomas Selby Tancred. Sir Thomas Tancred (his title was inherited and owed nothing to his engineering career) also worked on railway projects before meeting up with Falkiner in New Zealand. Falkiner and Tancred then returned to England and formed an engineering contracting business in the 1870s, predominantly on railway construction including working for John Fowler. Although they enjoyed a good reputation, they had little experience of building large bridges. Also, their tender, a round £1,600,000 gives the impression that they had not carried out any detailed examination of the work involved, whereas the other tenders look to have been assembled from more detailed work.

Vernon and Ewens started in business at the Central Ironworks in Cheltenham, where they manufactured boilers and steam engines. Later they branched out into construction, based in Liverpool. They completed several railway stations but their only experience relevant to the Forth Bridge seems to have been erecting the large roof of the Bishopsgate Goods Depot along with other iron roofs. Their unsuitability was illustrated two years later when they had to abandon work on the rebuilding of the Hammersmith suspension bridge, see Chapter 23.

Andrew Handyside and Company of the Britannia Ironworks in Derby were involved in a wide range of engineering activities from casting pillar boxes to building steam engines and bridges. The company had many years' experience of bridge building, both in Britain and abroad, including the Albert Suspension Bridge at Chelsea and large railway bridges in Australia and South Africa. The company may have been a serious contender but had by far the highest cost.

Finally, to John Dixon. John Fowler and Benjamin Baker were familiar with his record of successful international projects and he had submitted the lowest tender.

The rejection of John Dixon's tender

In spite of most authors claiming that William Arrol submitted the lowest tender, it was definitely John Dixon. He would surely have been seen as eminently qualified by virtue of his previous work. Yet the decision from the meeting at Westminster was an instruction to John Fowler to see if a combination of Arrol with Falkiner and Tancred could be arranged in the event of the Board deciding to let the whole work in one contract.

It would have made sense to engage two contractors on such a large project, particularly as William Arrol was already occupied on the Tay Bridge. But why choose Falkiner and Tancred ahead of John Dixon? One explanation lies in John's obituary, from the Proceedings of the Institution of Civil Engineers, which was probably written by Baker (he would have been one of the few people who knew of John's tender):

> 'Mr. Dixon's personal qualifications were those which go to the making of a great contractor. Original in conception as regards the practical carrying out of works, and guarded by his engineering training against mistakes of a theoretical nature, he faced difficulties with a light heart and found them but a stimulant to greater efforts. He tendered for the construction of the Forth Bridge, and was quite prepared to undertake that work single-handed, but the directors did not deem it prudent to entrust it to any one man.'

The excuse about undertaking the work single-handed does not stand up because the directors wanted two contractors involved, even in the case of William Arrol. Possible concerns about John's health can probably be discounted. The first reports of his failing health do not appear until 1888, but it is perhaps significant that for his last project, the rebuilding of Hammersmith suspension bridge tendered for in 1884, he worked with two partners. Age was not an issue; John was forty-seven, Arrol was forty-three, Falkiner was fifty-three and Tancred was forty-two.

A more likely factor is the assessment of John's competence. Thomas Harrison, chief engineer of the North Eastern Railway, was one of the engineers advising the Forth Railway Bridge Board. Harrison had taken over management of the construction of the Whitby to Loftus railway line

'Scotland for your Holidays' British Railways 1952 poster featuring a painting by Terence Cuneo. The title is somewhat ironic as the A4 60031 Golden Plover is hauling a south-bound express towards England. The construction of the bridge is clearly visible.
Reproduced by permission of the Cuneo Estate and the National Railway Museum (Science and Society Picture Library). NRM reference 1979-7908 BR(ScR).

in 1875 and inspected the viaducts, which had been designed by Dixon. He was very critical of their construction, although this was arguably more to do with shortcomings in the contractor rather than in the design. Nevertheless, Thomas Harrison would have questions in his mind about John's competence, which he would have passed on to his fellow engineers, if not the Forth Railway Bridge Board. Balanced against Harrison's opinions would be the (probable) favourable opinions of Benjamin Baker and John Fowler. Baker had worked closely with John Dixon on the project to bring Cleopatra's Needle to London, fabricating the iron vessel used to transport the obelisk and assisting John in its erection on the Embankment. From 1869 Fowler had worked with Baker on various civil engineering schemes in Egypt, including the construction of the first Aswan Dam, and he would be acquainted with John and Waynman's work in Egypt.

Awarding the contract

At the Board Meeting following the opening of tenders, held in Leeds on 4 November 1882, the minutes record that:

> 'With reference to the Minute of the last Board Meeting instructing Mr Fowler to communicate with Messrs Falkiner Tancred & Phillips and Messrs William Arrol & Company a joint tender by these firms offering to construct the bridge for the sum of £1,600,000 was submitted by Mr Fowler as the result of that communication and it was resolved to accept this tender ...'

The contract was signed on 21 December 1882. Falkiner and Tancred had now been joined by Joseph Phillips. Joseph Phillips (1828-1905) had a long career, first as a professional engineer and then as a contractor, and a first-class reputation as a builder of bridges. He had previously worked with Tancred and was entrusted with much of the detailed work on the bridge. His son kept a photographic record of the construction work. Falkiner left Tancred and Phillips in 1886. This time the steel was to come from Britain rather than Germany, with the Steel Company of Scotland supplying the steel plates.

Construction of the cantilever bridge

The construction of the Forth Railway Bridge and its subsequent history has been well chronicled elsewhere, particularly by Wilhelm Westhofen, and with John Dixon not involved with the enterprise little more need be written here. There is however one small contribution John made to the Forth Bridge. During construction, temporary tie bars were fixed between the vertical columns and the lower tubes of the cantilevers. These temporary tie bars consisted of the old wrought iron suspension links removed from the Hammersmith Suspension Bridge during its rebuilding in 1884-87. The main contractor for this rebuilding had been John Dixon.

The Forth Railway Bridge was opened on 4 May 1890, when John only had only nine months to live. Whether he ever saw the completed bridge is not known.

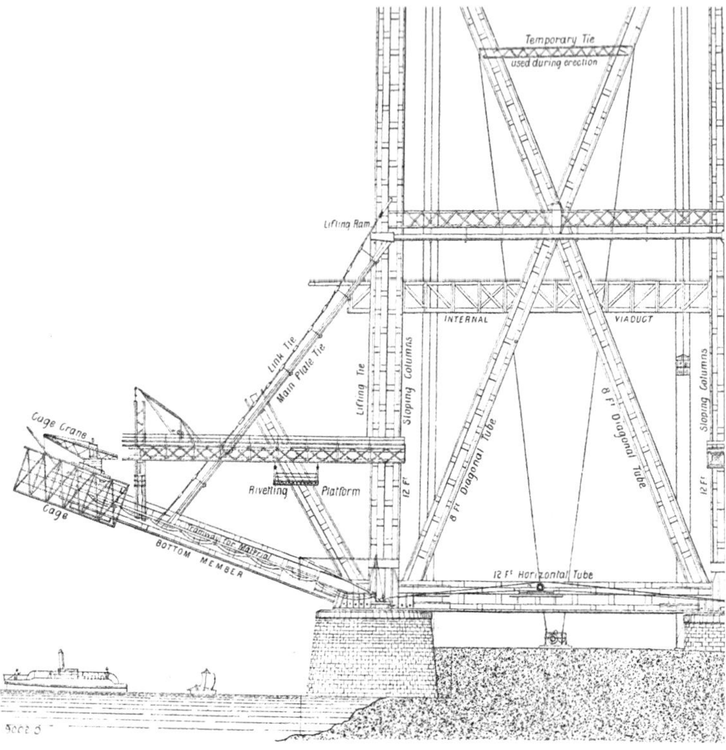

The only tangible connection John Dixon had with the Forth Bridge! Some of the links that he had removed from the original Hammersmith Suspension Bridge were used as temporary supports for the lower cantilevers during construction. One of them is identified as 'Link Tie' in the drawing. Engineering, London, 28 February 1890, page 52

'The Silver Forth' London and North Eastern Railway 1935 poster by Norman Wilkinson. Norman Wilkinson (1878-1971) from Cambridge was a maritime and poster artist and was also the inventor of dazzle camouflage used on British naval ships in the First World War. This view is looking west from the vicinity of Burntisland.
The bridge is many miles away, as far out of reach to us as it was to John Dixon.
Reproduced by permission of the National Railway Museum (NRM Pictorial Collection / Science and Society Picture Library). NRM reference 1978-9160.

Acknowledgements

Jane Jamieson, Historical Search Room Archivist, National Records of Scotland, Edinburgh, for advice on searching Forth Bridge Railway Company records.

References

The Forth Bridge
Reprinted from 'Engineering' February 28, 1890
Wilhelm Westhofen
Offices of 'Engineering' Bedford Street, London 1890
The definitive work on the bridge, an excellent work. Makes no mention of the tendering procedure. Westhofen himself worked on the construction. It includes drawings of the planned James Anderson suspension bridge of 1818.

The Life of Sir John Fowler
Thomas Mackay
J Murray, London, 1900
Good descriptions of the railway ferry over the Forth, the background to the bridge and the construction. Contains Fowler's distrust of the Tay Bridge and his comment about the 'Holbein straddle.'

Battle for the North, the Tay and Forth Bridges and the 19th century railway wars
Charles McKean
Granta Books, 2006
A popular history of the two bridges, but not always accurate.

The Curate, a Vicar and Five Engineers
J Michael Taylor
Pont Island News, 11th Edition, 2014
Ponteland Local History Society, Ponteland,
Newcastle upon Tyne
Pages 13-15 have a good biography of John Furness Tone.

The Forth Bridge Railway Company
The Saturday Press, Dunfermline, 14 November 1863, page 1
Notice that the company was to apply for Act of Parliament for a new line between the Edinburgh and Glasgow Railway and the North British Railway line on the north bank of the Forth.

The Daily News, London, 23 November 1863, page 5
Plans for a bridge between Blackness and Charlestown for the North British Railway

Bound Plans and Sections of Forth Bridge Railway from Pardovan, crossing the Forth near Blackness, to Charlestown
Book of Reference
George R. Stephenson and John F. Tone of
Newcastle upon Tyne
National Records of Scotland,
Reference RHP42326

Railway Meetings - North British
The Scotsman, Edinburgh, 21 May 1864, page 7
Report on the special shareholder meeting to consider the two proposals for a Forth Railway Bridge but decision deferred until the outcome of the Parliamentary Bills was known.

North British Railway
The Morning Journal, Glasgow, 10 June 1864, page 3
Virtual merger of the Edinburgh and Glasgow Railway and the North British Railway.

The Forth Railway Bridge
The Dundee Courier and Argus, 15 June 1866, page 3
Comprehensive description of Bouch's first design and the timber raft foundations.

Proposed Bridge across the Forth at Alloa
The Alloa Advertiser, 11 January 1868, page 2
Comprehensive description of the case for the bridge and Thomas Bouch's design.

In Parliament - Session 1874. Forth Bridge Railway
The Scotsman, Edinburgh, 14 November 1873, page 1
Details of the Second Parliamentary Bill extending the powers of the North British within the Forth Bridge Railway Company.

The North British Railway Company
The Edinburgh Evening News, 6 March 1874, page 3
Stormy meeting of North British shareholders with directors unwilling to put the bridge to a vote.

Laying the Foundation Stone of the Forth Bridge
The Glasgow Herald, 1 October 1878, page 3
Report of the ceremony on Inchgarvie.

Forth Railway Bridge
The Dundee Courier & Argus and Northern Warders,
7 August 1879
Specifications complete and construction put out to tender.

The Forth Bridge Contracts
The Scotsman, Edinburgh, 3 October 1879, page 4
After much deliberation contracts awarded to William Arrol for the construction and Vickers and Son for the chains.

The Forth Bridge
The Engineer, London, 24 October 1879, pages 313-5
Description of Thomas Bouch's design with illustration.

The Forth Railway Bridge
The Edinburgh Evening News, 17 December 1879, page 2
Circular sent to shareholders in the four railway companies forming the Forth Railway Bridge Company stating there will be 111,600 shares of £10 each with a guaranteed dividend of 5% during construction and 6% thereafter.

The Forth Railway Suspension Bridge (from our Edinburgh Correspondent)
The Times, London, 26 December 1879, page 8
Full description of the suspension bridge with a glowing report on the merits its design.

The Forth Bridge
Engineering, London, 6 February 1880, page 113
Editorial critical of the directors or concealing the risks to potential shareholders.

The Forth Bridge
Engineering, London, 13 February 1880, page 131-2
Detailed description of the Bouch suspension bridge casting doubts on its design.

The Forth Bridge
Engineering, London, 20 February 1880,
page 153-4 and 27 February 1880, pages 173-5
Max am Ende's steel arch bridge.

The Forth Bridge - To the Editor of Engineering
Engineering, London, 27 February 1880, pages 168
Andrew Barclay's design for a Forth Bridge.

Meeting of the Forth Bridge Railway Company - Abandonment of the Forth Bridge
The Dundee Advertiser, 14 January 1881
Justification for the inevitable decision to scrap Thomas Bouch's bridge and John Waddell's re-election as a director.

The Forth Bridge
The Dundee Courier & Argus, 21 June 1881, page 4
The new bridge is definitely going ahead.

The New Forth Bridge Scheme
The Dundee Courier & Argus, 1 July 1881, page 2
Guarantee of £2 million from the railway companies.

Forth Bridge Railway Company, the bridge to be built
The Dundee Courier & Argus, 12 July 1881, page 5
Extraordinary general meeting of the company, on 11 July 1881, withdrew the abandonment bill and sanctioned the new bridge to John Fowler's design.

The Forth Bridge
Engineering, London, 11 November 1881, page 475-8
Comprehensive history of continuous girder or cantilever bridges, concluding that the design was as old as the suspension or arch bridge. Description of the four designs considered for the Forth Bridge and the rejection of a modified Bouch design.

Advertisements and Notices
The Times, London, 13 September 1882, page 1
Notice requesting tenders for the new Forth Bridge at Queensferry. Plans can be seen at John Fowler's office in Westminster.

Forth Bridge Railway Company Minutes of Board and General Meetings
Reference Forth Bridge Railway, 1873-1948, BR/FOR/1/8
National Archives of Scotland, 2 Princes Street, Edinburgh
Hand-written record of meetings, with details of tenders and action on John Fowler to seek combination of contractors. The minutes were hand-written on absorbent paper such that the ink has spread out making them illegible. However, on the reverse side of the paper, the line made by the steel nib is clearly visible and the minutes can be read from the reverse via a mirror.

List of tenders received for the Forth Bridge
Sub-piece 13, Box BR/FOR/4/3
National Records of Scotland, Edinburgh
Rough list of the tenders, John Dixon is referred to as 'Dickson'.

Obituary, John Dixon
Proceedings of the Institution of Civil Engineers, volume 104, January 1891, pages 309-311
Gives the official reason for John Dixon's tender being rejected.

The Forth Bridge Contract
The Edinburgh Evening News, 13 November 1882, page 2
Contract awarded to Tancred and Arrol for £1.6 million over 5 years.

The Forth Bridge
The Engineer, London, 7 November 1884, page357
Paper by Benjamin Baker read to the British Association. Includes details of tenders.

The Forth Bridge (continuation of above paper)
The Engineer, London, 21 November 1884, page 388, also 5 December, page 422

Great Bridge Builder - The Late Mr. Joseph Phillips
The Folkestone Herald, 4 November 1905, page 15
Account of the life of Joseph Phillips, who died at Folkestone, by a life-long friend.

The Contractors
Hugh Ferguson and Mike Chrimes
Institution of Civil Engineers Publishing, London, Thomas Telford Limited, 2014
Includes a biography of Sir William Arrol 1839-1913.

Forth Bridge Illustrations 1886-1887
No.27 General View from Dalmeny Park
National Library of Scotland, Shelfmark RB.l.229
These are the photographs taken by Joseph Philip Phillips, son of Joseph Phillips. Text accompanying the photograph explains the use of the ex-Hammersmith Bridge suspension links as tie bars.

23 Rebuilding Hammersmith Suspension Bridge

John Dixon's last large project, as contractors Dixon, Appleby and Thorne, was the rebuilding of the Hammersmith suspension bridge from 1884 to 1887. The original suspension bridge had become overwhelmed by vastly increased traffic and was rebuilt to a design by Sir Joseph Bazalgette and his son, with elaborate cast iron panels on the towers and forged steel links for the suspension chains. After the failure of the first contractors, John and his partners took over the work. Before the main bridge could be rebuilt, a temporary crossing was constructed. John's work was favourably received but, as all too often happens, the engineering challenges were largely unappreciated. One newspaper even went so far as to say that the engineering skill involved in reconstructing the bridge was extremely interesting 'but of course the interest is chiefly for engineering experts and could hardly be made intelligible to general readers.'

The original bridge

The original Hammersmith Suspension Bridge was designed by William Tierney Clark (1783-1852), who had been appointed by John Rennie as engineer to the Hammersmith Waterworks. Clark's plans were accepted in 1824 by the Hammersmith Bridge Company, attracted to 'a bridge of suspension with a view to the strictest economy.' The planned opening ceremony and celebratory dinner, on 6 October 1827, had to be abandoned when at the last minute three dukes, a marquis and four lords all declined their invitations. Fortunately, this did not prevent the opening of the bridge, with music and fireworks replacing the absent peers.

Hammersmith was the first of London's suspension bridges over the Thames. With the convenience of the new crossing and its elegant design, the bridge was much appreciated and admired. It was claimed that the total length of the carriageway supported by the chains was longer then Telford's famous bridge over the Menai Straits, opened the previous year. A local press report read:

> 'This is really a most magnificent piece of architecture, and unlike some modern improvements, is as useful as it is ornamental. When viewed from the land, in a right line with the bridge, it is far more beautiful and imposing in its appearance than any other bridge either in London or its vicinity.'

Suspension chains, made up of wrought iron links, were carried on two masonry towers, each with an archway through which traffic passed. These openings were only fourteen feet wide, certainly adequate for the time it was built but, as the vehicles crossing became larger and more numerous, they formed an unacceptable bottleneck. Although there were footpaths along the outer sides of the carriageway, these footpaths ended at the towers and people had to negotiate their way through the narrow arches along with the horses, carriages, wagons and other traffic. But the greatest inconvenience to travellers was the imposition of tolls, ranging from a ha'penny for a person on foot or with a wheelbarrow to four pence for a carriage drawn by a single horse, with three pence extra for every additional horse.

Freeing the bridge from tolls

Before 1879 most of the bridges over the Thames had been in private ownership and tolls charged. In February 1870 a motion in the Houses of Parliament to free the Thames bridges had been defeated by 162 votes to 21, an example of how English law has usually given much more weight to the interests of property owners than to those of the general public. Over the next seven years pressure grew for free crossings and in 1877 the Metropolitan Board of Works succeeded with a bill in Parliament enabling them to purchase bridges and allow free use. Ten carriageway bridges, several foot-bridges and a ferry were taken over. The last three bridges to be purchased were the Hammersmith Suspension Bridge and the bridges at Wandsworth and Putney, with the price determined by arbitration. Optimistically the Hammersmith Bridge Company claimed £160,000 for their bridge, £40,000 for approach roads and toll houses, and £1,000 to wind up the company, making a grand total of £201,000, but they had to settle for £112,000. The example of the Hammersmith Bridge Company makes it clear why it took so long to wrest control of the bridges from their owning companies. Over the period 1870-79 annual toll income averaged about £6,000, enabling the company to pay an annual dividend around 6%. Shareholders would be reluctant to lose this sort of secure and lucrative investment.

The Metropolitan Board of Works had not been able to make any detailed inspection of the Hammersmith Bridge before taking it over. They may

'The Oxford and Cambridge Universities' boat-race, Hammersmith Bridge on a race day' engraving by M W Ridley. Matthew White Ridley (1837-1888) from Newcastle gave up a career as an architect to become an artist and had an art school in London. The Illustrated London News commented that Clark's bridge was 'a favourite place for those not afraid of the fatigue and exposure to cold in long waiting'. The Philips Wigan building was the old Mortlake Brewery.
The Illustrated London News, 23 March 1872, pages 288 and 289 © Illustrated London News Limited/Mary Evans.

have put their faith in an engineering report commissioned by the Hammersmith Bridge Company in 1869 which confidently declared the condition of the bridge 'exceptionally good, with evidence of very careful repair and supervision.' However, it went on to state that the suspension rods were not of first class quality and the masonry towers were not far off sliding into the river; criticisms which would be repeated in later surveys by Sir Joseph Bazalgette, engineer to the Metropolitan Board of Works. When Bazalgette wisely questioned the soundness of the structure in 1877, he was told by the company that a traction engine with a train of carriages weighing 35 tons had safely passed across. On the other hand, the Hackney District Board of Works was of the opinion that the bridge had been in a dangerous condition for years and concerns had long been expressed about its safety. These concerns had greatly increased after 1870, when an estimated 12,000 people had crowded onto the bridge to watch the Boat Race. There is evidence that the owners of the bridge were privately concerned about its safety. In 1872 they commissioned the bridge designer Rowland Ordish (1824-1886) to examine the structure with reference to overcrowding during the Boat Race, expressing every confidence in him. His report has not come to light.

It had cost the Metropolitan Board of Works the huge sum of £1.4 million to take over ten of the Thames bridges, but the expense did not end there. In the aftermath of the Tay Bridge disaster (December 1879), the Board of Trade sent a letter to railway companies and public authorities owning bridges, prompting the Metropolitan Board of Works to make a thorough inspection of their newly-acquired structures. In May 1880 Bazalgette, presented his report. Much to the public's concern, these inspections revealed that another £0.6 million would be needed to restore the bridges to a safe condition. Given that the previous owners of the bridges would have maximised short term income, it is hardly surprising that they had neglected maintenance, particularly as the campaign for free crossings had been around for many years, leading to a 'make hay while the sun shines' attitude. It was said that the tax payers of London had been fleeced to the extent of 6½d in the £1.

Sir Joseph Bazalgette's concerns about the safety of the bridge

Hammersmith Bridge was far from the worst of the bridges, although Bazalgette was sure that its closure at the time of the Boat Race was absolutely necessary. The press suggested that the privileged few allowed on the bridge would be advised to take life belts with them. Bazalgette's report contained many recommendations: serious consideration should be given to replacing the cast iron beams supporting the carriageway with wrought iron beams, the timber trusses introduced to stiffen the roadway should be replaced by wrought iron trellis girders and wrought iron plates should replace the timber planking of the carriageway. But his over-riding concern was the strength of the wrought iron links forming the suspension chains. The inner chains were twice the strength of the outer ones but carried five times the width of platform. He proposed installing an extra chain over each inner chain to reduce their loading. Finally, the bridge should be cleaned and painted. These works were estimated to cost £15,000. It was not surprising that the Hammersmith Bridge was in a poor state; average maintenance expenditure for the previous ten years had only been around £250 and nothing had been done to strengthen the structure to handle the considerable increase in traffic, which now included heavy traction engines.

No repair work could be done until the Metropolitan Board owned the bridge, and then priority was given to keeping the bridge open. There were official openings of the Thames bridges freed from toll. In contrast to the opening of Tierney Clark's bridge in the absence of nobility, this time there was a royal presence. On 26 June 1880 the Prince of Wales headed a grand procession to open Wandsworth Bridge at 3:30pm, Putney Bridge at 4:00pm and Hammersmith Bridge at 4:30pm. Not everything went to plan, with the royal party arriving half an hour late and a thunderstorm drenching the proceedings. On Hammersmith Broadway a thousand schoolchildren sang 'God Bless the Prince of Wales' and the band of the West Ashworth Schools played the national anthem. On the Hammersmith Bridge hooligans threw the tollgates into the river and smashed the windows of the toll houses to celebrate the end of paying to use the bridge.

The Metropolitan Board of Works finally realises the dangerous state of the bridge

Once Hammersmith Bridge had been freed from tolls, Bazalgette's report seems to have been set on one side. The Metropolitan Board of Works might justifiably be accused of silence to avoid public fury over the excessive price paid for the bridge, given its serious shortcomings. The dangerous state of sections of the bridge was clearly evident when, in November 1881, the wooden walkway gave way under Police Constable Bullock, who fell forty feet onto the mud below. He was taken, unconscious, to hospital where he recovered but was left unfit to continue work as a constable. And a few weeks previously some horses had been injured when their hooves went through rotten boards. In March 1882 Bazalgette tried to shake the Board out of their complacency with an urgent letter. On examining the bridge, he had found four of the rods anchoring the roadway to the suspension chains to be fractured and concluded that the structure was of insufficient strength to carry the increased traffic following freedom from tolls. This shows Bazalgette's political acumen. By putting the blame on the increased traffic consequent on the lifting of tolls, he avoided any accusation that the Board should have inspected the bridge more thoroughly before acquiring it, or that remedial work should have been done immediately after its acquisition. His letter had the desired effect and the question of the bridge was on the agenda for the Metropolitan Board of Works meeting on 17 March 1882.

A detailed examination of the bridge by divers had revealed that scouring by the current had undermined the footings of the masonry tower on the Barnes side of the river. Each masonry tower had originally been built on a massive timber raft carried on 246 timber piles driven into the river bed. These foundations now required additional underpinning. Given the questionable strength of the suspension chains and inadequacy of the carriageways and footpaths, Bazalgette's recommendation to rebuild the entire bridge was accepted. When the original bridge was dismantled and the rotten state of the platform revealed, there was amazement that the bridge had been immune from serious accident. A tongue-in-cheek comment was made that 'the authorities must have calculated to a nicety - perhaps within the margin of safety - the duration to be assigned for such immunity.'

Sir Joseph Bazalgette, and his son Edward, produced a novel design for the replacement bridge. They reasoned that, if the weight of the towers

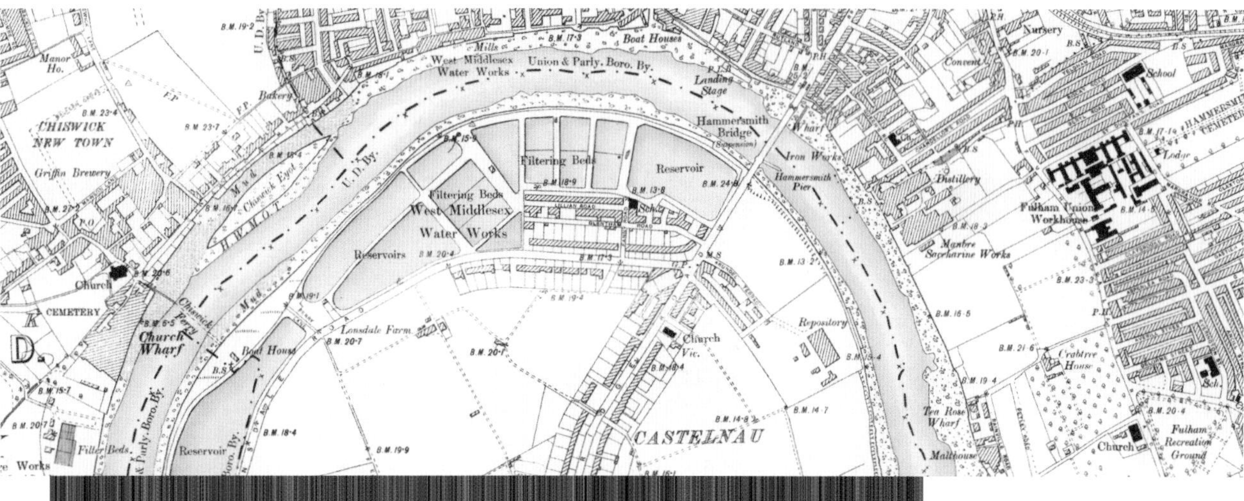

Hammersmith Suspension Bridge. Ordnance Survey Six Inch Series Revised 1891-94, published 1898, Surrey II.SW. Reproduced by permission of the National Library of Scotland.

could be reduced, then the original bases of the towers could be retained provided the underpinning mentioned above was carried out. Weight reduction was achieved by fabricating slimmer towers with a wrought iron framework clad in cast iron panels, much lighter than conventional masonry. New chains using steel rather than wrought iron links would carry a wider carriageway, with arches 21 feet wide through the towers for horses and vehicles and separate footpaths. Bridge deck clearance above water-level was increased by 4 feet. The estimated cost would be about £80,000 and the work was put out to tender.

The ornate appearance of the towers may have been due to George John Vulliamy (1817-1889), architect to the Metropolitan Board of Works. Drawings exist of fanciful designs, including Indian Raj and Italianate themes, which seem more likely to have come from Vulliamy, the architect of the Embankment lamp standards with their ornate sturgeon fishes, rather than from Bazalgette, the sober designer of London's sewers.

An alternative means of crossing the river was necessary while the old bridge was dismantled and the new structure erected. The Metropolitan Board of Works planned to provide two ferry boats, each holding a maximum of twelve persons, only operating during the hours of daylight. This raised an outcry from the residents of Castelnau on the Surrey side of the bridge. A public meeting was told that in September 1882 alone, over 86,000 pedestrians and nearly 20,000 vehicles had crossed the bridge. The proposed ferry boats would handle at best 14,000 passengers a week. A resolution was passed demanding a temporary bridge. Then unexpectedly, and to their further embarrassment, the Metropolitan Board of Works discovered that it had a statutory duty to maintain a crossing and no powers to close the bridge. They would have to seek authority from Parliament to construct a temporary bridge, a procedure which delayed the start of the rebuilding by two years and added £10,000 to the costs. The Board took £2,000 off the contract price, the estimated cost of providing the ferry boats, now no longer required. The necessary bill cleared Parliament on 26 June 1883.

The contract with Vernon, Ewens and Company

In April 1884 the contract for the rebuilding of Hammersmith Suspension Bridge was awarded to Vernon, Ewens and Company with their tender of £74,920. The contract included the structural wrought iron, the suspension chains and the cast iron cladding, which would come from the Central Ironworks.

It is quite surprising that Vernon, Ewens and Company were given the contract to rebuild the Hammersmith Bridge as their precarious situation at the start of 1884 could surely not have been hidden from even rudimentary enquiry. Perhaps their low tender, resulting from desperation for new business, proved too hard to resist. The highest tender had been £250,000, more than three times the Vernon, Ewens and Company tender.

Unsurprisingly, within two months of signing the contract, Vernon, Ewens and Company failed and an official receiver was appointed. Not for the first time, John Dixon came to the rescue of works halted by the failure of the contractors (as with the Rio Tinto ore-loading facility in Spain and the Minho District Railway in Portugal). John had formed a partnership with Charles James Appleby and Alfred Thorne, both long-standing colleagues, to carry out the Hammersmith Bridge work. Their tender of £82,177, 10% higher than that of Vernon, Ewens and Company, was accepted in October 1884.

Alfred Thorne and John Dixon had just finished rebuilding the Solway viaduct, and John would have welcomed a project so near to home, although he was no friend of the Metropolitan Board of Works. Six years earlier he had been angry with their refusal to give proper recognition to men in Egypt, particularly his brother Waynman, who had been involved in ensuring Cleopatra's Needle was despatched to London. He was also annoyed with the Board for managing to position the sphinxes, on either side of the obelisk's pedestal, facing the wrong way around.

Who's who?
Vernon, Ewens and Company

Thomas Vernon and Paul Ewens started in partnership at the Central Ironworks in Cheltenham, where they manufactured boilers and steam engines. Later the business expanded, with a construction operation based in Liverpool and an engineering consultancy office in Westminster. Their experience in bridge building was limited, although they submitted an unsuccessful bid for the Forth Railway Bridge two years earlier.

For many years Vernon, Ewens and Company had difficulty in covering its costs, and became mired in questionable legal and financial dealings. In 1877 the Cheltenham works was mortgaged to a firm of rogue solicitors in London, Frederick Searle Parker and John Searle Parker, for £1,500. Two years later the Parkers negotiated loans totalling £55,000 for Vernon and Ewens from the Worcester City and County Banking Company, using the engineering company and various insurance policies as securities. In 1882 Vernon and Ewens sold the engineering company to a solicitor, Edward Francis Davis, and then promptly entered a partnership with him to operate the company. The next year Davis retired and Vernon, Ewens, and Company was converted into a limited liability company. It failed to raise sufficient capital to continue in business and by June 1884 was in receivership but was involved in the complex legal proceedings precipitated by the Parkers' bankruptcy, allegations of misconduct and their absconding abroad to escape the British courts. It also transpired that an accidental fire had conveniently destroyed the company's accounting books.

Who's who?
Charles James Appleby (1828-1908)

Charles James Appleby trained as an engineer in his father's iron foundry at Chesterfield. After working in Russia for eight years he set up in business in London, where he was soon joined by his brother, Thomas Hodgson Appleby (1826-1899), building cranes and contractors' machinery. In 1874 the Appleby Brothers were awarded a five-year contract with the Egyptian Government for the supply of materials and rolling stock for the Sudan Railway. By 1877 responsibility for the contract had passed to the Governor General of Sudan, Gordon, who defaulted on payments to the Applebys. John Fowler, advisor to the Khedive on a variety of engineering matters at the time, stepped in to arbitrate between the Egyptian Government and Appleby Brothers in 1878. The Appleby brothers would in all probability have been known to John and Waynman Dixon from their work in Egypt in the 1870s.

Over the years the brothers amalgamated with several other businesses and became Appleby Brothers (Limited) in 1886. Charles stepped back from the day to day affairs of the business to pursue his literary interests but died at the age of eighty from heart failure.

Materials for the new bridge

Work started in November 1884. To obtain the materials for rebuilding the bridge, John turned to companies he knew and trusted. There were two suppliers of wrought iron, Thomson and Gilkes of the Millfield Iron Works, Stockton-on-Tees and the Thames Iron Works. Following the demise of Hopkins, Gilkes and Company (largely as a consequence of the Tay Bridge disaster) Edgar Gilkes joined the firm of Thomas J Thomson and Company at Stockton in 1881, from when the business became Thomson and Gilkes. The Thames Iron Works had fabricated the 'Cleopatra' vessel to transport the Egyptian obelisk. Iron castings were from the Whessoe Foundry at Darlington, previously Charles I'Anson and Son, who had supplied the castings for the Rio Tinto ore-loading facility in Spain. In 1860 Charles I'Anson had taken over an iron foundry and locomotive construction business in Darlington from his cousin Alfred Kitching. He moved to a new site on Whessoe Lane, where it became known as the Whessoe Works, operating as Charles I'Anson and Son Company until Charles's death in 1884.

At the time steel was a relatively new material and there were few potential suppliers of the forged links that would form the suspension chain. John Brown and Company had pioneered Bessemer steel manufacture in Sheffield at their Atlas Works in the 1850s. John Brown was knighted in 1867 but left the business in 1871. In spite of his departure, the business expanded and in 1899 moved into shipbuilding on the River Clyde where the name of Sir John Brown is well known. The Atlas Works in Sheffield had the necessary machinery for forging the links, the largest being over sixteen feet in length. John Dixon spent nine months in 1885 searching for a possible supplier of the links. Initially John Brown had declined but, by the end of the year when they were short of work, it was decided to accept. One of the Hammersmith Bridge links featured on the John Brown stand at the Liverpool International Exhibition opened by Queen Victoria on 11 May 1886.

Even the John Brown forge-masters found the task of producing the links far from straightforward. Each link was tested at David Kirkaldy's works in Southwark to a tensile stress of 29 tons/in^2. In July 1886, 100 of the

844 links delivered that month had to be rejected. Kirkaldy had designed the hydraulic testing machine, installed at his works in 1865, which became the premier testing facility for Victorian engineering components. He had demonstrated several deficiencies in the Tay Bridge structure following its collapse in 1879; many of the lugs on the cast iron columns fractured due to porous castings and some of the wrought iron sections failed at a tensile load of only one third that specified by Thomas Bouch.

The only maker's name visible on the bridge today is 'Cadogan Iron Works, Stanley Bridge, Chelsea', on the central lamp standards. Cadogan Iron Works, another business in serious financial trouble, supplied the 22 lamp standards. Original lighting was by gas but converted to electricity some twenty-three years later.

The temporary bridge

John's first task was to construct the temporary wooden bridge on the upstream side of the existing bridge. At first rapid progress was made and it was predicted that the work would be complete a month early, by the end of February 1885. In the event it was not completed until 22 April 1885 when traffic was diverted from the old bridge and subjected to an 8 ton weight limit. The temporary bridge was a substantial structure with a carriageway 23 feet wide carried on timber uprights with two wrought iron central spans, each 50 feet long, to allow for river traffic to pass relatively unimpeded. Pedestrians were provided with a separate footway but, as this was on the upstream (western) side, they were denied a clear view of the rebuilding work. This resulted in a fatal accident in April 1886 when an inquisitive man crossed the carriageway to obtain a better view of the works and was crushed against the eastern parapet by a passing vehicle.

There was adverse comment in *The Engineer* about several serious accidents to people

'The Present Hammersmith Bridge, London, under construction, showing the Temporary Bridge, 1886' painting by John Archibald Webb. John Archibald Webb, born in 1866, was a painter of marine and canal scenes, and also a book illustrator. His father was artist James Webb (1835-1895), his uncle artist Byron Webb (1831-1867) and his grandfather artist Archibald Webb (1793-1883). To add to the confusion Archibald Bertram Webb (1887-1944) was yet another artist! This painting shows the temporary bridge which John Dixon had to build before he could start dismantling Clark's bridge.
Reproduced by kind permission of the Richmond Borough Art Collection, Orleans House Gallery.

crossing the carriageway to look at the construction work. John's reply was so typical of the man that it is worth reproducing here:

> 'In your paragraph you seem to forget the fact that the traffic, both foot and horse, had to go through the 12ft. arches of the towers, as the footpaths were not carried round the outside. Now there is a good roadway for double line of traffic and a wide footpath as well. If stupids chose, against regulation, to cross the road, climb on the kerb and railings, and stick themselves in the way of danger, the man himself is alone to blame; at least the contractors have no option.'

It had been rumoured that, owing to the temporary wooden bridge restricting the passage of river craft, the course of the 1885 Boat Race would have to be altered. The rumours proved unfounded, and each crew was allocated a specific one of the 50 feet central spans to pass through, giving the Surrey side a distinct advantage and making the winning toss critical for success. The same arrangements were made in 1886, by which time the entire fabric of the old bridge had been removed and the new suspension links were in position. Work was still incomplete at the time of the 1887 event. Meanwhile there was growing discontent with the state of the temporary wooden bridge which was condemned as being woefully inadequate. These complaints seem misguided as John's temporary bridge was shown to be a sturdy construction during the International Sculling Sweepstakes, held on the river in September 1886. The umpire's paddle steamer *Lotus* managed to smash into one of the temporary bridge's piers, demolishing a paddle box and paddle but leaving the bridge intact.

The piles supporting the temporary bridge caused considerable scouring of the Surrey bank and a stone revetment had to be constructed to protect the bank.

Starting the rebuilding work

All that was to remain of the old bridge were the lower parts of the two towers (below road level) and the abutments on either bank. The carriageway was dismantled leaving the chains, suspension rods and carriageway support girders in position to maintain a balanced loading on the towers. Masonry was then taken off the top of the towers down to the level of the chain bearings, when dismantling of the chains could begin. Access staging was erected under the chains and links were removed, one row at a time, to be lowered into barges below. With the suspension chains removed, the remaining masonry was taken away down to the level of the carriageway.

It had been reported as early as April that piles were being driven around the southern abutment as part of the widening and lengthening of the approach roads. In September John's men were removing the old anchorage blocks and excavating new chain tunnels and anchorage chambers at each end of the bridge, which were 40 feet below the surface at their lowest point. The increased load capacity of the Bazalgette bridge can be gauged from the much greater volume of concrete forming the anchorages, more than ten-times the volume specified by Clark. Each end of the suspension chains was to be connected by steel forgings to massive plates embedded in concrete anchorages at an angle of 60° away from the river.

The serious work to the stone foundations of the towers could not begin until the weight of masonry had been removed. A timber cofferdam was then constructed around the base of the southern (Surrey bank) and the water pumped out. A series of passages was excavated in the clay beneath the lowest course of stonework and filled with brickwork on a bed of cement. The clay between this brickwork could then be removed and replaced with more brickwork, with the result that the lower course of the original masonry now rested on 6 feet deep brick footings. The northern (Middlesex bank) foundation was not affected by scouring and was left alone.

The pier stonework was then rebuilt to accept the cast iron base plates for the new towers, and assembly of the wrought iron framework forming the new towers began in June 1886. During August the wrought iron saddles, over which the chains ran on a series of steel rollers, were installed ready for the erection of the new chains. Given the weight of the steel links, this was a difficult operation. Links from the original chains were attached to the towers and adjusted to the length of the new chains. Timber working platforms were erected along the path of the new chains, John Mowlem and Company being given a £7,562 contract for this work. John Mowlem had set up a paving business in London which, after his retirement in 1845, was developed by his wife's family, keeping John Mowlem's name. The business grew into the famous civil engineering contractors who, in more recent times, built the forty-storey NatWest Tower in London, London City Airport and the Docklands Light Railway.

The steel links were lifted up from barges on the river and pinned together, working down from either side of the towers and using the old chains as supports. At the same time the ornate cast iron panels forming the outer surface of the towers were bolted into place. By February 1887 the new towers, chains, suspension rods and carriageway girders were complete. Creosoted timber decking was laid, covered with tarred felt and wooden paving setts. The weight limit was set at fifteen tons spread over four wheels. Footways were built along the outer sides of the bridge, with teak handrails. The entire project, including construction of the temporary bridge, had taken thirty months. Painting and installation of the gas lighting standards were not completed until after the official opening of the bridge. For its first year the bridge was illuminated by open gas jets mounted on wooden posts, surely a hazardous arrangement but considered acceptable at the time.

'Hammersmith Bridge on the River Thames, London' by Ray Art Graphics. Hammersmith Suspension Bridge is one of the few John Dixon structures remaining intact. Its ornate cast iron cladding disguises a relatively light-weight bridge designed by Sir Joseph Bazalgette and his son Edward to reduce loading on the river bed.
© Alamy Images reference D2NXBH.

Opening the rebuilt bridge

The rebuilt Hammersmith Suspension Bridge was opened at 3:30pm on 18 June 1887 by Prince Albert Victor of Wales and his cousin Prince George of Greece. In marked contrast to the exuberance which accompanied the freeing of tolls, this re-opening was a quiet affair. Hammersmith vestry had decided that it would be a waste of money to decorate the streets, but some shops and private houses bravely put up flags and there were banners and portraits of the Queen on the bridge itself. Another contrast with the 1880 event was the weather, which was beautifully fine. In a remarkably short speech Prince Albert said that this was the first opening ceremony he had undertaken in London (he was twenty-three years old) and that it had been his father and mother who had declared the bridge free from tolls seven years previously. Sadly, but all too typically, he made no mention of the engineers responsible for the design and construction of the new bridge. The only exuberance of the day was in the evening, when the Hammersmith Varieties Music Hall celebrated with a grand evening event.

Although the new bridge remained open during subsequent Boat Races, there was a prohibition on persons, horses or vehicles remaining stationary on the carriageway during the race.

Disposal of the old bridge

The timbers, ironwork and the Pooley's Patent 10-ton weighbridge, which had been necessary to enforce the weight limit on the temporary crossing, were auctioned in July 1887. Wrought iron girders from the old bridge were reused in a footbridge at Teddington. Some of the wrought iron bars from original suspension links were taken to Scotland and used as temporary tie bars during the construction of the Forth Railway Bridge. This was John Dixon's only fleeting involvement with the Forth Bridge; his tender for the construction was rejected in spite of being the lowest bid. The remaining ironwork from the old Hammersmith Bridge was sold for £500.

The Hammersmith Bridge since 1887

The rebuilt bridge, quite capable of handling late 19th century horse-drawn traffic and the occasional traction engine, suffered with the greater stresses of 20th century motor vehicles. Not only that, but dissident Irish groups seem to have harboured a grudge against the bridge, making several assaults on the structure. Irish nationalists attempted to blow it up in March 1939 with two suitcases filled with explosives. A quick-thinking passer-by threw one suitcase into the river, but the other exploded causing damage to the central links on the upstream side. The steel braces introduced to make good the damage can still be seen today. The Provisional IRA planted thirty pounds of Semtex under the south side of the bridge in April 1996, but a faulty detonator prevented significant damage. The third attempt was by the so-called Real IRA in June 2000, their bomb necessitated closure of the bridge for two years while repairs were carried out.

Gradual deterioration by the damp climate and heavy traffic has been countered by periodic major repairs and a succession of different weight limits. The bridge was overhauled in 1952 (by John Mowlem and Company), in 1973 and again in 1997. The original weight limit of 15 tons was reduced to 12 tons in the 1960s, temporarily to 5 tons prior to the major overhaul in 1973 following which it was set at 12 tonnes (11.8 tons). In 1984, after damage due to an overweight lorry, it was reduced to 3 tonnes apart from buses. Following the 1997 overhaul, the limit was raised to 7.5 tonnes with a traffic control system for buses.

In the 1960s the rebuilt bridge came close to suffering the fate of Tierney Clark's bridge, with consideration given to its possible replacement by a completely new structure. London County Council, which had taken over the responsibilities of the Metropolitan Board of Works in 1889, was faced with a critical engineering report on the state of the bridge. Prevailing opinion of the time was to replace outdated structures with modern designs. Plans were drawn up for a new four-lane crossing, the only nod to the past being a recognition that local opinion might favour another suspension bridge. With the arrival of the Greater London Council in 1964 these plans were quietly forgotten. The future of the bridge now seems secure; it is Grade II* listed and now under the London Borough of Hammersmith and Fulham who, presumably, have more local interest and limited resources for major capital projects.

After the unsuccessful Real IRA attempt to blow up the bridge in 2000, the structure was repainted in its original green colours with gold highlights, along with the seven coats of arms at each end of the bridge which, until then, had been painted in their proper heraldic colours.

Acknowledgements

Assistance of staff at the London Metropolitan Archives, 40 Northampton Road, with records of the Metropolitan Board of Works.

References

Hammersmith Bridge
Engineering, London, 2 April 1872, page 78
Directors of the Hammersmith Bridge have commissioned an inspection by R M Ordish.

An East and West End Work - Freeing the Bridges over the Thames
East London Observer, 31 May 1879, page 5
Progress in the campaign to obtain free crossings of the Thames.

Metropolitan Board of Works, Metropolitan Bridges
Report by Sir J W Bazalgette C.B. as to Repairs Urgently Necessary
Printed by Order of the Bridges Committee,
26 May 1880, No.955
London Metropolitan Archives, London, reference MBW 2417, page 50
Inadequate strength of inner suspension chains and other repairs needed to Hammersmith Suspension Bridge.

Accountants' Reports, Proofs and Tabulated Accounts &c., in the matters of freeing from tolls Waterloo Bridge, Charing Cross and Cannon Street foot-bridges, Lambeth Bridge, Vauxhall Bridge, Chelsea Suspension Bridge, Albert and Battersea Bridges, Wandsworth Bridge, Fulham or Putney Bridge, Hammersmith Bridge, Deptford Creek Bridge, Grand Junction Canal foot-bridges, Poplar and Greenwich Ferry Company
London Metropolitan Archives, London,
reference MBW 2020, pages 28-48
Detailed accounts of the Hammersmith Bridge, including tolls taken, repair costs, dividends paid, etc.

The Freeing of the Bridges
The Daily News, London, 23 June 1880, page 6
Ceremony to mark the free opening of Hammersmith Bridge on Saturday 26 June after purchase by the Metropolitan Board of Works.

Programme for opening Hammersmith Bridge free from toll, 26 June 1880, by H.R.H. Prince of Wales
London Metropolitan Archives, London, reference MBW 2417, page 12
Includes map of route taken by procession, etc.

An Account of the Metropolitan Bridges over the Thames by Sir Joseph Bazalgette C.B., Engineer to the Board.
London Metropolitan Archives, London, reference MBW 2417
Report on Bazalgette's own hand writing of the last three bridges to be freed from tolls. Again the weakness of the Hammersmith suspension chains was highlighted.

Decayed bridges
The Dundee Courier and Argus, 31 July 1880, page 2
The state of the Thames bridges in the light of the Tay Bridge disaster.

Hackney Board of Works - The Thames Bridges
The Borough of Hackney Express and Shoreditch Observer,
31 July 1880, page 3
Local knowledge was that the Hammersmith Bridge was far worse than the Metropolitan Board of Works believed.

Dangerous state of Hammersmith Bridge
Pall Mall Gazette, 7 November 1881, page 7
Police constable fell through rotten woodwork.

Notes
St James's Gazette, 18 March 1882, page 5
Metropolitan Board of Works plan to reconstruct the bridge at an estimated cost of £80,000.

Science and Arts
The Illustrated London News, 19 August 1882, page 194
On 11 August the Metropolitan Board of Works accepted a tender of £74,920 for rebuilding Hammersmith Bridge.

Thames Bridges
The Edinburgh Evening News, 26 August 1882, page 4
Tender for £70,000 accepted, bridge to be closed for two years.

The stoppage of Hammersmith Bridge
The Daily News, London, 5 September 1882, page 6
Letter to the editor about the lack of an alternative crossing while the work was done.

Notes upon Passing Events by the Man-in-the-Moon
The Cheltenham Mercury, 16 September 1882, page 2
Messrs Vernon and Ewens have just accepted a contract for rebuilding the Hammersmith Bridge. The casting and other work will be undertaken at the Cheltenham Iron Works.

The Central Iron Works Excursion
The Cheltenham Mercury, 11 August 1883, page 2
Report on the works excursion to London. Some took a penny boat on the Thames, passing beneath the Hammersmith Bridge which is shortly to be pulled down and replaced, the contract having been given to Vernon and Ewens.

Occasional Notes
Pall Mall Gazette, 19 September 1882, page 3
Public meeting about the bridge closures with data on number of crossings in a week. The ferry boat scheme was 'preposterous and cannot be persisted in.'

London, Monday, September 25
The Standard, London, 25 September 1882, page 5
Public meeting on the blockade of Castelnau. Tenders for the rebuilding of the bridge ranged from £75,000 to £250,000. The Prince of Wales was reported to have taken up the case for a temporary bridge.

Occasional Notes
Pall Mall Gazette, 30 September 1882, page 3
Metropolitan Board of Works discovered it has a statutory duty to maintain a river crossing.

London, Saturday, October 14
The Standard, London, 14 October 1882, page 5
Temporary bridge will cost £10,000 but the notional cost of providing ferry boats, £2,000, will be deducted from the contract price. The blockade of Castelnau had been averted.

The Thames Iron Works 1837-1912: a major shipbuilder on the Thames
Daniel Harrison
Museum of London Archaeology and Crossrail Limited, 2015
Reproduction of a page from the *Thames Iron Works Gazette*, No.13, 1897, showing a selection of civil engineering projects undertaken at the works, includes the Hammersmith Bridge.

Cleveland Iron Trade
The North-Eastern Daily Gazette, Middlesbrough,
12 December 1881, page 3
Edgar Gilkes of Middlesbrough was to join T J Thomson and Company, iron and brass founders, at Stockton-on-Tees.

Gloucester News - Local Failure
The Citizen, Gloucester, 14 June 1884, page 4
Failure of Vernon Ewens and Company Limited with the comment 'the firm, though for a long time in poor credit, has done extensive business.' Receiver appointed.

High Court of Justice, Chancery Division (Before Vice-Chancellor Bacon) in re Vernon, Ewens, and Company (Limited)
The Times, London, 25 February 1886, page 3
Account of the convoluted legal cases arising from the bankruptcy of Messrs Parkers, solicitors, and the mortgage taken out by Vernon, Ewens and Company.

Editorial - The Putney and Hammersmith Bridges
The Engineer, London, 6 February 1885, page 108
The contractor was making rapid advance with the piled bridge for a temporary crossing. The scheduled completion was end of March, but it seemed that the work would be done by end of February.

Notes
St James's Gazette, London, 25 March 1885, page 5
Effect of the temporary wooden bridge on the Boat Race.

Closing Hammersmith-Bridge
The Times, London, 23 April 1885, page 8
Temporary bridge opened yesterday. Contractors had already started driving in piles into the river at the southern end of the bridge.

Editorial - Hammersmith Bridge
The Engineer, London, 12 June 1885, page 463
The platform of the old bridge platform was in a poor state and there should be sincere thanks that there had not been a serious accident.

Editorial - Hammersmith Bridge
The Engineer, London, 4 September 1885, page 184
Contractors engaged on excavations for concrete anchor blocks on either end of the bridge, having removed the original anchorages. Some accidents on the temporary bridge due to the single footway.

Letters to the Editor - The Hammersmith Bridge
The Engineer, London, 11 September 1885, page 206
John Dixon's blunt reply to criticism of the safety of the temporary bridge.

Metropolitan Bridge - building and repairing
Daily News, London, 11 December 1885, page 3
Details of the modifications to the Hammersmith Suspension Bridge.

The Hammersmith Temporary Bridge - To the Editor of *The Standard*
The Standard, London, 16 April 1886, page 3
Letter from a resident of Barnes who witnessed the fatal accident on the temporary bridge.

The International Sculling Sweepstakes - Final Heat - Accident to the Umpire's Steamer
The Daily News, London, 2 September 1886, page 2
The *Lotus* collided with the temporary bridge.

The Queen's visit to Liverpool - Opening of the 'Shipperies' Exhibition
The Sheffield Daily Telegraph, 12 May 1886, page 3
Description of the Liverpool International Exhibition. Messrs John Brown had a very imposing exhibit which included a link for the Hammersmith Bridge.

Editorial - Hammersmith Bridge
The Engineer, London, 21 January 1887, page 52
Great progress being made, ornamental towers almost complete, platform being built on the Surrey side.

Two New Thames Bridges
Daily News, London, 3 May 1887, page 3
The engineering skills involved would be unintelligible to the general reader.

Two New Thames Bridges
Daily News, 3 May 1887, page 3
Rebuilding specification with contract cost £80,000, but quoted elsewhere at £70,000.

The New Hammersmith Bridge
The Engineer, London, 22 April 1887, page 309 and a supplement
Detailed drawings showing the construction of the bridge and the casings of the towers.

The New Hammersmith Bridge
The Engineer, London, 29 April 1887, pages 330-31
Detailed drawings showing the construction of the internal wrought iron structure of the towers, the chain saddles and concrete anchorages.

The New Hammersmith Bridge
The Engineer, London, 20 May 1887, pages 391-94
Detailed drawings showing the chains, anchorages and towers, accompanied by a comprehensive description.

Hammersmith Suspension Bridge
The Times, London, 9 June 1887, page 9
Hammersmith vestry decided that it would be a waste of money to decorate the streets for the opening of the bridge.

The New Metropolitan Bridges
The Times, London, 20 June 1887, page 7
Detailed account of the bridge and the re-opening ceremony. Wrongly describes the towers as being of masonry.

Hammersmith Bridge
Charles Hailstone
Barnes and Mortlake History Society and Fulham and Hammersmith Historical Society, London, 1987
A comprehensive history of the bridge, but with much more detail on Tierney Clark's bridge than on the rebuilding to Joseph Bazalgette's design.

New Hammersmith Suspension Bridge
The Graphic, 18 June 1887, page 638, with illustration on page 645
Description of works, contractors Messrs Dixon, Appleby and Thorne.

The New Metropolitan Bridges
The Times, London, 20 June 1887, page 7
Description of the opening ceremony on 18 June by Prince Albert Victor of Wales.

Forth Bridge Jottings
The Dundee Advertiser, 3 March 1890, page 2
Re-use of some of the wrought iron bars in the new Forth Railway Bridge.

Obituary, Charles James Appleby, 1828-1908
Minutes of the Proceedings of the Institution of Civil Engineers, Volume 172, 1908, pages 307-308

24 Hawkesbury Bridge tender, Australia

In 1885 John Dixon was one of the eight British engineers to submit tenders for the design and construction for the large railway bridge across the Hawkesbury River in New South Wales. Much to the consternation of the British engineering establishment, the contract was awarded to an American company. Due to the uncertain nature of the river bed, construction proved challenging, but the bridge opened in 1889. John's subsequent criticism of the lightweight American design may have been justified for the bridge required strengthening and was replaced by a new structure in 1946.

Call for tenders

The Hawkesbury Railway Bridge was the final link in the Australian railway network between Adelaide, Melbourne, Sydney and Brisbane. Prior to its construction, passengers and freight were transferred onto a paddle steamer for the crossing. Bridging the Hawkesbury was going to be a challenge as the river was nearly 3,000 feet wide and fast flowing with tidal currents. A crossing between Long Island and Mullet Creek was chosen, and in December 1884 it was decided to advertise for tenders for the design, construction and one year's maintenance of the bridge. It was to be a span of 2,896 feet between abutments, and to be constructed in steel and carrying two lines of standard gauge (4 feet 8½ inch) track, although the line on either side of the bridge was single track. Not surprisingly, this resulted in the bridge being used as a convenient passing place for trains which increased the weights the bridge had to carry. Clearance above high water level was to be 40 feet.

The Australian Ministry of Public Works published a prospectus inviting tenders, at the cost of one guinea. Their comprehensive specifications included a detailed profile of the river bed based on eleven trial borings. Solid bedrock was never reached, the borings ending in 'very hard sand' which was taken as the base of the piers. At the southern end of the crossing this 'very hard sand' was not reached until a depth of 170 feet. The specifications did not include a maximum pressure on the foundations, resulting in a great variation of pier cross-sectional area in the different designs.

Tenders were to be delivered to the Westminster office of the agent-general for New South Wales by 1 June 1885, giving just over four months for them to be put together. Because of the costs involved and typically five months needed for the round voyage from England to New South Wales, non-Australian bidders could not have visited the site. John Dixon submitted a tender for a conventional girder bridge of ten spans. Each pier was made up from four steel cylinders, each 12 feet diameter, set 25 feet apart and filled with concrete. His drawings showed their diameter was increased significantly at the base to reduce the pressure on the ground beneath. It can be speculated that, had the prospectus specification not been so exact, John Dixon might have used the solution to the problem of building a stable structure on an unstable river bed that he and George Barclay Bruce had developed at Huelva in 1874, using submerged platforms bolted to the pier columns. This would have been feasible since each group of eight columns at Huelva was tested to a load of 400 tons, while the Hawkesbury Bridge specification was for a load of 900 tons per span, equivalent to 450 tons on each group of four (much larger diameter) columns.

Fourteen tenders were received. That from the Phoenix Iron Works, which had submitted a wrought iron structure contrary to the specifications, was immediately rejected. The tenders were unusual in their wide variation on costs, but the American companies were clearly the cheapest:

Three American tenders from £280,000 to £327,000
Eight British tenders from £377,500 to £584,898
Two Australian tenders from £403,367 to £702,384
One French tender for £685,000

John Dixon's tender was for £486,100 and William Arrol's tender, possibly the most reliable British design, was £580,000.

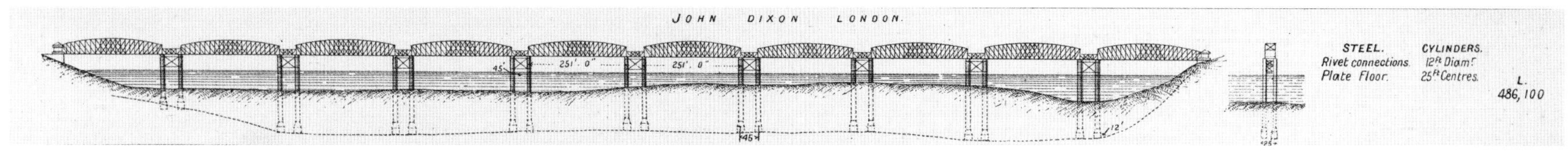

John Dixon's design for the railway bridge. There is a lack of definition about how the piles will be sunk into the river bed.
Engineering, London, 16 April 1886, page 367

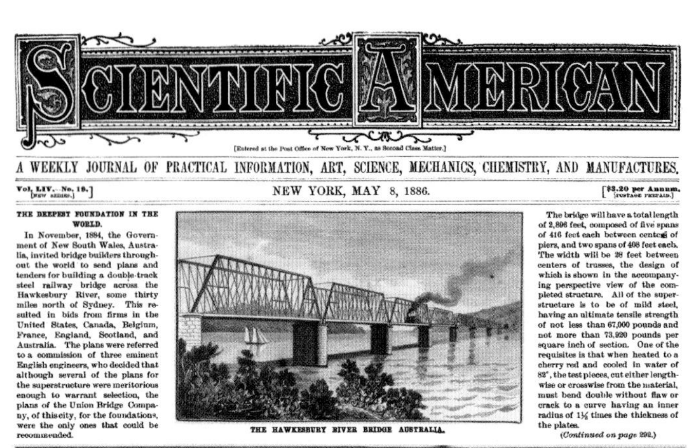

SCIENTIFIC AMERICAN

[Entered at the Post Office of New York, N. Y., as Second Class Matter.]

A WEEKLY JOURNAL OF PRACTICAL INFORMATION, ART, SCIENCE, MECHANICS, CHEMISTRY, AND MANUFACTURES.

Vol. LIV.—No. 19. [NEW SERIES.] NEW YORK, MAY 8, 1886. [$3.20 per Annum. [POSTAGE PREPAID.]

THE DEEPEST FOUNDATION IN THE WORLD.

In November, 1884, the Government of New South Wales, Australia, invited bridge builders throughout the world to send plans and tenders for building a double-track steel railway bridge across the Hawkesbury River, some thirty miles north of Sydney. This resulted in bids from firms in the United States, Canada, Belgium, France, England, Scotland, and Australia. The plans were referred to a commission of three eminent English engineers, who decided that although several of the plans for the superstructure were meritorious enough to warrant selection, the plans of the Union Bridge Company, of this city, for the foundations, were the only ones that could be recommended.

THE HAWKESBURY RIVER BRIDGE AUSTRALIA.

The bridge will have a total length of 2,896 feet, composed of five spans of 416 feet each between centers of piers, and two spans of 408 feet each. The width will be 28 feet between centers of trusses, the design of which is shown in the accompanying perspective view of the completed structure. All of the superstructure is to be of mild steel, having an ultimate tensile strength of not less than 67,000 pounds and not more than 73,920 pounds per square inch of section. One of the requisites is that when heated to a cherry red and cooled in water of 82°, the test pieces, cut either lengthwise or crosswise from the material, must bend double without flaw or crack to a curve having an inner radius of 1½ times the thickness of the plates.

(Continued on page 292.)

THE DEEPEST FOUNDATION IN THE WORLD.—SINKING THE PIERS FOR THE HAWKESBURY RIVER BRIDGE, NEW SOUTH WALES, AUSTRALIA.

The cover page of Scientific American, 8 May 1886. Scientific American first appeared in 1845 as a weekly newsletter. It later became a monthly journal and is the oldest continuously published monthly magazine in the United States. At the time much was made of the Hawkesbury Bridge having the deepest foundations in the world. The engraving clearly shows how the piers were sunk into the river bed. Alluvial material was excavated through the three internal cylinders.
Image from Macmillan Publishers Limited, Springer Nature, Springer International Publishing AG.

Judging was by a committee of three British engineers, who unanimously decided that the Union Bridge Company design met all their requirements and was considerably cheaper than the majority of tenders. Sir John Fowler, retained as consulting engineer to the colony of Australia, agreed. The decision to award the contract to an American company caused dismay in Britain, in spite of it having been made by British consulting engineers.

The position of Fowler is interesting since he was employing Arrol on the Forth Bridge at the time and Arrol was also building the replacement Tay Bridge. William Arrol was clearly a highly competent bridge-builder but, perhaps fortunately for Fowler, his high tender ruled him out and thus avoided any concerns that Fowler may have entertained about over-stretching even Arrol's almost boundless energy.

Union Bridge of America wins the contract

The Union Bridge Company of New York was awarded the contract, although in the event they only machined the eye-bars and pins themselves, engaging a range of subcontractors for the majority of the work. William Arrol, whose own tender for the entire bridge had been rejected, fabricated the girders using steel from Colville of Glasgow, while Head Wrightson of Stockton supplied the boiler plate for the caissons. A Sydney-based company built the stonework of the piers above water level, and two American contractors provided the labour for sinking the columns and assembling the bridge.

John Dixon, as will be seen later, identified the piers as a critical feature of the design, although his own tender used conventional cylindrical columns filled with concrete. The specification called for them to be sunk to a depth of 170 feet below water level, far greater than for any previous bridge and, as John noted, beyond the working limit of divers. It is not clear how he proposed to sink the piers for his bridge. On the other hand, the Union Bridge tender included an ingenious design to overcome the problem. The under-water section of each pier was formed from a rectangular caisson fabricated from ⅜ inch thick steel boiler plate, with rounded ends and slightly flared out over its lower twenty feet. Its bottom edge was fitted with hardened and sharpened steel cutting shoes. Inside the caisson were three similarly-fabricated cylinders which flared out over their lower length such that they met the bottom edge of the outer caisson. By excavating riverbed material from the insides of the three cylinders, using pontoon-mounted grabs, the entire assembly gradually descended into the river bed. As it descended additional sections were added, working from barges alongside, and the space between the three cylinders and the outer caisson was filled with concrete. Therefore, the outer caisson never had to withstand any significant water pressure and the weight of the pier gradually increased so as to assist its fall through the sediment. However, difficulty was experienced in keeping the caissons vertical and in position during the descent, and some misalignment was inevitable. On completion, the space inside the three cylinders was filled with concrete.

With the caissons completed, masonry piers were built above the concrete to carry the bridge. Each of the spans was assembled on a pontoon, resting on a trestle 50 feet high constructed on the pontoon. The pontoon was then positioned between a pair of piers at high tide so that, as the water level fell, the span came to rest on the piers.

Construction was completed in thirty-four months, four months longer than anticipated due to technical problems and a dispute over working hours; the American contractors demanding a ten-hour day, the Australian government recognising an eight-hour day. Thorough tests were carried out to check the deflection of the bridge under the specified 900 tons load. The bridge was opened amid much political fanfare in May 1889.

Bridge design, America v Britain

The fact that the cheapest tenders were all from America, and that the contract was awarded to the Union Bridge, caused much consternation among British engineers and contractors. American companies were already constructing most of the bridges in the Americas and even some in the British colonies, and the Hawkesbury contract was an unwelcome indication of what the future might hold.

Although British engineers had largely accepted steel as a replacement for wrought iron, their approach to bridge design was still based on wrought iron design practice. Each span was conceived as an inherently rigid structure of riveted steelwork. Girders had to be riveted together on site, a time-consuming operation requiring skilled workers. In contrast, American engineers favoured pre-fabricating components in workshops, using steam driven riveting equipment. These were then connected together on site by pins, a rapid and unskilled operation. This technique, together with the use of trusses (small cross-section members under pure tensile loading), greatly simplified accurate stress analysis. By these means the Americans were able to exploit the stronger and more consistent properties of steel, resulting in much lighter, and hence cheaper, structures.

For many years the Board of Trade regulations on maximum permitted stresses had hampered English engineers from exploiting the superior properties of steel over wrought iron. Twelve years before the Hawkesbury Bridge the journal *Engineering* had criticised the Board of Trade rules for encouraging English engineers to use 'old-fashioned ponderous girders of common iron' in contrast to 'the leading engineers on the other side of the Atlantic, who are now so boldly bridging the magnificent rivers of America.'

John Dixon questions the American design

John Dixon started a lengthy correspondence on the lessons of the Hawkesbury Bridge contract in the *Engineering* journal. While he claimed to be a supporter of free trade he thought it a questionable precedent for Australia to settle on an American design. Australia owed its existence to England and came to England to borrow all its money, so why had they turned their back on British bridge designers? It was a questionable precedent. The Union Bridge design

'Hawkesbury Bridge' from the Royal Australian Historical Society Osborne Collection. This detailed photograph shows how the American engineers exploited the strength of steel to produce a light weight, and consequently low cost, bridge. The design was criticised by British engineers, including John Dixon.
© Alamy Images reference E9CWKK

was a very much lighter structure than English engineers were accustomed to, and John had heard it referred to as cheap and nasty. He also implied that the American firms were short of business and were willing to work for negligible profit.

More thoughtfully, John pointed out that the wide discrepancy in costs was due to the uncertainties of the river bed. This point was picked up by the anonymous foreman of one of the other British companies tendering. He had seen the American drawings for the pier cylinders and was astonished at their thin walls, which he likened to milk cans. This criticism was dismissed by another anonymous correspondent remarking that both the Tay Bridge and the Forth Bridge used caissons of similar thickness. Another letter singled out the unnecessary precision demanded by English Board of Trade Inspectors as increasing costs significantly. He quoted examples such as the underside of deck plates having to be planed, rivet heads having to conform to a specific shape and complete spans having to be trial-assembled in workshops, only to be broken up, transported to site and reassembled.

Troubles start almost immediately

Defects were soon apparent in the stonework of the piers. Problems were also experienced with the spans, and in 1925 it was decided to strengthen the decks. Further problems appeared in the 1930s and when a serious crack was found in one of the piers in 1938 it was decided to build a new bridge. The inherent weakness of the original structure was assumed to be the impossibility of reaching bedrock for the base of the piers, compounded by bridge loadings which exceeded the design specifications.

There was another defect. In the Union Bridge design, the under-water steel caisson was intended only to form a mould for the concrete infill, which would become the structural member when solidified. Corrosion of the steel plates should not matter, since the weight of the bridge would be carried on the concrete column. But the subcontractors had just filled some of the steel cylinders with rubble, echoing the problem faced by John on the viaducts for the Whitby to Loftus Railway. The inevitable corrosion of the outer steel plates was therefore critical.

Work began on a replacement bridge in 1940, with completion in 1946. A report in 2016 found faults in the piers and the spans of the replacement bridge which, it had been claimed, had a design life of 200 years.

References

Innovations in Bridge Engineering Technology
Edited by Khaled M Mahmoud
Taylor and Francis, London, 2007
Chapter 25 'Hawkesbury Railway Bridge near Sydney, Australia' by Kirti Gandhi is a comprehensive description of the bridge.

The Hawkesbury River: A Social and Natural History
Paul Boon
Commonwealth Scientific and Industrial Research Organisation Publishing, Victoria, Australia, 2017
Chapter 12 on railway crossings has a history of the first bridge.

Hawkesbury River Rail Bridge and Long Island Group
Office of Environment and Heritage, New South Wales Government, Australia
www.environment.ns.gov,au?heritageapp/ViewHeritage ItemDetails.aspx?ID=4800130
History of the original and replacement bridges.

The Hawkesbury River Bridge was designed to last 'at least 200 years'
The Sydney Morning Herald, 11 May 1946
The old American-designed bridge lasted less than 60 years, the new Australian-designed bridge will last at least 200 years.

The Use of Steel
Engineering, London, 26 September 1873, pages 251-2
Editorial critical of Board of Trade rules and English engineers not exploiting steel.

Contracts open - Borings for the Hawkesbury Bridge
The Engineer, London, 20 February 1885, page 155
Call for tenders for design, detailed specification and construction of the crossing.

American Affairs (From our Own Correspondent)
The Birmingham Daily Post, 19 April 1886, page 4
American firms confident of winning contract for bridges in preference to English firms. Their pin-jointed construction means that most construction can be done in the workshop with easy assembly on site. In contrast riveted structures require much on site work.

Hawkesbury Bridge - To the Editor of Engineering
Engineering, London, 23 April 1886, page 400
Letters from John Dixon and 'Cosmopolite' who supported American design practice.

Hawkesbury Bridge - To the Editor of Engineering
Engineering, London, 30 April 1886, page 431
Letter from foreman of a tendering company questioning thickness of American steelwork.

Hawkesbury Bridge - To the Editor of Engineering
Engineering, London, 7 May 1886, page 458
Further correspondence. Complaints were sour grapes by unsuccessful tenderers.

Hawkesbury Bridge - To the Editor of Engineering
Engineering, London, 14 May 1886, page 482
More letters including complaint that entries had not even been acknowledged or the unsuccessful plans returned and problems of over-zealous inspectors.

The Deepest Foundations in the World
Scientific American, Boston and Philadelphia, Issue 19, 8 May 1886, Volume 54, pages 287 and 292
Description of sinking the caissons with good engravings.

The Hawkesbury River Bridge; New South Wales
Engineering, London, 8 April 1887, pages 318-9 with fold out drawings
Description of the structure by Union Bridge Company and Sir John Fowler.

Foundation Caissons for the Hawkesbury River Bridge
Engineering, London, 27 April 1887, pages 370-372
Description of the sinking of the caissons.

25 Mining interests

John Dixon had at least three episodes as a director of a mining enterprise, and all ended in tears, at least for the unfortunate investors. He was a director of the Pen'Allt Silver-Lead Mining Company in Wales from 1870 to 1871, chairman of the Rio Malagón Mines in Portugal from 1881 to 1882 and a director of the Crooke's Mining and Smelting Company, operating in America, from 1882 to 1885. All three companies failed.

John Dixon's interest in mining

Like many of the Victorian engineers, John Dixon had business interests outside his main profession. The latter half of the 19th century saw a spectacular growth in business activities, with enticing new company prospectuses in the advertising columns of every newspaper. Not surprisingly, the wonderful opportunities offered by many of these prospectuses often failed to materialise, but only after the unfortunate investors had parted with their money, mining ventures being particularly risky. John would have learned about new ventures with a reasonable chance of success and the prospect of good returns through his business contacts in London and abroad, his membership of the Freemasons, and through his engineering colleagues. He seems to have had a penchant for mining companies; perhaps he had inherited something of the spirit of the past generations of the Dixons of Cockfield Fell with their extensive coal mining interests.

Although there was an insatiable demand for raw materials to feed industry, and mining procedures and equipment were well developed, geological investigation was in its infancy and there was no guarantee that a new mine would reach profitable seams. If one was a director, with a strong belief in capitalism, the free market and the survival of the fittest, one could use inside knowledge to divest a personal shareholding before doubtful prospects became general knowledge. While not wishing to accuse John of sharp practice, he does not appear to have the strong sense of ethics prevalent among the traditional Quaker businesses.

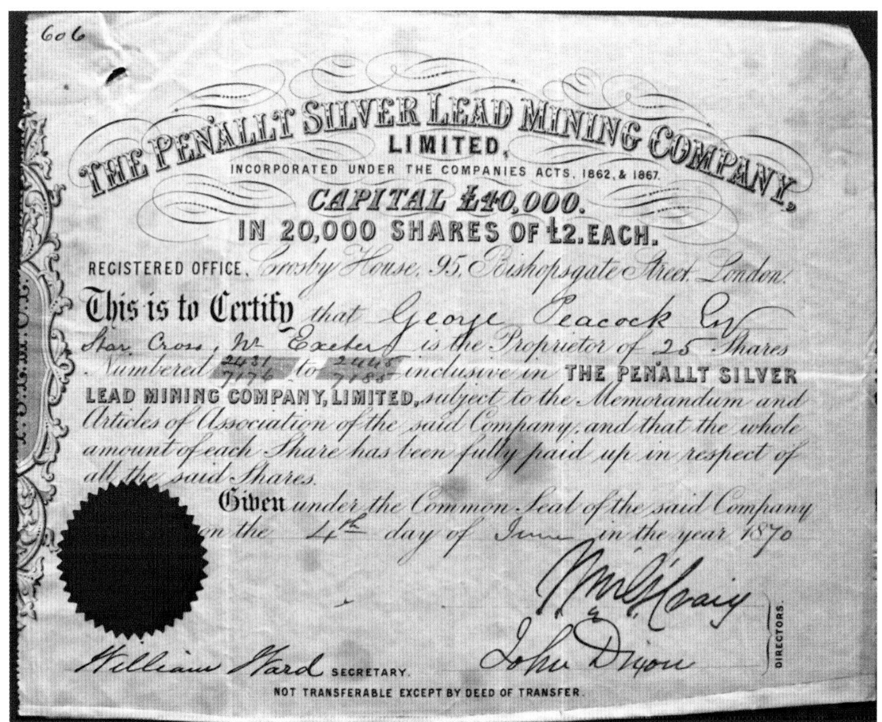

606

THE PEN'ALLT SILVER LEAD MINING COMPANY, LIMITED,
INCORPORATED UNDER THE COMPANIES ACTS, 1862, & 1867.
CAPITAL £40,000.
IN 20,000 SHARES OF £2. EACH.

REGISTERED OFFICE, Crosby House, 95, Bishopsgate Street London.

This is to Certify that George Peacock Esq Star Cross, nr Exeter is the Proprietor of 25 Shares Numbered 2431 / 7176 to 2445 / 7188 inclusive in THE PEN'ALLT SILVER LEAD MINING COMPANY, LIMITED, subject to the Memorandum and Articles of Association of the said Company; and that the whole amount of each Share has been fully paid up in respect of all the said Shares.

Given under the Common Seal of the said Company on the 4th day of June in the year 1870

W G Craig
John Dixon
DIRECTORS.

William Ward SECRETARY.

NOT TRANSFERABLE EXCEPT BY DEED OF TRANSFER.

Share certificate for the Pen'Allt Silver Lead Mining Company, with John Dixon's signature as one of the directors. Captain George Peacock (1840-1883) served in the Royal Navy before commanding a steamer service along the Pacific coast of South America. Ferdinand de Lesseps used Captain Peacock's survey of the Panama isthmus for his canal. Captain Peacock bought at least fifty £2 shares in the mine.
Reproduced by courtesy of the Liverpool Record Office, Liverpool Libraries. National Archives reference 387 PEA/9/5.

Mining in Wales

In 1870 share certificates for the Pen'Allt Silver-Lead Mining Company Limited appeared, carrying the names of two directors: W G Craig and John Dixon. There is no doubt about the identity of this John Dixon since he sent his younger brother Waynman to construct a mine tramway there in 1870. The name of the mine has alternative spellings (Pen'Allt, Penalt or Benalt), all deriving from 'pen' meaning head or top and 'gallt' meaning hill and, just to confuse matters further, is sometimes known as Nentlle Vale.

It is situated Penygroes, near Caernarfon. Although there was extensive slate extraction in the area, there were also a few mineral mines, principally for lead.

In the 1840s the Pen'Allt mine was a single adit penetrating just over a hundred yards into the hillside to reach a three-foot vein of copper, mundic (iron-pyrites) and Black Jack (zinc-blende). By 1870 the huge success of lead mines in Shropshire and at Llanidloes in mid-Wales made it easy to raise the capital for a new lead mine. John Dixon, William G Craig of Surbiton and W H Bond of Lewisham set up the Pen'Allt Silver Lead Mining Company Limited, acquired the existing mine and issued shares.

No fewer than four independent surveys were published, promising up to 101 ounces of silver for each ton of lead. Shares were quickly taken up and Captain Thomas Glanville appointed mine manager. By July 1870 an extensive mill near the river was largely completed. Three new adits had been driven, crushing rolls driven by a water-wheel and a steam-driven stone breaker installed, and a building was being put up to house German ore dressing machinery. It was at this time that John sent Waynman, who had by now joined his office at No.1 Laurence Pountney Hill, to the site to construct a tramway on a self-acting incline between the lowest adit and the stone-breaker.

The directors were enthusiastic about progress, claiming that 'the works will, when in full operation, present a scene of animation and industry not to be equalled in the Principality.' Captain Glanville, the mine's resident manager, assured investors of immense quantities of ore awaiting treatment. In January 1870 he reported that 'splendid stones of silver-lead are now being broken from the winze sinking below the No.3 Cross Cut, better than any yet seen in the mine.' Anticipating the start of a useful output, the directors appointed Mr G S Clement to act as broker to handle the sales of ore. On 8 February, at their first meeting, the shareholders were told by William Craig that the mine had been operating for four months. Lumps of ore with an abundance of silver crystals were passed round and admired, while the assayers had reported an average of sixty-six ounces of silver per ton of lead, and the lead was of high quality.

Shareholders were invited to a meeting at the mine in November 1870, when they could see the incline operating and inspect the modern dressing machinery. However, there was no output from the mine, even though Captain Glanville claimed:

> 'Judging from the present appearance of the lode and the specimens of rich silver-lead ores broken from it, I have every confidence that as the level gets deeper into the hill the lode will increase in richness. I have never seen such good indications at so shallow a depth.'

Over the following months, Captain Glanville continued to deliver encouraging reports. By the end of 1870 a very large pile of ore had been partly dressed by the patent German dressing machinery, from which between fifteen and twenty tons of lead ore were ready for market, but it was not proposed to make any sales until the end of January. By mid-January all the machinery was complete, there were now fifty tons of lead ore ready for sale, 'the mine had never shown a better appearance' and there was 'no limit to the ore coming out of it.'

By April 1871 the real state of affairs became all too apparent. The £3,000 expenditure on machinery was denounced as premature, and Glanville was called upon 'to explain the wonderful discrepancy between his estimates and the actual results.' It was also revealed that Glanville had been dealing in shares in the venture. There is little doubt that Thomas Glanville had difficulties in recognising truth and reality. He was later a leading figure in the Talybont Mine, where he was said to have given what must have been some of the most outrageous assertions ever made about the prospects of a mine. At Pen'Allt Glanville was replaced by Robert Casement, from the Laxey Mine on the Isle of Man, a man already known to John and Waynman when they were constructing the pier at Douglas during the previous year. Casement, who had been described as a practical rather than a professional man, had been supervising work on the masonry breakwater at Douglas while John was building the iron pier in 1869. This appointment is interesting since it implies that John was taking an active role in the running of the mine, and therefore cannot escape all blame for its misleading of shareholders. Robert Casement laid out the true situation; prospects for the mine were bleak.

On 12 July 1971 John presented a petition to the Master of the Rolls in the Court of Chancery to wind up the Pen'Allt Silver-Lead Mining Company Limited, after just over a year's existence. That it was John himself who presented the petition again suggests that he had an active role within the company. James William Thomas, of Tilly and Thomas, was appointed as the official liquidator in September.

There was a protracted legal action taken against the directors who, undeterred, promoted a new venture, the Great Mountain Silver-Lead Mine Company, to acquire the site for £2,000. The mine was now to produce paint pigment in addition to metal ores. By February 1873 a few tons of lead and zinc ores were ready for sale. A deeper adit was driven, but proved disappointing, and the second company collapsed with another Court of Chancery case. This seems to have been the end of John's interest in the mine, but there were several subsequent attempts to establish mining companies at Pen'Allt, in 1878, in 1906, in 1917 and in 1925.

Certainly, the Pen'Allt company attracted men of dubious ethics. In 1872 a Mr Fothergill attempted to sell another mining property to the Pen'Allt company. Quite separately he had already contracted to subscribe to 1,000 shares and, rather than give Pen'Allt the money for the shares, he attempted to use part of the value of the property as payment. He was taken to court by the company. In another legal case two years later, the liquidator, James William Thomas, was accused of fraudulently endorsing a cheque for £47, intended for one of the creditors, and paying it into his own account!

Rio Malagón (Sulphur, Copper and Silver) Mines Limited, Portugal

In July 1881 notices appeared in the press from Brighton to Aberdeen for an undertaking 'believed to be quite removed from the class of speculative mines, with the uncertainties and disappointments so often attending such projects, as by the arrangements already entered into it is expected to rank among dividend mines of the highest class immediately the mines are opened out.' The Rio Malagón mine was situated some thirty miles west of the Rio Tinto Mines in south west Spain. The Rio Malagón Mines chairman, John Dixon, was said to have been engaged for some years in constructing extensive works for the Rio Tinto Company and to be well acquainted with the Rio Tinto, the San Domingo and the Tharsis mines, neighbours of Rio Malagón. Bearing in mind that his experience with Rio Tinto had been constructing the ore-loading facility at Huelva, and his association with the mining operation had been minimal, this statement could be questioned. Some of the other directors hardly inspired confidence:

- Mark William Carr (1857-1886) was born in Gateshead and worked on railways in Wales and India before becoming the general manager of the Rio Tinto railway. John Dixon would have certainly known him well, and it looks likely that they were the promoters of the scheme, having learned that the mine might become available while they were working for the Rio Tinto Mines.
- Henry Arthur Herbert (1840-1901) inherited the large Muckross estate in County Kerry, originally created with money from copper mines in Kerry. His father and great grandfather had both represented Kerry in Parliament. Herbert was vice chairman of the Limerick and Kerry Railway (only forty-two miles long and operated by the Waterford and Limerick Railway) and an incompetent manager of the family fortune as the estate became insolvent in 1897.
- James Rennie, a director of London and Glasgow Engineering Company which built iron ships and steam engines at Govan in Glasgow. One wonders if potential investors might have confused him with the celebrated engineering brothers John and George Rennie.
- Hon Randolph Henry Stewart (1836-1920) seems to have spent much of his time at horse races, receptions and balls. He was a director of the Richmond Consolidated Mining Company established in 1871 to mine gold in Nevada, United States of America, and also a director of the Norway Copper Mines Company.

The prospectus made much of the agreement with Richards, Power and Company of Swansea to purchase the entire ore output of up to 12,000 tons annually for five years. By this time the company, which had started in shipping but moved into speculative ore trading, was probably in financial trouble and it failed in August 1883 with liabilities of £300,000. The mining engineer, Mr Richard White Rickard (1837-1887), considered the Rio Malagón Mine to be one of the best in the Huelva district. Rickard liquidated his ore smelting business in September 1883.

By the beginning of August all the Rio Malagón shares had been taken up and, as promised in the prospectus, an engineer was immediately despatched to inspect the mines. There was then an ominous silence from the company and by mid-1882 press notices appeared calling a meeting of creditors. At a meeting in July the disillusioned shareholders resolved to go into voluntary liquidation and appoint Horace Woodburn Kirby as the official liquidator. This meeting was chaired by James Rennie; it is not known whether John was merely unavailable or whether he had resigned from the board by this stage. In October Kirby was able to announce that he had managed to salvage £2 10s for each £5 share, followed by slightly better news of a further £1 per share in November.

Crooke's Mining and Smelting Company

As the Ute native Americans left what is now Hinsdale County in Colorado, white prospectors rushed in. In the autumn of 1870 the *Chicago Tribune* reported 'Fifteen hundred would be a low estimate of the people already arrived, where, one month ago, a single cabin was the only evidence of the white man.'

The area around what became Lake City contained some of the richest lead and silver mines in the San Juan Mountains. One of the mining centres was at Ute Ulay, named after the Ute chief who had negotiated the Brunot Agreement under which the Ute peacefully left the San Juan Mountains. The first claim to the minerals at Ute Ulay was registered in 1874 by four white prospectors, but they lacked the capital necessary to develop the site. The Crooke's Mining Company was formed in 1876 by the brothers John and Lewis Crooke, astute businessmen from the eastern United States. They bought the mining rights in 1876 for $125,000, and other mines in the Lake City area. This investment was followed by a smelter at what is now Crooke's Falls and accommodation for the miners. In 1878 they extracting 2,000 tons of ore from the Ute Ulay mines, at a net profit of $12 per ton. Lake City became a boom town with such amenities as seven saloons, six restaurants (two open all night), five blacksmiths, four Chinese laundries, three barber shops and two cigar factories.

The Crooke brothers must have realised that there were plenty of English speculators attracted by the prospect of making money from Colorado mines, not through toil with pick and shovel but through the purchase of shares in speculative mining companies. Enthusiasm for investing in

Colorado's mines shrugged off cautionary warnings such as that by a reporter for *The Times* in 1878:

> 'I am convinced that many of the English capitalists who have invested their funds in California, Utah, Nevada and Colorado, would have spared themselves much futile anxiety and painful disappointment had they simply thrown their money into the deepest part of the sea.'

It was against this background that a prospectus for the Crooke's Mining and Smelting Company Limited appeared in the press in the spring of 1882, seeking to raise £301,000 capital. The intention was to take over the mining properties and smelting works set up by John and Lewis Crooke in the Galena District of Colorado, United States of America. John Dixon of Laurence Pountney Hill was listed as one of the directors. Apart from John, the London-based directors were notable for their lack of experience in mining. His nine fellow directors had backgrounds in railways, banking, insurance, docks, brewing and tramways. The chairman was James Edwin Thorold Rogers, MP, an Oxford University economist and historian. He visited Colorado on behalf of the company and presented an optimistic report on its potential, stating that 'though I cannot assume the authority of a professional mineralogist, I was entirely satisfied with the reports of the experts sent out by the Board.'

The appointment of Professor Thorold Rogers is an extreme example of the need felt by new companies to appoint a chairman who would be seen as trustworthy. That an Oxford academic with little experience of business and none in mining, could lead an American mining venture was stretching credibility. Then for him to claim that, in spite of having no knowledge of minerals or mining, there were good prospects for the mine, is entering the realms of fantasy. Even discounting the competence of the chairman, John's other directors had little relevant experience between them.

Undeterred by the numerous failures of foreign mining enterprises, and in spite of the prophetic name of the company, there was a rush to take up the share offer, which was almost fully subscribed within a week, mainly from New York. At the first shareholders' meeting Rogers ventured that they had purchased the mining property at a very reasonable price and congratulated those present on the prospects that lay before them.

At first there was genuine progress, with the construction of a larger ore mill and a dam to meet the energy needs of the site. There were also real difficulties, as there was no railway to the area and the lake behind the dam froze every winter, cutting off energy supplies. But the greatest difficulties seem to have been at board room level. By 1885 it was becoming apparent that not all was well. There had been duplicity in establishing the company. Considering the frequent references in the newspapers to Thorold Rogers' political and academic work, his embarrassment over the Crooke's Mining and Smelting Company was kept fairly quiet. Only the *Pall Mall Gazette* reported it:

> 'When the chairman of a company with which he had been connected from the first, feels compelled to tell his shareholders that the concern has been "a gigantic swindle," matters must have arrived at a crucial point. Such has been the fate of Professor Thorold Rogers, M.P., who has been mercilessly exposing to view the early history of Crookes Mining and Smelting Company, of which he is the chairman. The gist of the matter seems to be that the promoters were one too many for the Oxford professor, who has been a little too confiding in human nature.'

Unlike the Rio Malagón Company, which had entered voluntary liquidation, the Crooke's Mining and Smelting Company had to be pursued into the Court of Chancery by their creditors. In September 1885 the High Court appointed an official receiver, none other than Horace Woodburn Kirby who had wound up the Rio Malagón Company three years earlier. He was able to pay the creditors the full amounts they were owed, but the shareholders must have lost most if not all their investment.

Who's who?
James Edwin Thorold Rodgers (1823-1890)

Thorold Rogers read classics at Oxford University and was ordained in the Church of England. His academic interests as an Oxford professor were the classics, philosophy and particularly economics, where he gained a good reputation for basing his economic theories on facts and statistics. He was Liberal MP for Southwark 1880-1885 and for Bermondsey 1885-86, although he was never greatly involved in Parliament preferring the academic life at Oxford. He became an archetypal academic historian, disliking government and the governing classes, sympathising with the working classes, and a pacifist, although he had led a privileged life himself. His practical experience of business was restricted being chairman of the National Liberal Land Company and a director of the Health Insurance Association. All in all, he could hardly be less well qualified to lead a mining venture in America.

Not surprisingly his obituaries made no mention of his unfortunate experience with the Crooke's Mining and Smelting Company.

The Ute Ulay complex was eventually sold to the American Lake City Mining Company, and the mines re-opened in 1887. In 1889 the Denver and Rio Grande Railroad arrived at Lake City, but optimism was short-lived since the Lake City Mining Company went out of business in 1890. The mines once again recovered but the next hundred years were characterised by boom and bust, and numerous changes of ownership. By the 1980s mining had ceased and today the site is being developed as a heritage tourism destination.

Were John Dixon's mining escapades unfortunate or unethical?

The early loss of all three ventures does bring to mind Lady Bracknell's observation on the loss of parents. It is difficult to believe that John did not take advantage of 19th century enthusiasm for investing in anything with a good prospectus. As a director he would probably not have lost money through the failures, either through preference shares or through using insider knowledge to dispose of his shares at the first hints of trouble. He was certainly not alone in taking advantage of the thirst for share acquisition in Victorian society, and there were plenty of warnings to potential investors in mining companies.

However, on balance it is hard to escape the view that John Dixon's mining forays did him little credit.

Top) Ute Ulay Mine and Mill, Colorado.
Images reproduced by courtesy of Hinsdale County Historical Society, Colorado, United States of America.

Middle) Building in Ute Ulay Lake City, Colorado.
Settled in 1874, Lake City became a boom town catering for all the needs of the miners.
Images reproduced by courtesy of Hinsdale County Historical Society, Colorado, United States of America.

Bottom) 'Pen-yr-Allt Lead Mine' a photograph taken inside the mine in June 1997 showing ghost marks of a tramway. Presumably this is taken in later workings of the PenAllt Mine, and is not the tramway laid by Waynman Dixon. Reproduced by courtesy of the Royal Commission on the Ancient and Historical Monuments of Wales, Ffordd Penglais, Penglais Road, Aberystwyth. Reference WMPT28_006 (C.588562).

Acknowledgements

David Franklin for explanation of Welsh place names.

Kristine Borchers, Lake City Downtown Improvement and Revitalisation Team, for assistance with the history of the mines in the area.

References

The Old Copper Mines of Snowdonia, third edition
David Bick
Landmark Publishing Ltd, Ashbourne, 2003
History of the Penalt mine, including the reproduction of a share certificate bearing John Dixon's name as a director.

Notes written for George Longstaff by Waynman Dixon, 7 March 1918
In private ownership
Includes a note about being sent to the Pen'Allt mine immediately after working on the pier at Douglas, Isle of Man. 'Thence to Nantle, Carnarvonshire to construct a mine tramway to Penalt Lead Mine.'

Commercial and Monetary
The Birmingham Daily Post, 31 January 1870, page 7
Reports of splendid stones being broken at the Pen'Allt Mine.

Money Market and City News
The Morning Post, London, 2 February 1870, page 8
Appointment of G S Clement of Throgmorton Street as broker.

Money Market and City News
The Morning Post, London, 8 February 1870, page 8
First meeting of shareholders in the Pen'Allt Mine Company.

Commercial and Monetary
The Birmingham Daily Post, 23 December 1870, page 3
Report from Captain Glanville of 15-20 tons of dressed ore.

Money Market and City News
The Morning Post, London, 21 January 1871, page 8
Now there are 50 tons of ore ready at the Pen'Allt Mine.

In the Matter of the Companies Acts 1862 and 1867
The Morning Advertiser, London, 14 July 1871, page 1
A petition for winding up the Pen'Allt Mine Company presented by John Dixon of Surbiton.

Mines
The Daily News, London, 1 September 1871, page 5
James W Thomas appointed official liquidator of the Pen'Allt silver Lead mining Company Limited.

Alltycrib (Allt-Y-Crib, Talybont, Tal-Y-Bont) Mixed Mine
http://www.aditnow.co.uk/Mines/Alltycrib-Mixed-Mine_7581/
Thomas Glanville described as a bent mine captain who conned investors.

Great Mountain Silver Lead Mining Company Ltd Receivers' Accounts
Reference C 30/3207
National Archives, Kew, London
Winding up of the second mining company.

Law Intelligence - Rolls Court - Dec. 14 Re Penallt Silver-Lead Mining Company – Fothergill's case
The Standard, London, 16 December 1872, page 6
Contract to purchase shares judged quite separate from contract to sell property to the company.

Charge of Forgery against an Official Liquidator
Jarrow Express, 3 October 1874, page 3
James William Thomas accused of pocketing a cheque for £47.

Money Market and City News
The Morning Post, London, 6 February 1879, page 2
Details of the Limerick and Kerry Railway which was to be worked and maintained by the Waterford and Limerick Railway.

Rio Malagón (sulphur-copper & silver) Mines (limited)
Pall Mall Gazette, London, 21 July 1881, page 16
Offer of first issue of 12,000 shares of £10 each.

The Money Market
The Manchester Courier and Lancashire General Advertiser, 6 August 1881, page 4
Letters of allocation sent out, an engineer will immediately proceed to the Rio Malagón mines to inspect them.

The London Gazette, 30 June 1882, page 3055
Notice of a meeting of creditors of Rio Malagón mines following a petition to the High Court, Chancery Division, by Henry Morier Evans, general advertising agent.

The London Gazette, 11 August 1882, page 3760
Extraordinary meeting of shareholders of Rio Malagón mines on 17 July resolved to go into voluntary liquidation and appoint Mr Horace Woodburn Kirby as official liquidator.

St James's Gazette, London, 6 October 1882, page 9
Mr H Woodburn Kirby, the official liquidator, announced a dividend of £2 10s per £5 share.

The Money Market
The Manchester Courier and Lancashire General Advertiser, 18 November 1882, page 4
Liquidator announced a further £1 per share bringing the total to £3 10s per share.

The London Gazette, 18 May 1883, page 2642
Notice of meeting of the Rio Malagón (Sulphur, Copper and Silver) Mines Limited to hear the liquidator's accounts.

The Failure of Messrs Richards, Power and Company
South Wales Daily News, 29 August 1883, page 3
Failure of company with £300,000 liabilities.

Local Liquidations
South Wales Daily News, 12 September 1883, page 3
Richard White Rickard's business in liquidation.

The New Colorado Mines
The Times, London, 5 October 1870, page 4
Article reproduced from *The Chicago Tribune* about the great excitement due to the discovery of silver and lead mining opportunities in Colorado.

The Colorado United Gold and Silver Mining Company
The Times, London, 14 June 1871, page 4
Prospectus for a London-based company to acquire the California Mine in Colorado.

Valuable and Extensive Mining Properties
The Times, London, 20 August 1872, page 1
Small advertisement from 'a practical businessman who has organised and managed in the United States one of the most successful of the Colorado Mining Companies' looking for an influential business partner to set up a company.

Mining and mines in Colorado
The Times, London, 6 September 1878, page 9
Describes the Colorado United Mine Company's business and the ease with which English investors can lose money in Colorado mines.

Prospectus, Crooke's Mining and Smelting Company Limited
The Standard, London, 19 April 1882, page 6
Company launched with offer of 60,000 shares of £5 each.

The Mining Market
The Manchester Courier and Lancashire General Advertiser, 24 April 1882, page 3
The launch of Crooke's Mining and Smelting Company had an excellent reception and lists will close on 26 April.

Money and Commerce
The Western Daily Press, Bristol, 16 August 1882, page 6
Report on the first shareholders' meeting of Crooke's Mining and Smelting Company.

The Money Market
The Standard, London, 10 September 1885, page 6
Mr H Woodburn Kirby appointed as official liquidator of Crooke's Mining and Smelting Company Limited.

City Notes
The Pall Mall Gazette, London, 2 June 1885, page 5
The embarrassment of Professor Thorold Rogers, MP.

Money Market and City News
The Morning Post, London, 17 August 1886, page 6
Creditors of Crooke's Mining and Smelting Company will be paid 20s in the pound.

Death of Professor Thorold Rogers
St James's Gazette, London, 14 October 1890, page 13
A typical obituary of Thorold Rogers.

A Brief History of the Ute Ulay
Casey Carrigan
Posted by Anna Macleod at https://static1.squarespace.com
Covers the history of the Ute and Ulay mines and the Crooke Brothers.

26 Falkland Islands properties

Rather mysteriously, John Dixon believed that he owned two lots of land in the Falkland Islands, numbers 11 and 12 on Villiers Street in Stanley. These were originally purchased by Captain Bracey Robson Wilson and then fraudulently used by his son as security for a loan, possibly from John. When Captain Wilson's son fled to America, John must have believed that ownership of the plots had transferred to him. In reality, ownership had remained with Captain Wilson. There is no known reference to John ever having worked in the islands or wishing to build property there.

Correspondence

On 11 March 1886 John Dixon wrote to the secretary of the Falkland Islands Company's London office:

> 'Dear Sir, I do not know whether you may remember me seeing you many years since as to two plots of land in Stanley. I thought that as at the time things were flat I should let them lie dormant with the exception of notifying my possession to the Colonial Government there. I turned them up the other day and shall be glad to know if you are now buyers or what you can recommend me to do. I don't know anyone out there.'

This prompted the London office to send a despatch to the head office in Stanley:

> 'Mr John Dixon, owner of two lots of land at Stanley Nos 11 and 12 Villiers Street, has again applied about them asking if we are buyers. I replied 'no' but requested him to name a price to be communicated to you; this is not done so we wish you to consider the matter and let us know the present value and if it would be a good purchase for this company.'

The reply from Stanley is not known, but the result was that John placed the disposal of the two plots with the company:

> 'Mr John Dixon about whom we wrote as possessing two Allotments of Land No 11 and 12 Villiers Street, Stanley, has entrusted certain papers and deeds relating thereto to us as per list enclosed in order that you may enquire whether he can dispose of the same, please therefore, enter into the matter carefully and let us have full particulars.'

The reference to 'certain papers and deeds' is a mystery since there are no entries in the Land Registers recording any sale to John Dixon. The Registers record that suburban lots 11 and 12 Villiers Street were bought by Captain Bracey Robson Wilson on 15 July 1852 for £30 each and later sold by him on 12 October 1889 for £32 each.

Matters are complicated by a despatch sent from the Colonial Manager of the Falkland Islands Company to their London Office later in 1886:

> 'Dixon's land question seems to me a singular one, and there are

(Copy) 1 Lawrence Pountney Hill E.C.

11 Mch 86.

Dr Sir Falkland Islands. I do not know whether you may remember me seeing you many yrs since as to two plots of land in Stanley—

VILLIERS ST

I thought that as at the time things were flat I should let them lie dormant with the exception of notifying my possession to the Col. Govt there—

I turned them up the other day & shall be glad to know if you are now buyers or what you can recommend me to do—I don't know anyone out there—

(Sgd.) John Dixon.

The Sec. F.I.Co

Co to Dixon 12 Mch 86.

Acknowledged above & asked for price but at present were not buyers—

John Dixon's letter describing what he believed was his property on Villiers Street.
Reproduced by courtesy of Tansy Bishop, Jane Cameron National Archives, Stanley, Falkland Islands.

'Port Stanley (b)' photograph from the Gustav Schulz collection 1887. Gustav Schulz (1849-1912) was born in Prussia but later took up residence in Brighton where he had a photographic studio. In 1887 he travelled to South America and the Falklands; Julius Klinkhardt of Leipzig published twenty of his Falkland photographs in South America No.1, The Falkland Islands. Image supplied by Tansy Bishop, Jane Cameron National Archives, Stanley, Falkland Islands.

> contradictions about it: I have read all the papers, and it appears that Captain Wilson's son, who was evidently a drunkard and apparently a thief, was in Mr Dixon's employ, and bottled to the United States without accounting for the £50 entrusted to him for business purposes, having previously borrowed over £100 on the security of two little deeds of property which he alleged had been presented to him by his father.'

In spite of the unusual name, it is difficult to identify the son who was named as Bracey Robson Wilson and described as a drunkard and thief. Captain Wilson's first son with this name was Bracey Robson Wilson (1833-1855). Although the Falkland properties were purchased by Captain Wilson in 1852, it is unlikely that this son, who died two years later, would have been employed by John, who was only twenty years old at that time and with no international business dealings. Captain Wilson was obviously anxious that his name should live on, and a later son, born in South America in 1875, was also named Bracey Robson Wilson. However, he would have surely been too young to have been entrusted with business dealings and a substantial sum of money by John. The most likely explanation is that there was yet another son named Bracey Robson Wilson, born soon after 1855 and deceased by 1875. Unfortunately records of Captain Wilson's many children are far from complete.

How did John Dixon meet Captain Wilson?

Seeking a close connection between Bracey Robson Wilson and John Dixon is far from simple. As far as is known, John did not work in South America until the 1870s, by which time Wilson was living in Peru as the British Vice-Consul. It is extremely unlikely that John would have visited Peru, given that his work was all on the east coast of Brazil. Both men had lived in Bishopwearmouth, but Wilson left in 1845 and John did not arrive until 1856. Wilson had been based in Swansea from about 1845 to 1868, but Dixon didn't work at Port Talbot until 1874 with his CwmAvon Ironworks involvement 1877-79. However, it must surely be that the two men did meet somewhere, when conversation would soon have established their mutual Wearside connections.

Why John should have entrusted a business assignment to Captain Wilson's son is a mystery, but he must have held some regard for the man to advance him £100, although perhaps caution meant that he demanded a security against the loan. When Wilson's son absconded to America, John must have believed that he then owned the two plots. However, the Falkland Island Company records clearly show that the two plots remained in name of Captain Wilson from 1852 to 1889. It is clear from John's letter of 11 March 1886 that he had been in direct contact with the Falkland Islands Company in London 'many years since'. At that time, on being told that the market was flat, he had done nothing until

1886. By this time Wilson was retired in Dundee, and probably out of contact with John. In 1889 Wilson, either himself or his executors after his death, sold the two plots.

Who's who
Captain Bracey Robson Wilson (1812-89)

Bracey Robson Wilson was at the very least a colourful character. Born in Bishopwearmouth, Sunderland, in 1812. Wilson married three times. His first marriage, in 1832, was to Elizabeth Ann Garbutt from South Shields. They had four children; the eldest son, also named Bracey Robson, died from cholera while aboard the sailing ship *Nimrod* in June 1855. Following the presumed death of Elizabeth in the late 1840s, Wilson moved to Swansea. There he married Louisa Hintze from America, and there were seven more children before she died in 1868. He then went to Uruguay and on to Peru, where he was appointed vice-consul, a position which he held until 1880 when loss of sight forced him to resign. Wilson married Elizabeth Kennedy from Dundee about 1870; he was in his late fifties, she was twenty years younger. There were at least two more children, including another Bracey Robson Wilson, who became a variety artist under the name of Jock Stuart and was described as an eccentric comedian.

Relinquishing the vice-consulship, Captain Wilson and his third wife, Elizabeth, moved to her native Dundee. In spite of his blindness, he took regular walks in the Dundee parks and sailed a model yacht. He wrote a series of newspaper articles for the *Newcastle Weekly Chronicle* from 1881 to 1889 in which he reminisced about his life in Sunderland and his sailing career, under the pseudonym 'Robinson Crusoe'. In 1889, Wilson died at the age of seventy-eight at Stonehaven. By then one of his sons, George Gordon Wilson, had become the vice-consul in Peru.

When sailing round Cape Horn, Wilson sometimes called in at Port Stanley in the Falkland Islands, where he and the Governor, George Rennie, appear to have struck up a friendship. When it was proposed to introduce a direct mail service from England to the Falklands, Wilson was recommended to command the Royal Mail packet *Amelia*, which was to operate the final link between Montevideo, Uruguay and Port Stanley, first arriving at Stanley on 1 July 1852, nine days out from Montevideo with general cargo and nineteen passengers. Wilson remained a supporter of the Falklands at a time when there was a move by the British Government to abandon them. He wrote an influential article on the islands in *The Nautical Magazine*, which was used to support the successful case to retain the islands.

The properties

The two properties are referred to as allotments of land, and there is no evidence that houses were ever built on them. When they were acquired by Captain Wilson the population of the Falklands was about 300, the majority probably in Port Stanley. By the time that John Dixon was enquiring about selling the plots, twenty years later, the overall population had risen to 1,850, with 650 living in Port Stanley. Although this was a significant increase in population, there was plenty of cheap building land, and there seems to have been little interest in the potential sale of the two plots.

Villiers Street in 2017. Villiers Streets is the road running up the hill from the sea front. Reproduced by courtesy of Robert Rowlands, The Falkland Collection.

Acknowledgements

Tansy Bishop, National Archivist at the Jane Cameron National Archives, Stanley, Falkland Islands, for providing documents and other information.

David Tatham, former ambassador and governor of the Falklands, for locating a copy of the Gustav Schulz book.

Robert Rowlands of Stanley for information and photographs of Villiers Street.

Teena Ormond of the Falklands Islands Museum and National Trust for searching for information.

Norman Kirtlan of the Sunderland Antiquarian Society for information on Captain Bracey Robson Wilson.

Alex and Beth Porteous for the initial information about the Falkland Islands properties.

References

Letter from John Dixon to the Secretary of the Falkland Islands Company dated 11 March 1886
Correspondence - Various - Falkland Islands Government Series EG General Correspondence Inwards/Outwards Reference FIC/EG2#1
Jane Cameron National Archives, Stanley, Falkland Islands
John Dixon's letter enquiring about selling the two plots.

Despatch 669 London Office to Stanley Office
dated 13 March 1886; paragraph 27
Jane Cameron National Archives, Stanley, Falkland Islands
John Dixon again asked the Falkland Islands Company were interested in buying the plots.

Despatch 670 London Office to Stanley Office
dated 25 March 1886; paragraph 8:
Jane Cameron National Archives, Stanley, Falkland Islands
John Dixon entrusted papers and deeds for the plots with the London office.

Despatch from Colonial Manager in Stanley to London Office, 1886
Jane Cameron National Archives, Stanley, Falkland Islands
Mysterious information about Captain Wilson's son being a drunkard and thief.

Death of Captain Bracey Robson Wilson
The Stonehaven Journal, 19 December 1889, page 2
Obituary. Captain Wilson died at his house Windsor after an illness of several months. He was survived by widow, four daughters and five sons.

Death of Captain Bracey Robson Wilson
The People's Journal for Dundee, 21 December 1889, page 9
Obituary. Mentions his ability to take walks around Dundee, including an occasion when he was lost in Baxter Park and took five hours to find the way out unassisted.

The Falkland Islands
Gustav Schulz
C Gross and Company, London (originally published by Julius Klinkhardt, Leipzig)
Comprehensive description of the islands with many photographs

Sunderland under sail, more recollections of the 1820s by Robinson Crusoe, an East End sea captain
Reprinted in five volumes
The Sunderland Antiquarian Society, 6 Douro Terrace, City of Sunderland.

27 Odds and Ends

Southampton jetty 1883

Southampton Harbour Board invited tenders for reconstructing and strengthening the '1871 jetty' in 1883. Dixon and Thorne submitted a bid of £9,210. Unusually for John Dixon's tenders, which were generally low, this was by far the highest, with ten other bids ranging from £4,755 to £7,850. Needless to say, he was unsuccessful.

Pier in Mexico

John Dixon's obituary by the Institution of Civil Engineers notes that the bridge at Cairo was 'followed by extensive drainage and sanitary works at Rio de Janeiro, and piers in Mexico and Parà on the Amazon.' No information has come to light about the pier in Mexico.

Raising sunken ships

HMS Vanguard was launched in 1870, one of four second-generation ironclads ordered by the navy following the success of *Warrior*. Ironclads had teak hulls enveloped in wrought iron plates. In the summer of 1875 all five ironclads were based at Dublin. On 1 September 1875 the ships left Dublin and sailed south, in close formation. In thick fog *Iron Duke* collided with *Vanguard*, sending her to the seabed ninety minutes after the collision. All the crew were rescued but the ship lay 120 feet below the surface.

On 31 May 1878 three German ironclads were steaming westwards through the English Channel. While attempting to avoid other vessels, *König Wilhelm* rammed into *Grosser Kurfürst,* which sank within eight minutes. Over half of the crew of 500 men were lost, with the *Grosser Kurfürst* 90 feet below the surface.

HMS Eurydice was a wooden frigate launched in 1843 and later converted into a training ship. Returning to Portsmouth from the West Indies, she was caught in a sudden heavy squall off the Isle of Wight on 22 March 1878. Under full sail and with open gun ports, she capsized with the loss of 364 lives and only two survivors.

John Dixon was one of many engineers who exercised their minds in devising ways of raising these three vessels. Most of the suggestions involved working from pontoons, but John recognised that waves and tides would render this virtually impossible. Movement of the sea near the surface hampered the initial descent of divers down to a depth of about 40 feet below which the water was relatively stable. In a remarkable forerunner of North Sea oil platforms, he suggested constructing two platforms supported on iron tubes of 10 to 15 feet in diameter, which would be towed out to the sunken vessel. With one over the bow and the other over the stern, water would be admitted to the tubes allowing them to drop to the sea bed, from where they would be filled with concrete to from a stable structure. From each platform, some 20 feet above the surface and clear of waves and tides, work could commence. An inner cylinder of 3 feet diameter inside each of the supports would provide safe access for divers to descend to the wrecks. The vessel would be lifted by hydraulic rams and on reaching the surface the water pumped out of the hull so that it floated up beneath the two platforms, which would then be carried by the raised vessel back to safe waters where they could be dismantled.

John estimated that it would take four months to raise the *Grosser Kurfürst* at a cost of £30,000. Because the supporting columns were to be filled with concrete in situ, much of the structures would not be reusable. Dixon's idea generated considerable interest. The main criticisms of the proposal were the difficulty in manoeuvring a structure with a draft of 30 feet and a height of 120 feet above the waterline and accurately positioning it above the sunken vessel. After much correspondence it was concluded that there was really no practicable method of raising these sunken vessels. The wooden *Eurydice* was raised in September 1878 but found to be so badly damaged as to be scrapped. The two ironclads remain on the seabed to this day.

Underground railway to Billingsgate

Congestion around Billingsgate Fish Market was causing problems in 1881. John proposed tunnelling through the London clay to drive a railway from the three London rail termini which received fish direct to beneath Billingsgate Market, with lifts at either end of the line to connect with the surface. This provoked much discussion and led to a deluge of correspondence arriving at No.1 Laurence Pountney Hill. He became more enthusiastic for the idea when he learned that there were spacious vaults beneath the entire area of the fish market which could be used to receive the wagons, but his enthusiasm was not contagious.

Sea front at Clevedon

In 1884 the authorities in Clevedon were considering repairs to the sea wall and improvements to the amenities. There was a proposal for a bathing pool, and a sketch was passed round with the comment that John Dixon C.E. had said £5,000 would be needed. John had also given an estimate of £3,000 to £4,000 for a boatman's slipway which would need a small breakwater alongside.

Breakwater at Grand Canary

The Canary Islands form an archipelago of volcanic origins in the Atlantic Ocean. In 1886 John Dixon was awarded a contract by the Spanish Government to construct a breakwater on the Island of Grand Canary (Gran Canaria), to provide a harbour for a large coaling station and for general shipping. The breakwater was about a mile long, in water from 25 to 50 feet deep. It was built from 30 ton concrete blocks, each set in place using a Titan crane running on rails. Titan cranes were manufactured by several manufacturers; perhaps the most likely source of John Dixon's Titan was Cowans, Sheldon and Company. They had supplied the cranes for his ore-loading terminal at Huelva, and John Cowans and Edward Sheldon had been apprentices with Robert Stephenson in Newcastle. The Titan crane and a concrete mixer were shipped from England to Grand Canary specifically for the work. Concrete was made up from local lava, rough gravel and lime, with the addition of 2% Portland cement to speed up the setting of the concrete. By the beginning of 1887, 1,200 blocks had been cast and 300 set on the sea bed.

The Waterford Free Bridge

John Dixon's obituary mentions 'bridges at Waterford in Ireland' but gives no further details. The first bridge over the River Suir at Waterford in Ireland was built in 1794. An Act of Parliament in 1786 had established the Waterford Bridge Commissioners, with powers to raise £30,000 by subscription towards building a bridge over the River Suir and buying out the ferry rights. Lemuel Cox, a noted American builder of wooden bridges, was invited to construct it. He brought American oak timbers and twenty skilled workmen from New England and started work on 13 April 1793. His 832 feet long wooden bridge opened nine months later. A drawbridge was added the following year to allow the passage of taller vessels, and this was enlarged in 1845 for the passage of paddle steamers. The structure was known as 'old Timbertoes' referring to the forty sets of oak piers which supported the crossing.

Postcard view of the old wooden bridge at Waterford known as 'Timbertoes'. William Ritchie and Sons of London and Edinburgh produced the 'Reliable' series of postcards in the early 20th century.

Tolls charged for using the bridge became a long-standing source of complaint. In 1851 calls were first made for the bridge to be purchased and made free, calls which were repeated many times over in the following decades. Another problem was that the drawbridge restricted shipping, and it had been deemed impracticable to further increase the opening section. Finally, the cost of maintaining the old wooden structure was ever-increasing.

Many proposals were made for a replacement bridge. It was probably in August 1890, when John Dixon was staying at the Imperial Hotel in Waterford, that he drew up designs for a replacement crossing incorporating a swing bridge giving two openings each of 50 feet width. This would have been one of John's last projects before his death the following January. He estimated the cost at £40,000 and the Commissioners gained Board of Works approval but, as no money was forthcoming from the Treasury, no action resulted. On 27 October 1896 a public meeting at Waterford endorsed a proposal to purchase the wooden toll bridge and build a new bridge. The meeting was told that the bridge rights could cost £70,000 and that, in 1890, John Dixon had estimated that a new bridge would cost £45,000. The apparent increase of £5,000 over the six years since 1890 was not all down to inflation, which would only account for about £1,200.

An authoritative article on Waterford's bridges, written in the 1920s by the owner and editor of *The Waterford News*, included descriptions of seven plans for new bridges drawn up between 1877 and 1902, but strangely with no mention of John's plans of 1890.

Eventually, in 1907, Waterford Corporation purchased the bridge for £63,000 and declared it a free crossing. The replacement John Redmond Bridge, in concrete, opened in 1913 but was in turn replaced in 1984 by the Rice Bridge. A cable-stayed bridge carrying the N25 Waterford by-pass was opened in 2009, the longest single bridge span in the Republic of Ireland.

John Dixon's obituary referred to 'bridges' implying that there was more than one bridge at Waterford. He may have built railway bridges. There were no fewer than five railway companies operating in Waterford:

- Waterford and Tranmore, completed in 1853
- Waterford, Limerick and Western, completed in 1854
- Waterford and Kilkenny, started in 1846, becoming the Waterford and Central Ireland in 1868 and completed in 1867 with a branch to Mountmellick in 1883
- Waterford, Dungarvan and Lismore, completed in 1878
- Dublin and South Eastern, the branch to Waterford was not completed until 1904.

Given the dates, it is probably only the Waterford and Central Railway and the Waterford, Dungarvan and Lismore Railway that might have employed John, but no references to him have been found.

Wire rope manufacture

Two firms manufacturing ropes and cables were located on opposite banks of the narrow Team River in Gateshead: Newall (R S) and Company and Dixon, Corbitt, and Company. They were on friendly terms, with Newall generally making wire ropes while Dixon, Corbitt used mainly hemp. In his history of the wire rope industry published in 1952, E R Forestiere-Walker states that Dixon, Corbitt was founded by the John Dixon who was born in 1796 and became a railway engineer under George Stephenson. Forestiere-Walker claims that John Dixon (1835-1891) was a later partner in the firm. The John Dixon who worked with George Stephenson was John's uncle. It is possible that John had an association with the rope works while he was still in the north east, before he went to London in 1865. Unfortunately, Forestiere-Walker gives no references, but there are three tentative clues for a connection between John and Dixon, Corbitt and Company.

In 1865 an attempt was made to lay a transatlantic telegraph cable using Brunel's ship *Great Eastern* which had been converted into a cable-laying vessel. After 1,200 miles the cable broke and fell to the ocean floor. A letter appeared in *The Times* advocating retrieval of this cable, signed 'John Dixon, City, 1st September 1865'. Its author went into details about a method of repairing the cable by bringing it up through a tube inserted amidships in the laying vessel and controlling its movement by use of the mechanism used on Fowler's steam plough winding drums, with a dynamometer to ensure that the cable was not under excessive tension. If John was indeed the author of this letter, it suggests that he had an interest in steel cables. Earliest records of John at Abchurch Yard are from 1866, but he could well have been in London by the late summer of 1865.

A second clue is in the cable used by the steamship *Olga* to tow the vessel bringing Cleopatra's Needle on its voyage from Alexandria. Forestiere-Walker wrote that the captain of *Olga* preferred to use an enormous hemp rope which he had used on previous occasions, and ridiculed the use of a thin steel hawser. But when the hemp rope broke on several occasions he tried a Newall's cable and had no further trouble. On 8 September 1877 John Dixon wrote to *The Times* explaining how he proposed to tow the obelisk vessel:

> 'She will probably be towed astern of a large merchant steamer, to which she will be attached by a three-and-a-half inch steel wire hawser specially manufactured for the purpose by Messrs Newall, and most courteously presented by the eminent head of that well known firm.'

Bearing in mind the amicable relationship between Newall and Dixon, Corbitt (as an example, George Dixon and John Corbitt were not only invited to the celebration banquet for Newall's completion of the first Atlantic cable in 1857 but were seated at the top table) it perhaps suggests that John had an association with the Gateshead rope makers.

The final clue comes much later. Newall and Dixon, Corbitt amalgamated in 1887, with Michael Corbitt becoming company secretary. He then acquired another rope works and set up the business as a limited company. One of the first subscribers of shares, and a director of Michael Corbitt & Sons Limited, was Sir Raylton Dixon of Gunnergate Hall. Was Sir Raylton a director because he was a prominent ship-builder or because his brother John had some earlier connection with Dixon, Corbitt? If Michael Corbitt wished to have a ship-builder on his board, and there was no connection with Raylton's family, surely he would have been more likely to turn to one of the many Tyneside or Wearside shipbuilders rather than go as far south as the Tees?

The steamship *John Dixon*

The iron screw-driven steamship *John Dixon* was built in 1872 by Schlesinger, Davis and Company at Wallsend on the River Tyne. She was named after one of her original owners, John Dixon of Jesmond, who was a Newcastle timber merchant. He was not related to John Dixon (1835-1891), but there is an incidental connection. In January 1881 the *John Dixon* was carrying iron ore from Huelva to the Tyne, ore which would have been loaded via the Muelle del Tinto built by John Dixon. On a cold misty evening the *John Dixon* rammed into the full-rigged sailing ship *Lenore* between Seaham and Hartlepool, causing her to sink with the deaths of eight of the crew of twenty-three. The *John Dixon* was virtually undamaged. The Board of Trade Inquiry thought that both vessels were more or less in default and suspended the certificate of the captain of the *John Dixon* for six months (the captain of the *Lenore* had been drowned). Later, a hearing in the High Court of Justice found the *John Dixon* was alone to blame, her speed had been excessive and her lookout inattentive.

Brighton dinner party with General Grant

In 1877 General Ulysses S Grant, ex-President of the United States of America, visited Brighton as the private guest of James Ashbury MP. Among the events held in his honour were a select dinner party for about thirty guests. John was the only engineer present, but why he was invited is a mystery. Another guest was Thomas Brassey (1836-1918), who was MP for Hastings and the son of the celebrated engineering contractor Thomas Brassey who had died in 1870. In the 1860s John had worked with Brassey senior on sewerage treatment works in Rio de Janeiro.

Acknowledgements

Sue McGaw, the great great grand-daughter of George Dixon, founder of Dixon and Corbitt, for information on the family and the business.

Celia Renshaw, family historian of the Corbitt/Corbett family.

References

Southampton - Harbour Board
Portsmouth Evening News, 4 September 1883, page 3
Tenders received for the Southampton Harbour Board jetty reconstruction. Dixon and Thorne, at £9,120 was the highest of eleven bids, the lowest bid which was £4,755 from Green and Burleigh of London. The Board had estimated the work would cost £5,327.

The Loss of the Grosser Kurfürst and its Lessons - To the Editor of The Times
The Times, London, 5 June 1878, page 5
Letter from John Dixon with his idea of using platforms supported on iron tubes. Immediately above his letter is one from Thomas Brassey on questions for the navy following the loss of the German vessel.

Raising Sunken Vessels - To the Editor of Engineering
Engineering, London, 14 June 1878, page 481
John Dixon's letter on his proposal to raise the two ironclads.

Raising Sunken Vessels - To the Editor of Engineering
Engineering, London, 28 June 1878, page 513
Letter proposing an alternative to John Dixon's structure.

Raising Sunken Vessels - To the Editor of Engineering
Engineering, London, 12 June 1878, page 33
Two more letters on the subject, both concluding it was virtually impossible to raise the vessels.

Railway Communication with Billingsgate - To the Editor of The Times
The Times, London, 31 August 1881, page 10
John Dixon's proposal for an underground railway to serve the fish market.

Billingsgate Market Railway Connections - To the Editor of The Times
The Times, London, 12 September 1881, page 8
John Dixon's letter about the underground vaults existing under the fish market.

The Sea Front at Clevedon - Local Government Board Inquiry
The Western Daily Press, Bristol, 1 February 1883, page 3
John's estimates for a swimming pool and a boatman's slipway.

Discussion on Concrete-work for Harbours
Minutes of Proceedings, Institution of Civil Engineers, volume 87, Issue 887, January 1887, pages 138-196
John Dixon was making 30-ton blocks for a breakwater at Grand Canary.

Waterford Bridge
The Waterford News and General Weekly Advertiser, 10 October 1851, page 1
Reproduces the Act of Parliament establishing the Waterford Bridge Commissioners.

Waterford and Limerick Railway Company
The Waterford Mail, 18 June 1851, page 2
First calls for the bridge to be made a free crossing.

Imperial Hotel - recent arrivals
Waterford Standard, Conservative Gazette and General Advertiser, 16 August 1890, page 3
John Dixon C E of London arrived at the Imperial Hotel.

Waterford Harbour Board
Waterford Standard, Conservative Gazette and General Advertiser, 12 October 1892, page 3
It was impracticable to widen the opening of the wooden bridge. Plans for a new bridge had been drawn up by the late John Dixon.

The Free Bridge Scheme
Waterford Standard, Conservative Gazette and General Advertiser, 28 October 1896, page 3
A public meeting resolved to purchase the bridge and ferry rights, and build a new bridge. In 1890 John Dixon had estimated a bridge would cost £45,000.

Waterford's Bridges
Edmund Downey
Waterford News (which he owned and edited)
Reproduced at
snap.waterfordcoco.ie/collections/ebooks/99263/99263.pdf
Gives the history of the proposals for crossing the river at Waterford, including the many plans for a replacement for the wooden bridge, but with no mention of John Dixon.

A History of the Wire Rope Industry of Great Britain
E R Forestiere-Walker
Federation of Wire Rope Manufacturers of Great Britain, 1952
North of England Institute of Mechanical and Mining Engineers, Newcastle upon Tyne.
Reference 622.6736 FOR
Pages 45-47 describe John Dixon's involvement with Dixon, Corbitt and Company, and the Newall's cable used to tow the obelisk vessel.

The Great Atlantic Submarine Telegraph
Liverpool Mercury, Liverpool, 12 June 1857, page 10
Celebration banquet for nearly 700 guests, with Messrs Dixon and Corbitt on the top table.

Letter to the Editor - The Atlantic Cable
The Times, London, 8 September 1865, page 150
Letter from John Dixon, City, about the telegraph cable.

Letter to the Editor, Cleopatra's Needle
The Times, London, 15 September 1877, page 10
Letter from John Dixon explaining that the vessel will be towed using a 3½ inch steel hawser supplied by Messrs Newall.

The Cleopatra Needle, transport from Alexandria to London and the erection on the Thames Embankment, second edition
Reprinted from *Engineering*, 1877-78, Offices of Engineering, London, 1878, page 6
Contains the quotation 'the splendid steel wire hawser, which Mr. Newall had specially manufactured and presented to Mr. Dixon for towing the Needle home.'

New Local Company
The Northern Echo, Newcastle upon Tyne, 4 December 1894, page 3
Announcement of a new business of Michael Corbitt & Sons (Limited). One of the first subscribers and a director was Sir Raylton Dixon of Gunnergate Hall. Michael Corbitt was managing director.

Local and District News - Iron shipbuilding on the Tyne
The Newcastle Courant, 23 August 1872
Description of the steamship *John Dixon*, named by Miss Blanche Edith Dixon, daughter of John Dixon who was one of the owners.

Terrible Collision off the Durham Coast - A Tyne-laden ship run down - Eight lives lost
Shields Daily Gazette and Shipping Telegraph, South Shields, 15 January 1881, page 3
First account of the collision between the *John Dixon* and the *Lenore*.

The Collision between Seaham and Hartlepool - The sinking of the Lenore - Decision against the John Dixon
Shields Daily Gazette and Shipping Telegraph, South Shields, 7 April 1881, page 4
John Dixon was alone to blame.

Visit of General Grant to Brighton (today)
The Brighton Herald, 20 October 1877, page 3
John Dixon invited to a dinner party with the ex-President of the USA.

28 Family and professional life

There is no doubt that John Dixon was a strong character, confident of his engineering abilities, direct in his dealings with others, always eager to make progress and take on new challenges and tenacious in pursuing anyone who might have taken advantage of him. These sides to his personality can be clearly seen in his work, but it is harder to gain any insight into his life outside work. What is known is that John married Mary England, that they had eleven children (two sons and seven daughters surviving into adulthood), and that John's health began to fail in his early fifties. His entire life seems to have been fully occupied with work, unlike his brothers, Raylton with his wide range of civic and political interests, and Waynman who enjoyed a long and happy retirement. John died at the age of fifty-six.

Childhood in Newcastle

John's parents, Jeremiah and Mary Dixon, had seven children, born over a ten-year period from 1835 to 1845. One son died in infancy, leaving three daughters and three sons, John being the eldest. At the risk of over-generalisation, the oldest child of a large family can find themselves acting as an unofficial mentor for those who follow, and consequently 'grows up' early. The Dixon children were brought up in what must have been a close-knit family living above the bank in Newcastle. John showed an interest in engineering from an early age. His sister Augusta described how the children spent much of their time in the three large rooms at the top of the bank building. One room contained a joiner's bench and two lathes where John 'always had many works going on'. In another room was a large bath which Raylton, known as Rally, who would later own the largest ship-yard on the River Tees, 'generally covered with boats and models of yachts of all sorts, which had to be removed and the water run off to the annoyance of those who came to bathe.' In another room was a large evergreen tree in a tub where Waynman, always interested in natural history, kept an owl, a merlin, a small hawk, siskins and snow buntings.

Mary Dixon, John Dixon's wife. Reproduced by courtesy of Ann Colville, great grand-daughter of Augusta Ann Richardson, one of John Dixon's sisters. From an original photograph by Herbert Bell of Ambleside.

Augusta wrote that John's closest boyhood friend was Henry Mennell. Henry Tuke Mennell (1835-1923) was born in Scarborough and brought up as a Quaker, attending Bootham School in York. His father, George Mennell, had a coke works in Newcastle upon Tyne from 1847 until the 1860s, so when not at the Bootham School the young Henry would have been in Newcastle. Henry's lifelong interest in natural history was no doubt encouraged by John Hancock, a frequent visitor to the Dixons, and by John's brother Waynman. Henry joined his mother's family tea business, first in York and later in London. Once in London, he married and was an active member of the Society of Friends, taking a leading role in the Quakers' foreign aid work during the Great War. From the 1870s to his death in 1923, Henry and his wife Maria lived in Croydon. At around the same time that John and Mary Dixon moved to 'High Towers' on Selborne Road, Henry and Maria Mennell moved into 'Red House' on Park Hill Rise, which was a continuation of Selborne Road to the north, with just a short walk between the two houses. Surely this cannot have been chance. In the last six years of John's life he would have been able to renew his boyhood friendship with Henry and contemplate the different directions life had taken them.

Meeting Mary England

John started his engineering career in 1856 when he began work at the Bishopwearmouth Iron Works in a senior position. It is likely that it was through this position that he would meet his future wife, Mary England. Her father, George England, owned the Hatcham Iron Works in London, and he may well have purchased iron from the Bishopwearmouth works, transported to London by sea. As a fellow Geordie, he could have formed a friendship

Who's who
George England (1811-95)

George England (1812-1855) was a native of Newcastle upon Tyne and the son of a blacksmith. His mother came from London, and at the age of fourteen George started an apprenticeship with John Penn and Son at Deptford, noted builders of marine steam engines. In 1839 he set up in business at the Hatcham Iron Works, about a mile west of Deptford. Initially, he manufactured screw jacks but soon turned to steam locomotives, building his first locomotive in 1849. In 1851 he exhibited a locomotive at the Great Exhibition in the Crystal Palace and was awarded a gold medal. At the Great Exhibition in 1852 his locomotive was reported as 'remarkable for the ingenious arrangement and good workmanship'. He used the 'cabbage garden' next to the works to experiment with his various locomotives.

Robert Francis Fairlie joined the business in 1860 as consulting engineer; he later designed the famous Fairlie articulated locomotives. Fairlie began courting George's seventeen year old daughter, Eliza Ann, but George expressly forbade the proposed marriage. The following year Fairlie eloped to Spain with Eliza Ann, prompting her father to recourse to the law. In the court case it transpired that George himself had run away with Eliza's mother while he was still a married man, although he had married her later, in 1856, after the death of his first wife. There may have been some truth in the rumour that George had installed a mistress in one of the terraced houses he had built for his employees, and had a secret tunnel connecting the house to his works! English law at the time considered a child born outside wedlock to belong to neither parent, and so Eliza Ann was free to marry whom she pleased.

There is no doubt that George England was a difficult man for, apart from his treatment of Robert Fairlie, he had been convicted of beating one of his apprentices and in 1863 a dispute with his employees over his strict application of works rules led to a strike which caused the cancellation of an order for twenty locomotives.

In 1869 George England retired due to ill health and went to live in France. The Hatcham Works passed to his son-in-law Robert Fairlie and became the Fairlie Engine and Steam Carriage Company. George's son, George England (1844-70), was a partner but he died the following year aged only twenty-five. The Hatcham works closed in 1872 with the machinery and plant auctioned. It was reported that 'most of the tools had been kept badly, and few were in what we would call really good condition.' Robert Fairlie set up as a consulting engineer in Westminster.

with the young John Dixon and perhaps invited him to his family home at Hatcham Lodge, where he would meet Mary. It is possible that the Dixon and England families were acquainted when both were living in Newcastle upon Tyne, but no evidence of this has come to light.

John Dixon's courtship of Mary England must have been impeded by the 250 miles between London and the north east. John was able to spend some time in London, for example he and Mary had taken her sister Eliza to the Crystal Palace just before Eliza's elopement. Mary was still in her teens, and seven years younger than her suitor. Given the strong personalities of John Dixon and George England, perhaps the marriage was partly an agreement between the two men? At least George approved of the match, unlike that between his daughter Eliza Ann and Robert Fairlie. This is not to imply that Mary was anything less than happy with the prospect of marrying John.

Marriage and the move to London

John and Mary were pronounced man and wife by Rev A K B Glanville at St James Church, Hatcham on 9 October 1862. He was twenty-seven years of age, she was just twenty. The years immediately before and after his marriage must have been difficult times for John and he would have much appreciated the support of his young wife. In 1861, with Jaspar Capper Mounsey, he was struggling to get the Bedlington Iron Works operational, then just as the factory reopened there was the appalling death of Jaspar's wife. Furthermore, business prospects did not look promising.

Following the wedding, Mary seems to have moved up to Consett to be with her new husband. Their first child, Sarah, was born exactly nine months after the wedding, in Hatcham. The fact that their first child was born in Hatcham can be explained by the common practice at the time of the daughter returning to her mother's house for support with the first child, and she was named after her mother. Sadly, Sarah died the day she was born, not unusual in Victorian times but a tragic opening to John and Mary's family.

Ten months later a son arrived and survived, to the relief and delight of John and Mary. He was christened George England Dixon, suggesting that John may have felt indebted to his father-in-law for helping him to become established in London.

With the failure of the Bedlington works, John and Mary moved to London in 1865. It seems likely that the move was encouraged, if not instigated, by George England, and that they lived in one of George's terraced houses adjacent to the Hatcham works. John and Mary's next two children were born at Hatcham, Augusta Mary in the summer of 1865 (named after his sister back in Newcastle) and Cornelia Clara in the autumn of 1866.

Moves to Kingston upon Thames and Croydon

In 1867, with increasing prosperity and perhaps an increasing desire to be independent of his father-in-law, John moved to Kingston upon Thames. George England, always irascible, was by then in poor health which would not have improved his temper. John and Mary, with their children George, Augusta and Cornelia, took up residence in 'St James Villa' on South Street (soon after renamed St Philip's Road and later part of Surbiton). This area immediately south of Kingston upon Thames and including the grounds of Surbiton Place, developed rapidly after the arrival of the London and Southampton Railway from Waterloo Station in 1838. Four pairs of semi-detached villas were built along the south east side of South Street, with the Dixon family home probably being the present No.13 St Philip's Road. Their neighbours included a surgeon, a stockbroker, a wine merchant, a bank manager and an army major. At some time in the 1870s, properties were built on the other side of South Street, then renamed as St Philip's Road. Remarkably, none of the residents in the eight villas recorded in the 1871 census were still there ten years later. The reasons for this exodus are not known, certainly the new properties had destroyed the view across open fields towards the river, and there was a loss of professional cachet with, for example, no fewer than seven widows and a lodging house keeper.

In 1870 John Castell Hopkins (1794-1871) moved from Darlington to 'The Firs' on Grove Road, Surbiton, just a short walk from 'St James Villa'. John Hopkins had been one of the early directors of the Stockton and Darlington Railway, and owned coalfields in Durham. Representing the Lords of the Admiralty, he was a Tees Conservancy Commissioner until the end of 1870. His eldest son, William Randolph Innes Hopkins, had been a close friend of John's brother Raylton since the latter started his shipbuilding business in Middlesbrough. No doubt Raylton told his brother than William Hopkins' father would be a near neighbour of his and, if so, John would have visited 'The Firs'. Within a few months of the move, John Hopkins died suddenly, and it is easy to imagine his son William staying with the Dixons when he came down for the funeral.

By 1875 the Dixon family was living at 'The Choubra' on the Portsmouth Road, named after the fashionable district in Cairo. John held some affection for Egypt since he was awarded the contract for the Nile bridge in 1870, and since his brother Waynman was still living in Alexandria. The Portsmouth Road ran along the east bank of the River Thames, and the house would have enjoyed fine views over the river towards Hampton Court Palace. 'The Choubra' was probably on the corner of Anglesea Road and Portsmouth Road, adjacent to St Raphael's Roman Catholic Church, and semi-detached with 'Shenton House'. These properties were demolished in the 20th century and replaced by a row of new houses.

John and Mary's final move was to Selborne Road, Croydon, in 1884. There is a letter dated 23 August 1884 in the National Archives from John Dixon on headed notepaper with 'The Choubra' crossed out and replaced with 'High Towers', East Croydon. Following the opening of East Croydon railway station in 1839, housing started to spread over the rural landscape. Building along Selborne Road came quite late, the 1881 census showed only one property, the 1891 census three properties and the 1901 census four properties. Extensive plots were available on Selborne Road, and it is likely that John had 'High Towers' built to his own plans, with many bedrooms for his large family, the very name 'High Towers' no doubt reflecting a grand design. The 1891 census includes four living-in servants (a cook and three maids) at 'High Towers'.

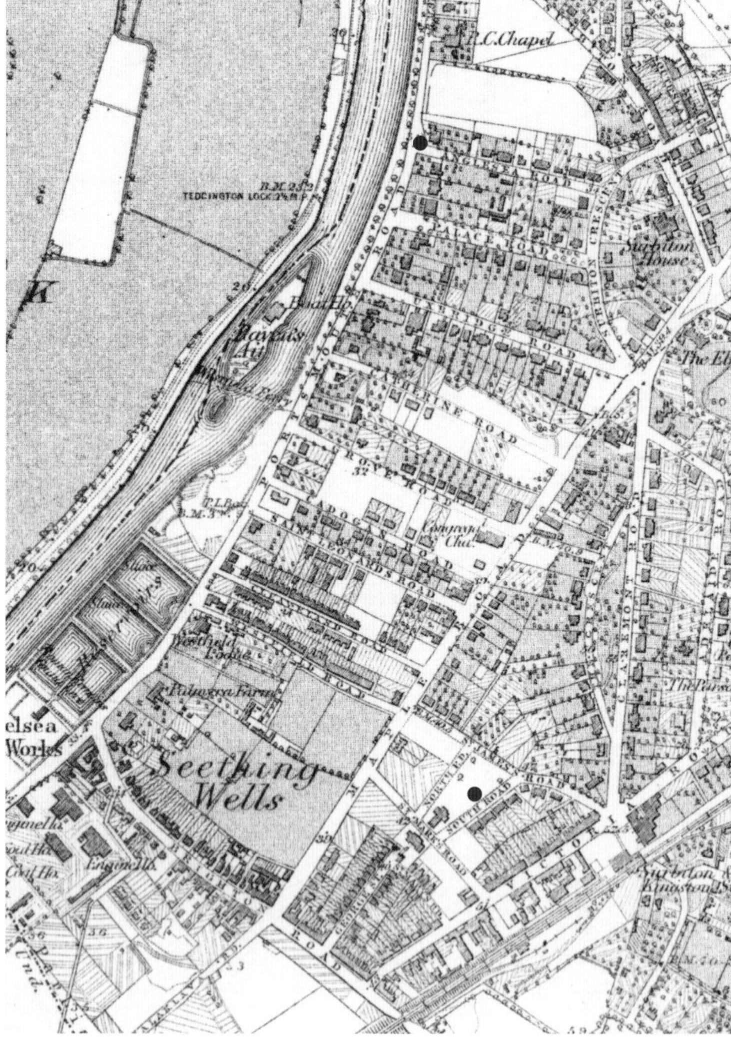

Map showing the location of John's house on the Portsmouth Road, Kingston upon Thames and his earlier house on South Street.
Ordnance Survey Six Inch Series Revised 1894-95, published 1898, Middlesex XXV.SE
Reproduced by permission of the National Library of Scotland.

Today only one of the original properties on Selborne Road, 'Thanescroft', remains, but has been extended and converted into apartments. All the other Victorian houses have been demolished to make way for high density development. The separate coach house at 'High Towers', included in the 1901 census, was probably added by George Gotelee, who purchased the house from Mary after John's death.

John and Mary's children

Given John's extensive travels around the globe, and lengthy absences from home, it is perhaps surprising that they managed to have eleven children, nine of whom survived into adulthood (two sons and seven daughters). It is not known if Mary accompanied her husband on any of his travels.

Sarah Dixon
Sarah was born on 14 July 1863 but Sarah died on the same day.

George England Dixon
George England was born on 12 May 1864 at Consett. John had ambitions for his oldest son, and he was sent off to Charterhouse School in 1878. If John wished George would take up an engineering career he was disappointed, his only contact with engineering was to be through marriage. In the 1891 census George was living with his widowed mother and working as a linen warehouseman. Ten years later he was visiting Alfred Springett, registrar to a mining company, in Croydon with his sister Ethel. Given that Ethel was with him, the visit was probably social rather than to do with business. At the time of the 1911 census, when he would be forty-six, George was boarding in Long Ditton, Surrey and working as a merchant. Late in life, in 1914, he married Elsie Kitty Punchard, known as 'Atta' within the family. He was forty-nine, she was thirty-one. Elsie's father was William Punchard, a civil engineer living in Kingston upon Thames. William Punchard and Edwin Clark were the contractors for the Rio Tinto railway from the mine to the ore-loading facility at Huelva constructed by John Dixon. After the marriage they lived at 'The Hermitage', Thames Ditton. There were no children and Elsie died in 1956, George having died some time previously.

Augusta Mary Dixon
Augusta Mary was born 2 July 1865 at Hatcham and was known as 'Gussie'. While living in Selborne Road, Croydon, she became very friendly with Charles and Marianne Fox who were neighbours at Thanescroft'. Charles Fox was a wealthy linen merchant. Gussie visited them when they moved to Ifield in Sussex and, following Marianne's death in 1913, Augusta lived with Charles Fox for many years at 'The Paddocks', Butlers Green, Cuckfield. In the 1939 Register she was described as his 'lady housekeeper' and in Charles Fox's obituary as 'his faithful companion'. They died within three weeks of each other in 1940, Charles was ninety-three, Augusta was seventy-four.

Cornelia Clara Dixon
Cornelia Clara was born 17 September 1866 at Greenwich. In the 1891 census she and her sister Maud were visiting their aunt Augusta Ann Richardson in Newcastle. On 4 August 1898 she married Richard Cooke-Yarborough in the Holy Trinity Church, Sloane Street, Chelsea. They had two sons, Richard and Francis. She died aged sixty-nine in 1935 in Bedford.

Nora Waynman Dixon
Nora Waynman was born 20 August 1867 at Kingston upon Thames. Waynman joined his brother's business in February 1867, so it appears that Nora was given the name to mark this event. In the 1891 census she was visiting William and Florence Tozer in Ecclesall Bierlow where William Tozer was a steel

Top) Silver Christening Cup presented to George England Dixon and engraved 'George E Dixon, from his uncle Raylton Dixon, 20th March 1866'. Reproduced by courtesy of Beth Porteous, great grand-daughter of John Dixon and photographed by Neil Crick ARPS of Smart-Ideas Photography.

Above) Norah Waynman Dixon, one of John and Mary Dixon's daughters. Original photograph by A. R. Perry, 13 Wellington Place, Hastings. Reproduced by courtesy of Ann Colville, great grand-daughter of Augusta Ann Richardson, one of John Dixon's sisters.

manufacturer. In 1901 she was boarding at 59 Wilton Road, Bexhill. A family photograph shows her in the uniform of a nurse. She died on 21 September 1914 in Kensington and was buried alongside her parents in Croydon.

Maud Marian Dixon
Maud Marian was born 9 August 1868 at Kingston upon Thames. In the 1891 census she and her sister Cornelia were visiting their aunt Augusta Ann Richardson in Newcastle. She married James William Pierce Wain, a merchant banker, on 12 September 1907 at Croydon. Maud and James seem not to have had any children and Maud died in 1933. For several years James employed a housekeeper, and then in 1940 he married Gertude Saunders. James Wain died in 1953.

Ethel Grace Dixon
Ethel Grace was born 9 January 1870 at Kingston upon Thames. She married Hamilton Bunce Northcote in 1912 at Herne Bay; she was forty-two, he was thirty-five. Hamilton Bunce Northcote was born in 1877 at Southsea, Hampshire, son of Colonel Samuel Northcote of the Royal Marine Artillery. Ethel died in Norwich in 1931, aged 61.

Alexandria Osman Dixon
Alexandria Osman was born 6 May 1871 at Kingston upon Thames. The 1911 census records her single and working as a governess for George and Barbara Bell in Hammersmith. George Bell was Borough Electrical Manager. On 28 August 1924 she married Beauchamp Orlando Chichele Orlebar at Kingston on Thames. Beauchamp Orlebar was born in 1864, son of Richard Orlebar of Hinwick House, Bedfordshire, Sheriff of Bedfordshire. He was educated at Repton School and Radley College, Oxford. He worked as an accountant and company secretary and was a keen actor in amateur dramatics. At the time of the marriage he was sixty, she was fifty-three. There were no children. After living at Hinwick, a village in Bedfordshire, for many years, in 1937 the couple moved to St Germans in in Cornwall. Beauchamp died in 1940, Alexandria died in 1951, age 80.

John Ralph Dixon
John Ralph, usually known as Ralph, was born 21 October 1872 at Kingston upon Thames. In the 1891 census he was boarding at Woolwich where he was an engineering apprentice. On 1 March 1898 he married Sophia Matilda Jennings, daughter of the late George Jennings, at St Paul's, Knightsbridge. The couple lived in the Manor House, Welford in Northamptonshire. Ralph died in 1928, age fifty-five.

Robert Dixon
Robert was born 11 October 1873 and died just five days later.

Hilda Monti Dixon
Hilda Monti was born 29 November 1875 at Kingston upon Thames. She seems to have moved with her mother to Bexhill-on-Sea, but there is no trace of her after 1901.

John Dixon's failing health and early death

In common with many other British engineers of the time, John Dixon died comparatively young. At the beginning of 1888 his doctor in Croydon, Peter Duncan, diagnosed incompetence of the aortic valve (a leaking heart valve) which caused breathlessness. With none of today's medical technologies available, Dr Duncan' s diagnosis would be based on detecting a heart murmur and a so-called collapsing pulse, where each beat feels abnormal, with a big surge and rapid fall-back. The abnormal heart valve may have been inherited, or it may have resulted from rheumatic fever. Although John was undoubtedly under pressures of work and business, his obituaries give the impression of a genial, self-confident man not obviously under stress, and in any case, lifestyle is not generally a significant factor in aortic incompetence.

In an attempt to improve his ailing health, John visited South Africa in 1888, not returning until late summer 1889. In the middle of January 1891 his breathing became more difficult, and on 18 January Dr Duncan diagnosed pulmonary oedema, where the lungs fill with fluid, a condition

Superintendent Registrar's District Croydon

Registrar's Sub-District Croydon

1891. DEATHS in the Sub-District of Croydon in the Counties of Croydon and Surrey

Columns:— 1.		2.	3.	4.	5.	6.	7.	8	9.
No.	When and Where Died.	Name and Surname.	Sex.	Age.	Rank or Profession.	Cause of Death.	Signature, Description, and Residence of Informant.	When Registered.	Signature of Registrar.
148	Twenty eighth January 1891 High Towers Park Hill Croydon U.S.D.	John Dixon	Male	56 Years	Civil Engineer	Disease of the Aortic Valve (incompetence) 3 years Bronchitis & Pulmonary Oedema 10 days Certified by P. J. Duncan MD	George Dixon Son present at the death High Towers Park Hill Croydon	Fourth February 1891	Edwin Bailey Registrar

John Dixon's death certificate. Image supplied by the General Register Office, Her Majesty's Passport Office, Southport.

Top) 'The Late Mr John Dixon C.E.' an engraving by R Taylor and Company of London. This portrait accompanied a short obituary.
The Illustrated London News, 14 February 1891, page 207 © Illustrated London News Limited/Mary Evans.

Above) John Dixon's grave at St John the Evangelist, Shirley, Croydon. John's wife, Mary, and his daughter Nora are buried in the same plot.
Photograph by John Anthony Dixon, who is descended from George and Sarah (née Raylton) Dixon, as was John Dixon and Jeremiah Dixon of Mason Dixon line fame.

usually caused by heart problems. John's condition deteriorated and he died at home on 28 January 1891, at only fifty-six. Dr Duncan gave the cause of death as 'disease of the aortic valve (incompetence)' and 'bronchitis and pulmonary oedema'. The bronchitis may have been a separate lung disease (it is not known if he smoked) or may not have been true bronchitis but rather an effect of the pulmonary oedema.

The funeral took place at St John the Evangelist, Shirley, near Croydon, on Monday 2 February 1891, with John's burial in the churchyard.

The probate value of John Dixon's estate was £11,019 11s. He had written his will on 4 February 1890 in his office at No.1 Laurence Pountney Hill, leaving his estate to his wife and appointing her sole executor. Should she have died before him, the executors were to be his eldest son George and his two eldest daughters, Augusta and Cornelia, with the estate divided equally between his children. The witnesses to the will were his clerk Herbert Wakeling and Edmund Appleby.

Herbert Lumley Wakeling (1859-1929), the son of a Camden Town upholsterer, acted as John Dixon's clerk and must have been intimately involved with his business. The 1891 census shows him at 'High Towers' immediately after John Dixon's death. It is quite possible that, particularly during the later stages of John's illness, Herbert lived with the family at 'High Towers' and he no doubt dealt with business matters after John's death. Herbert Wakeling later went on to work as a civil engineer in his own right. Edmund Gardner Appleby (1866-1927) was one of the sons of Charles James Appleby who had collaborated with John on the rebuilding of the Hammersmith Suspension Bridge. At this time, he was working with his father and brother Percy from premises at No.22 Walbrook. Although it was less than a five-minute walk between Walbrook and Laurence Pountney Hill, the fact that Percy was asked to witness the will is indicative of a continuing close friendship between John and the Appleby family.

Mary Dixon now a widow

After John's death his widow Mary and the children, apart from John Ralph who was boarding in Woolwich, continued living at 'High Towers' for a few years before moving to 'Villa Franca', Dorset Road, Bexhill on Sea. In the 1901 census Mary and her daughters Augusta and Alexandria were living at 'Villa Franca'. Nora was also living in Bexhill but boarding at No.59 Wilton Road in Bexhill. Why she was boarding rather than living with her mother is not known.

Towards the end of 1901 there are reports in the local paper of Mary and some of her children at grand balls in Bexhill. It is likely that the children were visiting their mother rather than living with her, apart from Hilda, since she alone had been at all the balls mentioned in the local paper.

Mary Dixon died on 23 March 1907, aged sixty-five. She was buried at Croydon alongside her husband.

Political and civic activities

Like his brother Raylton, John was a staunch conservative and was on the committee of the Kingston upon Thames Conservative Association. Unlike Raylton, he does not seem to have taken an active part in politics. Again, unlike Raylton, he apparently took little part in civic affairs, and only one example has come to light. In 1879 the Lord Mayor of London, Sir Charles Whetham, nominated twelve men, including John Dixon, for the new commission of lieutenancy for the City of London. This nomination should not be confused with the appointment of another John Dixon to this position on 30 December 1852, when John was only seventeen and long before he moved to London.

Freemasonry

Erasmus Wilson, recalling his first meeting with John Dixon to discuss the transportation of Cleopatra's Needle to London, wrote:

> 'A few days afterwards (we were then in November) I called upon Mr Dixon, whom I had never seen before nor heard of, save through Sir James Alexander. Sir James Alexander left him a few minutes before I entered. I soon found that Mr Dixon was a Freemason, hence, all formality and ceremony were at once banished.'

Palatine Lodge No.114 was the oldest Lodge in Sunderland, founded in 1757, and met in the Bridge Hotel, Sunderland Street, from 1860 to 1870. John Dixon, manager of the Bishopwearmouth Iron Works, was proposed by James Hamilton and seconded by W J Young in December 1860 and, after being approved by a ballot of Palatine Lodge members, attended his first meeting on 14 February. He gave his age as twenty-six, his address as 'Sunderland' and his occupation as 'iron merchant'. John's proposer and seconder were probably business associates. James Hamilton was a native of Sunderland then living in Bishopwearmouth and was a ship broker and coal exporter. William Joseph Young was a solicitor with offices in in Lambton Street, Sunderland. With his father-in-law he acquired the West Hartlepool Steam Navigation Company in 1866, when he left Sunderland for West Hartlepool. He was appointed chairman of the Hartlepool Port and Harbour Commission, a magistrate and a director of the North-Eastern Railway from 1882. On the retirement of Thomas Richardson, Liberal MP for Hartlepool, Young became the Conservative candidate for the election of 1875, but lost to the Liberal Isaac Lothian Bell.

Masonic records show that John ceased payments to the Palatine Lodge in the same year that he joined, 1861. There is no record of any Freemason activities in London (the John Dixon who was Worshipful Master of the Temple-bar Lodge in 1877 was a different Dixon). It must be assumed that Freemasonry was not to his liking, and he left almost as soon as he had joined. If this is the case, it seems strange that Erasmus Wilson should have eagerly embraced John as a fellow Freemason when his brief association with the brethren had been some fifteen years previously.

Institution of Civil Engineers

John Dixon was elected an Associate Member of the Institution of Civil Engineers on 7 December 1869. Throughout 1877-78 there was much controversy among the members of the Institution over the various classes of membership. It was felt that many men had joined the Institution with dubious credentials and some of the academic and professional engineers now objected to others associated with civil engineering, such as contractors, being given full membership. At the same time the governing council was seen to be out of touch, with few fresh faces around the table. There were proposals to resolve the dilemma by defining a second category of members, either an upper level of membership for the professional elite, or a lower level for those less well qualified. John, a professional engineer and a contractor, wrote to the editor of *Engineering* magazine urging the Institution to take action to remedy the matter. He thought that all engineers should be full members, while men who were merely concerned with engineering, such as 'lawyers, promoters of companies, stockbrokers, &c' should be associates. There should be no attempt to divide engineers into superior and inferior grades. At a time when many correspondents to the press sheltered behind nom-de-plumes, John's closing sentence is worth quoting.

> 'With the welfare of our old Institution cordially at heart, I have penned these suggestions, and disliking as I do all anonymous contributions, I unhesitatingly append my name and I am, Sir, Yours respectfully, John Dixon.'

Each year the Institution held a 'conversazione' with engineering items and works of art on display to an invited audience. From his teenage years above the bank in Newcastle upon Tyne, John had been a keen model maker. Within months of his election as an associate member, at the 1870 conversazione he had contributed several excellent models: his proposed floating swimming bath for river or sea bathing and two models of breakwaters, one extended into a pier and one constructed with braced wrought iron cylinders. He later used wrought iron cylinders to support piers and bridges in several of his contracts. At the 1879 conversazione he exhibited two beautifully made models relating to Cleopatra's Needle, one of the vessel used to transport the obelisk, the other of the gantry used to lift it into position on The Embankment.

There is no doubt that John was a highly competent and experienced engineer although, given his numerous commitments, he only occasionally attended meetings of the Institution. He could make pithy comments on the papers presented. In January 1876, there was a prolonged discussion of a paper on the ventilation of railway tunnels, chaired by none other than Robert Stephenson. The paper had detailed calculations on the composition and quantity of locomotive exhausts and the sizing of ventilation fans, and followed the near fatalities to a locomotive crew in the Mont Cenis tunnel.

> 'Mr John Dixon doubted the accuracy of some of the author's calculations. If the Channel Tunnel were once pierced the difficulties in the way of ventilation would soon be overcome, as similar difficulties had been in reference to other undertakings which had been regarded as impracticable. He believed that the Mont Cenis Tunnel had been badly ventilated when the system of fans, &c, was in use; but at present it ventilated itself, and that most effectually. It would be remembered that the same thing had occurred in reference to the Metropolitan railway, which now practically ventilated itself.'

The Metropolitan Line, London's first underground railway, was operated by steam engines from its opening in 1863 until the start of the 20th century.

On another occasion, when discussing the economics of a floating bridge in India, he was able to quote examples from Egypt, the Rhine and Mississippi where floating bridges had been superseded by permanent structures and questioned the estimate for a permanent bridge by presenting details of a bridge in similar ground conditions which had been built for a quarter of the estimated cost.

Never a great socialiser, unlike his brother Raylton, John attended the annual dinner of the Institution of Civil Engineers when he was in London. This was particularly so in the early days of his career when he would be keen to make himself known to the engineering establishment of the day.

Recognition as a civil engineer

John was awarded the CBE and was given an honorary degree from the University of Durham, but never enjoyed the fame of some of his contemporary engineers. At the time of erecting Cleopatra's Needle there was talk of honours for those involved, but none were forthcoming. Later, Erasmus Wilson was honoured, but his knighthood was for his medical work and not for his financial contribution to the Cleopatra's Needle enterprise. Honours were conferred on many Victorian engineers, although often rather late in their careers. Robert Stephenson turned down the belated offer of a knighthood in 1850.

While not given his due recognition, there is no doubt that John became a wealthy man. He had been prepared to risk £10,000 over the cost of transporting Cleopatra's Needle and the various legal cases over the salvage left him over £9,000 out of pocket. £10,000 in 1878 would be approximately £1 million today. He left £11,000 in his will.

John Dixon the man

Naturally most historical references to John Dixon are about his engineering work but, by 'reading between the lines' and searching out other source material, it is possible to understand John as a person. He was undoubtedly a highly capable engineer, displaying the usual traits associated with engineers, self-motivated, logically assessing data to arrive at practical decisions, then implementing them through careful planning.

The Institution of Civil Engineers commented in his obituary:

> 'Mr. Dixon's personal qualifications were those which go to the making of a great contractor. Original in conception as regards the practical carrying out of works, and guarded by his engineering training against mistakes of a theoretical nature, he faced difficulties with a light heart and found them but a stimulant to greater efforts.'

> 'His enthusiasm was contagious, and the hesitations and doubts of engineers and financiers were often swept away by his vigorous and cheery eloquence.'

As with all of us, John had good and not-so-good aspects to his personality. The following paragraphs attempt an objective view of the man, based on evidence from his life and work. Horace Walpole expressed Oliver Cromwell's instruction that his portrait painter should 'not flatter me at all, but remark all these roughnesses, pimples, warts, and everything as you see me,' and this principle has been applied here.

John was highly self-motivated. He was always ready to take action where others might have hesitated. While still in his twenties, he took on the semi-derelict Bedlington Ironworks with Jasper Mounsey. Later in life he stepped in with an offer of finance to save the first section of the Guimarães railway. Although in his eagerness for action he sometimes failed to weigh up all the consequences, generally his decisions were based on prudent analysis, as with the Guimarães railway where he made sure, as he thought at the time, that his investment was secure. On his own initiative, he set out to find fresh water in the Rock of Gibraltar. His desire for action sometimes overshadowed a due regard for the consequences, such as his plan to excavate an opening in the side of the Great Pyramid.

Incidents throughout John's life give insights into his personality. Something quite small in itself can provide many such indications, such as in a letter he had published in *The Surrey Comet* of 17 February 1883, summarised here. After three great floods of the River Thames that winter there had been an epidemic of throat infections. John said that local doctors, who should have known better, blamed the milk supplies, with an adverse effect on the Surbiton dairy. He pointed out that a neighbour, who used a different dairy, had her entire household afflicted by the ailment. All the sewers discharged into the river, but the high-water levels had backed up into the pipes trapping effluent for days on end and forcing noxious gases back into domestic properties. Chloride of lime and carbolic acid should be used as disinfectants, but 'not in homœopathic and useless doses of a pint'. It would need applications of gallons to effectively treat the 15 gallons of sewage produced per day by each member of the household. A proper sewage treatment facility was needed, but the district had recently refused to sanction £30,000 for a sewage farm, and experience showed that with existing chemical knowledge it was impossible to make sewage treatment pay. John concluded that the only answer was to increase rates and provide a proper treatment works as had been installed in Rio de Janeiro.

He accused doctors of jumping to rash conclusions for blaming milk supplies, quoting evidence for refuting this theory and then set out a logical explanation of the real causes of the infections. He was dismissive of homeopathy and showed it would be unrealistic to use disinfectants. While his conclusion, the need to install a proper treatment works and increase rates to pay for it, was undoubtedly logical it failed to recognise the political reality that the ratepayers of Kingston upon Thames and Surbiton would not agree to increased rates. John had been one of the contractors for the Rio scheme, and a letter from the engineers responsible, published a week later, shows that John had not weighed up all the evidence before writing his letter. They listed reasons why a Surrey scheme would be much cheaper than that at Rio. It might only cost ten shillings annually for a Surrey household, compared with John's figure for Rio of £5 10s.

In general John's correspondence was direct and to the point. This is clearly shown in the series of letters from both John and Waynman to Charles Piazzi Smyth, the Scottish Astronomer Royal in Edinburgh, over Egyptian matters. Waynman's letters are usually well over twice as long as John's, and range over several topics with good wishes for Mrs Smyth. In contrast, John's writing is minimal. A good example was when he was seeking information from Piazzi Smyth about the waters of the Red Sea, in a letter completely devoid of any social pleasantries:

> 'Dear Sir,
> Can you tell me what is about the temperature of the Delta water close inshore about halfway between Suez & Aden?
> I'm asked about a condensing apparatus for freshwater at Jeddah the port of Mecca to supply the Pilgrims.
> I'm off to Egypt beginning of week.
> Yours truly, John Dixon'

The 'vigorous and cheery eloquence ' of his obituary was kept for his professional dealings. As in his letters, at social gatherings John was not given to small talk. In the summer of 1884 he was in Newcastle for the wedding of his niece (James and Augusta Richardson's daughter Amelia) to Alfred Holmes. One of the guests, Emma Pumphrey, tried to engage him in light conversation appropriate for such occasions, but in a letter to her father she recalled that all John would talk about was the state of trade and the government. Business matters dominated his life, and he only seems to have taken a break from work in his later years, and then mainly in the hope that time away in a warm climate might improve his health. He had turned down the opportunity of accompanying his friends on the cruise up the River Nile in 1873, leaving it to his brother Waynman to host the party. His early departure from the Freemasons was possibly because he felt that the brethren spent more time on the ritual and social side of the craft, rather than on developing business contacts.

He had little time for anyone he thought intellectually inferior. Returning to the letter on sewage treatment, John wrote of the Surrey civic authorities' small-mindedness in rejecting the lessons from places such as Rio:

> It is all very well to pooh pooh it, but that has been done for years, and we are not such mighty clever people that we can afford to sneer at that example, which is better than all theory.'

Two other examples can be mentioned. In the matter of the floating swimming bath, Kingston upon Thames Corporation had minuted that John had been discourteous in every way, and had treated them in a contemptuous manner, as nobodies. Later John wrote that the poor man who was killed crossing the carriageway of the temporary bridge at Hammersmith was stupid and only had himself to blame. In stark contrast, when in the company of fellow engineers, he could be most courteous, as shown by his eloquent tribute to Théophile Seyrig at the London lecture on the Douro Bridge.

The episode with Kingston Corporation illustrates how John could become hostile when challenged or criticised. An unfortunate consequence of this trait was his tendency to resort to the law when faced with disagreement. He instigated legal action against Curwen Estate over the Windermere ferry, and William Burrell over salvage for Cleopatra's Needle. Losing both of these cases, it could perhaps be said that his personal sense of injustice clouded a realistic assessment of his chance of success. He was tenacious in pursuing claims he felt were justified, notably over non-payment for the section of the Guimarães railway in Portugal. He doggedly kept up his battle with the Portuguese authorities for seven years and was eventually successful.

Similarly, in engineering fields he would never admit defeat, and was adept in finding a way round difficulties. The way he overcame problems when driving piles for the ore-loading facility at Huelva shows how he was undaunted by unexpected obstacles. When the steam-powered machine for screwing the piles down into the river bed failed, he assembled huge manually-operated capstans to complete the work. With his resident engineer, Thomas Gibson, he devised the submerged timber platforms to anchor the piles on the underwater silt.

Ultimately, the contribution of a civil engineer is measured by the utility and integrity of the structures he creates. Although few of John's structures exist today this is no reflection on his work. The railway in China was dismantled by the authorities for political reasons. Promenade piers at Shanklin and Douglas were demolished when they became financially unviable. Lisbon Customs House piers were submerged in later waterside developments. Railway viaducts on the Whitby to Loftus line, and across the Solway Firth, were dismantled when their respective railway lines ceased operating. The 'Pont des Anglais' at Cairo and the Eau Brink Cut Bridge at King's Lynn were replaced when they became unable to handle modern traffic flows. At Guimarães the railway has been replaced in broad-gauge along a slightly different route.

Still standing are the Hammersmith Suspension Bridge, the pier at Llandudno, the ore-loading pier at Huelva in Spain and Cleopatra's Needle by the side of the Thames in London. All four are eloquent testimonies to a great, but admittedly not the greatest, engineer.

The only question mark against John's engineering reputation is his design of the Whitby to Loftus railway viaducts, but subsequent problems had more to do with shortcomings in construction rather than design. More questionable are the ethics of some of his business dealings, such as his ventures into mining and his stake in the asset stripping of the CwmAvon Works. But then he was operating in the almost unbridled capitalism and faith in private enterprise of the Victorian era, and it is unfair to apply today's standards to past times.

It would be wrong to assume that John was devoid of sentiment, although source material presents few examples to show a softer side to the man. Although he was immersed in his business affairs in London and abroad, he retained some affection for his youth in Newcastle. In 1884 the Natural History Society of Northumberland, Durham and Newcastle upon Tyne moved into a splendid new museum which would later be named the Hancock Museum. The Dixon children had known Albany and John Hancock well, and when John heard that Hancock was seeking funds to build the new museum he donated a hundred guineas.

After the loss of the six brave men from the *Olga* who had attempted to rescue Captain Carter and his crew from the obelisk vessel, John instigated a fund their dependents. He appointed Alfred Thorne, who was working at No.1 Laurence Pountney Hill at that time, as treasurer. John made the first contribution, £250, Erasmus Wilson gave £100.

John was an accomplished artist, as were his two brothers. Painting was a keen interest for, within a year of moving to London, he became a member of the Society of Arts. He generally painted in watercolours. It is not known how many paintings John completed, he had little spare time in which to indulge this hobby, and it is likely that some of his paintings are in unknown ownership. For example, his painting of the Iron Pier at Douglas is only signed with his initials, and its owners, the Manx Museum, were unaware of the painter's identity. His painting of Niagara Falls gained an honourable mention at an exhibition of 'vacation sketches in oil and watercolours' held at the Paragon Art Studio, Bath, in 1886. This suggests that he did take an occasional holiday which would give him time to paint. There are several watercolours of Cleopatra's Needle, both in Egypt and London, kept at the Museum of London. John was at a private viewing of the Royal Society of Painters in Water Colours in April 1889.

John Dixon's painting of Niagara Falls painted in 1884. It was included in an exhibition at the Paragon Art Studio, Bath, in 1886. Reproduced by courtesy of Ben Hopkinson, great grand-son of Augusta Ann Richardson, one of John Dixon's sisters.

Acknowledgements

John Robinson for seeking out John's properties in Kingston upon Thames and Surbiton.

John Dixon for seeking out the site of 'High Towers' in Croydon and John's gravestone.

Dr Jacqueline Cove-Smith for medical advice on John's health.

Peter Aitkenhead of the Library and Museum of Freemasonry, Great Queen Street, London.

Wayne Rumley of the Palatine Lodge, Sunderland for access to the records of John's membership of the Freemasons.

References

Census Returns, Births, Marriages and Deaths Records, Electoral Registers, 1939 Register

The Descendants of Ralph Dixon
Charles Pease
http://www.pennyghael.org.uk/Dixon.pdf
List of John and Mary Dixon's children with birth dates and infant deaths of Sarah and Robert.

Reminiscences of the Dixon Family
Recalled by Mrs Augusta Ann Richardson, 23 June 1911
Transcription owned by Ann Colville (née Richardson)
Contains an account of John Dixon's activities at the top of the bank building in Newcastle and his friendship with Henry Mennell.

Biographical Dictionary of British Quakers in Commerce and Industry 1775-1920
Edward H Milligan
Sessions Book Trust, York, 2007
Biographies of George and Henry Tuke Mennell.

Marriages
The Morning Post, London, 14 October 1862, page 8
Announcement of marriage on 9 October 1862 at St James, Hatcham, of John Dixon and Mary, daughter of George England of Hatcham Iron Works.

Marriages
The Newcastle Chronicle and Northern Counties Advertiser, 18 October 1862, page 8
Hatcham, St James, 9th inst, by Rev A K B Granville MA, John Dixon Esq of Bedlington to Mary, daughter of George England Esq of Hatcham Iron Works, London.

George England and the Hatcham Iron Works, established 1839
A Weatherley
Caro Group, Belvedere, Kent, 2001
Also available on-line:
http://digitalpages.digitalissue.co.uk/?userpath=00000082/00008121/00072489/
Detailed biography of George England. Has the age of his son George England at his death as thirty-six; in fact he was twenty-six.

George England, pioneer locomotive builder and the Hatcham Ironworks
Talk by Douglas Hills and Grahame Hood on 9 February 2011
Institute of Cast Metals Engineers
Summary at www.icme.org.uk/news.asp?ID=360
Biography of George England.

Sale of Engineering Plant at the Hatcham Ironworks
The Engineer, London, 31 May 1872, page 381
Auction of plant and equipment, much in poor condition.

The Great Exhibition
The Morning Post, London, 29 October 1852, page 3
Commendation of the locomotive shown by England & Company.

Central Criminal Court, March 7
The Times, London, 8 April 1862
Report on the trial of Robert Fairlie for misdemeanour in making a false statement with a view to procuring a marriage licence. When it emerged that England's daughter had been born out of wedlock, the verdict was not guilty. England mentioned John Dixon, who was courting another of his daughters at the time, but who had his approval.

4 January 1853
The Gazette, London, Issue 2, 21398, page 2
Appointment of a John Dixon as Deputy Lieutenant on 30 December 1852.

The Conversazione of the Institution of Civil Engineers - Docks, Harbours and Bridges
Engineering, London, 3 June 1870, page 398
John Dixon had contributed several excellent models.

The Conversazione of the Institution of Civil Engineers - Docks, Harbours and Bridges
Engineering, London, 3 June 1870, page 398

The Institution Conversazione 1879
Engineering, London, 30 May 1879, page 464
John Dixon showed two models relating to Cleopatra's Needle.

The Institution of Civil Engineers - To the Editor of Engineering
Engineering, London, 1 February 1878, page 82
John Dixon's letter on the membership debate at the ICE.

The Institution of Civil Engineers
Engineering, London, 8 November 1878, page 377-8
Editorial on the question of ICE membership.

Letter from Emma Pumphrey, 6 Summerhill Grove, Newcastle upon Tyne, to Thomas Pumphrey, dated 30 July 1884
Private collection of Marjorie Gaudie
John Dixon talks about trade and the government at the wedding of Amelia Constance Richardson to Alfred Holmes.

Letter from John Dixon, 1 Laurence Pountney Hill, London, to Charles Piazzi Smyth, Royal Observatory, Edinburgh, dated 27 September 1872
Royal Observatory Library, Blackford Hill, Edinburgh
File "DIXON, John, 10 Letters" ROE reference A11-48
Example of one of John Dixon's short letters.

The Lieutenancy of London
The Manchester Courier and Lancashire General Advertiser, 8 November 1879, page 6
John Dixon CE nominated.

The Royal Visit to the North - The New Museum
The Newcastle Courant, 22 August 1884, page 3
John Dixon is listed in the contributors to the new building 'John Dixon, London, £105.'

Letter written from 'High Towers' dated 23 August 1884
Foreign Office Correspondence: Further correspondence relating to Mr John Dixon's claim against the Guimarães Railway Company 1882-1884
Reference FO 63/1202 (April 1884 to July 1887)
National Archives, Kew
This is the first reference to John Dixon having moved into High Towers.

Deaths
The Evening Standard, London, 31 January 1891, page 1
Announcement of John Dixon's funeral arrangements.

Death Certificate of John Dixon
Central Register Office Reference: 1891 M Quarter in Croydon, volume 02A, page 176
Details of cause of death.

Marriages
The Morning Post, London, 2 March 1898, page 1
Marriage of John Ralph Dixon, John Dixon's second son.

Marriages
The Evening Standard, London, 8 August 1898, page 1
Marriage of Cornelia Clara Dixon, John Dixon's second daughter.

Bexhill Subscription Ball - Last Night - A Great Success - List of Guests
Bexhill-on-Sea Observer and Visitors' Register, 26 October 1901, page 4
The ball was attended by Mrs John Dixon, Miss Alex Dixon and Miss Hilda M Dixon.

Bexhill Subscription Ball - Last Night at the Hotel Metropole - Another Great Success
Bexhill-on-Sea Observer and Visitors' Register,
30 November 1901, page 5
Among those present were the Misses Alex and Hilda Dixon.

Bexhill Christmas Ball - Last Night at the Sackville Hotel - Brilliant Scene
Bexhill-on-Sea Observer and Visitors' Register,
28 December, page 5
Among those present were Miss Hilda Dixon, Mr George Dixon and Miss Ethel Dixon.

The Late Miss A M Dixon - Haywards Heath Resident's Funeral at Cuckfield
The Mid-Sussex Times, Haywards Heath,
13 February 1940, page 2
Augusta' funeral, Charles Fox was unable to attend due to indisposition.

Death of Mr Charles Fox
The Mid-Sussex Times, Haywards Heath,
19 March 1940, page 8
He was taken ill shortly before the death on 23 February of Miss Dixon, his faithful companion, and died on 15 March.

Bath Chronicle, 2 December 1886
John Dixon's painting of the Niagara Falls was exhibited at the Paragon Art Studio.

List of Carthusians 1800-1879
William Douglas Parish
Farncombe and Company, Lewes, 1879
Old scholars of Charterhouse. On page 61 is George England, son of John Dixon C E of Surbiton, as entering the school in 1878.

Mr Dixon CE on the Drainage of the Lower Thames Valley - To the Editor
The Surrey Comet, 17 February 1883, page 3
Letter suggesting there should be proper treatment of sewage, comparing the situation in England with that in Rio de Janeiro.

Drainage of the Lower Thames Valley - To the Editor
The Surrey Comet, 24 February 1883, page 4
Letter from Gotto and Beesley explaining that a Surrey sewage treatment scheme would be far less costly than that at Rio.

Picture Week
The Western Times, Exeter, 29 April 1889, page 3
John Dixon at private viewing of Royal Society of Painters in Water Colours.

Tees Conservancy Commission
The Evening Gazette, Middlesbrough, 6 December 1870, page 3
John Castell Hopkins resigns from the Commission.

Death of J. C. Hopkins Esq
The Evening Gazette, Middlesbrough, 17 April 1871, page 2
Death of John Castell Hopkins of 'The Firs' Kingston-on-Thames.

A Short History of the Egyptian Obelisks
William Ricketts Cooper
S Bagster and Sons, London, 1877
As an appendix to Chapter XXII Cooper reproduces on pages 140-143 the text of a letter written to him by Erasmus Wilson, dated 3 October 1877.

Minute Books of the Palatine Lodge, Sunderland
Record that in 1861 John Dixon was initiated on 14 February, passed on 2 May, and raised on 11 July. He gave his age as 26 and his address as Sunderland.

Minutes of the Festival of St John, 27 December 1860, Palatine Lodge, Sunderland
John Dixon, manager of the Bishopwearmouth Iron Works, proposed by James Hamilton and seconded by W J Young.

Minutes of the General Lodge, 10 January 1861
28 brethren present plus 10 from other Lodges. Ballots taken for Messrs Kelsey, Evans, Simey, Dixon and Wiseman who were all duly elected.

Death of Mr W J Young
Yorkshire Gazette, York, 7 November 1885, page 9
Obituary of William Joseph Young.

Temple-bar Lodge 1728
Shipping and Mercantile Gazette, London, 5 January 1878, page 8
Last night a new Masonic Lodge, styled 'The Temple-bar Lodge', was formally dedicated to Freemasonry and Mr John Dixon was installed as first Worshipful Master.

Boat's Crew of the *Olga*
The Times, London, 26 October 1877, page 6
Details of the fund for the dependents of volunteers lost in the attempt to rescue the crew of the *Cleopatra*.

Three of John Dixon's excellent watercolours:

Previous page, top) 'No.3 Calm on the Medway by John Dixon, 1 Laurence Pountney Hill, London E.6.' There is no date on the painting and the inclusion of 'No.3' suggests that he painted other similar scenes at the time.

Previous page, bottom) Watercolour of a ship at sea in moonlight by John Dixon.

Above) 'Tynemouth Priory in a storm' watercolour signed on the reverse side by John Dixon.

Reproduced by courtesy of Beth Porteous, great grand-daughter of John Dixon and photographed by Neil Crick ARPS of Smart-Ideas Photography.

Appendix: Engineering materials in the 19th century

Iron making

Iron was produced from suitable iron ores in a blast furnace. Blast furnace design had seen many improvements during the 19th century, with increasing scientific knowledge beginning to overtake experience in controlling the process. The blast furnace was a high cylindrical vessel with heat-resistant lining. Through an opening at the top the initial charge was loaded, with a layer of combustible material at the bottom, followed by ore mixed with limestone and coke. Once the furnace was alight, hot air, heated by the hot gases escaping from the top of the furnace, was blown up through the charge. The resulting chemical reactions separated the iron from the ore and drove off impurities as gases and slag. Liquid iron was tapped from the bottom of the furnace and run into moulds to form 'pigs'. When solidified, a pig was a block of iron containing up to 5% carbon with inclusions of slag. Pig iron was then further processed into cast iron or wrought iron.

Cast iron

To make castings, pig iron was reheated in a smaller furnace to which scrap metal might be added and poured into moulds made from special sand. Cast iron has a high strength in compression, but virtually none in tension and is brittle, properties which limited its use. Typically, the columns supporting a pier or a bridge, where the loading is purely compressive, would be made of cast iron. Castings had to be of reasonable thickness, so they were heavy. With the high carbon content of cast iron, components could be easily machined on a lathe.

Wrought iron

Wrought iron takes its name from the process of working the iron under a steam hammer followed by passing it through rollers. Before this could be done, excess carbon was removed in the puddling furnace. This involved melting pig iron in a small furnace and agitating it vigorously by stirring (rabbling) with iron rods to bring the molten metal into contact with air, thus removing the excess carbon as carbon dioxide. As the stirring continued, the molten mass thickened until the puddler could form it into large balls of white hot metal. These were immediately lifted out of the furnace and taken to a steam hammer where successive blows knocked out most of the remaining slag, to form bars of wrought iron. As might be imagined, the working conditions of the puddlers were extremely arduous, with the intense heat from the molten iron and the hard work of raddling and lifting the balls of white hot metal. Puddling was not only physically demanding but required a great deal of experience to be able to control the process and judge when the iron was ready to be formed into balls.

A number of wrought iron bars were then built into a stack rather like brickwork, and again hammered to weld them together. The resulting block of iron was then rolled to produce bars, plates, rails and other sections as required. Although not all the slag had been removed by hammering, what was left was in the form of strings after rolling and did not seriously weaken the iron.

Wrought iron withstood some tensile load, and so was used extensively for beams and boilers.

Bridge spans

The spans of a bridge or pier were built up from lengths of wrought iron plate and girders, fastened together with rivets. Robert Stephenson's brilliant design for the High Level Bridge at Newcastle upon Tyne used bow-like spans formed from arch-shaped iron castings, with the 'bowstring' of wrought iron links. The cast iron is in compression, the wrought iron in tension. Suspension bridges used chains fabricated from wrought iron links, purely in tension, with cast iron saddles on top of masonry towers in compression.

Limitations of wrought iron

Wrought iron was unable to withstand high stresses, and its quality was very variable. Quality variations were mainly due to the lack of high temperature measurement and any form of chemical analysis. Blast furnace operators and puddlers had to rely on experience to judge when the process was complete. Testing methods were extremely crude, and for many years merely consisted of a drop test where a weight was dropped onto section of bar supported at each end. All of this meant that the design was very conservative, generally using thick cross-sections resulting in heavy structures. However, it was possible to produce graceful designs, as in the Eiffel Tower. What is often called 'wrought iron' today, such as in garden gates, is not wrought iron but mild steel.

Advent of steel

Steel is an alloy of iron, usually containing about 2% carbon, and other elements. Steel had been made in small quantities for centuries, as for the renowned swords from Toledo and Japan, but was not available in large quantities until Henry Bessemer introduced his steel-making furnace in 1856. Molten pig iron was poured into the Bessemer Converter and air blown up through it to remove excess carbon as carbon dioxide, and to oxidise other impurities which formed a layer of slag floating on the molten metal. The resulting steel had much better properties than wrought iron, and these could be further improved by the addition of small quantities of alloying metals. Because the process was easier to control than the puddling furnace, the steel produced had uniform properties. Steel revolutionised structural design, and by the end of the 19th century wrought iron had virtually disappeared.

Riveting

Wrought iron structures were fastened together using rivets, short cylinders of iron with a domed head at one end. The red-hot rivet was inserted into holes punched or drilled into the components to be fastened, and then the protruding end was hammered over into a similar dome shape. The shrinkage as the rivet cooled pulled the components together to form a solid joint.

'Tapping the Blast Furnace'
etching by R S Chattock in 1872.
One of a series of prints by Richard Samuel Chattock (1825-1906) from Solihull, artist and engraver. This etching captures the moment the blast furnace is tapped, newly-smelted iron flows into moulds in the sand to form 'pigs'.
Reproduced by courtesy of Dudley Archives and Local History Service, reference 1944_51

'The Puddling-Furnace'
etching by R S Chattock in 1872. The puddling process judged complete, the puddler removes a ball of white hot iron from the furnace. Puddlers worked in extremely arduous conditions, even by the standards of the time.
Reproduced by courtesy of Dudley Archives and Local History Service, reference 1944_52

Index

References in Who's Who format listed in **bold** type.